Ratio decidendi

Comparative Studies
in Continental and Anglo-American Legal History
Vergleichende Untersuchungen zur kontinentaleuropäischen
und anglo-amerikanischen Rechtsgeschichte

Herausgegeben von

Helmut Coing (†), Richard Helmholz, Knut Wolfgang Nörr
und Reinhard Zimmermann

Band 25 / 1

Ratio decidendi

Guiding Principles of Judicial Decisions

Volume 1: Case Law

Edited by

W. Hamilton Bryson
Serge Dauchy

Duncker & Humblot · Berlin

Printed with support of the Gerda Henkel Stiftung, Düsseldorf

Bibliographic information published by the Deutsche Nationalbibliothek

The Deutsche Nationalbibliothek lists this publication in
the Deutsche Nationalbibliografie; detailed bibliographic data
are available in the Internet at http://dnb.d-nb.de.

Typesetting and printing:
Berliner Buchdruckerei Union GmbH, Berlin
Printed in Germany

ISSN 0935-1167
ISBN 3-428-12216-X
978-3-428-12216-5

Gedruckt auf alterungsbeständigem (säurefreiem) Papier
entsprechend ISO 9706 ♾

Internet: http://www.duncker-humblot.de

Preface

Although the problem of *ratio decidendi* concerns the essence of law and justice, very little comparative work between the Continental and Anglo-American legal systems has been done on the topic. Legal literature often repeats that it is one of the sharpest points of contrast between the two legal cultures. Within the English speaking legal system, multiple opinions, both concurring and dissenting, prevail where dissent among Continental judges only occurs behind closed doors: the published decision indeed is always presented as the single and incontestable opinion of the whole court. Historical reasons are generally put forward to explain that contrast. Where in the Anglo-American Common Law system judges are asked – and always have been asked – to present the materials and reasons upon which they based their judicial opinions, in Ancien Régime continental Europe it was not considered necessary to formulate the reasons of a decision and in most courts of the European Continent it was even formally forbidden to the judges, until the end of the eighteenth century, to write down or even communicate orally "the secrets of their discussions and deliberations".

To comparatists, this reveals two different cultures among judges and lawyers. In Continental Europe there is much emphasis on the idea of judging as a science which can be learned and reproduced with an impersonal rigour. The Anglo-American judge is not considered to be such a trained scientist, he is merely a practised craftsman. Can the history of *ratio decidendi* – but also the history of law and justice from the Middle Ages to the nineteenth century – therefore be reduced to a total contradiction between two legal cultures? Is there no possible comparison? As well in the Continental as in the Anglo-American legal system materials always have been presented and argued to the judges by the lawyers in order to persuade them to rule in favor of their clients and, exposed in public or not, the authorities put forward have always been used and discussed by those judges.

As it is the purpose of the *Comparative Studies in Continental and Anglo-American Legal History,* we thought one would gain new insight into the problem of *ratio decidendi* by studying the question in a historical comparative way in order not only to understand the guiding principles of judicial decisions in the Continental and the Anglo-American legal systems but also to search in their legal history why both systems have known separate evolutions. Studies are, of course, in hand on the history of court records, though these address the nature of the records rather than the jurisprudential problem of how and why decisions came to be accompanied by reasons. Our purpose is therefore to compare the Continental tradition – through the study of the Roman and Canonical doctrine, the commentaries of Ancien Régime jurists and in particularly the practice of the continental superior courts – with England and the American colonies and, after 1776, also with the federal courts and the states of the United States in order to search for an answer to some more particular questions including: the emergence of the practice of giving or recording reasons for judicial decisions, the forms which such records take, and the problem about their accurancy and the interaction between respect for rules (*stare decisis* or *non quieta movere*) and the critical re-examination of reasons for past decisions when put to a later court. Our focus in this first volume is to study the particular reliance on "Case Law Jurisprudence" through examples of constitutional, national, regional and local law.

Lille, 2005 *Serge Dauchy*

Contents

LAURENS WINKEL

Ratio Decidendi – Legal Reasoning in Roman Law

I. Introduction[1]

An analysis of *rationes decidendi* in Roman legal literature meets comparable difficulties as in modern common law: at first, the *ratio decidendi* in legal decisions is very often only implied. There are further in both domains considerable difficulties to define even the very notion of *ratio decidendi* and the border between *ratio decidendi* and forms of interpretation is equally quite vague.[2] Further, it is difficult to distinguish between the *dictum* and the *ratio decidendi*. An extra difficulty in modern common law is that the decision is made by several judges with their concurring and dissenting opinions. This difficulty is not present in Roman law.

But there is similar uneasiness and vagueness in Roman law: the relation between "Begründung" and subsumption under a rule is also there problematic. In Roman law this is also partly caused by the only gradually developing notion of analogy, upon which Arthur Steinwenter[3] has extensively published some fifty years ago. But there is also a reason that is not to be found in modern law: it is difficult to take into account the horizontal structure of the Roman legal order, linked with the predominance of the *ius honorarium*. Modern legal systems, common law and civil law alike, have a hierarchy which is lacking, at least in classical Roman law.

Many decisions of the Roman jurists are not motivated, or justified, and even words like *quia, cum* and *quod,* which grammatically could seem to refer to reasoning, are sometimes misleading. They often refer only to the factual circumstances of the case. Significantly, a more or less complete analysis of *rationes decidendi* was only in recent times carried out in the Roman legal literature of the pre-

---

1 This article is partially a further elaboration of a previous article, *The role of general principles in Roman law,* published in the South African review *Fundamina* 2 (1993), 103–120.

2 *C.K. Allen,* Law in the Making, Oxford 1964, 259 ff.; 291 ff.; cf. *S. Vogenauer,* Die Auslegung von Gesetzen in England und auf dem Kontinent, I, II, Tübingen 2001. No mention of *ratio decidendi* is made in the index of this work.

3 *A. Steinwenter,* Prolegomena zu einer Geschichte der Analogie, Studi in onore di Emilio Albertario, Milano 1953, II, 105 ff.; Studi in onore di Vincenzo Arangio Ruiz, Milano 1953, II, 169 ff.; Festschrift für Fritz Schulz, Weimar 1951, II, 45 ff.

classical period, the first century B.C., by Franz Horak.[4] He analyzed about 300 decisions ascribed to Roman jurists of that period. This is only a very small percentage of the available Roman legal literature! A promised second volume of his book, covering the period of classical Roman law till 250 A.D. never saw the light of day.

At first the Roman "case method" has to be examined, which can – as stated above – be compared with the case method in common law, but there are at least some differences, from which the "horizontal structure" of the sources is certainly here the most important.[5] Therefore we are first devoting attention to the structure of the sources of Roman law as such. Then we examine some of the possible *rationes decidendi* as found by Horak: he distinguished application of a legal norm; application of logic or linguistic rule (for examples *in maiore minus inest*[6]); *ratio decidendi* from earlier jurisprudence, where the jurist invokes the equal opinion of one of his predecessors; *ratio decidendi* found in a *regula iuris; ratio decidendi* found in a legal construction; *ratio decidendi* found in legal concepts; *ratio decidendi ex iure controverso; ratio decidendi* from ordinary language; *ratio decidendi* from the will of the parties or one concerned party; *ratio decidendi* from philosophy; *ratio decidendi* from decency; *ratio decidendi* from analogy; *ratio decidendi* from an example (simpler than the case); *ratio decidendi* from *deductio ad absurdum.* A.M. Honoré, who somewhat earlier wrote an instructive article on legal reasoning in Rome[7] distinguishes the arguments of the Roman jurists between "appeal to rules of law", "open arguments (topos or principle)", "the facts" and *"argumenta ex auctoritate"*. Quite often, he concludes, a *ratio decidendi* is lacking altogether.

We will concentrate in the following paragraphs on a few topics only: the hierarchy of sources in Roman law (Section II), the historiography of *rationes decidendi* in Roman law is dealt with in Section III; some pre-classical (Section IV) and classical *rationes decidendi* (Section V) will be discussed briefly, followed by a few remarks on the topic in medieval and later jurisprudence (Section VI). We end with some conclusions (Section VII).

---

4 *F. Horak,* Rationes decidendi – Entscheidungsbegründungen bei den älteren römischen Juristen bis Labeo, I, Innsbruck 1969.

5 Comparative studies in the Roman "case method" were done recently by the Italian Romanist Letizia *Vacca,* Contributo allo studio del metodo casistico nel diritto romano, Milano 1976, 2nd edition Milano 1982.

6 *R. Backhaus,* In maiore minus inest, Eine justinianische "regula iuris" in den klassischen Rechtsquellen – Herkunft, Anwendungsbereich und Funktion, ZSS rA 100 (1983), 136–184; *O. Behrends,* Die Wissenschaftslehre im Zivilrecht des Q. Mucius Scaevola pontifex, Nachrichten der Akademie der Wissenschaften in Göttingen, Phil.-Hist. Klasse, 1976, Nr. 7, Göttingen 1976. See lately *K. Tuori,* The myth of Quintus Mucius Scaevola: founding father of legal science?, TRG LXVII (2004), 243–262.

7 *A.M. Honoré,* Legal Reasoning in Rome and Today, South African Law Review 91 (1974), 84–94.

II. Hierarchy of Legal Sources

As has been said, a very important difference between old and modern case law is that the Roman legal order was not characterized by a clear hierarchy of norms, but a preliminary question is to find a full survey of sources of law. There are indeed some legal and non-legal texts in which such a survey of sources of law is given. The question is: are these sources really giving a complete survey or are they only giving examples? The question is acute, because sometimes a reference to custom seems to be lacking. Dieter Nörr has dealt with these texts in his important study *"Divisio und partitio"*[8] in which he showed that these texts conceived as *divisio* are supposed to be complete; conceived as *partitio* they can give only examples of sources of law and therefore may be incomplete. This is his ingenious explanation for the fact that in some texts no reference to customary law is made. The surveys of Roman legal sources are to be found mainly in Cicero and in the Digest.[9] These texts were analyzed by other scholars as well, primarily in order to investigate the role of customs and customary law, but all this research has been fruitful for the better understanding of the Roman legal order.

So we distinguish in classical Roman law statutes (*leges, plebiscita*), decisions of the Senate (*Senatus Consulta*), edicts of Roman magistrates, customary law, and finally opinions of earlier individual jurists, all of which exist side by side. As to the last category we meet the problem linked with the so-called *ius respondendi* on which again much has been written.[10] The question here is: are all jurists entitled to give their legal opinion or only the ones given the *ius respondendi* by the emperor? We must leave this question aside here. It is enough to say that all these sources can be referred to as a *ratio decidendi* in a case.

An important element is that the praetor has, at least until the codification of the *Edictum Perpetuum* about 138 A.D. in his edict, but also in a special injunction (*decretum*), the possibility to correct and to adapt the rules of the *ius civile.*[11] So he could set aside a rule from ancient (unwritten) *ius civile* or even an explicit provision of a *lex.* He can then provide one of the parties a legal remedy in the form of an *actio* or an *exceptio* against existing rules. A famous example of the latter is the introduction by the praetor Aquilius Gallus in 69 B.C. of the *exceptio doli.* This is

---

8 *D. Nörr,* Divisio und partitio, Bemerkungen zur römischen Rechtsquellenlehre und zur antiken Wissenschaftstheorie, München 1972 [= D. *Nörr,* Historiae iuris antiqui, II, Goldbach [2003], 705–774].

9 Pomponius, Ench. D. 1, 2, 2, 12; Papinianus, D. 1, 1, 7; *Cicero,* De inventione, 2, 22, 65.

10 *F. Wieacker,* Respondere ex auctoritate principis, Satura R. Feenstra, Fribourg 1965, 71–94. The dissenting opinion of J.W. *Tellegen,* Plinii min. Epistula VII, 24, 8, ZSSr.A.105 (1988), 278 ff., links the *ius respondendi* with the existence of the schools of the Sabiniani and the Proculiani, but this is not fully convincing.

11 See D. 1,1,7,1: Ius praetorium est quod praetores introduxerunt adiuvandi vel supplendi vel corrigendi iuris civilis gratia propter utilitatem publicam. Quod et honorarium dicitur ad honorem praetorum sic nominatum.

at first sight a possible start of hierarchical structure of the Roman legal sources. The freedom of the praetor to do this, however, was restrained already in the age of the Severian emperors at the end of the second century A.D. This follows from the recent research of J.-P. Coriat, who analyzed many imperial *rescripta* of that period.[12] In later classical and post-classical law these imperial legal measures (*rescripta, mandata, leges generales* and the like) become more and more the leading legal sources. From the *Lex citandi* of 426 A.D. of the emperor Theodosius II, we can deduce nonetheless that especially the legal literature remained an important source even then.

A survey of the sources of Roman law is at the least a first step in the discovery of possible *rationes decidendi.* Roman jurists, who were in the course of the Principate more and more integrated in the imperial administration, slowly formulated and developed general legal principles, like *natura rerum, ratio, regulae* and definitions that can be used as a *ratio decidendi.*

In the Digest, a part of Justinian's legislation, where fragments of the Roman literature are compiled, we find – in the first book in which a fragmentary survey of some philosophical ideas is given – some general legal principles, which are normally called the *praecepta iuris: honeste vivere, neminem laedere, suum cuique tribuere.* They are used in the famous definition of justice by Ulpian in (D. 1. 1. 10), but also very occasionally a Roman jurist vaguely refers to them.[13] Further examples of *rationes decidendi* can be found in legal principles as *bona fides, humanitas, benignitas, utilitas, aequitas.* But the list of possible *regulae* or *rationes decidendi* is still far from complete. In the first place, there are examples of other rules: *audite et alteram partem, noxa caput sequitur, favor libertatis, nemo auditur turpitudinem suam allegans; non venire contra factum proprium; plus est in re quam in existimatione mentis; plus est in opinione quam in veritate.* These last two examples clearly show that Roman *regulae* can be contradictory.

These examples may also suffice to show that Roman *regulae* appear in very different forms, sometimes they are denoted as such, either as *regulae, regulae iuris* or *regulae iuris civilis.* This threefold distinction was the starting point for research by Bruno Schmidlin,[14] who attributed to them an increasing normative value, where *regulae* are the least, and *regulae iuris civilis* the most normative. On this point he was rightly criticized by Dieter Nörr:[15] Schmidlin put too much emphasis on these rather loose qualifications and draws too far-reaching conclusions in the sphere of normative value. In other cases legal principles are only

---

12 *J.-P. Coriat,* Le Prince Législateur, La technique législative des Sévères et les méthodes de création du droit impérial à la fin du Principat, Rome 1997, 351 ff.

13 *E. Levy,* Natural law in Roman thought, Studia et Documenta Historiae et Iuris, XV (1949), 1–23 [= Gesammelte Schriften I, Köln / Graz 1963, 3–19], esp. p. 19, resp. 16 ff.

14 *B. Schmidlin,* Die römischen Rechtsregeln, Köln / Wien 1970.

15 *D. Nörr,* Spruchregel und Generalisierung, ZSS r.A. 89 (1972), 17–93 [= D. *Nörr,* Historiae iuris antiqui, II, 775–850].

implicitly considered as *regulae*. *Libri regularum* collecting legal rules as a form of Roman literature date only from the second century A.D. on, the first jurist of whom we know that he wrote such a work is Neratius. Books with definitions,[16] also likely to be used as *ratio decidendi*, are considerably older. They go back to Quintus Mucius Scaevola (± 100 B.C.) who is said to have written a book of definitions called *Libri Horōn*. The compilers of the Digest in the sixth century in their turn collected some more abstract rules in the last title of the Digest, D. 50. 17: *De diversis regulis iuris antiqui*. This Digest-title was very important in the long-term process of "abstraction" of legal science, away from case law, which on the European continent eventually led to codifications.[17]

III. Short History of Earlier Research

It may be interesting to devote a few words to the question why the research of *rationes decidendi* in Roman law is a rather recent phenomenon. A more theoretical attempt at changes in legal science was the consequence of the revival of Kant's philosophy at the end of the nineteenth century. The most important representatives of this revival were Hermann Cohen (1842 – 1918) and Rudolf Stammler (1856 – 1938). This so-called Marburger Schule did not only inspire a revival of philosophy in general, but also more specifically the theoretical approach of legal phenomena. This orientation implied at the same time an increasing interest for legal principles. These were largely neglected during Pandectism and Begriffsjurisprudenz. Illustrative of this is the lack of interest in notions like *bona fides* and *aequitas* in Savigny's *System des heutigen römischen Rechts*[18] and in Bernhard Windscheid's *Lehrbuch des Pandektenrechts*.[19]

Rudolf Stammler was the jurist of the *Marburger Schule*. He was a prototype of a jurist in legal science in transition. He became professor when the German Civil Code was already being made. His inaugural address was about the role of Roman law after the introduction of the Civil Code. The increasing interest in legal principles lies for example in the distinction made by Stammler between the concept of law (*Rechtsbegriff*) and the idea of law (*Rechtsidee*), or, to put it in his own words *"Die Idee des richtigen Rechts"* (The idea of the right Law). The idea of law is a measure for judging the positive law. Whereas the positive law always has gaps,

16 See the nearly simultaneously published books by *A. Carcaterra*, Le definizioni dei giuristi romani, 1966, and R. *Martini*, Le definizioni dei giuristi romani, Napoli 1966.

17 See for further references *P. Stein*, Regulae iuris, From Juristic Rules to Legal Maxims, Edinburgh 1966, 162 vv.; *idem*, The Digest Title 'De diversis regulis iuris antiqui' and the General Principles of Law, Essays in Jurisprudence in Honor of Roscoe Pound, Indianapolis / New York, 1 – 20 [= *P. Stein*, The Character and Influence of the Roman Civil Law, London 1988, 53 – 72].

18 In eight volumes, Berlin 1840 – 1863.

19 In three volumes, revised by *Th. Kipp*, 9th ed., Frankfurt / M 1906, reprint Aalen 1984.

the judge requires principles "of right law". These can be divided into principles of respect and principles of participation (*Grundsätze des Achtens und des Teilnehmens*[20]). Through these concepts of the idea of law, Stammler supersedes the positivistic legal science, in the German context, the consequence of the scientific positivism of the science by the Pandectists.[21]

Rudolf Stammler also had a strong influence on Dutch legal science of the beginning of last century, especially on Paul Scholten (1875 – 1946), one of the most important Dutch jurists in the first half of that century, well known for his plea for the study and application of legal principles. In Scholten's inaugural address we find many of Stammler's ideas, and these can also be found in the former's "General Introduction to Dutch Private Law", a book influential in the Netherlands until this very day.[22] There is still an older repetition of Stammler's ideas, when Scholten comments on the new Swiss civil code (1907) with its famous article 1, which allows the judge to apply the rule he would conceive as if he were a legislator in cases not foreseen by the statute.[23] Scholten here developed his theory about legal decision making, which he later elaborated in his "General Introduction".

At the same time as Rudolf Stammler, François Gény,[24] who devoted much of his attention to the task of the judge in a codified legal system, was in addition to Stammler responsible for opening the eyes of Romanists to considering Roman legal general concepts as *rationes decidendi*. This new trend also changed gradually the method of studying the Roman legal sources. For the first time, Roman law was a purely historical phenomenon after the introduction of the German Bürgerliches Gesetzbuch in 1900.

However, the historical – and we have to add the philological – approach towards the Roman legal tradition led at first to a in retrospect, rather unfruitful

---

20 *R. Stammler*, Die Lehre von dem richtigen Rechte, Berlin 1902, 201 ff.

21 See extensively *K. Larenz*, Methodenlehre der Rechtswissenschaft, above note 4, 88 ff.; differently, but in my view not appropriate: *F. Wieacker*, Privatrechtsgeschichte der Neuzeit, Göttingen 1967, 589, who speaks about "entschieden positivistische[n] Anwendungen des Neukantianismus". These characteristics certainly do not apply to Stammler.

22 *P. Scholten*, Algemeen Deel, C. Asser's Handleiding tot de beoefening van het Nederlands(ch) Burgerlijk Recht, 3rd ed., Zwolle 1974. This book has been translated into French by B.E. *Wielenga*, but, in spite of the preface by the famous French jurist Georges *Ripert*, never attracted sufficient attention outside the Netherlands: Traité de droit civil néerlandais: partie générale, Zwolle / Paris [1954].

23 "Das Gesetz findet auf alle Rechtsfragen Anwendung, für die es nach Wortlaut oder Auslegung eine Bestimmung enthält. Kann dem Gesetze keine Vorschrift entnommen werden, so soll der Richter nach Gewohnheitsrecht und, wo auch ein solches fehlt, nach der Regel entscheiden, die er als Gesetzgeber aufstellen würde. Er folgt dabei bewährter Lehre und Ueberlieferung."

24 Méthode d'interprétation en droit privé positif, 2 Paris 1919. See also the Recueil des Etudes sur les sources du droit en l'honneur de François Gény, Paris 1934; Gény seems to have been influenced by J.C. Bluntschli, Rudolf von Jhering and Gustav Radbruch.

period during which the search for interpolations was the main object of study and not the study of Roman legal principles or *rationes decidendi*. The starting point for the interpolationistic approach is to be found in a book by Otto Gradenwitz, which was published in 1887.[25] Following earlier attempts of purification of the texts during the period of legal humanism in the sixteenth century, scholars of Roman law emphasized a historical and critical approach of the texts of the sources and tried to detach from Justinian's legislation the pure classical Roman law of some 300 years earlier by purifying these texts from Justinian's alterations. They did not take into account that the preparation of Justinian's project took so little time (less than five years), and they idealized the style and the Latin of the classical jurists in a way that is, in retrospect, incomprehensible.[26]

Since roughly 1965 there is room for another, more structural historical analysis of the Roman legal sources. Again, scholars in modern legal theory gave fresh incentives to Romanists. Influential were at least two publications: those of Viehweg[27] and Esser[28] in the years following 1950. Esser could be considered as a late follower of François Gény, whom we already mentioned. Viehweg and Esser aimed at the importance of topical arguments and general principles for judicial decision-making. The echo in the world of studies in Roman law came a few years later, when one of the leading Romanists in the second half of the twentieth century, Max Kaser, wrote on the process of decision making by Roman judges.[29] In 1966 and 1970 Stein, Martini, Carcaterra and Schmidlin wrote their books on definitions and *regulae iuris*. Simultaneously, an important switch followed in the opinions of the leading Romanist Max Kaser. In his contribution to the conference "La Critica del Testo" in 1967, somewhat later elaborated in a book,[30] Kaser warned against the assumption of "additive" (sophisticated and time-consuming!) interpolations and pleaded for a more conservative approach to Justinian's Digest, taking the texts at their face value and assuming interpolations only when there is a substantive argument. For example: the explicit replacement of a classical institution by a Justinianic counterpart is a reasonable assumption of an interpolation: substitution of *mancipatio* by *traditio*, *fiducia* by *pignus* etc. Maybe this new approach does not help us very much directly in the investigation of *rationes decidendi* in Roman legal texts, but it is very remarkable that the above mentioned publications, together with Horak's book, were published in these same years.

---

25 *O. Gradenwitz*, Interpolationen in den Pandekten, Berlin 1887.

26 See for a comprehensive survey of the interpolation period: *J.H.A. Lokin*, The End of an Epoch, Epilegomena to a Century of Interpolation Criticism, in: Collatio iuris romani, Essays in honor of Hans Ankum, Amsterdam 1995, I, 261–273.

27 *Th. Viehweg*, Topik und Jurisprudenz, Ein Beitrag zur rechtswissenschaftlichen Grundlagenforschung, first published in 1954, ^{5}München 1974.

28 *J. Esser*, Grundsatz und Norm bei der richterlichen Fortbildung des Privatrechts, Tübingen 1956, 2nd ed., Tübingen 1967.

29 *M. Kaser*, Zur Methode der römischen Rechtsfindung, Nachrichten der Akademie der Wissenschaften in Göttingen (Phil.-Hist. Klasse), 1962, Nr. 2, Göttingen 1962.

30 *M. Kaser*, Zur Methodologie der römischen Rechtsquellenforschung, Wien 1972.

Horak combines insights of the two historical approaches to Roman law and very intelligently draws attention to the possibility that, in the process of copying the texts of Roman jurists between their first version in classical times and the epoch of Justinian, the *ratio decidendi* could have been added by the copyist.[31] This possibility can unfortunately neither be confirmed nor falsified, but it warns us strongly from drawing radical conclusions and also makes it more understandable that Horak did not write the last word on *rationes decidendi* in classical Roman law.

IV. Rationes Decidendi in Pre-Classical Roman Law

There is a contradictory idea about republican jurisprudence: on the one hand it is Quintus Mucius Scaevola (about 100 B.C.) to whom the credit of being the founder of Roman legal science is given,[32] because of the distinction made by him between *genera;* on the other hand we find in republican jurisprudence especially casuistic solutions for legal problems, and other sources from classical Antiquity give the honor of being the founding father either to Servius Sulpicius Rufus, a friend of Cicero, or to Cicero himself on the basis of his lost work *ius civile in artem redactum.*[33]

Illustrative of the Roman case method, and also of the difficult research on *rationes decidendi,* is an early text by Alfenus Varus, at least one generation later than Quintus Mucius Scaevola, where we meet the later famous expression *ius in causa positum* (D. 9. 2. 52. 2). This text is, strangely enough, not discussed by Horak. The case is one of the oldest reported traffic accidents on a very well-known spot: the Capitol Hill in Rome and the description comes from Alfenus Varus.[34]

D. 9. 52. 2. Alfenus Varus libro secundo digestorum.

In clivo Capitolino duo plostra onusta mulae ducebant: prioris plostri muliones conversum plostrum sublevabant, quo facile mulae ducerent: inter superius plostrum cessim ire coepit et cum muliones, qui inter duo plostra fuerunt, e medio exissent, posterius plostrum

---

31 *Horak,* Ratio decidendi, 291 ff.

32 See *O. Behrends,* Die Wissenschaftslehre im Zivilrecht des Q. Mucius Scaevola pontifex, Nachrichten der Akademie der Wissenschaften in Göttingen, Phil.-Hist. Klasse, 1976, Nr. 7, Göttingen 1976. See lately *K. Tuori,* The myth of Quintus Mucius Scaevola: founding father of legal science? TRG LXXII (2004) 243–262 and *L. Winkel,* Quintus Mucius Scaevola once again, Ex iusta causa traditum, Essays in honor of Eric H. Pool, Fundamina – Editio specialis, [Pretoria] 2005, 425–433.

33 See *M. Villey,* Recherches sur la littérature didactique du droit romain, Paris 1945; H.J. *Mette,* Ius civile in artem redactum, Göttingen 1954.

34 Biography of Alfenus Varus in *W. Kunkel,* Herkunft und soziale Stellung der römischen Juristen, Graz / Wien / Köln 1967, 29. Alfenus Varus was probably not only a jurist, but at the same time owner of a shoe factory in Cremona.

a priore percussum retro redierat et puerum cuiusdam obtriverat: dominus pueri consulebat, cum quo se agere oporteret. Respondi in causa ius esse positum: nam si muliones, qui superius plostrum sustinuissent, sua sponte se subduxissent et ideo factum esset, ut mulae plostrum retinere non possint atque onere ipso retraherentur, cum domino mularum nullam esse actionem, cum hominibus, qui conversum plostrum sustinuissent, lege Aquilia agi posse: nam nihilominus eum damnum dare, qui quod sustineret, mitteret sua voluntate, ut id aliquem feriret: veluti si quis asellum cum agitasset non retinuisset, aeque si quis ex manu telum aut aliud quid immisisset, damnum iniuria daret. Sed si mulae, quia aliquid reformidassent et muliones timore permoti, ne op-primerentur, plostrum reliquissent, cum hominibus actionem nullam esse, cum domino mularum esse. Quod si neque mulae neque homines in causa essent, sed mulae retinere onus nequissent aut cum coniterentur lapsae concidissent et ideo plostrum cessim redisset atque hi quod conversum fuisset onus sustinere nequissent, neque cum domino mularum neque cum hominibus esse actionum. Illud quidem certe, quoquo modo res se haberet, cum domino posteriorum mularum agi non posse, quoniam non sua sponte, sed percussae retro redissent.

Some mules were pulling two loaded carts up the Capitoline. The front cart had tipped up, so the drivers were trying to lift the back to make it easier for the mules to pull it up the hill, but suddenly it started to roll backward. The muleteers, seeing that they would be caught between the two carts, leaped out of its path, and it rolled back and struck the rear cart, which careened down the hill and ran over someone's slave-boy. The owner of the boy asked me whom he should sue. *I replied that it all depended on the facts of the case.* If the drivers who were holding up the front cart had got out of its way of their own accord and that they had been the reason why the mules could not take the weight of the cart and had been pulled back by it, in my opinion no action could be brought against the owner of the mules. The boy's owner should rather sue the men who had been holding up the cart; for damage is no less wrongful when someone voluntarily lets go of something in such circumstances and it hits someone else. For example, if a man failed to restrain an ass that he was driving, he would be liable for any damage that he caused, just as if he threw a missile or anything else from his hand. But if the accident that we are considering had occurred because the mules had shied at something and the drivers had left the cart for fear of being crushed, no action would lie against them; but in such a case, action should be brought against the owner of the mules. On the other hand, if neither the mules nor the drivers were at fault, as, for example, if the mules just could not take the weight or if in trying to do so they had slipped and fallen and the cart had then rolled down the hill because the men could not hold it when it tipped up, there would be no liability on the owner or on the drivers. It is quite clear, furthermore, that however the accident happened, no action could be brought against the owner of the mules pulling the cart behind; for they fell back down the hill not through any fault of theirs, but because they were struck by the cart in front.

The meaning of the expression *ius in causa positum* has especially caused controversy. The expression was never raised to the status of legal principle. It is missing from in the usual surveys of legal principles. Kaser,[35] Schmidlin[36] and Nörr[37] all consider this expression as a program of casuistic method in making a

35 *Kaser,* Rechtsfindung, 60 and fn. 60.

36 *Schmidlin,* Rechtsregeln, 118.

legal decision, whereas the meaning could be – as far as I can see, with much more probability – that legal responsibility lies in the causation (*causa*). We are here at the beginning of the problems of the interpretation of the *Lex Aquilia* (286 B.C. or around 200 B.C.), a statute that is the predecessor of many legal measures against torts.[38] The meaning of this expression is therefore dependent on the meaning of the word *causa*. *Causa* means – besides cause or causation – lawsuit, legal reason and concrete case.[39] However, it is unmistakable that interpretation and the making of a legal decision are not yet conceived as a problem. Therefore we can consider this case as what Honoré would have called the invocation of the facts. There is only one step from the facts to the application of the *Lex Aquilia*. This was already different for some older republican jurists, as for example Quintus Mucius Scaevola, one generation before Alfenus Varus. Maybe the latter was more a practitioner than the former.

V. Ratio Decidendi in Classical Roman Law

As been said, besides the *praecepta iuris* there is a second, more important group of legal principles in Roman law, like *aequitas* and *bona fides*. Especially the development of *bona fides* in classical Roman law gave rise to an enormous literature. Most likely the *bona fides* for private law was developed from an old Roman virtue *fides* that also played a role in the international relations of the city state of Rome.[40] The most important aspect of *bona fides* is the great liberty left to the *iudex* by the *praetor* in a well determined number of cases. After the fixing of the judicial program in the *litis contestatio*, the *iudex* has the power to condemn the defendant after the successful proof of the claims of the plaintiff to whatever the *bona fides* implies (*quidquid dare facere oportere ex fide bona*). In the later history of classical Roman law, we can see an increasing importance of the *iudicia bonae fidei*. Thus a certain number of actions originally provided with a *formula in factum concepta* and therefore *iudicia stricti iuris* are provided with a *formula in ius concepta*. Some legal remedies, for example the *actio pigneraticia in personam*, the *actio commodati*, or the *actio depositi* were originally creations of the

37 *D. Nörr*, Causa mortis, München 1986, 143.

38 See *R. Feenstra*, Vergelding en vergoeding, enkele grepen uit de geschiedenis van de onrechtmatige daad, Rechtshistorische Cahiers Nr. 6, [3]Deventer 2002. On the date of the Lex Aquilia see *L. Winkel*, Das Geld im römischen Recht, in: Roman Law as Formative of Modern Legal Systems, Studies in honor of W. Litewski, II, Cracow 2003, 251 – 258.

39 *H. Heumann/E. Seckel*, Handlexikon zu den Quellen des römischen Rechts, 11 Graz 1971, s.h.v. The word *causa* is also important as an early form of what is called later "Natur der Sache", see on this *Th. Mayer-Maly*, Romanistisches über die Stellung der Natur der Sache zwischen Sein und Sollen, Studi in onore di E. Volterra, II, Milano 1971, 113 – 124.

40 *D. Nörr*, Aspekte des römischen Völkerrechts, München 1989, 102 ff.; see also *D. Nörr*, Die Fides im römischen Völkerrecht, Karlsruhe 1991 [= *D. Nörr*, Historiae iuris antiqui, III, 1777–1844].

praetor and therefore belonged to the *ius honorarium*. This implied that the intention of the action was very much geared to the facts ((*in factum concepta*). Gradually the praetor introduced here a *formula* with an allusion to good faith, *bona fides*, giving in such cases a *formula in ius concepta*.[41] In this way, he created more liberty for the iudex to take the actual situation into account and to use *bona fides* as a *ratio decidendi*. This also implies a great freedom for the iudex to concretize the *bona fides*. Even the cases where the *intentio* of the *formula* already contained the clause with *bona fides*, for example, all the four consensual contracts (sale, hire, mandate and partnership) in pre-classical Roman law, the *bona fides* had the tendency to become more and more important. This is very clear in the field of application of the *actio empti*[42] in classical Roman law.

The role of *aequitas* has been a different one. Occasionally Roman jurists call upon *aequitas* in order to prevent an all too strict application of norms. According to Pringsheim, *aequitas* serves as a bridge between the formulation of a legal norm and its application.[43]

Here again, there is a striking parallel between contemporary jurisprudence and the study of Roman law. Sixty years ago, when a book by Hedemann on "Die Flucht in die Generalklauseln"[44] became very popular in German jurisprudence, scholars on Roman law adopted the view that only in post-classical times *aequitas* was used in Roman law. The use of *aequitas* became of some importance in the search for interpolations by the compilers of Justinian.[45] According to this view, classical Roman jurists would have been very reluctant to use "vague concepts". As soon as modern doctrine blames vague conceptions, the most outstanding jurists of all times, the Roman jurists, are supposed to have refrained from doing so. The unbiased study of the use of *aequitas* by the individual Roman jurists, no longer "fungibele Personen" as in the time from Savigny[46] until Fritz Schulz,[47] has only started recently and so far has given only provisional results[48]. Attention is

---

41 *M. Kaser / R. Knütel*, Römisches Privatrecht, [18]München 2005, 196–198.

42 *R. Zimmermann*, The Law of Obligations – Roman Foundations of the Civilian Tradition, Cape Town etc. 1990, 319 ff.

43 *F. Pringsheim*, Ius aequum und ius strictum, Gesammelte Abhandlungen I, Heidelberg 1961, 131 ff.

44 *J.W. Hedemann*, Die Flucht in die Generalklauseln: Eine Gefahr für Recht und Staat, Tübingen 1933.

45 *F. Pringsheim*, Ius aequum und ius strictum, Gesammelte Abhandlungen I, 1961, 131 ff.; (= note 43) Aequitas und bona fides, *ibidem*, 154 ff.

46 *F.C. von Savigny*, Vom Beruf unserer Zeit für Gesetzgebung und Rechtswissenschaft, 3 Freiburg im B. 1892, 18 and 96 (in the 1814 edition: 29–30, resp. 157).

47 *F. Schulz*, Prinzipien des römischen Rechts, Berlin 1934 / 1954, 73.

48 *P. Stein*, Equitable Principles in Roman Law, "Equity in the World's Legal Systems", Brussel 1973, 75–92; *L. Vacca*, Considerazioni sull'aequitas come elemento del metodo della giurisprudenza romana, Studi in memoria di Giuliana d'Amelio, I, Milano 1978, 397–424 [now also in Contributo allo studio del metodo casistico nel diritto romano, 2nd ed., Milano 1982, 163–190]; *Jan Maifeld*, Die aequitas bei L. Neratius Priscus, Trier 1991.

also paid in this respect to the concept of *utilitas*. Roman jurists are said to have called upon *utilitas* because they were so pragmatic and reluctant of using a fixed methodology.[49] Both *Benignitas* and *humanitas* could occasionally motivate exceptions to legal rules.[50]

Now we come to speak about a third possible category of legal principles, the *regulae* in the Roman sources. Of course we cannot give this subject full attention. As has been said, in accordance with the existing literature, we have to make some basic distinctions: some *regulae* are used in a wide range of contexts, others are found in the *libri regularum* of the jurists Neratius, Gaius, Cervidius Scaevola, Paulus, Modestinus and Marcianus. This latter category exists mostly in short fragments taken out of their original contexts. In spite of this, they have a very casuistic origin and they have therefore only a limited significance as legal principles. But also in the first category, we find *regulae* that are still so closely linked with a concrete case that we cannot categorize them as legal principles. As a third category we could consider some abstract rules in Roman law that are not denoted as *regulae*. Some of them come directly from Roman legal sources. Others were formulated as *regulae* only in later times in legal history, but contain a legal principle from classical Roman law.

This applies for example for the principle of *favor libertatis*. This principle only got the form of a *regula* because it was put in the Digest title 50, 17 *De diversis regulae iuris antiqui* by the compilers of Justinian:

D. 50. 17. 20. Pomponius libro septimo ad Sabinum.

Quotiens dubia interpretatio libertatis est, secundum libertatem respondendum erit.

When there are doubts about freedom, a legal advice has to be given in favor of freedom.

This principle is especially important when a slave is freed by testament and the testament is invalid. Another example is the principle *noxa caput sequitur* (see e.g. D. 2. 9. 2).[51] This principle means that old liability for the misbehavior of a slave is transmitted with the transfer of ownership of that slave. The same applies for the damage caused by a domestic animal. No formulation in the form of a *regula* ever occurred, but no one doubts its character as a legal principle in classical Roman law. A well-known legal principle, occasionally still found in modern law is *nemo auditur turpitudinem suam allegans* (no one can be heard in court who is alleging to his own turpitude). This principle is much later, in modern times, quoted for example by Rawls in his well-known discussion on the case Riggs v. Palmer.[52]

---

49 See *J.A. Ankum*, Utilitatis causa receptum, on the pragmatical methods of the Roman lawyers, Symbolae M. David, Leiden 1968, I, 1 – 31.

50 See *F.B.J. Wubbe*, Benigna interpretatio als Entscheidungskriterium, Festgabe A. Herdlitzka, München / Salzburg 1972, 295 – 314; see also *F.B.J. Wubbe*, L'humanité de Justinien, Tijdschrift voor Rechtsgeschiedenis LVIII (1990), 249, fn. 1.

51 See *Schmidlin* (1970), 94 ff.

52 *R. Dworkin*, Taking Rights Seriously, Cambridge, Mass., 1978, 23; see also *L. Winkel*, A Note on Regulae Iuris in Roman Law and on Dworkin's Distinction between Rules and

This rule is related to the principle *nemo contra factum proprium venire potest* (no one can go against his own deed).[53] This principle is the Roman foundation of the modern doctrine of derogation.

Principles on interpretation we find in two contradictory rules. The first is *plus est in re quam in existimatione mentis* (facts are more important than the individual state of mind), a principle of objective interpretation. The second is *plus est in opinione quam in veritate* (the personal opinion is more important than the truth), a principle of subjective interpretation.[54] The very fact that the Digest contains both maxims shows that Roman law, even in Justinian's time, had never become an axiomatic system. Topical arguments still form the great majority.

The principle of equal hearing, *audite et alteram partem,* is not found as such in Roman legal sources. The point of attachment is:

D. 48. 17. 1. pr. Marcianus libro secundo publicorum.

... *neque enim inaudita causa quemquam damnari aequitatis ratio patitur.*

... the principle of equity does not, as a matter of fact, allow that someone is condemned when he has not been heard in his case.

This principle is not specifically Roman, but it also occurs in other legal systems in Antiquity.[55]

A well-known separate legal principle is the *regula Catoniana,* possibly formulated by Cato in the second century B.C. According to this *regula* the validity of a legacy is evaluated exclusively at the moment of the making of the will. This *regula* is not always applicable, e.g. not in cases of a conditional legacy or a legacy with a *dies incertus.*[56] The *regula Catoniana* is still much more a fixed legal rule in the modern sense than a flexible legal principle. Another *regula* is the rule that *ignorantia iuris nocet* (ignorance of the law is harmful – D, 22. 6. 9. pr.). In another publication I have shown that this *regula* is of a rather late origin, was formulated initially in a different way (*ignorantia iuris non prodest*), and only got its formulation in the form of a legal rule with a distinct number of exceptions in the late classical period.[57] This development might be illustrative of a change in

---

Principles, in: J. *Cairns* & O. *Robinson* (ed.), Critical Studies in Ancient Law, Comparative Law, and Legal History in Honor of Alan Watson, Oxford 2001, 413–418.

53 *E. Riezler,* Venire contra factum proprium, Leipzig 1912; *H.W. Dette,* Venire contra factum proprium nulli conceditur, Zur Konkretisierung eines Rechtssprichworts, Berlin 1985. Cf. *L.B. Curzon,* A Dictionary of Law, Plymouth 1979, s.h.v., 228.

54 See *Ph. Lotmar,* Über plus est in re quam in existimatione und plus est in opinione quam in veritate, Festgabe J.J.W. von Planck, München 1887, 59–115. See also *A. Wacke,* Plus est in re quam in existimatione mentis, Tijdschrift voor Rechtsgeschiedenis LXIV (1996), 309–357.

55 See recently *L.M. Coenraad,* Het beginsel van hoor en wederhoor in het Romeinse procesrecht, [Deventer / Arnhem], 2000.

56 *M. Kaser* / *R. Knütel,* Römisches Privatrecht, [17]München 2003, 448.

the development of later Roman legal science and reinforces the above formulated supposition of Horak, that legal principles in classical Roman law underwent considerable change. There is, at least in the field of mistake of law, a tendency towards a more axiomatic approach: a fixed main rule with clearly defined exceptions. This observation, however, does not apply in every field of the law.

VI. Some Remarks on Medieval Roman Law and Ratio Decidendi

The glossators of Roman law in Bologna in the early twelfth century were confronted with great difficulties when they tried to conceive of Justinian's legislation as a coherent set of rules.[58] The many contradictions in the Digest and the Codex, the result of the short preparation time and also their complex structure, were solved by the method of defining *similia* and *contraria*, following the rules of medieval textual logic. By choosing some texts to be *similia*, it was necessary to recur to more abstract rules and the field of application of these texts was growing. Only occasionally older general legal principles could play a role; the *aequitas gosiana,*[59] named after the glossator Martinus Gosia, around 1140, was perhaps an exception. Also in later periods of medieval Roman law, the general use of legal principles was not common, as follows from studies in the doctrine of the Post-Glossator Baldus de Ubaldis[60]. It is only in the time of the Renaissance that principles like *aequitas* and good faith are being reconsidered, and it is not without reason that, only in this time, all contracts are to be executed in good faith. By this time, the old difference between *actio stricti iuris* and *actio bonae fidei* had finally been abolished.[61]

Theories of interpretation have only been considered as a part of jurisprudence since the sixteenth century juridical humanism, when there was a need for interpretation of Justinian's Roman law sources in their original meaning, apart from the daily application in that period, which was based on the methods of the Post-Glos-

---

57 See *Winkel,* Error iuris nocet, Rechtsirrtum als Problem der Rechtsordnung, I: Rechtsirrtum in der griechischen Philosophie und im römischen Recht bis Justinian, Zutphen 1985, 165–166.

58 *E. Genzmer,* Die Justinianische Kodifikation und die Glossatoren, Atti del Congresso internazionale di diritto romano, Bologna 1933, Pavia 1934, 347–430 [partly reprinted in: *E.J.H. Schrage* (ed.), Das römische Recht im Mittelalter, Darmstadt [1987], 5–53].

59 *J.J. Hallebeek,* Audi, domine Martine, over aequitas gosiana en het beding ten behoeve van een derde, Amsterdam 2000 [inaugural lecture Free University].

60 Cf. *N. Horn,* Aequitas in den Lehren von Baldus, Köln / Graz 1968.

61 First remark in this sense clearly by Baldus in his commentary to X 2,11,1, see H. *Coing,* Europäisches Privatrecht, I, München 1985, 400, n.. 1; later one could refer to *Grotius,* De iure belli ac pacis, II, 11, 6, where as far as I can see, the words *Sed harum distinctionum pleraeque veniunt ex iure Romano... Quaedam etiam non satis verae aut accuratae sunt* have this implication.

sators. This can be illustrated especially in the developments in the interpretation of the last title of the Digest, D. 50. 17, *"De diversis regulis iuris antiqui."*[62] The rise of a specialized *hermeneutica iuris* is the direct consequence of the attempts of historical understanding of the Roman law sources, which emerged first in the sixteenth century, but was also important in the seventeenth, eighteenth, and nineteenth centuries.[63] It is not without reason that the most important movement in nineteenth century German jurisprudence was called the *Historical* School. Here lies at the same time the most recent link between the modern theories of interpretation and Roman law. It may be useful to dwell for one moment upon Savigny's "Methodenlehre."[64] In this treatise, we find an outline of the scientific program of the Historical School. There the main question is how interpretation of legal rules, of "Jurisprudenz" is possible. Further on, Savigny deals with the relation between history and system, a question which he returned to in his later work "System des heutigen römischen Rechts"[65] in a much more elaborate way. General principles were, however, not very important in German jurisprudence in the nineteenth century.

VII. Conclusions

In the previous paragraphs, we described not only the history, but also a part of the historiography of the *rationes decidendi* in Roman law and we linked them with simultaneous changes of position in general jurisprudence. We saw that, at least in the last two centuries, there were remarkable parallels. It is noticeable also that, in modern time, *rationes decidendi* play a role in codified and uncodified legal systems alike. That all this discussion, as far as can be traced, started in Roman law in antiquity where the style of concrete legislation had remained quite primitive, is at the least remarkable. The often quoted phrase of Fritz Schulz: "Das Volk des Rechts war nicht das Volk des Gesetzes" and the fact that the style of legislation itself remained primitive in Rome[66] could at first sight not possibly

62 *P. Stein*, Regulae iuris, 162 ff.; *P. Stein*, The Digest Title 'De diversis regulis iuris antiqui' and the General Principles of Law, Essays in Jurisprudence in Honor of Roscoe Pound, Indianapolis / New York, 1–20 (above, note 17) [= *P. Stein*, The Character and Influence of the Roman Civil Law, London 1988, 53–72].

63 Jan *Schröder*, Recht als Wissenschaft; Geschichte der juristischen Methode vom Humanismus bis zur historischen Schule, München 2001, 48 ff. and 119 ff.; see also *G.C.J.J. van den Bergh*, Jedem das Seine, in: "Recht als norm en als aspiratie" (red. J.B.J.M. ten Berge e.a.), Nijmegen 1986, 258–265, especially 263.

64 *F.C von Savigny*, Juristische Methodenlehre (herausgegeben von Gerhard Wesenberg), Stuttgart 1951. This edition is based upon a manuscript of Jakob Grimm from 1802 / 1803. See also: *A. Mazzacane* (ed.), F.C. von Savigny, Vorlesungen über juristische Methodologie, 1802–1842, Frankfurt / M. 1993.

65 Quoted at note 18.

66 *H. Honsell*, Gesetzesverständnis in der römischen Antike, in: Europäisches Rechtsdenken in Geschichte und Gegenwart [= Fs Helmut Coing] I (1982) 129–148, especially 141.

have led to the astonishing development of the sophisticated use of arguments in the form of what can be called *rationes decidendi* in pre-classical, classical, and later Roman law[67].

67 I thank my colleague Tammo Wallinga for his useful comments. See also *R. Knütel*, Zur Rechtsfindung der Römer, in: Gedächtnisschrift für Meinhard Heinze, München 2005, 475–499, published aften completion of this article. Knütel's conclusions are close to mine.

JEAN HILAIRE

Ratio decidendi au Parlement de Paris d'après les registres d'*Olim* (1254–1318)

La source exploitée pour cette recherche – les quatre plus anciens registres des archives du Parlement de Paris[1] – a été choisie parce qu'elle permet de suivre l'évolution du processus de décision à travers l'importante mutation de la *curia regis* autour du souverain à la charnière des XIIIe et XIVe siècles.

En premier lieu, cet ensemble de registres désigné traditionnellement du premier mot de l'un d'entre eux, *Olim*, couvre l'époque où les séances judiciaires (*parlamenta*) de la *curia regis* donnent progressivement naissance à une nouvelle juridiction, la Cour de Parlement. Cette cour, constituant ainsi une juridiction distincte de la *curia regis* et étant par là une juridiction de justice déléguée, est au sommet de l'ensemble des juridictions royales; mais le roi peut toujours *retenir sa justice* pour l'exercer lui-même à la *curia*. Le Parlement est bientôt fixé à Paris tandis que la *curia* demeure itinérante en suivant la personne royale dans ses constants déplacements. Pour autant le roi – qui peut venir à tout moment tenir en personne sa cour de Parlement – est toujours censé y juger lui-même souverainement. Il en résulte enfin que le ressort territorial de compétence de cette nouvelle juridiction est ainsi celui du roi lui-même, c'est à dire l'ensemble du royaume.

Or la naissance du Parlement est, en fait, une des conséquences directes de la grande politique capétienne qui, menée de Philippe Auguste à Philippe le Bel en passant par saint Louis, a assuré en trois grands règnes la montée en puissance de la royauté surtout à partir du milieu du XIIIe siècle. Les accroissements territoriaux n'en sont d'ailleurs qu'un aspect. Dans ce cadre en effet les réformes procédurales de saint Louis ont grandement contribué à renforcer l'audience de la royauté dans le monde féodal, tout particulièrement par l'introduction de la procédure d'appel hiérarchique dans le domaine royal, en la substituant aux gages de bataille, et par le rôle d'incitation que le roi entendait lui faire jouer. Les affaires ont alors afflué de tout le royaume aux séances de parlement. D'une part, les *Olim* rendent parfai-

---

1 Les Olim ou registres des arrêts rendus par la cour du roi sous les règnes de saint Louis, de Philippe le Hardi, de Philippe le Bel, de Louis le Hutin et de Philippe le Long, publiés par le comte Beugnot, membre de l'Institut, Paris Imprimerie royale, t. I 1839 (1254–1273), t. II 1842 (1274–1318), t. III[1] 1844 (1299–1311), t. III[2] 1848 (1312–1318); Index sous la direction de *Jean Hilaire*, Centre d'Etude d'Histoire Juridique, Centre Historique des Archives Nationales, Paris 2003. On pourra également consulter l'*Index* sur le site du CEHJ http://www.u-paris2.fr/cehj/.

tement compte de l'énorme accroissement d'activité judiciaire sous l'autorité du roi d'autant que la distinction n'y était pas encore établie entre le criminel et le civil; d'autre part, ces registres permettent de suivre complètement l'évolution de l'organisation des séances judiciaires de la *curia regis* vers la constitution d'une nouvelle cour de justice, le Parlement.

Enfin ces séances judiciaires sont devenues, à cause de cet accroissement considérable et rapide d'affaires à trancher, une instance où le roi n'est plus venu siéger qu'exceptionnellement; plus précisément, dès la fin du règne de saint Louis la personne royale est devenue de moins en moins présente aux séances judiciaires de sa cour. Le travail des membres de la *curia regis,* appelés alors à juger et décider en l'absence de la personne royale mais sous le couvert de la souveraineté du roi, s'est nécessairement organisé en fonction de cette absence. D'un côté, les conseillers devaient apprendre à travailler et décider seuls tandis que les décisions ne pouvaient par principe être prises qu'au nom du roi. D'un autre côté, la prise de décision restait tributaire du cadre particulier de la souveraineté de la personne royale même dans le cadre de la délégation de pouvoir judiciaire[2]. Par la suite la cour de Parlement était ainsi appelée à rendre une justice à la fois déléguée et souveraine; mais en même temps elle ne pouvait disposer de la grâce à l'égal de la personne royale et devait apprendre à en reconnaître les limites[3].

Du fait de cette évolution, la recherche de la *ratio decidendi*[4] à travers les actes du Parlement ne peut donc être comprise que très largement. Il est nécessaire en effet d'explorer préalablement le développement du processus de décision à partir des séances judiciaires de la *curia regis* jusqu'aux sessions de la Cour de Parlement (I); seulement alors pourra-t-on, à travers les décisions, jugements et arrêts rendus dans le cadre de cette juridiction au cours de ce demi-siècle si déterminant dans l'histoire de la Justice royale, aller plus avant dans la recherche des raisons fondamentales, de la nature des motifs[5], qui guidaient les jugeurs (II).

---

2 *J. Hilaire,* „Le *Roi* et *Nous.* Procédure et genèse de l'Etat aux XIIIe et XIVe siècles", in: Revue Histoire de la Justice, n̄ 5 (1992), p. 3–18.

3 *J. Hilaire,* La grâce et l'Etat de droit dans la procédure civile (1250–1350), in: Suppliques et requêtes. Le gouvernement par la grâce en Occident (XIIè-XIVè siècle), Collection de l'Ecole française de Rome, 2003, p. 357–369.

4 Au sens donné à cette expression par les juristes contemporains: *expression latine signifiant „raison de décider", parfois utilisée pour désigner, dans le processus décisionnel d'une autorité,le motif décisoire, la raison décisive, la donnée déterminante de la décision* (*G. Cornu,* Vocabulaire juridique, Association Henri Capitant, PUF, 1987, v̄ ratio decidendi).

5 Sans pour autant retenir dans sa totalité la définition du *motif* telle qu'elle est donnée dans l'ouvrage cité ci-dessus: *raison de fait ou de droit qui commande la décision et que le jugement doit exposer avant le dispositif (NCPC, a. 455).* La référence ne peut s'attacher ici qu'à la première partie de la définition; la seconde qui souligne l'obligation de motiver relève de la tradition nouvelle dans le système français depuis les réformes révolutionnaires.

I. L'influence du cadre institutionnel sur le processus de décision

L'évolution du cadre institutionnel fait apparaître deux situations bien différentes suivant que le roi est présent ou absent dans les séances judiciaires de sa cour, *parlamenta.* Or cela a d'autant plus d'importance que, d'une part, les méthodes de travail et la prise de décision ne pouvaient pas être les mêmes dans les deux cas tandis que, d'autre part, si la présence royale était assez fréquente dans ces séances durant la première période, le règne de saint Louis, le roi s'en est écarté par la suite ce qui a préparé et suscité la création du Parlement.

1. La *curia regis* sous le règne de saint Louis

Dans la première situation, en effet, le roi entouré de ses conseillers jugeait en tenant dans sa cour des séances judiciaires; ou bien, au contraire, les conseillers tenaient la cour et prenaient une décision en l'absence de la personne royale laquelle était alors censée avoir tranché elle-même. Pour éclairer cette différence profonde il faut s'en remettre ici à la forme de la source de référence: les quatre registres d'*Olim* (X^{1A} 1 à 4) sur lesquels à partir de 1274 les greffiers ont commencé à résumer certaines affaires pour la commodité de la consultation car toutes les décisions d'une session étaient traditionnellement consignées à la suite les unes des autres sur un très long rouleau de parchemin de plusieurs dizaines de mètres d'un seul tenant, rouleaux aujourd'hui perdus. Les greffiers ont constitué ce genre d'archives, les registres, en remontant jusqu'en 1254 si bien qu'ils ont ainsi recensé des actes anciens en même temps que des décisions contemporaines. D'où l'intérêt qu'il faut porter à la manière dont ces greffiers ont rédigé ces textes, plutôt brièvement d'ailleurs pour les plus anciennes sessions à propos d'affaires auxquels ils n'avaient peut-être pas assisté, et aux formules qu'ils ont employées: on y décèle des nuances terminologiques fort éclairantes pour notre propos.

Saint Louis, en effet, était suffisamment présent dans les séances judiciaires de sa cour pour que son influence personnelle soit perceptible à travers les recensions des greffiers; il s'y comportait en souverain féodal qui, après l'exposé de la demande et l'instruction de l'affaire, sollicitait éventuellement des membres de sa cour le conseil que ces derniers avaient le devoir de lui apporter. Très pénétré de l'importance de sa mission et de l'*officium judicis* qui était le sien, il instruisait d'abord l'affaire en donnant une grande place à la procédure d'enquête qui a été un élément capital dans sa profonde réforme de la justice. Le recours à l'enquête était de sa part quasiment systématique et le greffier nous rapporte même que le roi, sans doute dans une affaire particulièrement délicate, avait *ex officio suo* prescrit une enquête pour soulager sa conscience avant de trancher[6]. De même, en 1261

6 Olim, I, 75, 19 (1258): ... *dominus rex ex officio suo fecit inde fieri inquestam ad alleviandam consciencism suam* ....

revient à la cour une enquête réalisée *de mandato domini regis* pour savoir si un certain chevalier ne s'était pas indûment, *de novo,* constitué une garenne sur les terres de ses voisins. Au cours de l'enquête les demandeurs n'ont rien prouvé contre le chevalier qui gardera sa garenne; ce point acquis, il est décidé que le roi n'en ordonnera pas moins une nouvelle enquête pour savoir si le chevalier n'aurait pas étendu abusivement sa garenne[7]. Il semblerait alors que la cour, prenant cette décision vraisemblablement en l'absence de la personne royale d'après le texte, s'est appuyée ici sur l'*officium judicis* du souverain. Un tel épisode montre parfaitement comment un long règne a permis à saint Louis de léguer à la *curia regis* et à la future Cour de Parlement une solide tradition pour la place et le maniement de cette procédure, en quelque sorte une culture de l'enquête dont s'étaient imprégnés les conseillers; le Parlement une fois constitué, les conseillers ordonnaient en effet des enquêtes avec la même fréquence et les jugeaient avec la même rigueur quant aux formes, n'hésitant pas au moment de les juger à annuler les procédures défectueuses[8].

Puis le roi sollicitait éventuellement le conseil de la part de tel ou tel membre ou de l'ensemble de ses conseillers avant de décider; cela se traduisait sous la plume des greffiers par: *habito consilio rex voluit.* Si les conseillers avaient le devoir de lui apporter ce conseil, le roi pouvait les consulter individuellement en secret. Cette tradition s'est conservée au début du XIVe siècle quand le roi ne venait plus qu'exceptionnellement tenir séance dans son Parlement pour y juger des affaires qu'il se réservait de trancher lui-même: une ordonnance précise alors que dans la salle d'audience les abords de l'estrade réservée au roi devront à ce moment-là être dégagés pour que le souverain puisse prendre conseil de tel ou tel en secret[9]. Ainsi apparaissait une autre tradition, celle du secret qui ne devait pas non plus demeurer sans conséquence.

A propos de certaines affaires le roi souhaitait interroger largement les membres de la cour[10] et même pour une affaire particulière le greffier a cru devoir le rapporter avec une solennité manifeste: il note que le roi a requis le conseil de nombreux conseillers dont, pour la plupart, il consigne les noms[11]. Dans leurs recensions des

---

7 Olim, I, 151, 7: ... *Quia nichil probatur contra predictum Guillelmum de Gisorcio, remaneat eidem Guillelmo garena sua in locis infrascriptis videlicet ... Verumtamen dominus rex, ex officio suo, faciet inquiri utrum idem Guillelmus extenderit garennam suam plus quam debeat.*

8 Olim, II, 436, 16 (1299): ... *et propter hoc predicta principalis inquesta per idem judicium fuit totaliter annullata et injunctum quod de predictis, iterato vocatis partibus, inquiratur* ... De même, II, 436, 17 (1299): *Inquesta facta inter regem et capitulum sancti-Petri-Puellarum-Bituris non est facta sufficienter et ideo partes iterato vocabuntur et audientur.*

9 Ordonnance du 11 mars 1345, art. 13: ... *quand le roi vendra en parlement que le parc soit tout vuide et aussi soit vuide la place qui est devant son siège si que il puist parler secrètement à ceuls qu'il appellera pour parler à luy*. . . .

10 Olim, I, 482, 16 (1260): ... *post multas inquestas ... de mandato domini regis factas, per dominem regem et totum consilium suum absoluti sunt de morte ipsius clerici* . . . .

Olim les greffiers ont parfois pris soin, en effet, de souligner que les conseillers avaient donné au souverain un avis particulièrement circonstancié vraisemblablement en raison de l'importance ou de l'urgence de l'affaire[12]; ils notaient les cas où le roi avait recueilli un avis unanime[13] ou l'opinion de quelques membres du conseil seulement[14] mais aussi ceux où étaient apparues des divergences d'opinions[15]. La forme et l'importance de la consultation ne dépendait que de la volonté du souverain, mais la consultation de l'ensemble du conseil pouvait apparaître aussi comme une esquisse de délibération, nuance que le greffier a commencé à introduire, en 1267, de manière encore très exceptionnelle dans une affaire traitée en présence du roi, en substituant ici la formule *deliberato consilio* à l'habituel *habito consilio*[16].

Enfin le roi décidait en souverain comme le montre le dispositif de la recension rédigée par le greffier. D'une part, les actes attestant la présence du roi dans sa cour ne comportent pas toujours la référence à l'avis des conseillers[17]. D'autre part, même ayant reçu le conseil le roi tranchait seul: *habito consilio rex voluit* ou *rex precepit.*[18] et cela même éventuellement contre l'avis de la majorité du conseil[19]. Il était vraiment le roi-juge et le greffier invoquera ici son *officium judicis*

11 Olim, I, 75, 19 (1258): l'enquête que le roi avait ordonnée pour soulager sa conscience arrivant à l'examen de la cour... *ea diligenter audita, dominus rex super ipsa inquesta requisivit et habuit consilium istorum quorum nomina scribuntur... Plures alii ad hoc interfuerunt. De unanimi consilio omnium istorum dictum et deffinitum fuit quod....*

12 Olim, I, 722, 20 (1268): ... *Demum dominus rex auditis premissis omnibus, intellecto etiam quod per domum ipsam si taliter remaneret non solum pax civitatis Matisconensis set totius illius terre posset turbari, habito diligenti consilio, precepit baillivo suo Matisconensi quod penitus dirueret domum fortem predictam.*

13 Olim, t.I, p. 418, n°3 (1254): ... *dictum fuit concorditer per totum consilium ....*

14 Olim, I, 762, 26, 1269.

15 Olim, I, 690, 29 (1267): après enquête ... *audito posmodum per baillivum quod de hujusmodi justicia vel consimili, nullum usum invenerat pro monachis aut pro Rege, visa etiam carta predicta, licet pluribus de consilio videretur quod per cartam ipsam non debebant habere justiciam hujusmodi in loco eodem abbas et conventus predicti, aliis de consilio et paucioribus contrarium sencientibus, voluit Rex quod ipsi abbas et conventus haberent hujusmodi justiciam in dicta villa de Sequacio ita tamen quod si alias posset ipsi domino Regi constare de jure suo quantum ad hoc illud, prout justum est recuperare valeret.*

16 Olim, I, 705,19 (1267): ... *Tandem audito quod ... visa etiam carta monachorum per quam hoc facere non poterant ut consilio videbatur, voluit rex deliberato consilio quod ....*

17 Olim I, 904, 57 (1272): ... *demum, viso diligenter privilegio antedicto, placuit domino regi quod usque ad voluntatem suam in scacario placiterent et respondere tenerentur.*

18 Olim, I, 712, 38 (1267): ... *dominus rex, habito consilio diligenti, super hoc dictum suum protulit in hunc modum videlicet quod ....*

19 Olim, I, 690, 29 (1267): ... *Tandem, dato in mandatis ipsi ballivo quod de usu parcium inquireret veritatem, et post, inquesta hujusmodi et predicta carta eorum ad curiam afferretur, audito postmodum per ballivum quod de hujusmodi justicia vel consimili nullum usum invenerat pro monachis aut pro rege, visa etiam carta predicta, licet pluribus de consilio videretur quod per cartam ipsam non debebant habere justiciam hujusmodi in loco eodem abbas et conventus predicti, aliis de consilio et paucioribus contrarium sencientibus, voluit*

auquel on fait appel pour le saisir. La plus grande fréquence des recensions faisant formellement état de la présence de la personne royale dans les séances judiciaires de la *curia regis* se situe sous le règne de saint Louis. Encore, il est vrai, les greffiers n'ont-ils attesté cette présence dans leurs recensions que dans les cas où le roi l'a manifestée par une intervention particulière ou inhabituelle. Mais pour autant, même sous ce règne nombre d'audiences ont certainement été tenues en l'absence du souverain, les conseillers examinant les affaires et les jugeant en son nom. Le fait que nombre de vacations de parlement soient tenues sans que le roi y assiste a des conséquences importantes sur la prise de décision. Sans doute à l'époque de saint Louis le roi n'en demeurait pas moins proche des conseillers, comme semble bien le marquer la formule plutôt familière que le greffier a ajouté à propos d'une enquête examinée en 1261: *Expedita fuit in hoc parlamento quantum ad consilium, et non quantum ad regem cum quo erat super hoc loquendum*[20]*;* les conseillers dans un cas délicat avaient instruit l'affaire et préparé la décision mais s'étaient tournés vers le roi avant de l'arrêter. Dans ce contexte deux remarques s'imposent. En premier lieu, s'il est indiqué parfois que le roi a consulté son conseil lors de la séance, en revanche lorsque sa présence n'apparaît pas le greffier s'en tient simplement, pour introduire le dispositif, à une formule impersonnelle: ... *determinatum fuit, pronunciatum fuit, judicatum fuit* etc. En second lieu, après un rapide exposé des faits ou des arguments des parties le greffier introduit presque toujours le dispositif par un terme annonçant des considérants fondant la décision: *quia* ... ou encore *considerato quod* ... [21]. Ainsi dans le jugement des enquêtes la *ratio decidendi* résulte le plus souvent de l'examen des preuves; une formule brève, *probatum est* ou *non probatum est,* justifie la décision dans la plupart des actes. Parfois est visée l'argumentation de l'une des parties: dans un bref dispositif l'incise *propter raciones premissas* se rapporte en réalité aux motifs de rejet de la demande présentés par les gens du roi dont l'avis a été suivi[22]. De même apparaît également parmi les motifs cités dans le dispositif le précédent judiciaire[23], ou encore l'avis formulé par le conseil à la demande du roi[24]. Enfin, autre aspect de cette esquisse

---

rex quod ipsi abbas et conventus hujusmodi justiciam in dicta villa de Sequacio, ita tamen quod si alias posset ipsi domino regi constare de juro suo quantum ad hoc illud, prout justum est, recuperare valeret.

20 Olim, I, 130, 10: le greffier a simplement désigné l'enquête ce qui cependant permet sans doute d'expliquer la prudence des conseillers ... *Inquesta cambellanorum domini regis et abbatis columbensis facta super palefredo quem cambellani petunt ab abbate quando est novus abbas.*

21 Olim, I, 781, 26 (1269).

22 Olim, I, 673, 18 (1267).

23 Olim, I, 624, 18 (1265): ... *invento ... quod etiam in consimili casu alias fuit pronunciatum* ....

24 Olim, I, 626, 21 (1265): le chapitre demandeur, saisissant le roi par voie de *supplicatio,* s'appuyait sur des lettres patentes lui accordant un privilège, mais le conseil rappela au roi que ces lettres avaient été rapportées: ...*habuit dominus rex consilium quod litteras ipsas [patentes] generales sicut capitulum Kathalanense petierat, revocaret et revocavit et fecit in*

de motivation, le dispositif précise dans certains cas le détail des raisons qui ont suscité la décision pour en souligner la force et l'accumulation[25].

Le style du greffier nous est d'autant plus précieux que dès le règne de saint Louis, à travers quelques signaux de plus en plus précis, il nous renseigne sur la tendance du conseil à prendre quelque autorité dans son rôle judiciaire en jugeant au nom du roi. Signes fugitifs et encore précoces, des recensions de 1259 présentent certaines sentences non plus de manière impersonnelle mais comme émanant du conseil et de la *curia*: ... *dictum fuit et ordinatum per consilium quod* ... [26] et aussi *curia tamen volens* ... [27]. En revanche, vers la fin du règne apparaît, en 1267, la locution *voluit curia*[28]. En 1267 également, autres faits nouveaux, tandis que parfois la *curia* décide *habito consilio* sans que le roi apparaisse[29], il est arrivé également que ce dernier, de son côté, décide *deliberato consilio* précisément en suivant l'avis des conseillers fondé sur l'examen des preuves produites[30]. Très significatif enfin est le dédoublement à propos de l'*officium judicis*: à côté de décisions du roi prises *ex officio suo* apparaissent des interventions *ex officio curie*[31]. En fait on est déjà entré dans une période de transition au terme de laquelle les sessions de parlement auront donné naissance à une nouvelle cour de justice. En 1276, en effet, apparaît subrepticement sous la plume du greffier une autre formule à propos du conseil: *nostra curia, pronunciatum fuit per nostre curie judicium*[32] ... Deux ans plus tard cette terminologie fait partie du style de la cour. Elle consacre

---

sua presentia cancellari ... *De revocatione vero specialium litterarum fuit responsum dicto capitulo quod* ....

25 Olim, I, 655, 13 (1266): ... *Tandem visa carta ipsius prioris in qua inter alia continebatur quod concessa erant pascua in dicta foresta pro propriis porcis suis, audito etiam quod usu erat super hoc dictus prior, necnon et quod ab ista eadem impeticione dictorum mercatorum in parlamento Penthecostis proxime preterito fuerat absolutus deteminatum fuit quod idem prior proprios porcos suos de nutriria sua vel quos emerit eodem anno a tali termino quod secundum consuetudinem ipsius foreste reputari debeant propria nutriria ponere poterat tempore pasnagii in dicta foresta et absolutus fuit ab impeticione eorumdem mercatorum.*

26 *Olim*, I, 447, 2; I, 449,6.

27 Olim, I, 448, 4 et 5.

28 Olim, I, 693, 35 (1267): ... *Tandem, inquesta super hoc facta et ad istud parlamenta delata, post multas altercationes mediantibus aliquibus de consilio domini Regis, facta fuit inter partes pax* ... *voluntas curie fuit* ... *Ceterum juravit idem Petrus* ... *Rege presente* ... Ainsi les parties peuvent mettre fin à la procédure par un pacte négocié sous l'égide de la cour et apparaît alors la *voluntas curie;* mais le greffier prend bien soin de rappeler également la présence du roi pour souligner la solennité de la prestation de serment.

29 Olim, I, 704, 17.

30 Olim, I, 705, 19.

31 Olim, I, 729, 11 (1268): ... *Vocato vero ex officio curie ipso ballivo, et ejus relatione audita, nichil inventum fuit per quod pronunciacio inqueste irritari deberet; et fuit dictum per curiam et ipsi Ysembardo responsum quod non audiretur sua peticio set staret judicium et pronunciatione facta per curiam in hac parte.*

32 Olim, II, 79, 5 (1276): *pronunciatum fuit per curie nostre judicium* ... .*et fuit expresse dictum quod* ....

par ce pluriel de majesté tout à la fois la distinction désormais clairement faite entre la personne royale et la cour (*Rex* et *nostra curia;* le *Roi* et *Nous)* et cependant la persistance du caractère souverain des décisions à travers la fiction de la présence physique du roi[33].

2. La transition vers la cour de Parlement

Le passage de la *curia regis* à la *cour de Parlement* en tant qu'organe de décision change les modalités de cette décision et en modifie l'expression. Le style du greffier consacre une situation de fait dans laquelle le *consilium* a donné naissance à une *curia* qui fait parler le roi d'elle-même comme si la personne royale ne faisait plus tout à fait corps avec l'institution[34]. Aussi bien la Cour de Parlement est fixée à Paris en 1303, ne suit plus le roi et son conseil dans ses déplacements; la royauté doit alors préciser l'organisation de cette nouvelle institution, particulièrement les devoirs des conseillers dans les méthodes de travail et la tenue des audiences (ordonnance de janvier 1278)[35]. Deux dispositions sont spécialement à retenir ici parce qu'elles consacraient directement l'éloignement de la personne royale et ont eu des conséquences importantes. D'une part, était exigé de ceux qui siégeaient *in consilio regis* à la fin du XIIIe siècle un serment garantissant au souverain, dans l'ensemble des causes qu'ils auraient à entendre, la loyauté et le secret du conseil qui lui était apporté[36]. D'autre part, quand les requêtes étaient reçues par les maîtres celles qui mettaient en jeu la grâce du roi devaient être distraites pour lui être soumises[37]. Or dans l'évolution de cette nouvelle institution ces deux dispositions, à propos du secret et de la grâce, se sont trouvées – de fait – étroitement liées.

Rappelons en premier lieu que, sous le règne de Philippe III, la cour est appelée de plus en plus couramment à décider seule en l'absence du roi mais toujours en son nom; dans ce cas, pour pouvoir donner ce conseil qui ne peut alors être qu'unique dans son expression, les conseillers devaient le formuler au terme d'une délibération clôturée par un vote où la majorité l'emportait. C'est le sens de la formule *deliberato consilio.* Une fois, à propos d'un jugement de 1318, le greffier nous a

---

33 *J. Hilaire,* Le *Roi* et *Nous* ... op. cit. p. 8–9.

34 Olim, II, 99, 6 (1277): ... *Auditis rationibus et defensionibus dicti Guillelmi, auditis etiam hinc inde propositis et plenius intellectis, et predictis partibus judicio nostre curie super hoc se supponentibus, habita deliberatione, idem Guillelmus, per judicium nostre curie ab impeticione dicti Johannis fuit absolutus et fuit idem super hoc silencium impositum.*

35 *Langlois,* Textes relatifs à l'histoire du parlement, p. 95 et s.

36 *Langlois,* op. cit., n° XCV, p. 127: *Nous jurons que nous serons leal au roi et le conseillerons leailment quant il nous demandera conseil et cèlerons son secré et son conseil en bonne foi; et es causes que nous orrons devant lui ou sanz lui par s'autorité nous li garderons sa droiture et l'autrui en bonne foi.*

37 *Langlois,* loc.cit., ord. de 1278, il est ordonné que *les requestes soient ouiez en la sale par aucun des mestres et seront portées au roi celles qui contandront grâce* ... (art. 16).

apporté la preuve de cette procédure en faisant état de la teneur de la délibération avec le détail des opinions émises (*Olim*, III^2 n° 84, p. 1312). Preuve fort utile, mais acte unique car c'est au contraire le secret des cours qui a dominé la tradition française. En effet la délibération n'en demeurait pas moins dans le cadre du conseil dû au souverain; en revanche, la décision fondée sur la notion de conseil au roi était souveraine comme si elle émanait du roi en personne. La conséquence semble bien avoir été plus ou moins directement que le secret du conseil a atteint en même temps les motifs qui fondaient les décisions. A partir de la fin du XIIIe siècle l'esquisse de motivation disparaît le plus souvent dans les recensions; la *ratio decidendi* ne sera plus guère exprimée ou même évoquée dans le dispositif.

Ainsi dès les années 1276–1277 l'expression d'un motif devient quasiment exceptionnelle[38] et le greffier s'en tient surtout à un simple visa des preuves avancées[39], en une formule très vite stéréotypée[40]. En revanche il est notable que se produit un véritable changement d'esprit dans la relation du greffier. D'abord, à mesure que les recensions se rapprochent de l'époque où les greffiers avaient entrepris ce travail de constitution de registres les textes sont plus longs. Ensuite, alors que le dispositif devient de plus en plus limité sur la *ratio decidendi*[41] l'exposé des prétentions, preuves et arguments, des parties devient plus complet passant de quelques lignes à plus d'une page; on peut retenir toutefois qu'une plus grande place est consacrée à l'argumentation de la partie en faveur de laquelle est prononcée la sentence. Enfin, s'il ne révèle guère la *ratio decidendi* le dispositif se fait insistant, d'ailleurs dans des formulations variables mais détaillées[42], sur le respect des formes procédurales devant la cour et la réalité de la délibération pour en souligner la rigueur[43].

Ces deux éléments, discrétion sur la *ratio decidendi* qui sera entendue plus tard comme le *secret des cours*, d'une part, affirmation de la rigueur de la procédure suivie devant la cour, d'autre part, semblent bien partir d'un même mouvement,

---

38 Olim, II, 86, 37 (1276): ... *visis litteris dictorum prepositi et conventus a dicto comite exhibitis per quam evidenter apparebat dictum comitem habere omnimodam justiciam in hominibus et villis dictorum prepositi et conventus sitis in baronia combralie* ....

39 Olim, II, 78, 1 (1276): ... *visa carta dictorum comitis et comitisse super dicta donacione, auditis hinc inde propositis, pronunciatum fuit quod* ....

40 Olim, II, 94, 29 (1277): ... *Auditis hinc inde propositis pronunciatum fuit* ....

41 Olim, III^1, 6, 9 (1299): ... *Tandem dictis partibus sufficienter auditis, visa etiam inquesta super predictis factis omnibusque rite actis, pronunciatum fuit per judicium curie nostre predictum episcopum intentionem suam sufficienter probasse* ....

42 Olim, III^1, 46, 10 (1300): ...*Tandem visa inquesta super hiis de mandato nostro facta et diligenter examinata, omnibusque sollemnitate que convenit rite actis inventum est* ....

43 Olim, III^1, 39, 55 (1300): ... *Tandem auditis partibus hinc inde, visisque processu predicto et quibusdam litteris ex parte dicti presbyteri productis habitaque deliberatione super hoc diligenti per judicium nostre curie dictum fuit et prononciatum* ...; III^1 59, 26 (1300): ... *Tandem auditis et diligenter discussis rationibus partium predictarum, visoque processu coram dicto preposito super hoc habito et ejus judicato predicto per judicium nostre curie dictum fuit* ....

avoir une même cause. En effet, l'éloignement de la personne royale dans la prise de décision a été mal admis par les justiciables, d'autant que le roi demeurait par le serment du sacre débiteur de bonne justice à l'égard de chacun de ses sujets. C'est là qu'intervient la grâce royale que les justiciables pouvaient implorer et dont le souverain restait le grand dispensateur.

Précisément faut-il rappeler, en second lieu, que la question de la grâce royale s'est posée nécessairement de manière plus aiguë à la cour à mesure que la présence du roi devenait plus exceptionnelle. Cette absence a fait, en effet, que peu à peu les interventions royales ont été beaucoup plus souvent liées à la grâce et plutôt destinées à opposer la volonté du roi aux décisions de la cour. Ainsi le souverain se réserve-t-il d'écarter la condamnation à mort pour un faussaire[44], de modérer une peine[45] ou de procéder lui-même à la taxation d'une amende[46]. Sans doute la cour peut toujours en référer au souverain[47] qui demeure le maître de la grâce[48] et une certaine concertation a lieu[49]. Mais en même temps elle est amenée aussi à décider elle-même pour une part d'affaires où la grâce royale peut intervenir comme un moyen de tempérer la décision. La cour commence alors, de son côté, à décider *de gratia* ou encore *de gratia speciali*[50]. Une formule s'imposera bientôt

---

44 Olim, II, 319, 26 (1290): *Quia Bertrandus de Manata falsarius per consiliarios domini regis clericos captus fuit pro suspicione dicte falsitatis, placuit domino regi quod non condempnetur ad mortem licet falsitas probata fuerit contra eum et de ea convictus fuerit et confessus.*

45 Olim, III[1], 282, 13 (1308): pour une affaire de destruction de biens immobiliers et mobiliers placés dans la main du roi la cour a prononcé une condamnation à une amende envers le roi et des dommages et intérêts envers la victime; le roi est intervenu par la suite: ... *Dominus rex postea de dicta emenda sua ... sibi adjudicata quitavit eidem militi de gracia speciali medietatem et de alia medietate dedit eidem respectum per terminos ....*

46 Olim, II, 491, 7 (1307).

47 Olim, III[1], 629, 4 (1311): *Inquesta ... super injuria que dicitur fuisse monialibus abbatie ... visa fuit sed non fuit judicata ex causa et fuit reportata in presencia domini regis;* III[1], 615, 107 (1310): ... *cujus emende taxacionem ad voluntatem domini regis curia nostra reservavit.*

48 Olim, II, 648, 4, (1317): la cour est incitée à la circonspection spécialement lorsque l'affaire peut susciter de la part du souverain des préoccupations politiques ... *et pro eo quod dicti major et jurati abusi sunt casibus et articulis predictis in prejudicium juris nostri, curia nostra dictam communiam et statum ejusdem per idem judicium posuit ad manum nostram ut super dicta communia et ejus statu omnino amovendis vel de speciali gracia remanendis, nostram faciamus totaliter voluntatem.*

49 Olim, III[1], 208, 35 (1308): la cour ayant condamné un voleur de troupeau à la restitution et à indemnisation, en réservant au roi la sanction au criminel ... *Tandem, curia nostra super hoc habita deliberacione nobiscum, et eidem R. in vita et membris parcendo propter clericorum nostrorum presenciam qui priori interfuerant judicato, sentencialiter pronunciavit omnia bona dicti R. tam mobilia quam immobilia tanquam commissa nobis esse integre applicanda.*

50 Olim, III[2], 1289, 67 (1318): la cour reçoit un recours par grâce car un appel a été fait d'une sentence de la juridiction des foires de Champagne devant les grands jours de Troyes puis de cette sentence d'appel devant le parlement ... *Auditis igitur in parlamento nostro*

sous la plume du greffier: *de gratia et ex causa*[51], c'est à dire par grâce en fonction des circonstances de la cause. En somme sous les successeurs de saint Louis le Parlement en arrive, au début du XIVe siècle, à assurer une sorte de gestion de la grâce royale mais toutefois dans des limites inévitablement imprécises, à la lisière du politique, dès lors que l'autorité royale était en jeu[52].

Mais la grâce offrait aussi une voie que les justiciables pouvaient exploiter contre les décisions du Parlement qui ne les satisfaisaient pas; ils pouvaient implorer le roi, puisqu'il n'y décidait plus en personne, d'exercer une sorte de contrôle sur sa cour. Cette voie était celle de la *supplicatio,* forme très générale de recours direct au souverain, explicitement fondée sur la grâce. La *supplicatio* est présente en effet dès le début des *Olim* et est devenue durant le règne de saint Louis une voie procédurale; voie de recours opposée à la voie ordinaire par action, elle ne pouvait être reçue tant que la voie ordinaire d'appel pouvait être empruntée. La *curia regis* avait donc à examiner toutes les *supplicationes* admises par grâce royale; en revanche la *supplicatio* n'apportait qu'une ouverture et l'affaire était reprise au fond en une nouvelle instance comportant des aléas pour toutes les parties au procès[53]. Un arrêt de 1265 est particulièrement éclairant sur la manière dont le roi comprenait et traitait la *supplicatio.* L'évêque de Chalons avait obtenu du roi l'autorisation d'affranchir des serfs pour pouvoir éteindre les dettes de l'évêché mais le chapitre estimant être victime d'une *lesio enormis* avait par voie de *supplicatio* demandé la révocation des lettres patentes et l'interdiction à l'évêque de procéder ainsi à l'avenir. Le roi fait ajourner l'évêque puisqu'il est concerné, en lui mandant de se munir de ces lettres. Or le roi a consulté le conseil apparemment sur le bien fondé de la supplique. Ayant en effet entendu les arguments de l'évêque et inspecté ses lettres, le roi décide en suivant l'avis du conseil rapporté ici par le greffier: il révoque les lettres, les fait canceller en sa présence et interdit à l'évêque de procé-

---

dictis partibus et magistris predictis super judicato predicto et ejus confirmacione, non ratione appellacionis predicte cum eamdem non admiserimus sed de speciali gracia, visisque processibus et judicatis predictis per curie nostre judicium dictum fuit predictos magistros bene judicasse . . . .

51 Olim, III[1], 619, 112 (1310): . . . *per judicium nostre curie dictum fuit . . . dictum Johannem male appellasse, curia nostra tamen de gracia et ex causa super hoc sibi remisit emendam.*

52 Olim, III[1], 707, 70 (1311): un sergent du guet avait commis une agression de nuit à l'égard d'un bourgeois parisien en l'attirant hors de sa maison comme s'il agissait dans le cadre de ses fonctions. Le prévôt l'ayant condamné à indemniser la victime, celle-ci en trouvant la taxation trop *modica* fait appel devant le Parlement qui l'augmente. Mais le roi se montre apparemment plus sévère que la cour sur le plan pénal: . . . *quantum ad emendam nostram curia nostra de voluntate nostra privavit eundem Petrum in prepetuum ab omni servicio et officio nostro et precepit quod cum hoc idem Petrus teneat ex nunc usque ad unum annum integrum et completum prisionem in Castelleto nostro parisiensi vel alibi ubi nobis aut curie nostra placuerit absque deliberacione vel recredencia super hoc facienda.* Il est possible d'ailleurs que cette dernière disposition ait été délibérée avec le roi.

53 *J. Hilaire,* Supplier le roi. Les voies de recours extraordinaires aux XIIIe et XIVe siècles, in: Revue historique de droit français et étranger (1996 – 1), p. 73 – 81.

der à de nouveaux affranchissements. En revanche il est répondu aux membres du chapitre que s'ils veulent agir contre les personnes affranchies qui sont également concernées ils devront les faire ajourner ...*et dominus rex libenter faceret jus eisdem*[54].

La royauté avait précisé en 1303 par voie d'ordonnance que les jugés, arrêts et sentences émanant de la *cour* ou du *commun conseil* étaient sans appel[55]; on ne pouvait en appeler du roi au roi. La cour elle-même prenait bien soin de rappeler le principe à propos des enquêteurs royaux tout en précisant que dans ce cas elle ne pouvait admettre le recours que par voie de *supplicatio* et non par voie d'appel[56]. La seule issue était effectivement la *supplicatio* qui, d'une part, offrait ainsi un exécutoire d'autant que les plaintes adressées directement au roi contre certaines décisions de sa cour prises en son absence ne pouvaient être éludées longtemps et, d'autre part, permettait aussi à la royauté d'exercer un certain contrôle sur la justice rendue par sa cour. Le roi a d'abord répondu en accordant, par grâce, le privilège à certains justiciables qui avaient perdu leur procès en appel devant le Parlement et le suppliaient, en invoquant une erreur, de provoquer un nouvel examen de l'affaire pour que la cour vérifie l'exactitude de sa propre décision.

La première proposition d'erreur retenue par le greffier dans ses recensions apparaît en 1309 et est fort révélatrice de l'attitude du Parlement. Le greffier a repris en effet en détail les propositions contenues dans la supplique et qui mettent en cause la procédure suivie dans l'examen de l'appel d'une sentence du prévôt de Paris. Cette procédure devant le Parlement serait entachée de graves défauts dans l'examen des preuves et d'éléments essentiels du dossier[57]. Le greffier qui fait ici parler le roi, insiste ensuite longuement sur la volonté du souverain de faire réexaminer l'affaire *de gratia speciali* et avec diligence pour corriger les erreurs éventuelles[58]. Dans le dispositif enfin, la cour, se prévalant de la plus grande rigueur et

---

54 Olim, I, 626, 21.

55 *Langlois,* op. cit., p. 173; toutefois l'ordonnance demeurait assez vague sur la procédure de correction d'éventuelles erreurs, celle-ci revenant *ad nos vel nostrum commune consilium vel ad majorem partem consilii nostri* ... .

56 Olim, III[1], 153, 31 (1304): les enquêteurs royaux envoyés dans la sénéchaussée de Beaucaire avaient condamné deux frères, de Béziers, lesquels ... *a judicato hujusmodi appellassent, dictosque fratres ad proponendum rationes suas contra judicatum predictum per viam supplicacionis, cum appellaciones a talibus inquisitoribus interpositas non reciperemus, de speciali gracia admisissemus et certos auditores super hoc dictis partibus dedissemus* ... .

57 Olim, III[1], 458, 67: ... *ceterum cum postmodum ex parte Nicolai, filii et heredis dicti Hervei, nunc deffuncti, nobis fuerit supplicatum quod cum curia nostra per facti ignoranciam, ut ipse dicebat, actis cause predicte ad plenum non visis consuetudinibusque notoriis et confessatis seu probacionibus dicti Hervei et substancialibus dicte cause per facti errorrem obmissis, predictum tulerat judicatum quatenus super hoc apponeremus remedium opportunum.*

58 *Nos vero omnem errorem tollere et corrigere cupientes de speciali gracia voluimus et mandavimus quod processus et acta tam principalis quam appellacionis causarum hujusmodi*

de la plus grande diligence dans ce nouvel examen, constate que nulle erreur n'a été commise au cours d'une procédure menée *rite et legittime* et décide de maintenir son jugement qui devra être intégralement exécuté[59].

On remarquera en premier lieu l'insistance de la formule employée pour affirmer la volonté royale de répondre aux suppliques des justiciables pour que les erreurs soient reconnues et corrigées sans retard. En second lieu l'affaire est rapportée en détail et le greffier ne paraît pas chercher à minimiser les défauts invoqués dans la procédure. En troisième lieu, la décision de la cour, ne comportant pour toute *ratio decidendi* que l'affirmation de la rigueur observée d'un bout à l'autre de sa procédure n'en paraît que plus tranchante en réponse à la *supplicatio*. Sans doute la procédure se cherche encore et l'année suivante une autre proposition d'erreur étant également rejetée, la formule du dispositif est simplifiée tandis que la cour prévoit une amende qui serait semblable ici à l'amende de fol appel, en réservant au roi d'en établir lui-même la taxation[60]; tentative infructueuse du Parlement pour décourager ce genre de recours? Toujours est-il qu'il ne sera plus question d'amende dans ce cas par la suite. En revanche cette affaire est intéressante à deux autres points de vue. En premier lieu en effet, des années plus tard, le demandeur expose qu'après ce premier jugement il a été porté à sa connaissance que son adversaire avait provoqué de faux témoignages; il obtient du roi qu'il soit procédé à une nouvelle enquête, laquelle est jugée au Parlement en 1318 mais il perd également son procès[61]. Il demeure que ce plaideur a donc pu provoquer une nouvelle procédure de révision à la suite d'une proposition d'erreur. Or, en second lieu, le greffier semble avoir attaché une particulière importance à cette affaire car, fait unique, il a rapporté le détail de la délibération avec les opinions de chacun des membres du Parlement qui étaient en séance.

---

iterato inspicerentur et diligencius examinarentur ut, si quid, in ipso judicato per facti errorem vel minus sufficientem visionem actorum et processuum predictorum inveniretur esse factum, illud corrigeretur et emendaretur et in melius reformaretur.

59 *Visis igitur et de novo omnibus processibus antedictis et per curiam nostram ad plenum et cum diligencia examinatis quia repertum est curiam nostram in aliquo non errasse in predictis nec per facti ignoranciam deceptam fuisse, sed eam rite et legittime judicasse, predictum judicatum iterato per curie nostre judicium extitit approbatum et eciam confirmatum et ex integro mandabitur execucioni ....*

60 Olim, III[1], 615, 107 (1310): ... *certum judicatum per curiam nostram in parlamento presenti latum fuisset contra Jacobum predictum [Jacobus de Chartaut], deinde dicto jacobo domino regi asserente curiam predictam errasse in compoto dictarum partium super hoc audiendo et obtenta licencia quod iterato raciones ejus super hoc audirentur: Vocatis igitur dictis partibus et auditis iterato omnibus que dicte partes hinc inde proponere voluerunt et deliberacione habita super hiis diligenti, per arrestum nostre curie dictum fuit quod, non obstantibus propositis ex parte dicti Jacobi predictum judicatum contra ipsum Jacobum ... ratum manebit et firmum et ex integro mandabitur execucioni et quod dictus Jacobus hoc emendabit, cujus emende taxacionem ad voluntatem domini regis curia nostra reservavit.*

61 Olim, III[2], 1312, 84 (1318): ... *asserens idem Jacobus falsitatem et subornacionem predictas ad sui noticiam devenisse post prolacionem judicari predicti ....*

Puis de la grâce royale on est passé à la reconnaissance à tous les justiciables du droit d'exercer des recours auprès du roi contre les décisions de son Parlement; ainsi sont nées des voies de recours extraordinaires à commencer précisément par la proposition d'erreur (d'où viendra plus tard la cassation). Les conseillers au Parlement avaient alors intérêt à faire du juridisme au moment de fonder leurs décisions pour ne pas risquer d'être contraints le cas échéant de se déjuger ouvertement.

Toujours est-il qu'une évolution sur ce point est perceptible dans les *Olim*. Dans les premières années rapportées la décision est assez souvent éclairée sinon motivée au sens technique du terme (par un visa formel), le dispositif commençant par *quia* ou un terme équivalent. A la fin du XIIIe siècle la décision de la cour rapporte simplement l'instruction de l'affaire (les parties ont été entendues, les pièces produites ont été examinées), les arguments des parties et le dispositif. C'est ainsi à travers la présentation de l'argumentation des parties que l'on peut, certes avec beaucoup de prudence, tenter de retrouver les motifs de la décision.

II. La nature des motifs de la décision

Les séances judiciaires de la *curia regis* puis le Parlement constituent la cour suprême de la royauté. C'est donc l'instance, comme on vient de le voir, où à la fois intervient la grâce royale avec son caractère exceptionnel qu'elle soit appliquée par le roi lui-même ou par ses conseillers en son nom, d'une part, et la justice royale déléguée qui contrôle par l'appel la vie judiciaire dans les juridictions royales et aussi dans les juridictions seigneuriales, d'autre part. Or la grâce est aux frontières de l'équité et le Parlement a toujours considéré comme un privilège de sa condition de cour souveraine de juger éventuellement en équité. La recherche de la *ratio decidendi* passe donc ici par les origines de cette tradition et entraîne ainsi à distinguer, d'un côté, les rapports entre la grâce et l'équité dans la décision et, d'un autre côté, le jugement en droit.

1. La grâce et l'équité

Sous le règne de saint Louis lorsque le roi est présent dans les séances judiciaires de sa cour, ce qui est assez fréquent, c'est donc alors lui qui juge; le greffier fonde éventuellement la décision du roi sur son *officium judicis* et les conseillers sont là pour l'éclairer sur le point de droit. Cela signifie d'abord que, au moment de la décision, il pourra aussi bien trancher par droit de grâce (*de gratia* ou *de gratia speciali*) et parmi les recensions où est attestée la présence du roi apparaît au premier chef la *ratio decidendi* résultant du droit de grâce attaché à la souveraineté royale.

Le propre de la grâce royale est d'aboutir à une décision qui s'écarte de la solution juridique qui a pu être présentée dans le cadre du conseil et de ne dépendre que de la volonté du souverain. Dès lors ce dernier sera guidé dans certains cas par des raisons d'humanité. Cet aspect de l'intervention du souverain-juge se manifeste spécialement dans les affaires où un justiciable a voulu s'adresser personnellement au roi pour se placer sous sa protection. Ainsi une recension très brève qui n'indique pas exactement la nature de la demande mais suppose cependant une véritable procédure montre la rapidité de décision du roi, apparemment en l'occurrence sans prendre le conseil; en 1260, durant des vendanges, un enfant avait été tué accidentellement par une charrette et les deux conducteurs avaient fui leur village de peur que soit engagée une action en justice contre eux: le roi décide alors d'écarter toute poursuite[62].

Mais il faut également retenir que les causes de la décision royale relèvent parfois d'une *ratio decidendi* fortement teintée d'opportunisme politique; ainsi apparaissent en particulier les raisons de certaines décisions prises par le roi, protecteur de l'Eglise, quand d'une manière générale les intérêts de l'institution sont en jeu, voire quand il y a conflit avec ceux de la royauté.

Dans une affaire jugée en 1262, le chapitre de Paris et les gens du roi se disputaient la possession d'une justice; l'enquête ayant révélé que la charte royale présentée par les demandeurs, le chapitre de Paris, n'était qu'un document fort suspect dénué de valeur probante, le roi a cependant tranché dans l'immédiat en faveur du chapitre *ex dono mero et gracia speciali,* en quelque sorte en renouvelant la donation avec toutefois la réserve d'usage quant à ses droits pour l'avenir[63]. Le roi ira même jusqu'à révoquer un jugement prononcé par la *curia regis* dans cette session de parlement au profit du demandeur à l'encontre d'une abbaye, cela à cause du précédent que ce jugement aurait pu constituer à l'égard des intérêts matériels des églises et, là aussi, selon des considérations d'ordre politique[64]. Mais le cas échéant il est bien marqué également que le roi n'entend pas répondre favorablement à toutes les sollicitations des établissements ecclésiastiques. En 1257 le

62 Olim, I, 487, 11: ... *Quia ipsi homines occasione ipsius facti patriam ac ipsam villam dimiserant, dominus rex audiens quod per infortunium evenerat et quod parentes pueri oppressi super hoc nichil petebant ab eisdem hominibus voluit ut ipsi homines secure quantum ad hoc possent redire ad villam predictam.*

63 Olim, I, 166, 17.

64 Olim, I, 492, 10, 1260: le dispositif arrêté par le conseil portait ... *quia prefatus Ingarrennus tenuit boscum ipsum post predictam diem ostensionis per decem annos et amplius absque reclamacione abbatis facta in curia domini, juicatum fuit quod non tenebatur eidem abbati super hoc respondere.* L'abbé perdait son procès malgré l'argument ultime qu'il avait invoqué justifiant son inaction: ... *licet idem Ingerrannus tenuit ipsum boscum per decem annos, non tamen prejudicabat ecclesie sue cum talis prescriptio non currat contra ecclesiam.* Le dispositif du jugement est suivi de la mention: *Hoc judicium fuit postmodum per dominum regem revocatum quia nolebat ecclesiam emittere per talem prescriptionem.* Les conseillers étaient sans doute bons juristes mais le roi n'entendait pas se laisser entraîner à couvrir une décision qui risquait de porter préjudice aux institutions ecclésiastiques.

jugement d'une enquête montre que si les demandeurs, un chapitre, n'avaient pas réussi à prouver le bien-fondé de leur prétention, l'appréciation du souverain dépassait manifestement les critères purement juridiques pour prendre en compte des aspects d'opportunité politique (*quare multi se opponunt et in dampnum plurium redundaret*) et ainsi rejeter la demande[65].

Deux autres affaires, concernant cette fois des laïcs, sembleraient également montrer que le roi utilise parfois la grâce en quelque sorte comme moyen de donner satisfaction au demandeur sans pour autant créer un précédent. Cette volonté s'imposera au besoin sans laisser la procédure aller à son terme, c'est à dire à un jugement. En 1261 un seigneur réclamait la haute justice sur une terre reçue du roi en Albigeois en interprétant les termes de la charte (*justicias et explecta*) et en invoquant l'usage en la matière; le sénéchal de Carcassonne s'y opposait pour de multiples raisons, notamment que la haute justice relevait du roi en pays de droit écrit. Ayant examiné la charte le roi ordonna au sénéchal de laisser le demandeur jouir de la haute justice mais le greffier précise très clairement à la fin de sa recension: *et fuit hoc factum de gratia non de jure quia non fuit inde factum judicium*[66]. Inversement il arrive qu'ayant laissé sa cour prendre la décision de rejet de la demande pour insuffisance de la preuve, le roi accorde une compensation d'importance *de mera gratia ob bonum servicium ... sibi impensum*, en raison d'un bon service fourni par le plaideur à la royauté[67].

Si la grâce dépend de la volonté royale, elle relève aussi de l'idée de miséricorde comme le rappelle parfois le greffier. Il y a ainsi dans la terminologie des *Olim* des distinctions entre différentes voies pour agir (par voie ordinaire, *petitio*, ou par voie extraordinaire, *supplicatio*) comme pour décider (par voie extraordinaire, *gracia*, ou par voie ordinaire, *judicium*). Or à partir de la *petitio* le greffier distingue à travers les décisions royales également deux voies: *per judicium* ou au contraire *per viam equitatis* comme l'indique un acte de 1267[68]; dans ce dernier

---

65 Olim, I, 18, 10: ... *Non est probatum quod capitulum ambianense debeat habere claustrum; nec intendit dominus rex ad presens super hoc facere graciam quare multi se opponunt et in dampnum plurium redundaret.*

66 Olim, I, 512, 14: le bénéficiaire d'un don royal en Albigeois entendant en interpréter les termes pour réclamer un nouvel avantage malgré l'opposition du sénéchal de Carcassonne ...*tandem dominus rex inspecta carta ipsius Lamberti injunxit senescallo quod ipsum Lambertum permitteret uti usque ad voluntatem suam, faidimentis et alta judicia, et hoc fuit factum de gratia non de jure, quia non fuit inde factum judicium.*

67 Olim, I, 610, 20 (1265).

68 Olim, I, 690, 30 (1267): ... *Audita peticione ... voluit dominus rex et ordinatum fuit non per judicium set per viam equitatis quod* ... Le demandeur réclamait à l'héritier des emprunteurs la restitution de la somme prêtée (3.200 liv. t.); il avait aussi produit des lettres constituant un *assignamentum* sur diverses terres à son profit; le dispositif ne donne pas satisfaction par une restitution immédiate de la somme mais oblige l'héritier à réaliser l'*assignamentum* au profit du prêteur: ... *quod dictus comes nivernensis permitteret ipsum Guidonem gaudere quodam assignamento quod dictus Odo comes nivernensis ei fecerat pro dicto debito post decessum comitisse uxoris sue eo modo quo sibi factum fecerat videlicet* ....

cas, en effet, il s'agissait bien de juger la *petitio* du demandeur (demande par la voie de droit ordinaire) et non pas une *supplicatio*[69]. Le recours à l'*equitas* est directement lié au *jus*: ainsi le roi ou la cour décident *per jus* ou encore *per judicium via juris*[70]. Le but de ce recours à l'équité est d'influer sur l'application de la règle juridique pour en atténuer la rigueur et le greffier traduit dans sa formule cet élément de la *ratio decidendi*, la décision ayant été prise ... *per ipsam curiam nostram equitatis motam mansuetudine* ... [71].

Lorsque le roi a préféré l'équité à l'application stricte de la règle de droit, la référence à l'équité n'apparaît pas toujours formellement mais les raisons qui ont fondé la décision royale peuvent se déduire de la recension et le greffier indique quelle règle le souverain a entendu écarter; ainsi en 1265 des plaideurs refusant de répondre à la demanderesse sous le prétexte qu'elle était mariée et que, selon la coutume de la cour, elle ne pouvait ester en justice hors la présence de son mari, elle avait objecté que son mari était trop vieux pour l'accompagner mais qu'elle avait son autorisation: il a plu au roi qu'on lui réponde même en l'absence de son mari *licet hoc esset contra consuetudinem hujus curie* ajoute le greffier[72]. De même encore le dispositif qui rapporte un accord conclu en 1259 entre les parties sous l'autorité de la cour, indique la *ratio decidendi* en équité qui a pour but d'écarter, parce que trop rigoureuse dans ses résultats, l'application de la coutume du lieu dans l'espèce présente[73].

A la limite de la grâce et de l'équité apparaissent parfois les préoccupations du roi dans des affaires où les manœuvres juridiques d'agents royaux ou de féodaux risquent de tourner à l'oppression des faibles par une occupation intempestive des terres. On peut déjà rattacher à la grâce, sans cependant que celle-ci soit expressément visée dans le dispositif, une décision de 1254 dans laquelle le roi décide en faveur des demanderesses, des moniales, sans doute en raison de leur condition; elles demandaient à conserver la jouissance du droit de paisson dans une forêt royale parce que, bien que ne disposant pas de titre écrit, elles en avaient eu un long usage: le roi décide que cette tolérance (*sufferencia)* sera maintenue[74]. De même le

---

69 *J. Hilaire*, Supplier le roi. Les voies de recours extraordinaires aux XIIIe et XIVe siècles, in: Revue historique de droit français et étranger (1996), p. 78–79.

70 Olim, III[1], 382, 23 (1309).

71 Olim, II, 491, 6 (1307).

72 Olim, I, 557,16 (1265): ... *ipsa vicecomitissa dicente a contrario quod propter hoc non debebat sua responsio impediri cum hereditas de qua agitur ex parte ipsius moveat et maritus adeo sit senex et debilis quod equitare et venire nequeat, ut dicebat, et maxime cum ipsa habeat auctoritatem petendi ab ipso marito suo* ....

73 Olim, I, 451, 13: ... *Concordatum fuit quod de equitate teneretur ipsa domina vendere terram suam set per consuetudinem terre non debet compelli ipsa domina ad vendendum nec compelletur vendere; set omnes exitus terre sue cedent in solucionem hujus debitorum ita tamen quod si domini feodales prius saisiverint pro rachatis suis bene teneant.*

74 Olim, I, 435, 9: *Moniales ... petebant pasnagium in foresta d'Andeine, dicentes quod illud habuerant a retro longis temporibus, nec super hoc cartam aliquam habebant. Dominus rex voluit quod quia ipse moniales habuerant per sufferenciam, adhuc habeant.*

roi se préoccupe des graves conséquences que pourraient avoir les procédures engagées par des féodaux pour s'approprier des pâturages sur lesquels des villageois avaient un droit d'usage depuis un temps immémorial. Devant l'assise des chevaliers les féodaux avaient eu gain de cause en arguant que ces terres relevant d'eux ils pouvaient se les approprier et que les villageois ne leur payaient aucune redevance. Les villageois avaient fait appel de ce jugement devant le roi. A l'audience, en 1264, ce dernier en a retenu que par un jugement de ce genre ces chevaliers tendaient à interrompre la *prescription* de villageois qui était *longue et pacifique* sur des terres sur lesquelles ils avaient un droit de pâturage *immémorial* et que *per hanc viam,* c'est à dire par une action de ce genre en justice, il serait possible de causer de grands dommages à de pauvres gens en divers lieux; en conséquence le roi a suspendu l'exécution de ce jugement tant qu'il n'aurait pas reçu pleinement le conseil sur cette affaire[75]. Outre l'expression savante et romanisante des notions juridiques que le greffier prête au roi, il apparaît surtout que le souverain entendait éviter, au delà des arguments juridiques, que la décision en appel puisse créer un grave précédent sur un plan très général pour l'équilibre social, en somme en considération de l'intérêt général; dans un tel cas la *ratio decidendi* ne serait sans doute pas d'inspiration purement technicienne.

Enfin à partir de l'époque où le roi ne participait plus aux séances de sa cour, celle-ci n'en avait pas moins recueilli un héritage, une tradition juridique qu'elle allait développer. Sans doute elle ne dispose pas totalement du droit de grâce qui, dans sa plénitude, appartient au roi seul, mais elle manie à la fois grâce et jugement en équité. Ainsi en est-il à propos des amendes dont la cour souhaite parfois tempérer l'application. Tantôt, comme on l'a vu, le dispositif porte simplement la mention de la grâce, voire *de gracia et ex causa,* tantôt une indication est donnée par le greffier par une note complémentaire, destinée au seul usage de la cour et révélant un motif qui demeure pour autant extérieur au dispositif: le demandeur ne devra pas l'amende parce que son appel était en partie justifié[76]; la cour ne veut pas que l'amende d'appel soit réclamée à un plaideur *pauper et gravatus*[77]; une note rappelant l'état de pauvreté d'un couple qui a perdu en appel, est ajoutée vraisemblablement en vue de la taxation de l'amende[78].

---

75 Olim, I, 595, 8: ... *dominus rex audito quod per hujusmodi judicium infringebant ipsi milites prescriptionem ipsorum hominum quantumcumque longa esset et pacifica, attendens etiam quod, per hanc viam, plurimum possent dampnificari pauperes homines in aisanciis et pasturagiis suis, in diversis locis, hoc judicium suspendit nolens quod firmitatem haberet quousque super hoc consilium habuisset.*

76 Olim, III², 1106, 37 (1317): note suivant le dispositif ... *Emendare non debet quia in parte bene appellavit.*

77 Olim, III², 857, 35 (1313): note suivant le dispositif ... *Curia noluit quod dictus Normannus de hoc solveret emendam quia pauper et gravatus.*

78 Olim, III², 1101, 35 (1316): *dictum fuit predictum ballivum bene judicasse et dictos conjuges male appellasse et quod ipsi hoc emendabunt.* Suit cette note du greffier: *Memoriale quod dicti conjuges simplices et pauperes sunt.*

Dans un débat où le roi est partie, en 1307, le Parlement ne parvenant pas à éclairer le point de droit posé par la prétention du demandeur malgré une procédure d'enquête décide en équité: le chevalier qui tenait la cour séculière de l'évêque et qui a perdu son office à cause de l'association entre le roi et l'évêque, affirmant que l'office lui a été conféré à vie, demande à y être rétabli ou à recevoir une compensation suffisante; les gens de l'évêque et du roi opposent que l'office a seulement été conféré *ad voluntatem dantis*. La cour lui accorde une pension sa vie durant à prendre sur les émoluments de la cour séculière commune entre l'évêque et le roi[79].

Une attention particulière doit être portée à un acte d'ailleurs unique parce qu'il éclaire la procédure selon laquelle s'est dégagée la *ratio decidendi* en l'espèce. Cet exemple déjà cité (ci-dessus note 60: *Olim*, III^2 n° 84, p. 1312, 1318) est en effet le seul où le greffier a révélé la teneur de la délibération. Il s'agissait de juger une enquête effectuée dans le cadre d'une procédure de proposition d'erreur. Rappelons que le demandeur prétendait avoir été condamné par un précédent arrêt de la cour à cause de la production de faux témoignages par la partie adverse mais n'avait eu connaissance de cette manœuvre qu'après la proclamation du jugement; il avait alors obtenu du roi qu'une nouvelle enquête soit faite. Le jugement de cette seconde enquête lui donna également tort[80]. Le greffier a tenu à indiquer à propos de cette affaire que dans la cour alors garnie de 22 personnes, la décision de rejet de la demande avait été prise par 19 opinions concordantes; mais il précisait aussi qu'un membre de la cour avait répondu *sub dubio*, un autre *nihil dixit, ex causa*, tandis que le dernier s'était prononcé *de rigore juris contra Jacobum* (demandeur), *sed de equitate pro ipso*. Or il est intéressant de noter que la réponse *sub dubio* émanait d'un ecclésiastique, que celui qui avait renoncé à émettre une opinion était un seigneur et qu'enfin la réponse balancée entre *rigor juris* et *equitas* était celle d'un maître, c'est à dire d'un juriste.

Dans les premières années du XIVe siècle, de même que la cour fait appel à la grâce royale, comme on l'a vu, avec des formules telles que *de gratia speciali* ou *de gratia et ex causa*, elle se réfère aussi, il est vrai beaucoup moins souvent, à l'équité dans l'application du droit à travers des décisions prises *equitate suadente*[81] ou

---

79 Olim, II, 491, 6: ... *cum autem per inquestam hujusmodi non potuerit ad plenam sciri veritas super hujusmodi debato, per ipssam curiam nostram equitatis motam mansuetudine et de consensu dicti episcopi sic extitit ordinatum qod in recompensacionem dicti officii de quo amotus est idem miles ... dictus miles quamdiu ipse vixerit anno quolibet habebit viginti libras turonenses capiendas super emolumentis secularis curie communis inter dominum regem et episcopum supradictum.*

80 ... *Inquesta igitur super premissis per dictos commissarios, vocatis partibus, facta et completa et dicte curie nostre remissa, partibusque presentibus et auditis, ad judicandum tradita et recepta, tandem visa diligenter examinata inquesta predicta per curie nostre judicium dictum fuit predictum Jacobum intencionem suam super predictis ab eo propositis minime probavisse, et quod eisdem propositis non obstantibus, judicatum predictum contra dictum Jacobum latum ex integro mandabitur execucioni.*

81 Olim, III^2, 728, 17 (1312); 821, 1 (1313).

encore *equitate pensata*[82], et plus complètement encore *ex officio suo et equitate pensata*[83]. Le Parlement paraît ainsi assez clairement distinguer la grâce fortement teintée de miséricorde et l'équité destinée essentiellement à rétablir un équilibre qui aurait pu être compromis par la rigueur du droit. Loin sans doute des théories des glossateurs sur les fondements de l'*aequitas scripta* et *non scripta* cette expression très mesurée de l'*equitas* par rapport à la *gratia* pourrait cependant attester aussi d'une certaine influence du droit savant.

2. Le jugement en droit

On en arrive ainsi au jugement en droit qui est évidemment l'hypothèse la plus fréquente. D'abord il faut rappeler une fois encore que la distinction entre deux époques, celle où le roi semble dominer les séances judiciaires de sa cour et celle au contraire où il n'y vient plus guère, est essentielle. Dans les recensions concernant le règne de saint Louis en effet, même en l'absence du roi une esquisse de motivation éclairait presque toujours sur la *ratio decidendi*. Plus tard, lorsque la cour de Parlement en est arrivée à juger en permanence en dehors de la présence de la personne royale, il est remarquable qu'elle éludait le plus souvent l'indication sur les motifs de ses décisions dans le dispositif de l'arrêt. En revanche la manière dont sont rapportés les faits et les arguments des parties en présence peut fournir un indice puisque très souvent les arguments le plus complètement transcrits sont ceux de la partie qui a gagné le procès c'est à dire, peut-être, ceux qui ont convaincu les conseillers. En second lieu, si par principe le roi était dispensateur-né de la grâce souveraine il n'en était pas moins respectueux du droit. Mais par opposition le rôle des conseillers était d'abord celui de l'application du droit, hypothèse ordinaire; ils paraissaient alors représenter la rigueur ou étaient d'autant plus portés à s'y attacher.

En premier lieu, le Parlement a toujours été très soucieux du respect des règles de procédure, surtout ayant le plus souvent à juger en appel. Il est remarquable qu'après l'ordonnance de 1278 qui insistait sur les devoirs des conseillers dans l'audition des parties, le dispositif de l'arrêt insiste particulièrement sur la rigueur de la procédure suivie devant la cour: à la fois sur l'audition des parties[84], sur la prestation et l'examen des preuves, sur la diligence observée dans la délibération[85]; si bien que la rigueur procédurale est présentée en quelque sorte comme si

---

82 Olim, III², 1019, 72 (1315): ... *tandem hinc inde propositis, curia nostra equitate pensata quantum ad eam pertinebat racione impedimenti predicti certos commissarios ordinavit qui coram se, vocatis dictis partibus, summarie et de plano inquirerent de dicto impedimento ...* .

83 Olim, III², 825, 7 (1313): ... *curia nostra non processit ad judicandum informaciones predictas sed ex officio suo et equitate pensata super debato hujusmodi taliter ordinavit quod ...* .

84 Olim, III¹, 59, 26 (1300): ... *Tandem auditis et diligenter discussis rationibus partium dictarum ...* .

elle constituait déjà un fondement de la *ratio decidendi* et l'on peut y voir de surcroît un luxe de précautions face au risque de recours extraordinaire par *supplicatio* auprès du souverain[86], recours que le Parlement aurait lui-même à examiner et à juger. Cependant, dans certains cas peut-être particuliers, le dispositif indique les motifs de la décision de la cour, par exemple lorsqu'elle décidait que le prévôt puis le bailli de l'évêque de Paris avaient mal jugé[87], ou bien encore parce qu'elle sanctionnait le non-respect de l'effet suspensif de l'appel par le bailli[88]; dans d'autres cas, inversement, alors que le dispositif n'a pas été motivé l'opposition est implicite mais très claire entre l'exposé des arguments de la partie gagnante et l'absence complète de précision sur ceux de la partie adverse[89].

Il suffit de rappeler ici, en quelque sorte au centre de la procédure, la place de l'enquête et l'héritage reçu de saint Louis dans ce domaine. Le Parlement a suivi cette voie en y recourant *ex officio suo* systématiquement; les conseillers se montraient intraitables sur la validité de la procédure, non seulement en ordonnant le cas échéant un supplément d'enquête[90] mais aussi en prononçant de nombreuses annulations[91]. Dans le jugement de l'enquête le dispositif reposera le plus souvent sur la constatation que l'une des parties a mieux fait sa preuve que l'autre et en conséquence gagne le procès[92].

---

85 Olim, III[1], 39, 55 (1300): ... *Tandem auditis partibus hinc et inde, visisque processu predicto et quibusdam litteris ex parte dicti presbyteri productis, habitaque deliberacione super hoc diligenti per judicium nostre curie dictum fuit* ....

86 Olim, III[1], 46, 10 (1300): ... *Tandem visa inquesta super hiis de mandato nostro facta et diligenter examinata, omnibusque sollemnitate qua convenit rite actis, inventum est omnia et singula supradicta in querimonia seu facta narracione dicti decani contenta bene et sufficienter probata, propter quod per curie nostre judicium* ....

87 Olim, III[1], 656, 25 (1311): ... *Visis igitur per curiam nostram actis et processibus dicte cause deposicionibus testium et litteris in modum probacionis a partibus productis plenius intellectis, quia inventum est dictam Thomassam ex legittimo titulo, in possessione dicte domus, jardini et pertinenciarum ejusdem longe ante dictam vendicionem factam ... extitisse per curie nostre judicium dictum fuit dictos prepositum et ballivum male judicasse* ....

88 Olim, III[1], 505, 1 (1310): ... *dictum fuit in causa principali predicta bene sentenciatum et male appellatum fuisse et quod predicta revocacio attemptarum firma manebit quia, dicta appellacione pendente, dictus senescallus suam exequi sentenciam non debebat* ....

89 Olim, III[1], 258, 45 (1307): il s'agit de l'élection controversé de consuls à Rodez ... *pars autem dictorum hominum asserebat dictam litteram immo pocius debere annullari propter plures rationes ab ipsis hominibus propositas* ....

90 Olim, III[1], 80, 19 (1301): ... *Tandem, auditis hinc inde propositis per arrestum curie dictum fuit quod super dictarum domorum destructione et dictorum scabinorum ac aliorum quorum interest deffensionibus, factis et consuetudinibus, curia faciet inquiri plenius veritatem; et interim dormiet inquesta predicta; qua facta super hoc faciet curia id quod videbitur racionabiliter faciendum.*

91 Olim, III[1], 622, 106 (1311): ... *Tandem, visa inquesta predicta, cum plures defectus in ea reperti fuerint, per curie nostre judicium dictum fuit quod obmissis totaliter appellatione predicta ac processu predicto in causa dicte appellacionis habito, dicte partes super principali causa predicta ad examen ballivi Silvanectensis revertantur qui in hujusmodi negocio via ordinaria procedat.*

Or l'instruction de l'affaire ne passait pas seulement par l'établissement des faits; elle passait aussi par la détermination du droit applicable qui avait autant d'importance, en particulier avec les problèmes de preuve que posait fort souvent le droit coutumier; les *Olim* en rapportent du début à la fin de très nombreux exemples qui appelleraient à eux seuls une étude substantielle. Citons simplement, à propos d'une affaire de récompense dans la communauté entre époux en cas de vente par le mari d'un propre de l'épouse avec le consentement de cette dernière, une enquête effectuée *de mandato domini regis* pour en connaître les règles dans la coutume du Vexin français; cette enquête était effectuée apparemment pour vérifier les allégations des parties sur la question telle qu'elle avait été tranchée en assises[93]. Dans le même but en 1270, à propos du relief qu'une veuve entendait ne pas payer la cour décide de rejeter la demande parce que rien n'a été suffisamment prouvé de sa part tandis que la coutume invoquée par la partie adverse s'est avérée notoire et générale[94].

Il y avait d'ailleurs à déterminer non seulement le contenu de la coutume mais également son aire d'application et à juger en appel de nombreux procès intervenus à ce propos entre les seigneurs et leurs hommes. En 1268, le frère du comte de Vendôme prétendant que trois villes qu'il possédait en Normandie suivaient les us et coutumes d'Anjou, les habitants opposaient qu'elles relevaient de la coutume de Normandie; l'enquête ordonnée par le roi ayant manifestement montré que la justice était rendue dans ces villes depuis plus de soixante ans selon la coutume d'Anjou, il fut décidé que cette coutume continuerait à y être appliquée[95]. La cour a eu également à trancher les questions de ressort et l'on retiendra ici un exemple se situant à la lisière des pays de coutumes et des pays de droit écrit. Un arrêt de 1299

---

92 Olim, III^1, 526, 25 (1310). Le texte visé ici est tout à fait caractéristique de la construction habituelle de la recension dans ce cas par le greffier. La demande est rapportée longuement: les hommes d'un village affirment être en saisine du droit de pêcher dans une rivière et se plaignent d'être injustement troublés dans leur saisine par les gens de l'évêque qui les arrêtent; la défense de l'évêque est rappelée de la manière la plus brève (... *dicto episcopo contrarium asserente*). Le dispositif est fondé sur la qualité de la preuve rapportée par les gens du village: ... *Visa igitur inquesta super hoc de mandato nostro facta per nostre curie judicium dictum fuit dictos majores et homines intencionem suam super hoc sufficienter probasse et inhibitum fuit ne dictus episcopus eosdem impediat de cetero in saisine predicta* ....

93 Olim, I, 149, 4 (1261): la question sur laquelle portait l'enquête concernait les actes scellés du sceau du mari et de celui du seigneur à propos de ce genre d'opération pour savoir si la validité d'un tel usage n'aurait pas été écartée en assises ... *et utrum judicatum fuerit in assisiis quod hujus modi littere non valerent: non est probata hujus modi consuetudo; valeat escambium hujus modi consuetudine nonobstante.* L'acte est suivi de cette note: *Facta fuit ista inquesta pro causa que vertebatur inter Johannem de Stratis militem et Johannem de Bantellu.*

94 Olim, I, 339, 11: ... *quia nichil inventum fuit sufficienter probatum pro dicta domina Johanna et consuetudo a parte adversa proposita notoria et generalis esse dicitur in illis partibus* ....

95 Olim, I, 730, 16: ... *Qua inquesta* ... *relata, quia liquide inventum fuit quod dicte ville justiciaverunt se continue ad usus et consuetudines andegavie, per sexaginta duos annos* ....

nous apprend que la cour avait déjà déclaré que la ville d'Ussel dépendait du bailliage d'Auvergne pour le droit féodal et du bailliage de Brive pour le ressort de justice qui était régi par le droit écrit. Le seigneur d'Ussel demandait que la cour ajoute à son arrêt précédent que les dépendances de la ville soient rattachées également au bailliage de Brive; la cour ordonne au bailli d'Auvergne d'enquêter sur la coutume du lieu et si les dépendances de la ville d'Ussel étaient bien *ab antiquo* dans le ressort de Brive il devra s'y conformer[96]. Là encore la *ratio decidendi* résulte directement de l'enquête.

Sans pour autant prétendre à un catalogue exhaustif des problèmes de détermination du droit coutumier qui pouvaient se poser devant le roi, il faudrait aussi préciser que les plaideurs savaient le cas échéant invoquer le *jus commune* pour soutenir leurs prétentions. Le comte de Blois en 1267 se plaignait que le bailli d'Orléans l'empêchait de jouir du droit de bâtardise dont il avait l'usage *de jure communi* dans sa châtellenie et demandait au roi de lever cet empêchement. Le bailli opposait que c'était le roi qui était en usage de ce droit de temps immémorial dans cette châtellenie comme ailleurs dans son baillage. L'enquête ordonnée par le roi n'ayant rien révélé au profit de ce dernier les bâtards seront rendus au comte, *maxime cum pro se jus commune haberet* décide la cour[97].

Le Parlement suivant cette orientation en matière coutumière a eu recours à la procédure d'enquête systématiquement, allant même jusqu'à relever en appel l'insuffisance de la preuve de la coutume qui avait été appliquée devant la juridiction inférieure et jusqu'à effectuer sa propre enquête sur cette coutume avant de décider. Ainsi devant le prévôt de Paris un plaideur demandant à son frère de procéder au partage des acquêts effectués par ce dernier depuis la mort de leur auteur commun avait perdu sa cause. L'affaire arrivant en appel devant le Parlement, la cour s'aperçoit que le prévôt ne s'était pas préoccupé de la preuve des coutumes alléguées devant lui; elle ordonne immédiatement une enquête au vu de laquelle cependant il est décidé, en 1300, que le prévôt avait bien jugé. Le dispositif est clairement motivé. D'un côté, la preuve de la coutume a apparemment été la *ratio decidendi* essentielle, puisque c'est bien sur les résultats de sa propre enquête sur la coutume que la cour a fondé sa décision suivant laquelle l'affaire avait été bien jugée. Cependant, d'un autre côté, cela donnerait à penser aussi que pour admettre l'allégation sur la coutume sans en provoquer une nouvelle preuve le premier juge, s'il a bien jugé, en avait une connaissance suffisante; peut-être d'ailleurs avait-elle déjà été reconnue en justice et même éventuellement par le prévôt lui-même? Or, s'agissant pourtant du prévôt de Paris la cour ne lui a pas fait ce crédit[98], rigueur

---

96 Olim, II, 435, 15.

97 Olim, I, 668, 10: ... *audita postmodum relacione ballivi quia invenerat comitem usum fuisse habere bastardos in dicta castellania et nullum super hoc invenerat pro rege, deliberati fuerunt bastardi dicto comiti in castellania sua Blesensi maxime cum pro se jus commune haberet.*

98 Olim, III[1], 59, 27 (1300): ... *Tandem in causa dicte appellacionis ... visoque processu coram dicto preposito super hoc habito quia per ejusdem processus inspectionem curie nostre*

extrême apparemment et qui peut ouvrir des perspectives particulières à la réflexion des historiens.

On aurait pu attendre enfin que la référence au précédent judiciaire dans le processus de preuve de la coutume tienne une place plus grande dans les *Olim*, d'autant que dans le dispositif des jugements et des arrêts du Parlement la cour vise surtout ses propres sentences[99]. Peut-être convient-il cependant d'observer ici que précisément la rédaction du dispositif ne comporte fort souvent que la simple mention globale de la preuve rapportée au cours de l'enquête et apparemment retenue comme élément essentiel dans la décision des conseillers; la rareté des allusions au précédent judiciaire dans le dispositif pourrait s'expliquer en partie de cette manière. Toujours est-il que dès cette époque le Parlement non seulement puise dans cette procédure un des fondements de la *ratio decidendi* en la matière mais esquisse déjà le rôle qu'il a rempli à partir du XIVe siècle, à la faveur des causes d'appel venant de tout le royaume, en utilisant le pouvoir d'appréciation du roi gardien des coutumes c'est à dire en exerçant un véritable contrôle sur le droit coutumier[100].

L'examen de la *ratio decidendi* offre un vaste champ de recherche et l'on ne saurait passer en revue les principes juridiques qui ont explicitement ou implicitement fondé la décision; tout au plus peut-on ici retenir quelques grandes tendances. Si l'on a insisté sur la manière dont la cour abordait le droit coutumier, il faut aussi considérer les rapports avec les droits savants, droit romain et droit canonique. Sans doute l'influence qu'ils ont pu avoir sur les décisions du Parlement n'est-elle pas en soi une découverte. En revanche il est plus délicat d'en prendre vraiment la mesure, car on ne saurait s'en tenir au seul dispositif des jugements et arrêts. Pour autant si, passé 1270, le secret des cours s'installe peu à peu dans la construction du dispositif, du moins la rédaction de l'ensemble de l'acte à travers le style du greffier peut-elle être utile dans la mesure surtout où il semble bien que le développement des arguments de la partie gagnante est délibéré.

En un temps, il est vrai, où les actes du Parlement étaient rédigés en latin et pas encore en français la terminologie utilisée que nous restitue la plume du greffier montre en particulier que les conseillers ont une connaissance certaine des droits savants, ce qui ne préjuge pas nécessairement d'une exacte utilisation des concepts

---

constitit quod dictus prepositus super quibusdam consuetudinibus hinc inde propositis coram ipso nec probationem nec informctionem aliquam recepit, curia nostra super eis diligenter informavit; visa igitur informatione facta super hoc per curie nostre judicium extitit pronunciatum dictum prepositum bene judicasse ....

99 Olim, I, 878, 33 (1271); I, 913, 80 (1272): ... *presertim cum hoc in consimili casu fuisset in domini regis curia judicatum ...;* I, 932, 23 (1273); II, 317,19 (1290); II, 381, 7 (1295): ... *visis cartis et privilegiis, judiciis et arrestis curie nostre ab utraque parte exhibitis ...;* II, 387, 16 (1295).

100 *J. Hilaire*, La procédure civile et l'influence de l'Etat. Autour de l'appel, in: Droits savants et pratiques françaises du pouvoir (XIe-XVe siècles) sous la direction de J. Krynen et A. Rigaudière, Presses universitaires de Bordeaux, 1992, p. 151 – 160.

eux-mêmes. La remarque s'impose à l'évidence pour la terminologie procédurale et l'on peut citer ici, pour ne retenir que cet exemple parmi bien d'autres, la *supplicatio* bien éloignée de l'institution romaine. Si la cour utilise à la fois les termes *saisina* et *possessio,* elle maîtrise parfaitement la distinction entre *possessoire* et *pétitoire*[101]. En revanche, dans la partie la plus ancienne des *Olim* le greffier paraît bien mettre sur le même plan *possessio* et *saisine*[102]. Tout au plus peut-on remarquer qu'au début du XIVe siècle les deux termes ne sont plus utilisés indifféremment dans le même acte. Dans ces nombreuses affaires où l'on se bat sur la saisine ou possession en évitant dans l'immédiat la question de propriété, apparaîssent les notions de possession immémoriale[103], longue[104], longue et pacifique[105] de même que celle d'interruption de la saisine[106]. On pourrait retenir en même temps qu'en matière d'association entre marchands le Parlement ne fait référence qu'à la *societas* sans faire la distinction entre les types de sociétés pratiqués à cette époque, *commande* et *compagnie,* alors que cette distinction semble perceptible à travers les affaires traitées[107].

Enfin on ne saurait achever ce trop rapide tour d'horizon sans examiner la *ratio decidendi* dans les affaires relevant du droit public. Soulignons d'abord que les

---

101 Olim, I, 39, 23 (1258): *Inquesta facta utrum Philippus de Lorrico habeat constumam ad brancham pro igne suo in foresta de Mereio et quomodo pater suus et ipse Philippus usi fuerint, reponatur idem Philippus in saisina usus ad branchas, salvo jure proprietatis.*

102 Olim, I, 29, 8 (1257): *Inquesta facta super hoc quod prior Sancti-Martini de Campis parisiensis dicebat se et antecessores suos fuisse et adhuc esse in possessione et saisina justicie apud Noisiacum-Grandem ... prepositis parisiensibus dicentibus a contrario quod rex est in saisina ipsius justicie: rex nichil probat, prior habeat saisinam ipsius justicie.* De même, I, 34, 7 (1258): *Inquesta facta super eo quod capitulum Sancti-Frontonis Petragoricensis dicebat esse in possessione ... recipiendi videlicet vendas terrarum et possessionum que in dicta villa ... vendebantur, burgensibus ejusdem ville contrario dicentibus se ... esse in possessione predictorum et non capitulum: probatur saisina pro capitulo et nichil pro burgensibus, habeat capitulum saisinam ipsarum vendarum.*

103 Olim, I, 36, 11 (1258): ... *dicens quod dominus rex erat in possessione ... a tempore a quo non est memoria ....*

104 Olim, I, 198, 8 (1264): ... *in possessione .... a tempore a quo potest haberi memoria, qua possessione longa probata ....*

105 Olim, I, 105, 5 (1260): ... *tenuerant et possiderant pacifice a longis temporibus retroactis ....*

106 Olim, I, 250, 1 (1267): *Conquerebantur major et jurati de Brueriis et alii homines dicti loci quod, cum ipsi essent et fuissent in saisina utendi pasturagio ... tanquam in pasturagio communi, fratres milicie Templi impediunt possesionem eorum ... templarii vero nagabant possessionem eorum et quod pacifice usi non fuerant de eodem. Tandem inquesta facta de mandato curie ... inventum est quod dicti major et homines sunt in saisina ... tanquam in pasturgio communi nec sufficienter probata est interrupcio quam Templarii proponebant contra ipsos homines ....*

107 Ceci réclamerait une étude approfondie mais il est rermarquable que le contentieux marchand arrivant au Parlement et dans lequel apparaît une *societas* concerne surtout des marchands italiens dont les sociétés étaient essentiellement constituées sous forme de compagnie.

conseillers qui siégeaient à la *curia regis* puis au Parlement ont été crédités par les historiens d'une défense très attentive de la souveraineté et des intérêts de la royauté. Or, ils n'apparaîssaient pas moins comme des juristes particulièrement rigoureux dès lors qu'il s'agissait de la défense des intérêts des particuliers face aux représentants du roi, l'absence de ce dernier ne faisant que le souligner.

Il est remarquable en effet que les entreprises excessives des agents royaux sont réprimées systématiquement et que les baillis et les sénéchaux royaux sont les premiers à être l'objet d'un contrôle sévère à travers les causes d'appel, comme on l'a déjà vu à propos du droit de bâtardise dans le comté de Blois (ci-dessus, note 97). Sans doute les agents royaux ont été les artisans de la primauté de la justice royale par l'abaissement des autres juridictions, mais les *Olim* montrent aussi que la cour, de son côté, contrôlait strictement leurs entreprises menées dans ce domaine. D'un côté, les conseillers rejettent les prétentions présentées au nom du roi si elles ne sont pas parfaitement fondées tandis que, d'un autre côté, un sévère examen des chartes royales délivrant des privilèges est un élément important de la prestation des preuves. Par exemple, en 1270, le bailli de Senlis, prétendant que cela relevait de la justice royale, s'était emparé de faux-monnayeurs que le maire et les jurés de la ville avaient arrêtés. Le maire et les jurés objectaient que cette justice leur avait été donnée par le roi, ce dernier n'ayant retenu pour sa propre justice que la compétence en matière de rapt, meurtre et homicide. La cour tranche en leur faveur à la fois sur l'exactitude de leurs dires et en fonction du principe selon lequel la fausse monnaie relève non de la haute mais de la basse justice[108]. Le cas échéant la décision est motivée fort rigoureusement à l'égard de la tentative de l'agent royal. Le dispositif est parfois même très sévère, comme celui d'un arrêt de 1273 par lequel la cour impose silence au bailli en accumulant des motifs qui présentent son action comme un abus caractérisé: la justice contestée appartient *de jure communi* au comte; rien n'est certain quant à une saisine du roi sur cette justice contrairement à ce qui a été affirmé; la cour invoque également un précédent par lequel en pareil cas elle a elle-même remis la justice au seigneur[109]. Autre exemple significatif, en 1295 la plainte de l'évêque d'Orléans au sujet des ajournements auxquels le bailli royal d'Orléans fait procéder indûment aux dépens de la juridiction ecclésiastique: la cour a déjà sanctionné les entreprises de ce bailli et rend un nouvel arrêt contre lui[110].

---

108 Olim, I, 818, 10: ... *visa carta eorum per quam apparuit ea que dicebant sibi concessa fuisse, considerato etiam quod expendere falsam monetam non ad altam set solum ad bassam justiciam pertinebat, reddita fuit eis per curiam justicia mlefactorum ipsorum non tanquam alta justicia, sicut premissum est, set ut bassa.*

109 Olim, I, 932, 23: ... *Demum, quia de jure communi ad dictum comitem spectabat hec justicia, nec certum erat de usu regis immo contrarium asserebatur pro certo et in casu consimili alias per hanc curiam deliberata fuerat justicia domino Castri-Radulphi, impositum fuit super hoc silencium ipsi ballivo et ei preceptum quod dictum comitem gaudere permitteret justicia antedicta.*

110 Olim, II, 387, 16: ... *Auditis racionibus hinc et inde, visaque quadam littera nostra, de quodam arresto nostro alias nuperrime super consimili casu pro dicto episcopo contra dic-*

Passons, en second lieu, de la défense des droits des particuliers à la défense et à l'affirmation des droits régaliens. Si les conseillers en rappellent les limites aux agents du roi, comme à propos de la fausse monnaie, les conseillers savent également en imposer le respect aux sujets. Un abbé se plaignait, en 1269, que le seigneur de Châteauroux avait créé une foire sur ses terres au même lieu et au même jour que la foire de l'abbaye, interdisant en outre à ses hommes de fréquenter ce dernier marché. Le seigneur objectait que l'abbé ne disposait pas d'une foire mais que quelques marchands seulement se réunissaient là sans que l'abbé ait d'ailleurs levé à ce propos une redevance; de surcroît en tant que baron, affirmait-il, il était en saisine comme ses prédécesseurs de créer des foires sur sa terre et de les concéder aux églises et établissements religieux. Or le dispositif présente fort nettement la *ratio decidendi*: le seigneur est effectivement en saisine de créer des foires mais il a institué celle-ci sans autorisation royale; aussi il devra la supprimer non à cause de l'action introduite par l'abbé mais parce que nul ne peut créer une foire dans le royaume sans cette autorisation. L'arrêt précise que certains membres du conseil ont rappelé ce principe[111].

Les conseillers savent également analyser le point de droit avec précision et habileté. Ainsi fondent-ils leur décision, dans une affaire jugée en 1270, sur la distinction entre souveraineté et suzeraineté. Ils doivent en effet se prononcer sur la demande des habitants de Châlons qui prétendent que leur ville est en situation difficile faute d'échevins en nombre suffisant. Les habitants étaient en conflit avec leur seigneur, l'évêque de Châlons, sur la désignation des successeurs des échevins décédés, l'évêque entendant y pourvoir lui-même en tant que seigneur de la ville; cet évêque étant mort *lite pendente*, les habitants demandent au conseil de nommer de nouveaux échevins: la cour décide effectivement, devant les difficultés dans l'administration de la ville, que des échevins seront désignés par le roi, mais en tant que seigneur suzerain et non pas au titre de la régale[112]. Et l'on pourrait citer un dernier exemple, de 1254, particulièrement significatif. La comtesse de Nevers demandait que le bailli du roi vienne dans la Marche tenir son plaid en cas de contentieux entre ses sujets et ceux du bailli, plaid qui serait terminé là; il a été décidé à l'unanimité par le conseil que le roi ne sera pas tenu d'envoyer son bailli tenir des assises dans la Marche mais qu'à l'occasion, ainsi à propos d'une enquête, il

tum ballivum prolato, per curie nostre arrestum fuit pronunciatum dictam citacionem seu adjornacionem esse adnullandam.

111 Olim, I, 762, 26: ... *Demum audito quod feriam hujusmodi fecerat sine licencia et mandato domini regis, licet ipse bene allegaret saisinam suam et predecessorum suorum ut dictum est, tamen quia eam fecerat sine auctoritate domini regis, cum nullus in regno talia possit facere absque assensu et mandato domini regis, ut dicebant quidam de consilio, non propter instanciam predicti abbatis, dictum fuit ballivo quod cadere faceret feriam antedictam.*

112 Olim, I, 798, 2: ... *intellecto periculo seu dampno dicte ville et patrie in tanto scabinorum defectu ordinavit curia quod, lite super hoc pendente, novi ponerentur ibidem scabini per dominum regem tanquam superiorem et regem, non racione regalium, salvo in omnibus jure partium.*

pourra y envoyer son bailli: ce sera toutefois non pour cause de nécessité mais seulement pour cause d'utilité[113]. Certes cette dernière distinction à cette époque n'était pas une nouveauté; elle montre du moins parfaitement que l'apport des glossateurs à propos de la *necessitas publica* et de l'*utilitas publica* était bien connu des gens du conseil et qu'ils l'utilisaient non sans subtilité pour ménager les intérêts du roi[114].

*

* *

En conclusion il apparaît assez clairement, en premier lieu, que la *ratio decidendi* n'avait pas exactement les mêmes fondements suivant que la décision émanait du roi lui-même ou de sa cour en son absence. Dans la décision prise par le souverain-juge la frontière entre le judiciaire et le politique, notamment du fait de la grâce royale, pouvait être indécise dans certaines affaires, même si le roi se montrait constamment soucieux de référence aux principes juridiques quitte à en tempérer l'application par l'équité.

La cour de Parlement, quant à elle, lorsque la présence du roi n'était plus qu'une fiction dans le cadre de la souveraineté royale, a dans la pratique tiré toutes les conséquences des réformes procédurales de saint Louis. Dans les limites de l'*officium judicis* qui était le sien, ses membres, même s'ils ont conservé l'héritage royal du jugement en équité, se sont montrés des juristes rigoureux manifestement imprégnés de droit savant. Et dans la construction d'une justice étatique la procédure a été un levier essentiel entre leurs mains. Cela d'autant plus que cet accroissement de technicité dans le traitement des affaires a favorisé l'influence des conseillers-maîtres devenus de véritables professionnels de la justice.

Plus encore, un grand enseignement de l'étude des décisions retenues dans les *Olim* est que si le Parlement a été dès sa formation un ardent défenseur des droits et des intérêts de la royauté c'est précisément par un juridisme cultivé et exercé rigoureusement à l'égard de tous les justiciables, fussent-ils le roi lui-même ou plus exactement la partie royale, c'est à dire les agents agissant au nom du roi et qui étaient sanctionnés pour leurs erreurs et leurs abus de la même manière que les seigneurs ou leurs agents. De ce point de vue, à la charnière des XIIIe et XIVe siècles l'action judiciaire du Parlement a très largement contribué à la construction d'un Etat de droit.

---

113 Olim, I, 418, 3: … *dictum fuit concorditer, per totum consilium, quod rex non tenetur mittere ballivum suum in Marchia pro placitis tenendis; verum si qua fuerit inquesta facienda super aliquo facto vel pro pacificando aliquo facto, poterat mittere ballivum suum in Marchia, non causa necessitatis set causa utilitatis.*

114 La question, est maintes fois abordée dans l'ouvrage de *A. Rigaudière,* Penser et construire l'Etat dans la France du Moyen Age (XIIIe-XVe siècle), Comité pour l'histoire économique et financière de la France, Paris 2003.

Summary

The ratio decidendi of the early decisions of the *Parlement de Paris* did not have exactly the same foundations whether the judgments were pronounced by the king himself or, in his absence, by the court. The king showed particular concern for references to legal principals; nevertheless he could temper the enforcement of law by resorting to equity or by granting a pardon. When the presence of the king became nothing more than a fiction within the framework of royal sovereignty, the court of *Parlement* drew conclusions from the reforms of the civil procedure introduced by King Louis IX. During the period covered by the so called *Olim* (the registers of decisions concerning the years 1254 – 1318), the judges rigorously used civil procedure as an instrument for establishing a state controlled judicial organization. Although they had conserved the royal inheritance of equity, they cultivated a systematic legalism towards the king's subjects, in particular the feudal lords and royal officers, and in this way they greatly contributed to the construction of a modern legal monarchy.

PAUL BRAND

Reasoned Judgments in the English Medieval Common Law 1270 to 1307

I.

In a case heard by the justices in eyre in Yorkshire in 1279 Denise, the widow of William of Wath, claimed her dower share of one third of a holding of a messuage, one hundred acres of arable land, ten acres of meadow and a rent of eight and a half marks in the village of Thornhill against one William of Longfield.[1] William made a defence of a common type. Since her husband had not been seised of the tenements as of fee on the day of marriage or afterwards, she was not entitled to dower. She claimed that he had been seised. This issue of fact went to a jury. It did not give a straight yes or no, but told a story, leaving it up to the court to apply the relevant law. Denise had originally been betrothed to William during the lifetime of his father by words of present consent, and she had borne William children. The couple had, however, never been formally married. When William had inherited his father's land, he had decided that he could do better, and had contracted marriage with a second Denise in a full ecclesiastical ceremony. His original wife initiated church court proceedings to assert the validity of her own prior marriage. She had succeeded in that suit. William had been required to resume cohabitation and marry her in a formal marriage ceremony. William had been excommunicated three times before finally agreeing to do this. He had previously leased these same tenements to William of Longfield, and before marrying Denise in the formal ceremony he had enfeoffed William of the land to spite her and to stop her getting dower. On the face of it, then, Denise was not entitled to dower, since William had given up seisin of the land prior to their (formal) marriage.

The justices probably discussed the matter, and perhaps even took some outside advice, before reaching their judgment. All the record shows, however, is the judgment the court eventually made. Denise was, after all, to recover her dower. The record gives the reasoning that the court provided in justification. In the particular circumstances of this case, the court held, the date from which entitlement to dow-

---

1 A full record and report of this case will be printed (and translated) in the forthcoming volume III of *Paul Brand,* Earliest English Law Reports [hereafter EELR], III, 82–83 (79–81 Yorks.5).

er should be reckoned was not (as was generally the case) that of the ceremony at the church door, but rather the day of the sentence upholding the validity of the prior, informal marriage, for this was when William had come under a legally enforceable obligation to marry Denise. No specific authority was cited for this radical departure from the normal rule. There was no reference to prior precedent or statutory authority, merely a general invocation of 'God and all right' (*secundum Deum et omnia jura*). This can be read as a tacit admission that there was no prior authority and that the court was creating its own precedent. Denise was entitled to dower because on that day William had held these tenements in fee. A second argument was, in essence, one of policy. The enfeoffment of the current tenant had been made to ensure that Denise did not get her dower, and the law should not support such deliberate evasions of a wife's right to dower. William's resistance to the sentence of the church court, characterized in the judgment as 'rebellion against God and the Church' (*Deo et ecclesie rebellandi*), had been motivated by the wish to ensure that his wife, if and when she became his widow, should not enjoy her dower. Others should be discouraged from any similar resistance in the future by the frustration of William's plans.

Royal justices had by 1279 been giving judgments in litigation determined in the king's courts for over a century (since c. 1176), and it seems likely that some record of their judgments had been kept since around the same date. The earliest surviving record of litigation heard in such courts, however, comes from 1194, almost two decades later.[2] Most early judgments were on matters of process, authorizing the next stage of process against an absent defendant, or authorizing the holding of a 'view' of the land in dispute or the like, and received no kind of justification. The same was often true even of final judgments, where judgment followed almost automatically from the verdict given by a petty or even a grand assize jury. There was some room for justification or explanation in a few early cases. When given, it was normally recorded laconically. In a case brought in 1199 by Bernard Grim against Lucy of Cockfield, for example, Bernard claimed eight messuages on the basis of his own possession of them during the reign of Henry II. He offered to prove his seisin by a 'free man' of his, who was supposed to have been a witness of that seisin and also to be willing to fight battle as his champion. Lucy denied Bernard had ever been seised and offered to prove this by her own champion. The court gave judgment for Lucy because the man Bernard had produced 'as his witness ... had not offered to prove against the same Lucy, but had remained wholly silent' (*ut testem ... non optulit probare versus ipsam Luciam set omnino obmutuit*).[3] Some justification is offered for the judgment. It was based on a failure of proof on the part of the claimant, and the rules of proof being invoked are evidently (but only implicitly, not explicitly) those laid down by legal custom in cases of this kind where battle was being offered.

---

2 *Paul Brand,* 'Multis Vigiliis Excogitatam et Inventam': Henry II and the Creation of the English Common Law' in The Making of the Common Law (London, 1992) at pp. 77 – 102.

3 Curia Regis Rolls, I, 71.

Over time, enrolled judgments giving reasons for judgments seem to have become less laconic, though the 1279 judgment with which this paper started is atypically generous. What did not change was the way in which the plea rolls continued to record such judgments as wholly impersonal and anonymous. When we begin to get the first surviving unofficial law reports, from c. 1270 onwards, it quickly becomes the normal convention to ascribe speeches and judgments to the individual serjeants and justices who delivered them. We then begin to see that it was the invariable practice of the courts for a single justice to give judgment, without recorded assent or dissent from other justices, even though the courts were multi-member courts with multiple justices. From the summer of 1291 reports begin to survive in much larger numbers, often as part of collections of reports belonging to a particular term or pair of terms or to a particular eyre visitation. Some evidence in these reports, however, suggests that even when judgment was pronounced by a single justice, it might be the outcome of a prior, and apparently private, process of discussion with his colleagues. In a report of a 1303 case, for example, we are told of a discussion between the justices as to whether or not the plaintiff was entitled to recover damages;[4] and in a case of 1293 chief justice Mettingham is reported as rehearsing the arguments of both parties and then explaining (before giving judgment) that 'we have spoken to our colleagues and they are advised and I am too that ...'.[5] A few reports even purport to give us a record of some of what was said in these private discussions;[6] or tell us that judgment was given by a particular justice, but only after he had consulted one or more of his colleagues in the court.[7] Very occasionally a reporter may even note a difference of opinion among the justices.[8] In general, the reports give us the words of judgments in direct speech and in the language (insular French) in which they were given in court, as opposed to the indirect speech and Latin translation found in the enrolment. Since each source is independent of the other, they are a valuable complement to each other.

---

4 'Fut demande parentre les justices si il dust recovere damages': BL MS. Egerton 2811, f. 43v [Trinity 1303].

5 'A quel jour Meting' rehercea lour resouns de une part e dautre e dit 'Nous avoms parle a nos compaignon e lour est avis e a moy aussint qe...': BL MS. Harley 25, ff. 63v-64r.

6 For an example see LI MS. Miscellaneous 738, f. 15v [1303 Hilary] (Hengham and Howard).

7 For examples see YB 33–35 Edward I, p. 77 (Hengham consulto Bereford); YB 33–35 Edward I, p. 381 (Stantone (Hengham, Howard et illo adinvicem consultis)); YB 33–35 Edward I, p. 423 (Stantone consulto Hengham); YB 33–35 Edward I, p. 440 (Stantone ... consultis Hengham et Howard); YB 33–35 Edward I, p. 499 (Stauntone consulto Hengham); YB 33–35 Edward I, p. 503 (Mallore consulto Howard, Hengham et Stauntone); YB 33–35 Edward I, p. 515 (Mallore consulto Hengham et Stantone).

8 'E agard fut par Hengh' invito Hou' ': BL MS. Additional 31826, f. 282v [Trinity 1303].

II.

Courts could, and did, give formal and reasoned judgment at various different points in proceedings. A few were medial judgments which did not dispose of the case, but allowed it to proceed notwithstanding a challenge,[9] or decided, for example, that a vouchee was obliged to warranty, after which pleading proceeded.[10] More common, however, were reasoned judgments disposing of a case. These were of two kinds. Some were based on facts alleged or admitted in pleading; others on facts found by a jury or other fact-finding mechanism.

In some cases where judgment was based on pleadings alone, cases were dismissed on what look to modern eyes to have been procedural grounds. Judgment might be given against a claim, for example, because the writ used to initiate litigation was inappropriate. This might be because the writ was addressed to the sheriff of the wrong county,[11] or because the count had revealed that the 'kinsman' on whose seisin at death the claimant was basing his claim was his great great grandfather and thus a direct, not a collateral, ancestor and so not a 'kinsman' as required for this action (of cosinage);[12] or because the defendant was now claiming ownership of the horse he had allegedly taken in distraint from the plaintiff and the action of replevin was not the appropriate action to determine rival claims to property.[13] A judgment might also dismiss a case because the plaintiff(s) or the defendant(s) named in the writ were not proper parties to the litigation. A plaintiff could not bring an action of ravishment of ward without joining his wife because his claim to the wardship was by virtue of a lordship he held jointly with her;[14] a plaintiff could not bring replevin to challenge the seizure of animals which were in his custody as a cowherd in common pasture when they had been seized by defendants who claimed the pasture as their several pasture.[15] Judgment might also be given against a plaintiff for want of jurisdiction, for example, if the land for which an assize of novel disseisin had been brought was appurtenant to an ecclesiastical office and the underlying dispute about possession of that office was one for the ecclesiastical courts alone to determine.[16]

---

9 For an example see 1286.13 in EELR, II, where a count in an action of cosinage that had been challenged in the Lincolnshire eyre of 1281–4 was eventually held good in the Common Bench by Brunton and other justices *par mult des resuns.* It seems unlikely, however, that any of these reasons were actually given in court.

10 For an example see BL MS. Additional 37657, f. 100v (and record at CP 40/105, m. 7) [Easter 1295].

11 For examples see CP 40/109, m. 32d; BL MS. Additional 5925, f. 44r [Michaelmas 1297].

12 BL MS. Harley 2183, f. 37v. The related enrolment (CP 40/122, m. 54d) simply records the claimant as unable to deny the objection made by the tenant.

13 CP 40/150, m. 217d [Hilary 1304].

14 EELR, II, 304 (1288.4).

15 BL MSS. Additional 5925, f. 32v, Additional 31826, f. 176v, Harley 493B, f. 61r (enrolled in CP 40/134, m. 115) [Trinity 1300].

More complex and more interesting were final judgments based on rules relating to proof. Judgments were given against litigants for failing to produce a specialty (sometimes just meaning written evidence, sometimes rather more) to support their case. Thus judgment was given against plaintiffs who failed to produce a charter or other written evidence proving the assignment of the whole of an advowson to the youngest coheir when they were claiming the right of presentment to a church at the first vacancy against a stranger without their coheirs;[17] or against a creditor who failed to produce a bond (rather than just a tally) to demand a debt against a debtor's executors.[18] Judgments might also be based on the failure of a litigant to displace a presumption created by a written document produced in court. A final concord made under the auspices of the court created the strongest presumption. A claimant in a 1272 case asserted that she had been under age when she had granted a manor, but the tenant pleaded a final concord confirming his title. The claimant was not allowed to plead that she had also been under age when that final concord was made and had been under age when she had appointed an attorney to levy the final concord on her behalf.[19] In a 1301 case a woman claimed land on the basis she had granted it away in return for an unfulfilled promise of marriage. She was not, however, allowed to prove her assertion because the final concord by which the land had been transferred had created the presumption of an unconditional gift. The justice explained that she would have been allowed to prove her assertion had the conveyance been by charter, and the reasons for this different treatment.[20] A charter created a weaker presumption. In 1298 a claimant in formedon in the descender alleged that her parents had been given land in fee tail and that she was their heiress but produced no charter. Her opponent showed a charter granting the claimant's father the land in fee simple and alleged a subsequent acknowledgement of that charter and its enrolment in the king's court in 1265. On this basis the court dismissed her claim without allowing it to go to a jury.[21]

Judgments given on the basis of pleading alone might also be based on something closer to rules of substantive law. One sub-group of such judgments related to the use of distraint to enforce obligations ranging from a rent seck secured on land,[22] to the services owed to the lord of a tenement who had himself acquired

---

16 CUL MS. Dd.7.14, f. 408v: '*Sodinton.* Terra pertinet ad preposituram et est ejus accessorium et ipse Nicholaus non est in possessione prepositure quod est principale sed ipse Thomas possidet et ideo consideramus quod Nicholaus nichil capiet per breve suum sed de prepositura cum suis accessoriis procedat contencio coram ordinariis.' The record is much less specific and merely records the plaintiff as being unable to deny the defendant's objection: JUST 1/1011, m. 29.

17 EELR, I, 19 (1274.1).

18 EELR, II, 281 – 2 (1287.4).

19 KB 26/207, m. 12.

20 BL MS. Harley 493A, ff. 283v-284r (enrolled in CP 40/135, m. 178d).

21 BL MSS. Additional 5925, f. 85v, Harley 25, f. 70v (enrolled in CP 40/125, m. 24).

22 EELR, I, 70 (1276.7).

part of that tenement.[23] Other judgments were based on substantive rules relating to incidents of tenure: disallowing a claim to a heriot where the lord had already received relief and the deceased tenant had not been resident on the holding of the lord concerned;[24] allowing a claim to relief on the death of the plaintiff's brother even when he had died on the same day as their father and had performed no homage or fealty or service and the plaintiff had himself already paid relief on the death of his father.[25] Others were based on substantive rules of land law: that a son who had survived his father and committed felony (whether in his father's lifetime or afterwards) forfeited his father's holding, whether or not he had ever gained seisin of it;[26] or that it was not permissible after a tenant had held lands and died in possession of them to challenge his title to them by alleging that he had been a bastard.[27] Substantive rules relating to pensions were invoked in judgments holding that payment of a pension by one church to another time out of mind was a sufficient title even in the absence of a specialty attesting the assent of the patron and the bishop;[28] or that a clerk granted a pension till presented to a suitable benefice forfeited it by marriage.[29] The general rules about the interpretation of royal franchisal grants were invoked in another judgment in an action challenging the seizure by burgesses of Stafford of woolskins offered for sale by a burgess of Newcastle under Lyme. The Newcastle burgess relied on a charter of Henry III granting freedom to trade and travel throughout England; the burgesses of Stafford on a prior charter of King John granting them their customs, which included a right to restrict retail trading in Stafford. The court held that the later grant could not prejudice the earlier, especially where it had been regularly applied in the interim.[30]

Reasoned judgments given after fact-finding seem to have been much less common, since this normally left little for the court to do other than to apply clear and well accepted law to the facts. A reasoned judgment was, however, required in a case in the 1268 Dorset eyre where the parties to an assize *utrum* had joined issue as to whether or not a particular rector of the church of Gillingham in John's reign had been in possession of eight acres of land before alienating them. The jury confirmed that he had only ever been in receipt of rent owed for this land, but then added that an earlier rector had alienated the land. The court adjudged that the plaintiff recover.[31] The judgment explained that the real issue in the assize was

23 BL MSS. Additional 31826, ff. 362r-v, and Additional 35116, ff. 150r-v (enrolled at CP 40/86, m. 232) [Michaelmas 1290].

24 EELR, II, 268–71 (1287.2).

25 CP 40/110, m. 47d.

26 JUST 1/275, m. 45 (1268–9 Gloucestershire eyre).

27 EELR, I, 128–31 (1283.6); CP 40/31, m. 97d.

28 CP 40/96, m. 114 (Michaelmas 1292).

29 BL MSS. Egerton 2811, f. 109v, Harley 493B, f. 50v, Harley 572, ff. 193v-194r, Additional 35116, ff. 265r-v, Stowe 386, f. 148r (enrolled in CP 40/113, m. 15).

30 CP 40/64, m. 144 (1286).

31 JUST 1/202, m. 3d.

always the basic question of free alms or lay fee; that no count was necessary other than by way of explanation (*ad evidenciam et declaracionem*) and thus (by implication) that the facts cited in the count were not an essential part of the claim; that no prescription period applied in the action since the right was not that of the claimant but of his church (and thus by implication that it did not matter when the predecessor had been seised). Thus a finding that the land had once been the church's free alms should determine the outcome. Reasoned judgment of some sort was also the obvious requirement where an assize jury found a special verdict, setting out the facts but drawing no overall conclusion from them. This was the position, for example, in an assize of mort d'ancestor probably heard in the 1271–72 Lincolnshire eyre where a jury found that the claimant's father had impleaded the tenants in the Common Bench and they had acknowledged his right and made a formal surrender, but that he had fallen sick on the way home and died before being put into seisin by the king's bailiff. The court held this did not matter and that he had in law died in possession of them and so the claimant was entitled to succeed in the assize.[32] Nor was it only in assizes that special verdicts were given. In 1305 master Henry de Bray brought an action of covenant against John fitzReginald for ejection from the manor of Chinnor, which he held by his lease for a five year term. The jury found that master Henry had evacuated the manor when he had heard that John's wife (whose right the manor was) was coming with armed force to retake it. She had then taken possession. John had nothing to do with it. The jury asked for the help of the justices. They decided that the wife's action was in law the action of her husband and that master Henry should therefore recover his damages.[33] In another case the same year Walter of Kelk alleged that Roger Ughtred had forcibly entered his house and taken two bonds belonging to a third party which had been entrusted to him. The jury found that Roger had come with a single groom and had tricked Walter's wife into handing over the bonds. He had pretended to have a letter from her husband authorising her to do so and had promised to return the bonds if necessary when Walter returned home. The jury again sought the assistance of the court. Chief Justice Hengham decided that even though no force had been involved the deception justified the court in ensuring that Roger returned the bonds and paid damages.

III.

Reasoned judgments in the early common law had, of necessity, to be based, either explicitly or implicitly, on some kind of underlying authority, the application of some pre-existing (or less commonly, newly created) rule or rules of law to the facts of the particular case to produce the outcome stated and recorded in the judgment.

---

32 CUL MS. Ll.4.18, ff. 230r-v (copy of enrolment but not yet found on the rolls of that eyre).

33 CP 40/145, m. 288.

The main, if not quite the only, *written* rules to be invoked or applied in judgments were those which had been enacted and proclaimed in legislation. From the second half of the thirteenth century onwards, statutes began regularly to authorise the creation of new forms of legal action to enforce their provisions, and the writs brought to initiate such actions normally specifically cited that legislation.[34] Even where the statute did not refer to the creation of a new form of action, chancery might still create one. This would then normally refer to the relevant statutory authority for the rule the action was created to enforce.[35] When such cases led to a final judgment, it was rare for them to explicitly rehearse the statute on which the action was based, but the judgment implicitly applied the rules of the legislation. Occasionally, however, they do so explicitly because the judgment is based not on that part of the legislation cited in the statutory writ, but on some other part. For example, in 1285 an action of *cessavit* was brought (under c. 4 of the statute of Gloucester) to claim the reversion of a tenement for the tenant's failure to perform services for a period of two years during which it had been impossible to distrain that tenement for services. The defendant admitted owing seven years arrears. He then left court without paying them or damages or finding any surety for future performance. The judgment adjudging the tenement to the plaintiff specifically cited that part of the statute relating to forfeiture for failure to meet any of these conditions rather than the part cited in the statutory writ grounding the claim simply on failure of performance of services for two years.[36] The wording of the statute might also be explicitly invoked in a judgment in a different kind of context, where a justice dismissed an action allegedly brought under its provisions, but where the wording of the writ was not in fact warranted by the statute.[37]

Statutes were also explicitly invoked in judgments in non-statutory litigation. Part of c. 6 of the statute of Marlborough of 1267 stated that no enfeoffment of an eldest son by his father during his lifetime was to bar the lord from claiming his wardship of that heir.[38] The legislation was specifically recited in an action of

---

34 Examples include the action of *contra formam feoffamenti* created to enforce c. 1 – 3 of the Provisions of Westminster of 1259 (which was later re-enacted as c. 9 of the statute of Marlborough of 1267) about suit of court (on which see *Paul Brand,* Kings, Barons and Justices: The Making and Enforcement of Legislation in Thirteenth-Century England (Cambridge, 2003), pp. 43 – 53, 109 – 115, and chapter 8); and the actions of *cessavit* and entry *in casu proviso* created by cc. 4 and 7 of the 1278 statute of Gloucester: Statutes of the Realm, I, 48.

35 For examples see *Brand,* Kings, Barons and Justices, pp. 263 – 71, 277 – 81, 288 – 93, 296 – 7, 348 – 61, 369 – 75.

36 'Et quia in statuto illo continetur quod si aliquis teneat terram qualencunque in forma predicta et noluerit vel contempserit reddere arrearagia hujus terre sic dimisse nec eciam dampna ante judicium redditum quod ipse amittat eandem terram inperpetuum, ideo consideratum est. . . .': *Wiggenhall v. Mortimer:* CP 40 / 57, m. 7.

37 For a good example see *Brand,* Kings, Barons and Justices, p. 210 and note 11, and for the background see pp. 208 – 12.

38 For this legislation and its background see *Brand,* Kings, Barons and Justices, pp. 196 – 98.

wardship brought by Chief Justice Weyland in his own court in 1288 where judgment was given for his recovery of the wardship of the land he claimed 'because the said John acknowledges that the said Juliana had enfeoffed the said heir of the said land, which is contrary to the same statute [of Marlborough]'.[39] In a trespass case heard in the 1287 Gloucestershire eyre twenty men were sued for knocking down a hedge and grazing the meadow it enclosed. The jury cleared them but the court then specifically invoked the provisions of c. 46 of the recent statute of Westminster II which had provided that, if anyone with the right to make an enclosure did so and erected a ditch or hedge and had it demolished, the four nearest villages were liable and had to remedy the damage and to pay damages and it made an order accordingly.[40]

The courts might also explicitly extend, or allow the extension of, the application of a statute beyond its specific terms. Chapter 12 of the Provisions of Westminster of 1259 (re-enacted with small amendments as c. 17 of the statute of Marlborough of 1267) had declared that the close kinsmen who held the wardship of lands held by socage tenure were to be answerable for their profits to the heirs when they came of age.[41] Nothing was said about lords or others who usurped such wardship likewise being held responsible. A statutory action of account citing the legislation had been created by 1278.[42] A special variant for use against a lord was created and used in a case of 1286,[43] but in 1293 a writ of the standard form was brought against a lord who had held the wardship.[44] Counsel for the lord argued that the statute did not apply and that the statutory action was inappropriate. The court forced him to answer over, but without (in the enrolment) spelling out the reasons. The reports suggest that a reason may have been given, but that it did not amount to a full-scale defence of this extension of the statute and the statutory remedy. In a second case of 1298 it seems to have been the precedent set by the 1293 case that persuaded the justices to allow the action.[45] Chapter 36 of the statute of Westminster II of 1285 was concerned with the use of distraint to secure the appearance of defendants in local courts to answer litigation brought against them there. It was concerned with the possibility that sheriffs, bailiffs, and the

39 *Weyland v. Brampton:* CP 40/70, m. 55.

40 JUST 1/283, m. 20.

41 For this legislation and its background see *Brand,* Kings, Barons and Justices, pp. 66–69, 190.

42 *Brand,* Kings, Barons and Justices, pp. 348–49.

43 *Brand,* Kings, Barons and Justices, p. 349.

44 *Stretlinges v. Bishop of Worcester:* for full references see *Brand,* King, Barons and Justices, p. 352 and note 21, and for a summary of the arguments pp. 359–60.

45 In an unascribed speech at the end of the report of this case we read *E le play le evesqe de Wyncestr' [sic] regarde semblable a cest cas ou la partie respundi nemye countre esteaunt lavantdite excepcion, par quey avis fut a justices qe il devereit estre respondu.* Nothing is said of the objection in the enrolment. For the references see *Brand,* Kings, Barons and Justices, p. 353 and note 27.

lords of private courts might procure third parties to bring such litigation as a way of harassing those subject to the court's jurisdiction and allowed such harassment to be pleaded in answer to any avowry of a distraint made for this purpose. If found to be true, this was to lead to the awarding of triple damages and the ransoming (by fine) of the defendant.[46] In a case of 1291 a plaintiff against whom a distraint had been made by virtue of a presentment made against him attempted to claim the (extended) authority of the statute to plead that this presentment was false and had been maliciously procured by the court's bailiff. This evidently gave the court pause. It was not until more than a year later that the court rejected this plea on the grounds that presentments made in leets were not covered by the statutory provision, and it awarded a return of the distress.[47] A report of the case shows that the judgment was given by Chief Justice Mettingham and that it included a restatement of the legal status of such presentments as matters of record, as well as the point about the statute not covering this particular case.[48] The court evidently later changed its mind, allowing just such an extension of the statutory replication in an unreported case of 1299 (without any recorded judgment specifically on this point).[49] The same point also came up in a reported case of 1302 where the same plea was again eventually allowed, though we know that it did not go without a challenge. Here we know that judgment was eventually given for the plaintiff after a jury verdict in her favour.[50]

There were other occasions where the courts specifically decided that certain statutory provisions should not be applied. This too might require the giving of reasons. Legislation of 1234 summarised (not wholly accurately) in c. 10 of the standard text of the Statute of Merton of 1236 allowed any free man who owed suit of court to a local court to appoint an attorney to perform his suit for him.[51] By the second half of the thirteenth century there was a statutory writ for the enforcement of this provision. In a 1296 case John Lewyne sued the prior of Barnwell for refusing to accept his attorney to perform suit to the prior's court at Chesterton. The prior pleaded that the manor was ancient demesne of the Crown and John held an ancient demesne socage tenement and that this disentitled him to the privileges of free tenants, including the right under the statute to appoint an attorney to perform

46 Statutes of the Realm, I, 89.

47 The enrolled version of the judgment runs 'quia pluribus racionibus et de causis quarum una est quod in statuto quod predictus Willelmus allegat nulla fit mentio de presentacionibus factis in letis videtur curie quod ballivi predicti Roberti justam fecerunt districcionem in hac parte': *Mortimer of Attleborough v. Tattershall:* CP 40 / 89, m. 26d.

48 BL MS. Additional 31826, f. 56v.

49 *Silke v. Thirsford:* CP 40 / 127, m. 137.

50 *Berenger v. Faukes:* CP 40 / 141, m. 16d. The challenge is recorded in the reports of the case in BL MSS. Additional 37657, f. 148r, and 5925, f. 32v, and in Harvard Law School Library MS. 193, f. 76r.

51 The original legislation is Close Rolls, 1231–34, p. 551. The summary is printed in Statutes of the Realm, I, 4.

suit. Although the court delayed giving judgment for about a year it eventually dismissed the suit on the basis of John's own acknowledgement that he was a sokeman of the ancient demesne. This meant that 'he was not entitled to use or enjoy the common law as a free man in respect of the said tenements in this case'.[52] The clear implication was that the statute did not apply to ancient demesne tenants. A different reason for not following a statutory provision or allowing a remedy provided by one was pleaded in a case of 1277. An attaint was brought to reverse the verdict of a jury given in the 1274 Middlesex eyre. The defendants' claim was that the attaint was only being allowed under the provisions of c. 38 of the statute of Westminster I of 1275 and that the statute did not apply to verdicts given before the passing of the statute.[53] The court duly dismissed the case as unwarranted by the statute but only after information had been given by John de Lovetot, one of the court's justices, that it was not the king's intention, nor had it been when the statute was enacted, that it should apply to jury verdicts given before its enactment.[54]

The only other kind of written, or perhaps semi-written, 'rules' to be applied in the cases of this period were some of the very general principles of the learned law which were summarised in *regulae juris*. These seem to have been applied not because of any general sense of the applicability of the learned laws in the common law courts, but because they embodied acceptable general rules. The general principle that men should not be allowed to benefit from their own deceit was pithily embodied in the learned law tag *fraus et dolus nemini debent patrocinari*. This was quoted, for example, in the final judgment in a detinue of chattels case of 1290. The action had been brought by an ex-wife separated from her husband by the judgment of an ecclesiastical court when he was claimed on grounds of precontract by another woman. It justified the decision that she should recover the valuable chattels given on marriage by her father.[55] A general preference for written evidence that could be produced in court over verbal allegations which would need to go for jury trial was summed up in the phrase *credibiliora sunt opera sermonibus et preferenda* (literally 'works are more believable than words and are to be

52 '... legi communi tanquam liber homo uti non debet nec gaudere quo ad predicta tenementa in hoc casu': CP 40/115, m. 185.

53 CP 40/21, m. 63d.

54 'Et quia non est intencionis domini regis nec existit tempore confeccionis statuti predicti quod hujusmodi jurate transirent super inquisicionibus ante predictum statutum captis, prout J. de Lovetot recordatur, immo post idem statutum concessum, consideratum est...'.

55 'Et quia ex fraude et malicia ipsius Edmundi que, si detecte fuissent in matrimonio inter ipsum Edmundum et predictam Agnetem contrahendo racione prioris contractus, predicta catalla eidem Edmundo liberate non fuissent, nec remanere deberent, maxime cum fraus et dolus nemini debent patrocinari, consideratum est quod predicta Agnes recuperet predictas sexaginta et sex libras et dampna sua que taxantur per juratores ad sexdecim libras': *Brok v. Navestock:* CP 40/81, m. 48d. The many surviving reports of this case report it only as far as the joinder of issue. For another enrolled judgment of 1292 in which the same tag is quoted see CP 40/93, m. 75d.

preferred'). This phrase is found in a number of enrolled judgments in debt cases of the 1290s both in situations where the defendant claimed to have had a written acquittance that had been accidentally destroyed;[56] and where the defendant claimed to have given collateral satisfaction for a debt.[57]

Much more commonly, however, the rules applied in cases are those of custom, of unwritten law. It is relatively rare for that custom to be a local one. The only such custom to be applied with any regularity was the custom of Kent.[58] Generally, the court simply accepted implicitly the statement of Kent custom agreed by the parties or formulated by a jury or agreed by the county and applied it to the facts agreed by the parties or found by a jury. There is, however, at least one case of 1288 where tenants claimed that Kent custom barred a widow from claiming dower because she had committed fornication after her husband's death and borne her lover a son, but the court (without any further enquiry) held that the 'custom of Kent is such, that women thus giving birth, must be taken in the act of giving birth by the levying of the hue, so that the neighbourhood should know it'. Since this had not been alleged she was entitled to her dower.[59] A different kind of special custom sometimes explicitly appealed to by litigants and applied in judgments was that of the 'law merchant'. In the second half of the thirteenth century the most common context in which this was invoked was that of the law of proof as applicable to actions of debt in which the plaintiff produced a tally, not a written bond, to attest the obligation. Here the courts regularly held that 'law merchant' allowed the plaintiff to prove his debt by producing suit (witnesses to the transaction) and gave judgment against the defendant if he refused such proof.[60]

The unwritten custom most commonly invoked, however, was the custom of the country, the 'common law of England'. Sometimes this was spelled out in the judgment by explicit references to what was 'in accordance with the law of the land' (*secundum legem terre*);[61] or 'in accordance with the law and custom of the realm' (*secundum legem et consuetudinem regni*);[62] or to what was 'the custom of the

56 For examples see *Essex v. Hales:* CP 40/103, m. 47; *Chategrave v. Surlingham:* CP 40/103, m. 139.

57 *Executors of Lovel v. Barri:* CP 40/106, m. 221d. Part of the phrase appears earlier in a case in the 1284 Leicestershire eyre (*Danby v. Preston*): JUST 1/460, m. 1.

58 On which see *Nelly Neilson,* 'Custom and the Common Law in Kent', in Harvard Law Review, 38 (1924–25), 482–98.

59 'consuetudo Kancie talis est quod mulieres sic parientes debent in pariendo comprehendi per uthesium levatum, ita quod patria illud scivit...': CP 40/75, m. 6 (*Chapman v. Clerk*).

60 For an explicit application of law merchant in a debt case in the 1299 Cambridgeshire eyre see, for example, the enrolled judgment in *Comberton v. Comberton* (JUST 1/96, m. 25d).

61 For a judgment in King's Bench in 1260 quashing wager of battle in a seignorial court in a land action because the record did not show that there had been any count *secundum legem terre* and because the claimant had waged battle in person but could not make proof on his own behalf *secundum legem terre* see *Pavilly v. Gascelin:* KB 26/167, m. 22.

realm' (*consuetudo regni*).[63] Despite the rather different vocabulary used, it is perhaps also unwritten English common law that is being referred to when a judgment refers to something as 'not in accordance with right' (*non est juri consonum).*[64] But in practice it is very much more common in the judgments of this period to see legal rules being invoked and applied without any specific description of the nature of those rules or their origin. We are simply left to deduce that these are the rules of the common law.[65]

Knowledge of unwritten common law rules must normally have depended, for both justices and the serjeants arguing before them, in part on their memories of previous decisions, though also in part on memories of what had been accepted in prior arguments. Sometimes counsel cited specific cases as precedents. The earliest is one to be found on the plea roll recording argument in 1281 about a case originally heard in the 1279–81 Yorkshire eyre which was being reviewed in King's Bench (*Maulay v. abbot of Whitby).* The abbot's counsel was arguing for the court's ability to seek additional information from the justices who had heard the case which was not recorded on their enrolment. Maulay's counsel cited a prior judgment in the court in 1274 in a case between Edmund of Lancaster and Robert de Ferrers for the principle that a royal official could add nothing to his record after ceasing to act.[66] For later evidence of the citation of precedents by counsel,

---

62 See the judgment given in 1279 in *le Breton v. Slolegh'* (CP 40/31, m. 97d): 'Et quia predictus Petrus cognoscit quod predicta Juliana obiit seisita de predictis tenementis post cujus mortem predictus Henricus intravit in eisdem ut filius et heres et ea tota vita sua pacifice tenuit et inde obiit seisitus nec predictus Petrus aut antecessores sui ipsum Henricum de predictis uncquam implacitaverunt per quod posset, si bastardia ei fuisset objecta, legitimacionem suam in vita sua probasse, nec idem Henricus potest aut debet *secundum legem et consuetudinem regni* post mortem suam bastardari ...'.

63 'Et quia *consuetudo regni* talis est quod post mortem antecessoris soror antenata habet beneficium quod primo debet presentare ad ecclesiam et predicti Robertus et Amabilia nichil ostendunt de specialitate ...': EELR, II, 215 (1285.8).

64 For an example in a judgment dismissing a criminal appeal brought by a child see CP 40/153, mm. 338–338d [Michaelmas 1305]: 'Et quia *non est juri consonum* quod quis infra etatem existens ad appellum prosequendum in regno regis admittatur ...'.

65 For a good example see the final judgment in an action of waste brought against a widow in 1301 where the jury verdict found that waste had only been committed in the time of her now deceased husband and the court held that she could not be held liable for this: 'Et quia per predictam inquisicionem compertum est quod predictus Eymo quondam vir etc. fecit predictum vastum in predictis tenementis postquam predictam Aliciam desponsavit, de cujus injuria predicta Alicia dampnum reportare non debet in hoc casu, consideratum est quod predicta [Alicia] eat inde sine die': CP 40/130, m. 329d. Two reports of the same case are no more explicit about the nature or origin of the rule being applied: '*Hengham.* Pur ceo qe wast fut fet en le tens son baroun e les chateus en tel cas sunt a baroun mesqe ele fu joynte en le purchaz vous ne poez la femme de cel wast charger...' (BL MS. Additional 37657, f. 143r) or 'Par quay *Hengh'* reherca le ple e dist: pur ceo qe trove est par enqueste qe le wast que fut fet si fut en tens le barun e en cest cas si naveit mye la femme parmy le purchas franc tenement que autre serreit par cas si agard la curt...' (BL MS. Additional 31826, f. 117v).

66 Case 64, *G. O. Sayles,* Select Cases in the Court of King's Bench, Selden Society, LV, pp. 86–90.

however, we are dependent on case reports.[67] Case reports also tell us of the citation of past cases by justices in the course of argument. In 1295, for example, Chief Justice Mettingham cited an unnamed case heard several decades earlier by his predecessor Gilbert of Preston for the proposition that the tenant of a manor did not need to show seisin by his ancestor of the right of presentment to a church but only seisin of the manor, if the advowson was appendant to the manor.[68] Courts sometimes specifically looked for past precedents when considering a judgment. The best example from this period relates to the claim of Margery, the wife of the disgraced and exiled Chief Justice Weyland, to the manor of Chipping Sodbury, of which she had been jointly enfeoffed with her husband, and to the earl of Gloucester's resistance to her claim. This was heard before the king's council in Parliament in 1290–91 where the search for precedents was requested by the earl.[69] Once discovered the precedent did indeed help to determine the outcome of the case. Usually we know of such a search only from the report of the case, not from its enrolment. In a 1295 customs and services case the plaintiff's count was challenged for asserting that his ancestor had been seised of scutage 'in demesne' as of fee and right. The serjeant who had made the count (Howard) asserted that the older practice of the court supported him. Only the reporter notes that the case was adjourned because 'the court wanted a search of the old rolls to discover how one used to count' *(la court voleyt sercher auncien roules coment en soloit counter)*, whereas the enrolment simply records an unexplained adjournment.[70] There is no record of what, if anything, was found. Past cases might also, as we can see from at least one early fourteenth century report, be cited by one justice to others in the course of their private discussions before judgment even when other reports and the record make no mention of those precedents.[71] The number of cases, however, in which prior judgments are cited as precedents in the judgments themselves seems to be relatively small. Something close to the direct citation of a precedent seems to have occurred in a case of 1291, where the issue at stake was whether a valid release in fee to a lessee could be made simply by a valid charter of feoffment, or needed some kind of formal ceremony changing the estate of the lessee publicly. There are six reports of this case. Only in one do we read of Chief Justice Mettingham citing (shortly before adjourning the case for consideration) a specific

---

67 The earliest seems to come from the 1286 Cambridgeshire eyre: '*Selby*. En meme cel cas voudreit homme aver voucher vers Johan Peverel e ne pueit estre resceu sil ne le garante avaunt le statut': Bodleian MS. Holkham Misc. 30, f. 39r.

68 LI MS. Miscellaneous 87, f. 92r.

69 SC 9/1, m. 12.

70 BL MS. Additional 37657, f. 100r; CP 40/109, m. 3d.

71 '*Heng*'. Pur coe qe ele ad clame en lenter plus haut estat qe ele ne fet ore en disheritance le eyr, si agard qe ele ne preigne rien par son bref etc. *Ber*' secrete allegga 3 jugemens in simili casu': BL MS. Additional 31826, f. 170r. All that is recorded in the enrolled judgment is 'Et quia predicta Elena alias clamavit integrum predictorum tenementorum ut predictum est etc. videtur curie quod eadem Elena dotem inde clamare non potest etc.': CP 40/136, m. 166.

judgment given before himself that had already determined this point,[72] and in the judgment itself he seems to have promised, if necessary, to show precedents supporting his point, rather than directly citing them.[73] In a 1304 cosinage case Justice Bereford dismissed an objection and made the tenant answer over with reference to the court's decision in the case of David of Flitwick, which had been decided the previous term.[74] The use and citation of precedents is also occasionally revealed in plea roll enrolments. In a 1282 King's Bench case relating to rival claims to the manor of Handsworth forfeited by William de Parles on his conviction for felony the justices of the court with the assistance of their Common Bench colleagues decided that Roger de Somery did not have to answer the rival claim brought by the prior of the Hospitallers and that the prior's seisin since the felony could not ground any entitlement. As authority for their decision they referred to several prior decisions to the same effect. Evidently, however, they did not cite them by name, promising only to do so if and when it was required.[75] In a 1287 assize of mort d'ancestor removed into the Common Bench and adjourned for judgment, and where the claimant then defaulted, the court (strengthened for the judgment by the addition of the King's Bench justices) decided to give judgment on the basis of the verdict as though the claimant was present. The plea roll enrolment noted that the justices cited as a precedent for this what had been done in the reign of Henry III before Martin of Littlebury and his colleagues in the presence of Richard of Middleton then chancellor, Walter of Merton, and others of the king's council in a plea of dower between Clemence, the widow of Stephen de Menyl, and Nicholas de Menyl, as was to be found in the plea roll for Trinity term 55 Henry III.[76]

---

72 '*Mett*'. Nus veymes en meme coe cas devont nus memes (et assigna entre qy) ou le feffour fist une chartre de feffement durant le terme al termer e pus ousta cely issi feffe e il porta la assise de novele disseisine e recoveri e issi ne chaunga unqe son estat. Mes pur coe qe lentre est conu de une part e de autre si ny ad nent plus a fere for soulement ver mon si la chartre pusse luy tenir si son estat ne euste change hors del terme en fee e sur ceo atendez vous jugement': BL MS Hargrave 375, f. 49r.

73 '*Met*'. Quaunt Willem entra a terme le maynour fut a luy du soyl e donqe ne demurra en la persone Renaud fors qe le franc tenement e le fee, les queus choses ne sunt mye corporeaus eynz choses nent mainables les queus choses pount meus estre done par especialte qe par livere de seisine e de ceo saverium dire ensample etc., par qai agarde etc.': BL MS. Hargrave 375, f. 49r.

74 '*Berf*'. Vus estes ouste e espleite quaunt a tele excepcion en autel bref avant ces houres etc. Teste David de Fletewyk' en queu cas hom put aprendre la cause de cel agard. E pur ceo dites outre etc.': BL MS. Hargrave 375, f. 27v.

75 'sicut contingit in multis casibus quos viderunt justiciarii temporibus suis et de quibus habuerunt evidentissima exempla que alias cum necesse fuerit satis habuerunt prompta': Case 76, *G. O. Sayles*, Select Cases in the Court of King's Bench, Selden Society, LV, pp. 103–111 at 106.

76 EELR, II, p. 185–187 (1285.1).

IV.

Reasoned judgments in the early common law varied quite markedly in their complexity. The very simplest of them simply referred to certain facts as agreed or found by a jury verdict but without any implicit invocation of any legal norm and deduced from that a judgment favouring one or other of the parties.[77] Slightly more complex are judgments which stated facts and then explicitly applied law or legal rules to them in order to reach the dispositive part of the judgment through a process of logical deduction.[78] More complex still are judgments which in giving a reason for the judgment also specifically dealt with one or more possible objections. A good example is provided by a replevin action of 1276 in which the abbot of Osney challenged the distraint made by the prior of the Hospitallers to enforce a rent-charge granted by Ralph Daundely and secured on all his lands in two villages, to whomsoever's hands they came, and part of which had subsequently come to the hands of the abbot. The judgment noted the valid creation of the original rent-charge and the prior's seisin of the rent-charge at the hands of the grantor but explicitly rejected the abbot's argument that the prior could not distrain because he had never been seised at the abbot's own hands.[79] In other judgments we see a process of deductive reasoning. In an assize case of 1295 the question was whether or not a tenant *pur autre vie* had a free tenement that was protected by the assize of novel disseisin. Chief Justice Mettingham held that such a tenant's estate was protected: 'It has to be that the free tenement rests in someone. But when a woman holding in dower grants the whole of her estate without reserving anything to herself she has given up everything she had and the reversioner has nothing except the fee and the right of reversion after the death of the doweress. The free tenement is never vacant and so it has to be that it resides in the person who holds the tenement for the term of another's life. So we tell you that he has free tenement as well as he who holds for the term of his own life. So the court adjudges . . . .[80]

V.

Reasoned judgments are certainly to be found in the early English common law. This paper has concentrated on final judgments which disposed of litigation, either on the basis of undisputed facts or after fact-finding, normally by a jury. Some rules discussed and applied in such judgments were rules of procedure, others rules relating to proof, still others rules of substantive law.[81] Some were written rules,

77 For one example out of many see above, p. 56.

78 See above, p. 61.

79 EELR, I, 70 (1276.7).

80 LI MS. Hale 174, ff. 40r-v.

81 Above pp. 58–60.

mainly rules provided by legislation, as extended and interpreted by the courts,[82] but also in some cases general rules derived from the Romano-canonical tradition.[83] Others were primarily unwritten rules, though these might be rules of local custom, law merchant, or general rules of the common law, either explicitly described or implicitly accepted as such. By the last quarter of the thirteenth century explicit statements of certain rules were coming to be associated in some instances with decisions in specific cases, which therefore served in some limited sense as precedents, but the cases seem often to have been themselves a matter of living oral memory; it was only in a small number of cases that the courts searched their own records for written precedents to guide them, so that prior decisions became themselves a written source of law.[84] The actual rhetorical structure of judgments, too, was quite varied: from the quite elliptic to the basic syllogistic application of law to a set of facts, to the jugment dealing with certain specific objections, to something that looks rather like a process of deductive reasoning. It would be wrong, however, to suggest that the English law in this period was embodied only in reasoned final judgments of this kind, and that it was only through such judgments that English law itself developed. Much of English law was embodied in assertions about the rules of law made by litigants and accepted by their opponents and by justices and it was through such consensual, but changing, agreements about what English law was that English law continued to develop outside the formal channels of decisive and reasoned judgments. Reasoned judgments are part of the history of English law and the development of English legal doctrine; they are not the whole story.

---

82 Above pp. 62–65.

83 Above pp. 65–66.

84 Above p. 68.

RICHARD H. HELMHOLZ

The *Ratio Decidendi* in England: Evidence from the Civilian Tradition

I. Introduction

The immediate purpose of this paper is to examine the place of the *ratio decidendi* in the history of the English ecclesiastical courts, where the European *ius commune* provided most of the applicable procedural law. Its second, and broader, purpose is to raise the question of whether these courts and the law they administered played any role in the development of the English common law's distinctive reliance on that concept. I entered into this investigation with high expectations. For legal historians who believe, as I do, that connections long existed between the *ius commune* and English common law, the very term – *ratio decidendi* – attracts immediate interest. So prominent in the history of the common law,[1] the phrase savors of the learned world of the European *ius commune*. It sounds like a term shared with the civilians.[2] It is easy to suppose that it might have been. The existence of dissimilarities in styles of judicial decisions between English and Continental courts in the modern world does not mean there were no historical links.[3]

A comparative study ought to begin by pursuing the Latin phrase itself, and initial examination of the medieval canon law is encouraging. A text in Gratian's *Decretum* (c. 1140) proclaims that "What lacks a *ratio,* is of necessity to be rooted out".[4] Another states that prelates must always be ready to *reddere rationem* for every doctrine when anyone asks for their help.[5] A canon found in the *Decretales*

---

1 See, e.g., *Rupert Cross,* Precedent in English Law, 3d ed. Oxford 1977, pp. 38 – 102; *C. K. Allen,* Law in the Making, 7th ed. Oxford 1964, pp. 259 – 68; *H. F. Jolowicz,* Lectures on Jurisprudence, London 1963, pp. 252 – 61. The concept was, however, slow to get started, both in form and in substance; see *J. H. Baker,* The Law's Two Bodies (Oxford 2001), pp. 1 – 31.

2 See the analogy drawn in *Peter Stein,* Regulae iuris: From Juristic Rules to Legal Maxims, Edinburgh 1966, p. 103; he does not, however, attribute the term to the Roman law, and his analysis of the problem seems to accord with the conclusions reached in this paper. See *Peter Stein,* Civil Law Reports and the Case of San Marino, in *idem,* The Character and Influence of Roman Civil Law: Historical Essays, London and Ronceverte 1988, pp. 115 – 30.

3 On the current situation, see *Folke Schmidt,* The Ratio Decidendi: A Comparative Study of a French, a German and an American Supreme Court Decision, Stockholm 1965.

4 Dist. 68 c. 5: "Et quod ratione caret, extirpari necesse est".

5 d.p. Dist. 36 c. 2: "Parati esse debetis reddere rationem omni poscendi".

Gregorii IX (1234) similarly stated the importance of giving a legitimate reason for any obligation that was imposed on those who were subject to the church's law. Thus a tax for which no discernible reason could be given was one that need not be paid.[6] The phrase was also no stranger to procedural practice in the courts of the church. For instance, witnesses were to be examined as to the reasons for their testimony; they were to *rationem reddere*, not just state their conclusions.[7]

This obligation to give a *ratio* was not simply a matter of language. It reached into the heart of making decisions in contested cases. The medieval canon law developed something very like a concept of procedural due process; the *ordo iuris* was meant to guarantee that litigants would receive their due.[8] Paying attention to the *ratio decidendi* of decided cases appears to be a natural part of this process. What is more due to litigants, what is more necessary for justice to be done, than requiring a judge to state the reasons for his rulings? To modern eyes, it seems axiomatic that they should always be given.[9] Parties, particularly losing parties, have the right to hear the reasons behind the judge's decision. Appellate judges need a way to review the decisions of lower courts.

The process by which the classical law of the church was formulated also encourages the supposition that the *ratio decidendi* was an essential element of court practice in the *ius commune*. Most of the decretals included in the *Decretales Gregorii IX* and the later books of the *Corpus iuris canonici* grew out of actual legal disputes.[10] Only a few were legislative enactments. And in the decretals, the reasoning that lay behind the law was brought to the fore. Explaining what law should be applied to the facts of a case submitted to the pope as judge was exactly what most papal decretals did. It is natural to suppose that lesser judges might have followed the papal example.

Moreover, judicial sentences in individual cases, although not exactly "precedents" in the sense that term would later be used in the English common law, were not without value in the *ius commune*. The later *Decisiones* are one sign of their

6 X 3.39.5: "[Census] cuius causa ignoratur solvi non debet".

7 Gl. ord. ad X 1.3.5: "[H]ic est argumentum bonum de omnibus esse rationem reddendam ... et valet ad testes examinados ut causam sui dicti reddant alias valere non videtur testis dictum".

8 See generally *Brian Tierney*, The Idea of Natural Rights: Studies on Natural Rights, Natural Law, and Church Law, 1150–1625, Atlanta 1997; *Kenneth Pennington*, The Prince and the Law, 1200–1600, Berkeley and Los Angeles 1993; *Charles J. Reid, Jr.*, The Canonistic Contribution to the Western Rights Tradition: An Historical Inquiry, in: Boston College Law Review, vol. 33 (1991), pp. 37–92.

9 E.g., U.S. Fed. R. Civ. P. § 52(a); requires judges in non-jury trials to make a separate statement of their findings of fact and also to state their conclusions of law. For commentary, see *Charles Alan Wright* and *Arthur Miller*, Federal Practice and Procedure: Civil 2d § 2577, discussing the power of appellate courts to vacate judgments that do not comply with this requirement.

10 See *Eric W. Kemp*, An Introduction to Canon Law in the Church of England, London 1957, pp. 19–22. I owe this point to Professor K. W. Nörr.

potential value, but in years during which the classical canon law was being formulated a more immediate example was their use in establishing a custom. The *communis opinio* among the jurists held that, "Two judicial acts within ten years' were sufficient to establish the existence of a lawful custom.[11] Knowing this, judges would naturally have been motivated to state explicitly upon what basis they had decided a particular case. Otherwise, their own judicial act would have been ambiguous and of doubtful value in establishing any custom's existence.

This being said, one must also recognize the warning signs in the texts and handbooks from the medieval *ius commune* – indications that the common law's *ratio decidendi* had no exact parallel with the canon law. First, the Roman law heritage of the canon law was at best ambiguous in encouraging judicial statements of *rationes decidendi.*[12] Many decisions of the classical jurists expressed no special reason for reaching a specific result. They simply announced the outcome.[13] The same was true for the *iudex* in classical Roman law. Second, the apparent encouragement for stating a *ratio* was very often balanced by opposed doctrines in the *ius commune.* For example, the law created a strong presumption that a valid *ratio* existed when the jurisdiction of the judge had been established and the proper procedure followed.[14] Third, in very many of the places where the phrase *reddere rationem* was used in an obligatory sense in the law, it meant "render account" rather than "provide a juridical reason". Often it was an obligation fastened to an office, as in the case of a testamentary executor or a bailiff.[15] It thus required producing facts and figures, not telling what legal reasons lay behind the decisions the official made. It was used in the texts, for example, to describe the account of our lives and stewardship of our talents we must one day present before God.[16]

The commentaries of the medieval jurists are also ambiguous on the place of a *ratio decidendi* in the *ius commune.* On the one hand, they often approached interpretation of the texts by asking – What is the "mind" of this papal decretal or that imperial rescript? They searched for its underlying reason, one might say, in much the same way English common lawyers would search for the *ratio decidendi* of a judicial opinion, distinguishing its core meaning from the judicial language that was merely *obiter dicta.*[17] On the other hand, the medieval canonists and civilians

---

11 See gl. ord. ad Dig. 1. 3. 32 s.v. inveterata. I also own this point to Professor Nörr; see generally *Kozo Ogawa,* Gerichtsurteile und Gewohnheitsrechts im mittelalterlichen gelehrten Recht, ZRG, Kan. Abt., vol. 87 (2001), pp. 484–90.

12 See the essay by L. Winkel, which is printed above.

13 See generally *Franz Horak,* Rationes Decidendi: Entscheidungs-begründungen bei den älteren römischen Juristen bis Labeo, Innsbruck 1969.

14 E.g., *Panormitanus,* Commentaria in libros Decretalium, Venice 1617, ad X 2. 26. 20, no. 32. See also *Jacobus Menochius,* De praesumptionibus, coniecturis, signis, et indiciis, Venice 1587, Lib. II, praes. 67, nos. 2–4.

15 See, e.g., X 1.19.1, dealing with executors and guardians of infants.

16 E.g., X 1.25.1.

17 Gl. ord. ad X 5. 33. 26 s.v. sola verba: "[C]onsideranda est mens potius quam verba".

did not normally use the same terminology and method the common lawyers would. Drawing a distinction between *dicta* and the *ratio,* so that the former could be discounted, was not their habitual way of dealing with the texts they discussed. They usually sought to squeeze everything they could out of the language used in *canones* and *leges.* In other words, their approach to their texts seems to have been different from that of the English common lawyers.

The difference is all the more prominent when one looks at the *ratio decidendi* from the perspective of the judge making the initial ruling. What the judge in the English common law tradition says in his opinion furnishes the starting point for any search for the *ratio* in his decision.[18] This was not true in the *ius commune.*[19] Consider the academic commentaries about judicial sentences used in court practice – at first sight the most immediate and obvious equivalent of the modern judicial opinion; they positively discourage any search for a *ratio decidendi* in judicial sentences. When one looks, for example, at one of the better early *ordines judiciarii,* that of Tancred of Bologna, one finds a formal approach to the nature of a judge's sentence.[20] Tancred tells his readers that in giving sentence the judge must be sitting in his accustomed, or at least in an honest, place. He tells them that the judge should state what the plaintiff's petition was and what the defendant's response was. Then he instructs the judge to say, "Having seen and heard the confessions, attestations, instruments, reasons, and allegations of each party, and having diligently investigated and understood [them], with the counsel of many learned men, I condemn or I absolve". That is all. Tancred's judge is apparently not obliged to inform his listeners, the parties or their lawyers, of the reasoning process that lay behind the sentence of condemnation or absolution.

Tancred died in 1236, but later proceduralists do not differ materially from his presentation of the subject. The influential treatise of William Durantis (d. 1296), for example, includes full and strong material on the formal elements of a judicial sentence. The judge's sentence should state – *Deliberatione cum peritis habita,* for example – but except in special circumstances, it need contain no information about the exact contents of that deliberation.[21] A definitive sentence must contain six elements: the name and source of authority of the judge, the names of the litigants, the tenor of the plaintiff's petition, the nature of the procedural steps followed, notation of whether the parties were present or absent by contumacy, and the formal condemnation or absolution of the defendant.[22] There is, however, noth-

---

18 I have adopted this admittedly ambiguous definition in order to avoid the arguments and difficulties in determining the exact role of the judge's own words; see *J. L. Montrose,* The *Ratio Decidendi* of a Case, Modern L. Rev., vol. 20 (1957), pp. 587–95, A. *W. B. Simpson,* The *Ratio Decidendi* of a Case, Modern L. Rev., vol. 21 (1958), pp. 155–60; *Arthur Goodhart,* The *Ratio Decidendi* of a Case, Modern L. Rev., vol. 22 (1959), pp. 117–24.

19 *James A. Brundage,* Medieval Canon Law, London and New York 1995, p. 134.

20 See *Pillius, Tancredus, Gratia,* Libri de iudiciorum ordine, Pt. 4; Tit. 1, ed. F. C. Bergmann, Göttingen 1842, repr. 1965, p. 273.

21 See Speculum iudiciale, Lib. II, Pt. 3, tit. De sentencia § 5 (Qualiter), no. 13.

ing about anything like a *ratio decidendi* in the treatise's description of a judicial sentence. For the historian, it would seem a fruitless task to seek for the *ratio decidendi* of a judge who was all but instructed to keep silent about the subject. Later English commentators of course never confined themselves to a judge's words in the search for the *ratio decidendi* of a case, but at least they had the judge's explanation as a place to start, and this seems not to have been true in the *ius commune.*

The absence of legal reasoning from sentences does not mean that the judges in courts governed by the *ius commune* did not *have* a reason for deciding as they did. It assuredly did not mean that judges were to pay no attention to the learned laws and the commentaries. Most judges in the ecclesiastical courts had been trained in them in the university law faculties. The connection between academic learning and the decision of actual cases is clear enough. Witness the *consilia* literature that held such a significant place in the *ius commune.*[23] It shows the ties between litigation and academic learning. The absence did mean, however, that judges were positively discouraged from giving their reasons when formulating their sentences. Nor did they receive any encouragement to state the facts they had considered important in reaching a decision.[24] The formal nature of the procedural law of the church thus seems to have precluded any search for the *ratio decidendi* in any individual case. It makes establishing any firm connection between the *ius commune* and the English common law on this point difficult.

II. Medieval Practice

Moving beyond the academic literature and into the court books and records of the English ecclesiastical courts confirms the conclusion drawn from Tancred and the later proceduralists. It only deepens the puzzle and confounds the expectation that the *ratio decidendi* should have played a part in medieval jurisprudence of the *ius commune.* A typical sentence used in practice seems more ceremony than substance. It began: *In dei nomine Amen. Auditis et intellectis meritis cause que veritur inter A, ex parte una, et B, ex parte altera.* Then it wound through a series of pious and conventional phrases, confined to generalities about the rectitude of the actions taken, to arrive finally at a statement that A either had proved his *intentio*

---

22 Ibid., no. 16. See also *Jo. Petrus de Ferrariis,* Aurea practica, Venice 1610, tit. De forma sententiae diffinitivae, listing many reasons for invalidity of a sentence, but not the absence of reasons, except, at no. 47, if a false *causa* were given in a sentence, the sentence was a nullity.

23 See *Guido Kisch,* Consilia: Eine Bibliographie der juristischen Konsiliensammlungen, Basel 1970; *Peter Riesenberg,* The Consilia literature: A Perspective, Manuscripta, vol. 6 (1962), pp. 3–22.

24 The facts as understood by the judge are treated as the key to the ratio in the most famous article on the subject: *Arthur Goodhart,* Determining the *Ratio Decidendi* of a Case, Yale Law Journal, vol. 40 (1930), pp. 161–183.

or else had failed to do so.[25] Sentences recited the procedural steps the judge had taken in the particular case – i.e., lawfully summoning witnesses, publishing their depositions, hearing allegations by both parties, and so forth. Of the substantive law in each case and the significant facts revealed in the depositions, however, they tell the reader virtually nothing. Indeed, the practice grew up of having each side submit a "draft sentence" to the court; the judge in turn accepted the one or the other and "porrected" it publicly – a system all but designed to keep any of the judicial reasoning process out of the official records of instance litigation.[26]

How is this apparently strange system of rendering sentences to be explained? Did it make sense at the time, and does it help us to explore the history of the *ratio decidendi* in the *ius commune?* From the perspective of the judge who promulgated the sentence, the absence of legal reasoning did make immediate practical sense. It protected his decision from being attacked. The canon law treated a sentence as a nullity if it contained an express error in law.[27] Where the error was not patent, however, it could only be corrected by an appeal, which in canonical practice required a virtual retrial of the case *ab initio*. Thus it is easy to see why the judges in English ecclesiastical courts might have preferred not to state their reasons or even their interpretation of the significant facts of any case. This explanation is, however, an argument from judicial self-interest. What about the perspective of the goals and policies of the law? Did the system serve those goals and policies?

At this stage, I cannot answer the question with confidence. The procedural system characteristic of the *ius commune* seems foreign to most modern ways of thinking about a judge's duty to the litigants and appellate judges. They were left with no statement of reasons. The most I can say is that the uninformative sentences used in English practice accorded with some other features of the *ius commune*. First, the sentences used in practice accorded with the formality and objective character of the law itself. The classical canon law put its faith in compliance with objective processes of law.[28] Balancing policies and weighing the merits of permissible alternatives in terms of desirable social policy was not what judges were supposed to do. Observance of the law's *ordo iuris* was the objective. That is

---

25 See, e.g., *Cyriel Vleeschouwers* and *Monique van Melkebeek*, Liber Sentenciarum van de Officialiteit van Brussel 1448–1459, 2 vols. Brussels 1982–83; *Norma Adams* and *Charles Donahue, Jr.*, Select Cases from the Ecclesiastical Courts of the Province of Canterbury c. 1200–1301, Selden Society vol. 95, 1981 for 1978–79, pp. 55–56; *Stanley Chojnacki*, Valori patrizi nel tribunale patriarcale: Girolamo da Mula e Marietta Soranzo (Venezia 1460), in *Silvana Seidel Menchi* and *Diego Quaglioni*, Matrimonio in dubbio: Unioni controverse e nozze clandestine in Italia dal XIV al XVIII secolo, Bologna 2001, pp. 244–45.

26 See *Anne Tarver*, Church Court Records, Chichester 1995, p. 21.

27 Gl. ord. ad X 2.27.1 s.v. contra leges: "Item sentencia contra leges ... ita quod hoc in sentencia exprimatur, nulla est ipso iure et citra appellationem rescinditur".

28 See generally, *K. W. Nörr*, Prozeßzweck und Prozeßtypus: der kirchliche Prozeß des Mittelalters im Spannungsfeld zwischen objektiver Ordnung und subjektiven Interessen, ZRG, Kan. Abt., vol. 78 (1992), pp. 183–209.

exactly what the sentences used in practice emphasized. Second, individual cases did not have special value as precedent.[29] The relevant law was in the relevant *Corpus iuris* and the commentaries built upon it. As was so often said, in the *ius commune* conclusions were to be made *legibus non exemplis.*[30] To allow sentences to become expositions of the law might thus have subverted an assumption upon which the law was based. Third, the nature of trials and appellate practice in the *ius commune* reduced the utility of a statement of reasons from the judges. Juries did not decide questions of fact, as at common law. Judges did. The most common form of evidence, the testimony of witnesses, was taken outside of court, reduced to written form, then submitted to the court. From the depositions, considered along with any other evidence submitted, judges made their decisions. This meant that if there were an appeal, the full range of evidence from the trial of first instance could also be put before the *iudex ad quem.* The distinction between law and fact, although well known in civilian practice, did not require that the two be kept separate and preserved in case of appeal.[31] The appellate court could – in fact was required to – make its own evaluation of the evidence. It was in just as good a position to do so as was the court from which appeal had been taken. It was thus unnecessary that the sentence have separated law from fact.

III. Later Medieval Developments

This procedural system governed practice into the sixteenth century and beyond in the *ius commune.* It was also applied in the English ecclesiastical courts. Not everything remained unchanged, however, and it is fair to say that by the late Middle Ages there must have been some dissatisfaction with the lack of importance accorded to judicial decisions and the absence of legal reasoning in them. The beginning of the compilation of *decisiones,* which collected together significant cases decided in particular courts, was a manifestation of that development. *Decisiones* from the *ius commune* were not, of course, the first example of this kind of collecting. Collections of the decrees of the Parlement of Paris in the *Olim* or the English Yearbooks come to mind as earlier examples.[32] Within the world of the *ius commune,* however, collecting started with the *Rota Romana* in the mid-fourteenth century. Auditors began to assemble and circulate decisions given by the branches of this most authoritative tribunal of the church. The habit spread elsewhere. It should be said that these *Decisiones* could be as fully elaborate and academic in

---

29 See *A. W. B. Simpson,* The Ratio decidendi of a Case and the Doctrine of Binding Precedent, in: Oxford Essays in Jurisprudence, ed. A. G. Guest, Oxford 1961, pp. 148–75.

30 On the role of this maxim in English law, see *Alan Harding,* A Social History of English Law, Baltimore 1966, pp. 221–223.

31 See *Peter Stein,* Civil Law Reports (above note 2).

32 See generally *J. H. Baker,* Dr. Thomas Fastolf and the History of Law Reporting, Cambridge Law Journal, vol. 45 (1986), pp. 84–94.

their presentation of the legal issues as were many contemporary *Consilia*, and they sometimes obscured the facts of particular cases as completely as did the *Consilia*. They were not, therefore, wholly alien to the traditions of the *ius commune*.

Nonetheless, *Decisiones* did bring individual cases and judicial reasoning into greater prominence than had been true before. *Decisiones* came out of particular cases brought before a specific court, and they explained the legal reasons for the judge's decision. In some sense, therefore, they must have been motivated by the conviction that what happened before a court was legally valuable; law as developed in actual cases could explain the customs and authorities that were accepted as law under the *ius commune*. *Decisiones* might also contain *singularia*, matters not adequately explained in the commentaries of the jurists.[33] As such, they have at least a connection of sorts with the history of the *ratio decidendi*.

The full history of *Decisiones* remains to be written.[34] However, it is clear that *Decisiones* were important and that they were known and used in later medieval England, as they were in Continental courts.[35] Those taken from the archbishop's court in Toulouse, and also those compiled by Guido Papa, Matthaeus de Afflictis, and Nicholas Boerius were particularly prominent in England, as were the *Decisiones* of the Roman *Rota*. How they were regarded by the English judges cannot be ascertained with certainty, and they did not stand as authority apart from the traditions of the *ius commune*. They were connected with judicial opinions in actual cases in a way the academic commentaries were not, however, and their reception in England marked an advance.

IV. English Developments

Developments within Continental legal traditions made a difference in the ecclesiastical forum in England. There are two general points to be made. First, the formal system in procedure described above, which excluded any legal reasoning from the sentences issued by the courts, long continued in England, as it did on the Continent. Second, English civilians, the lawyers who practised in the ecclesiastical and maritime courts, must have felt that their own system was incomplete, for

---

33 So stated in *Guido Papa*, In Senatu Gratianopolitano Decisiones, Geneva 1667, Proem.

34 See *Gero Dolezalek / K. W. Nörr*, Die Rechtsprechungssammlungen der mittelalterichen Rota, in Handbuch der Quellen und Literatur der neueren europäischen Privatrechtsgeschichte, ed. *Helmut Coing*, Munich 1973–6, vol. I, pp. 851–56; *J. F. von Schulte*, Die Geschichte der Quellen und Literatur des canonischen Rechts, Stuttgart 1875, repr. Graz 1956, vol. II, pp. 479–80.

35 For a fuller description, see *Mario Ascheri* (Italy), Rechtsprechungssammlungen, in *Coing*, Handbuch, (above note 33), vol. II:2, pp. 1113–1194; *Gerhard Walter* (France), ibid., pp. 1223–63; *Johannes-Michael Scholz* (Spain and Portugal), ibid, pp. 1271–1309, 1319–38; *Heinrich Gehrke*, (Germany), ibid., pp. 1343–72; *Udo Wagner* (Low Countries), ibid., pp. 1399–1417.

from the mid-sixteenth century, they themselves began to compile what might be called *decisiones* from their own courts. By this means, legal reasoning came to the fore to a greater extent than had once been true.

In this aspect of their history, the courts of the church (and the admiralty too) ran along parallel tracks with both the *ius commune* and the English common law. The parallel is clear in the nature of the court records. The judgments entered on the plea rolls of the royal courts kept to their ancient forms. They remained "highly formulaic, using stereotyped Latin phrases in place of detailed assertions, omitting the evidence, the arguments of counsel, and the reasons for judgments."[36] The same remained true of the sentences in the ecclesiastical courts. They too kept to their formulaic standards. Although specific cases were occasionally mentioned in the procedural literature of English ecclesiastical lawyers, the cases were not collected separately or organized to bring out the reasoning that lay behind them.[37] The medieval system, which excluded all but the most determined search for a *ratio decidendi* in decided cases, lasted as long as the English ecclesiastical courts exercised their traditional jurisdiction over marriage and divorce, testaments and defamation, that is, into the nineteenth century.[38]

The parallel is also evident in the growth of new kinds of law reporting that laid greater stress on legal reasoning. For most practical purposes, the ancient form of law reporting in the royal courts was eclipsed by the rise of nominate law reports, beginning during the Tudor era,[39] and new procedural techniques gave legal issues greater prominence in the decision of many individual cases.[40] Nothing so dramatic happened in the ecclesiastical forum, but again there was a parallel. Beginning in the reign of Elizabeth I, English civilians began to compile reports of cases heard in the ecclesiastical and admiralty courts. A fairly typical example, now kept in the Bodleian Library, was entitled "Certain adjudged cases in the Civil Law".[41] It was a modest and a miscellaneous effort, but like the others, it is a manifestation of contemporary discontent with the older, formal system of the *ius commune*. In this limited sense, one may discern something like a search for a *ratio decidendi* among the English civilians.

---

36 *J. H. Baker,* An Introduction to English Legal History, 4th ed. London 2002, pp. 178, 182–86.

37 See Queen's College, Oxford (15th century), MS. 54, fols. 32–35v, mentioning for example, "causa Hugonis contra episcopum Lincoln' pro ecclesia de Coltesworth". F. Donald Logan, who is editing this text for the Canterbury and York Society, was kind enough to provide me with a copy.

38 See *G. I. O. Duncan,* The High Court of Delegates, Cambridge 1971, pp. 173–74.

39 *L. W. Abbott,* Law Reporting in England 1485–1585, London 1973.

40 See *S. F. C. Milsom,* Historical Foundations of the Common Law, 2d ed. London 1981, pp. 70–81.

41 Bodleian Library, Oxford, Lit. MS. Eng. Misc.f.473, containing twenty-nine pages of miscellaneous notes and cases on ecclesiastical law from the 1620s and after.

The history of this English "case literature" remains to be investigated fully. Only a preliminary list of those compiled from before the 1640s, when the ecclesiastical courts were closed in the wake of the English civil war, has so far been made.[42] None of the early reports has ever been printed – the first printed reports from the ecclesiastical courts come from the middle of the eighteenth century.[43] However, the amount of this "case literature" that existed in manuscripts and was kept in ecclesiastical repositories is not negligible. It must have circulated widely at the time, because many of the same cases turned up in manuscript repositories spread throughout England. Evidently a need for these reports was felt among the English civilians at the time. Enough remains to show that reporting civilian cases was not the peculiar interest of a tiny group of them.

For the years after the Restoration of the monarchy in 1660, virtually nothing has been done with this "case literature". Clearly, the reporting continued. It apparently grew in numbers and scope. But little about its character is certain. For example, there is the large and lurking question of the influence of the English common law in the spiritual courts. Before 1640, the reports show very little influence. The authorities and reasoning of the *ius commune* retained their dominant place in argument and practice. But was this true afterwards? Or did the post-Restoration English civilians accord a greater place to the authorities of the common law,[44] rejecting the cosmopolitanism of their predecessors? And how much attention was given to judicial reasoning? In the present state of research, no exact answer to the questions can be given.[45] Still less is it now possible to make good the gap in scholarship.

However, it is possible to take an example of this literature, one that sheds some light on the theme of this volume. It comes from a collection of reports now kept in the library of the Columbia University Law School in New York City.[46] How the manuscript got there is unknown, but it is similar to most of the other examples so far discovered. The manuscript covers the years between 1670 and 1707 and deals with cases from the London courts, principally the Court of Arches. It contains 118 folios that cover ecclesiastical causes, which are in turn followed by

---

42 See *R. H. Helmholz,* Roman Canon Law in Reformation England, Cambridge 1990, pp. 198 – 199. The most significant additions have been the Trumbull MSS. now in the British Library in London.

43 It was compiled by *Sir George Lee,* Reports of cases argued and determined in the Arches and Prerogative Courts of Canterbury, 2 vol. 1832 – 1833.

44 This was the view of *F. W. Maitland,* Church, State and Decretals, in: Roman Canon Law in the Church of England, London 1898, pp. 95 – 96: "[T]hey were easy Englishmen, and year by year they were becoming more English and less cosmopolitan" ... "Our civilians were fast acquiring what we may call the common law mind".

45 There are signs of greater common law influence; e.g., Tunstall c. Salmon (1671), All Souls College, Oxford, MS. 230, a testamentary cause, contains about an equal number of common law and civilian citations.

46 MS. M 315; it is listed in *J. H. Baker,* English Legal Manuscripts in the United States of America, Part II: 1558 – 1902, London 1990, No. 263.

cases taken from the Court of Admiralty. In most but not all instances, the report contains the names of the parties to each case, the names of the advocates, some at least of the facts behind the litigation, the legal arguments advanced (usually those of each side), the authorities they relied upon, and the decision, which was normally a simple notation that sentence was being given for one or the other of the parties.

A fairly typical example of a statement of facts, taken from a testamentary dispute found early in the manuscript,[47] begins:

> Ezekiel Langston sent for Mr Haggott a counselor of law to come to make his will. Haggott took instructions for a will in minutes, no one with the decedent at [the] taking of these instructions but Mr Haggott. Before Mr Haggott could reduce the same minutes into writing and return with them, the decedent died.

This death-bed scenario was a frequent one, it turns out, in the practice of courts hearing testamentary causes in England. The decedent intended to make a written will, and there was indeed a written will introduced into probate. However, the document had not been completed prior to the decedent's death. A nuncupative testament was therefore a possibility. They were perfectly valid under English law, and it could be one informed by the minutes Mr Haggott had taken. However, he was the only witness to the oral statement of the decedent's last wishes, and in the civil law two witnesses were regularly required to prove any fact. This was a common case, and one not adequately covered by statute or decretal law. It was no wonder that an English civilian should have noted it, therefore, and preserved it for the future. He also would want to have more than a sentence in favor or against; he would need some legal reasoning to help him understand the problem and the solution.

The manuscript report provides this. It went on to give the legal reasoning on both sides. Dr Mylles spoke first, in favor of validity.[48] Admitting that the will did not meet the requirements of the civil law, he nonetheless argued that it could be treated as valid *in foro animae* according to the *lex naturae* and the *lex gentium*, if it was undoubted that it contained the true last wishes of the testator, as he asserted this will did. For this proposition he cited four authorities: Franciscus Mantica (d. 1614), *De conjecturis ultimarum voluntatum*, Liber II, Tit. 14, no. 23; Simon de Praetis (d. c. 1590), *De ultimarum voluntatum interpretatione*, Liber II, fol. 195, no. 41; Paulus de Castro (d. 1441), *Consilia*, Vol. 1, cons. 456, and *Brown* v. *Sackville* (KB 1552), 1 Dyer 72a, which was a case from the Court of King's Bench interpreting the Statute of Wills (32 Hen. VIII, c. 1, 1540). This range of citations is typical of those found in this manuscript. The majority of them came from the European *ius commune*, and one in this case from a jurist who had died more than

47 Ibid., f. 5. The date was 1671.

48 On Mylles, who was admitted to Doctors' Commons in 1650, see *G. D. Squibb*, Doctors' Commons: A History of the College of Advocates and Doctors of Law, Oxford 1977, p. 177.

two centuries prior to the English case, but that preference did not exclude citation of a case from the common law that supported the advocate's argument. *Brown* v. *Sackville* did in fact bolster the case for the validity of this particular will, although it was distinguishable in that the will in that case had been reduced to writing prior to the death of the decedent, but had not been read back to him for his confirmation prior to his death. The other citations, those from the civil law, seem also to have supported the argument as a matter of substance, though none was exactly in point. To this argument, Dr Mylles added a second: Singular witnesses may constitute full proof *cum conjecturis*. The two-witness rule in the civilian tradition had many exceptions, and this was one; here he supplied five citations, all drawn from the *ius commune*, to establish the point. Nothing from the common law would have been available.

Next followed a second advocate arguing for the validity of the will, Dr Edward Master. He made two legal arguments, both buttressed by citation to commentaries on the Roman and canon laws. The first: that a testament not in solemn form may be valid *inter liberos;* the second, that *indicia* may serve for "a certain form of proof". These were weaker points, but they did tend to show that the law did not always require proof in strict form. He had two laws from the Codex and commentaries to them by Baldus and Bartolus, the two greatest civilians from the Middle Ages, to back him up.

The manuscript goes on to record that an advocate for the other side, the takers by intestacy, then spoke. He was identified only by his initials R. W., and who this was, we cannot be sure. Sir Robert Wiseman (d. 1684) is a possibility. Wiseman was active as an advocate during these years and no other advocate of the day had the same initials. He was the author of a work designed to spread greater knowledge of Roman law, *The Law of Lawes* (1st ed. 1656); itself a description and encomium of the principal features of the civil law.[49] His argument in *Langston's Case* (if it may be so called), however, was that although the will might be valid under the English common law, if backed by the verdict of a jury, it was not sufficient to pass the personal estate under the civil law applicable to the case, because "the several circumstances here are not to the substance of the will and therefore not sufficient". For this he supplied no legal citations of the sort just mentioned. He simply ascribed the difference to the Statute of Wills and to the extra weight supplied by the verdict of an English jury, which were of course absent from this cause. It might have been possible for an advocate to have found support for his arguments in the treatise literature of the *ius commune,* but this particular advocate produced none; his answer nonetheless gave a straightforward reason for his position, and in the event his view prevailed.

The case was evidently being heard before the Court of Delegates, because the Columbia manuscript records that the judges were Sir William Moreton (d. 1672), one of the justices of the King's Bench, Timothy Littleton (d. 1669), a baron of the

---

49 The Law of Lawes (1657), Preface (no pagination).

Exchequer, a prominent civilian, Dr Richard Lloyd (d. 1686), and two other civilians who so far remain unidentified. Unlike most ecclesiastical courts, the Court of Delegates was made up of judges appointed individually for each appealed case, and the panels were normally drawn from the ranks of both civilians and common lawyers. Their apparently joint decision, a notable one, drew upon the traditional distinction between lands and chattels, reaching a result that made it easier to devise land than to bequeath chattels. In so doing, the court expressly rejected the *ratio decidendi* contained in the Continental authorities cited by the will's proponents. It appears that this decision might have effectively settled a point of law that arose with some regularity in practice and also been a means of harmonizing temporal and spiritual law. Would it have been a precedent for the future? Perhaps not in a strict sense, but it would have been a step in establishing the customary practice of the ecclesiastical courts.

V. Conclusion

Langston's Case is no more than an example. Many more such cases could be drawn from the reports of the English civilians in the years both before and after the Restoration. However, it is a good and a typical example, one worth contemplating. From it and cases like it may be drawn tentative conclusions for this project in comparative legal history. There are at least two, one positive, the other negative.

First, if we adopt a broad meaning of the term *ratio decidendi,* the lawyers practising in the courts of the church and in the Admiralty shared the same desire for greater legal precision that was felt in the common law during the sixteenth century and thereafter. Something like what S. F. C. Milsom called "the ancient pattern of the law suit", in which legal reasoning was kept from view in the court records, can also be found in the medieval the ecclesiastical courts.[50] This pattern was gradually and partially superseded by procedural innovation in the royal courts – motions in arrest of judgment, demurrers to the evidence, and special verdicts.[51] No such procedural changes occurred in the ecclesiastical forum, but the creation of a body of reports from these courts shows that a similar movement occurred in that world. The English civilians must have desired a closer connection between legal reasoning and decided cases.

Second, if we adopt instead a narrower and more careful definition of *ratio decidendi,* it seems idle to speak of anything like the doctrine's existence in the ecclesiastical courts. The cases decided there were without value as precedent; they were rarely cited or used as such by the civilians.[52] The texts in the *Corpus iuris,*

50 See *Milsom,* Historical Foundations (above, note 40), pp. 38 – 39.

51 On these developments, see *J. H. Baker,* Oxford History of the Laws of England 1483 – 1558, Oxford 2003, vol. VI, pp. 385 – 407.

augmented by statutes and constitutions, were what supplied the applicable law. There was no need for the careful distinction of holding from dicta in prior, authoritative decisions that made it necessary to search for the *ratio decidendi* of the particular cases in the common law. A measure of change did occur within the ecclesiastical courts, but no move towards treating decided cases as binding precedents or searching through past cases for an underlying *ratio.* Sentences remained as formal as ever they had been. Such changes would probably have puzzled, if not horrified, the civilians. So the two legal systems in England remained distinct. The possibility, raised at the outset of this paper – that the *ratio decidendi* was a shared institution – turns out to be misleading.

[52] See generally *Alain Wijffels,* References of Judicial Precedents in the practice of the Great Council of Malines (ca. 1460–1580), in Miscellanea Consilii Magni, vol. 3 (1988), pp. 165–186.

VÉRONIQUE DEMARS-SION ET SERGE DAUCHY

La non motivation des décisions judiciaires dans l'ancien droit français: un usage controversé

Dès le XIIIe siècle, en France, les bases d'une justice «moderne», rationalisée et centralisée, sont jetées. Désireux d'imposer sa souveraineté, le roi favorise l'abandon de l'ancienne procédure féodale, accusatoire, formaliste et ignorant l'appel à laquelle se substitue une nouvelle procédure, de nature contradictoire: la procédure d'enquête. Cette procédure – dite romano-canonique – s'inspire de l'exemple des cours d'Eglise qui ont elles-mêmes emprunté au modèle romain. Quant au système de l'appel, il se développe à la suite de la création, au milieu du XIIIe siècle, du parlement de Paris. L'une des grandes innovations introduites à cette époque tient au fait que les décisions de justice sont désormais consignées par écrit[1]. Il faut cependant attendre la seconde moitié du XIVe siècle pour qu'un système développé d'écritures s'instaure de façon permanente dans le monde judiciaire, tout au moins dans les juridictions les plus importantes[2]. A partir de là, toute la question est de savoir comment les décisions sont rédigées et, plus particulièrement, si elles contiennent une motivation. Une telle motivation est en effet considérée comme essentielle dans notre droit positif: comme le souligne fort justement Tony Sauvel, *«il n'est pas un Français aujourd'hui qui ne soit intimement convaincu ... qu'une décision, pour être valable et s'imposer, ait besoin être motivée»*[3]. Il en va tout autrement dans notre ancien droit où l'absence de motivation constitue la règle. Dans les premières décennies de son existence, le parlement de Paris semble pourtant avoir eu le souci d'expliquer ses décisions[4] mais sa pratique a rapidement évo-

---

1 En la matière, l'exemple semble avoir été donné par l'Echiquier de Normandie dont les décisions commencent à être inscrites sur des feuilles de parchemin conservées en rouleau dès 1196. La même pratique apparaît à Paris vers le milieu du XIIIe siècle mais, dès 1260, les notaires et greffiers attachés à la Cour substituent des registres aux rouleaux (les premiers registres constituent les célèbres *Olim*). Cf. *J. Hilaire / C. Bloch,* Connaissance des décisions de justice et origine de la jurisprudence, in: J.H. Baker (éd.), Judicial Records, Law Reports, and the Growth of Case Law, Berlin 1989, p. 47–68 (p. 53–54).

2 Sur les conditions de la lente pénétration de la civilisation de l'écriture dans le monde judiciaire, voir *J. Hilaire / C. Bloch*, art. cit., p. 54–55.

3 *T. Sauvel*, Histoire du jugement motivé, in: Revue de droit public et de la science politique en France et à l'étranger, 71 (1955), p. 5–53, cf. p. 5.

4 Ce souci se révèle à travers l'insertion dans ses arrêts de la formule explicative *«judicatum est quod ... quia ...»* (sur ce point voir *T. Sauvel*, art. cit., p. 11 sq. et *Ph. Godding,* Jurisprudence et motivation des sentences, du Moyen Age à la fin du XVIIIe siècle, in: Ch. Perelman / P. Foriers (ed.), La motivation des décisions de justice, Bruxelles 1978,

lué et, dès le XIVe siècle, la solution inverse a prévalu: dans les années 1330, toute trace de motivation disparaît[5]. Cet abandon se perpétuera jusqu'à la Révolution, tant et si bien qu'on présente traditionnellement la non-motivation comme l'un des traits caractéristiques de la justice dÁncien Régime, voire comme l'une de ses «*plus étranges particularités*»[6]. Certains auteurs en sont même arrivés à considérer que, dans l'ancienne France, il était, par principe, interdit aux juges de faire connaître les motifs de leurs décisions[7]. Mais en allait-il vraiment ainsi? Ce n'est pas certain. L'étude des sources montre qu'aucun texte n'a formellement consacré cette prétendue interdiction que la doctrine n'a pas davantage entérinée. Ainsi, rien ne permet d'affirmer qu'avant 1789 il était par principe interdit aux juges de faire connaître les motifs de leurs décisions mais il n'en est pas moins vrai qu'en pratique ils s'abstenaient de le faire. A défaut d'un principe contraignant, il existait donc un usage bien établi auquel les juges resteront fidèles jusqu'à la fin de l'Ancien Régime[8]. Cet usage ne s'est pourtant pas imposé sans difficultés. La tendance à la non-motivation, révélée par les arrêts du parlement de Paris dès le XIVe siècle, ne fait pas l'unanimité. Elle finira cependant par l'emporter et, au XVIe siècle, tout laisse penser qu'elle a triomphé (I). Ce triomphe reste cependant relatif car la pratique ne tarde pas à prendre conscience des inconvénients de l'usage qu'elle a imposé et, dès le XVIe siècle, elle contribue elle-même à introduire des dérogations dont l'importance ne cessera de croître au cours des deux derniers siècles de l'Ancien Régime (II).

---

p. 37–67 (p. 50–51). Cependant – comme l'a fort justement souligné J. Hilaire – il ne s'agit pas alors d'une véritable «*motivation ... au sens moderne, c'est-à-dire une motivation visant les textes sur lesquels la décision est fondée*», *mais plutôt de «justifications». Cf. J. Hilaire,* Jugement et jurisprudence. Le procès, in: Archives de philosophie du droit, 39 (1995), p. 181–190 (p. 183). Voir aussi *T. Sauvel*, art. cit., p. 14 et *F. Aubert*, Histoire du parlement de Paris de l'origine à François Ier (1250–1515), 2 t. en 1 vol., Réimpression de l'édition de 1894, Genève, t. 2, p. 124: la Cour indiquait simplement, jusqu'au second quart du XIVe siècle, «*ce qui avait été prouvé* (et) *ce qui ne l'avait pas été*».

5 Cf. *P. Guilhiermoz*, Enquêtes et procès, Etude sur la procédure et le fonctionnement du Parlement au XIVe siècle, suivie du style de la chambre des enquêtes ..., Paris 1892, p. 154. Voir aussi *T. Sauvel*, art. cit., p. 18 sq et *Ph. Godding*, art. cit., p. 51.

6 Cf. *A. Lebigre*, „Pour les cas résultant du procès". Le problème de la motivation des arrêts, in: Revue d'Histoire de la Justice, 7 (1994), p. 23–37 (p. 23).

7 Voir, par exemple, *Ph. Godding*, art. cit., p. 53 et *S. Dauchy*, Les recueils privés de „jurisprudence" aux Temps Modernes, in: A. Wijffels (éd.), Case-Law in the Making. The Techniques and Methods of Judicial Records and Law Reports, Berlin 1997 (*Comparative Studies in Continental and Anglo-American Legal History*, bd. 17/1), vol.1: Essays, p. 237–247 (p. 244).

8 Voir *S. Dauchy/V. Demars-Sion*, La non-motivation des décisions judiciaires dans l'ancien droit: usage ou principe?, in: Revue Historique de Droit Français et Etranger (R.H.D.F.E.), 82.2 (2004), p. 223–239.

I. La lente affirmation de l'usage

Si la non-motivation a eu tant de mal à s'imposer c'est que, contrairement à ce qu'on a parfois écrit, le législateur ne s'est jamais prononcé sur la question (I.1). Quant à la doctrine, sa position est loin d'être unanime (I.2).

1. Le silence des textes

Les historiens contemporains s'accordent pour rattacher la non-motivation au principe du secret des délibérés. A les en croire, ce secret permettrait de justifier l'absence de motivation des décisions de justice[9] voire l'interdiction de motiver ces décisions[10].

Le principe du secret des délibérés a été posé, pour la première fois, par l'ordonnance du 11 mars 1344 qui y voit une conséquence du serment prêté par les magistrats[11]: le jour de leur réception au Parlement, les magistrats s'engagent expressément à «*tenir ses délibérations secrètes*»[12]. Mais y a-t-il là vraiment matière à expliquer le défaut de motivation des décisions? C'est peu vraisemblable pour deux raisons tenant à la mauvaise observation du principe du secret et à l'objet de ce secret.

L'application du principe du «*secret des cours*» s'est avérée difficile. Contraint lui-même à admettre que ce secret n'est guère respecté[13], le législateur a dû intervenir à de multiples reprises entre 1344 et 1549[14]. Dans l'espoir de mieux le proté-

---

9 C'est ce que semblent penser J. Hilaire et C. Bloch qui voient dans cette absence de motivation une simple conséquence du secret des cours (cf. art. cit., p. 50). Pour plus de détails sur ce point voir notre article à la R.H.D.F.E., précité.

10 Les auteurs qui affirment l'existence d'une interdiction de motiver établissent un lien de cause à effet entre cette interdiction et le secret des délibérés imposé par la législation royale; cf. *Ph. Godding*, art. cit., p. 53 et *S. Dauchy*, art. cit., p. 244. Voir aussi *J.P. Dawson*, The oracles of the Law, University of Michigan 1968, p. 286–287.

11 *Isambert* e.a., Recueil général des anciennes lois françaises ..., t. 4, p. 498 sq., voir article 14, p. 503: «*Depuis que les arrests sont prononciez et publiez, il ne loist à nul, quel que il soit, dire, ne reciter, de quel opinion li seigneur ont esté. Car en ce faisant, il enfraindroient (sic) son serment que il a fait, de garder et non reveler les secrez de la cour*». L'interdiction de «*révéler les secretz de la cour*» est également en vigueur aux Pays-Bas où elle a été affirmée par Philippe II dans son ordonnance de 1559 fixant le *Style* du Grand conseil de Malines. Le même secret s'impose aux membres du Conseil de Brabant en vertu d'une ordonnance de 1604. De manière générale, les cours souveraines de la plupart des pays d'Europe occidentale ne motivent pas leurs arrêts (*Ph. Godding*, art. cit., p. 59 et p. 63 note 81).

12 Voir, à titre d'exemple, les formules du serment en vigueur au parlement de Flandre rapportées par *G.M.L. Pillot*, Histoire du parlement de Flandre, 2 vol., Douai 1849, t. 1, p. 299–300.

13 Cf. art. 15 de l'ord. de 1344, art . 110 de l'ord. de 1453, art. 36 de l'ord. de 1535.

14 Ordonnances du 28 octobre 1446 touchant le style du Parlement (art. 4); ordonnance pour la réformation de la justice d'avril 1453 (art. 110 et 112); lettres de novembre 1507

ger, il se préoccupe d'abord de punir «*les infracteurs*». En 1446, pour la première fois, il les menace de la privation de leurs gages, voire de la privation de leur office. Cette menace est réitérée en 1453 et 1507[15] puis, au XVIe siècle, la sanction s'alourdit: en 1535, les contrevenants sont frappés d'une incapacité définitive d'exercer un office royal[16] et déclarés passibles «*d'autres grandes peines pécuniaires et corporelles selon l'exigence des cas*»[17]; l'édit de 1549 viendra préciser le montant de l'amende applicable, fixé à «*dix mille livres*». Parallèlement, le législateur s'efforce de définir de manière très contraignante les obligations imposées aux officiers des parlements au titre du nécessaire respect du secret. Dès 1446, il introduit une obligation de délation[18] puis, par différents textes, il précise à l'égard de qui, quand et comment s'impose le secret[19]. Cette répétition des textes et leur sévérité croissante témoignent des difficultés du législateur à se faire obéir et on ne voit pas très bien comment, si elle découlait d'une obligation aussi mal respectée que le fut manifestement le secret des délibérés, l'absence de motivation aurait pu constituer la règle pendant plus de cinq siècles !

Un autre argument, bien plus péremptoire, milite contre la thèse de ceux qui voient dans le principe du secret des délibérés l'origine de la non-motivation des décisions judiciaires sous lÁncien Régime. Cet argument tient à l'objet même du secret imposé aux magistrats. Cet objet est clairement défini dès l'ordonnance de 1344 aux termes de laquelle il est interdit à quiconque de «*dire, ne reciter de quel opinion li seigneur ont esté*»[20]. Le magistrat astreint au secret doit donc seulement

relatives à la justice en Normandie (art. 51 et 53); ordonnance d'octobre 1535 sur l'administration de la justice en Provence (art. 36 et 44); édit de mars 1549 portant règlement de la justice au parlement de Paris (art. 14): *Isambert,* op. cit., t. 9, p. 151 et p. 245; t. 11, p. 478; t. 12, p. 432 et t. 13, p. 157.

15 Textes précités. L'ordonnance de 1446 limite la privation de gages à un an tandis que les deux autres textes parlent de «*privation de gages*» sans autre précision.

16 «*Sur peine de privation d'offices et d'estre inhabiles à jamais tenir offices royaux*».

17 L'article 110 de l'ordonnance de 1453 contenait déjà une allusion aux «*grandes peines corporelles...imposées contre les révélateurs au temps passé*».

18 Art. 4 de l'ord. de 1446 précitée: «*qu'il soit enjoint ... à tous les presidens, conseillers et autres officiers* (de la cour), *sur le serment qu'ils ont à nous et à nostredicte court, que s'ilz, ou aucun d'eux, savent aucuns qui doresnavant révèlent les secrets d'icelle, qu'ilz le dient à nostredicte court ou aux présidens en icelle, le plutost qu'ils pourront*» ... Cette obligation sera rappelée en 1453 et 1507. Voir aussi l'ordonnance de 1535 (art. 36) qui s'efforce de stimuler le zèle du président du parlement de Provence dans la poursuite des «*transgresseurs*» qui pourront lui avoir été dénoncés.

19 Sur ces trois points, il fait preuve d'une grande rigueur: les officiers ne doivent rien révéler «*aux parties, advocats, procureurs, solliciteurs et autres quelconques personnes quelqu'ils soient*» (ord. de 1535, art. 36), «*soit durant le jugement soit après*» (ord. de 1549, art. 14), «*par eux ne par autres directement ou indirectement*» (ord. de 1535, art. 36).

20 Dans le même sens, voir l'art. 14 de l'édit de mars 1549 précité: «*défendons aussi très-étroitement de ne révéler les opinions, soit durant le jugement ou après ...* ». Voir aussi l'article 13 de l'édit de juillet 1501 portant établissement du parlement de Provence (*Isambert,* op. cit., t. 11, p. 428): cet article interdit la présence des avocats et procureurs à la visitation des

s'abstenir de révéler son opinion ou celle des autres juges qui ont participé avec lui à la décision d'une affaire. Le secret ainsi conçu vise à protéger à la fois la Justice et les juges. Il serait en effet inconvenant de laisser apparaître les divisions des juges alors que la décision est censée être l'expression de la Justice, qui ne peut parler que d'une seule voix. Par ailleurs, les juges doivent pouvoir s'exprimer sans être exposés à aucune pression extérieure et sans craindre d'éventuelles représailles. Il s'agit donc de garantir «*la dignité et la force de la justice*» tout en préservant «*la liberté des opinions*» et «*la sécurité des juges*»[21]. Cette conception somme toute très restrictive du secret est toujours en vigueur à la fin de lÁncien Régime, comme en témoignent les propos de Guyot qui rapporte que «*Les opinions qui se donnent, soit à l'audience ou au rapport, doivent également être secrètes: il est défendu par les ordonnances aux juges, greffiers et huissiers, de les révéler*»[22]. Dans ces conditions, il faut renoncer à justifier l'absence de motivation des décisions sous lÁncien Régime par le secret des délibérés. Et s'il était besoin d'une preuve supplémentaire du caractère parfaitement compatible de ce secret avec la motivation, ne suffirait-il pas de rappeler qu'aujourd'hui encore tout nouveau magistrat, avant son entrée en fonction, prête serment «*de garder religieusement le secret des délibérations*»[23], ce qui ne l'empêche pas d'être obligé de motiver ses décisions?

Ce n'est donc pas dans la législation royale qu'il faut chercher l'origine de l'absence de motivation. En réalité, le seul texte à caractère réglementaire évoquant, dans l'ancien droit français, la question de la motivation des décisions est le *Style de la chambre des enquêtes* du parlement de Paris, rédigé vers les années 1336–

---

procès au motif que «*s'ils sont presens ... ils peuvent maintefois facilement cognoistre les opinions des juges et conseillers ...* ».

21 *Henrion de Pansey,* De l'autorité judiciaire, in: Œuvres judiciaires, Paris 1843, p. 533: *Des devoirs des juges et des règles qu'ils doivent suivre dans l'exercice de leurs fonctions*; *G.-M.-L. Pillot,* op. cit., t. 1, p. 11. Certains textes royaux montrent bien que le principal objet du secret imposé au magistrat est de préserver sa liberté: dans l'art. 110 de l'ordonnance de 1453 (dont le texte est textuellement reproduit dans l'art. 51 des lettres de 1507), le législateur déclare intervenir «*pour ce que par révélation des secrets de nostredicte court, se sont ensuivys et ensuyvent plusieurs maux et esclandres, et en a esté et est empeschée la liberté de délibérer et juger en icelle nostre court*».

22 Répertoire universel et raisonné de jurisprudence, Paris 1784, 17 vol., t. 12, au mot *Opinion.* La formulation de Merlin, dans sa nouvelle édition du *Répertoire* de *Guyot* (Paris, 1827–1828, 18 vol. + tables; voir t. 11, au mot *Opinion*), est encore plus explicite: «*Nos plus anciennes ordonnances font un devoir sacré aux magistrats de ne pas révéler leurs opinions respectives après la prononciation des jugemens qu'elles ont concouru à former*» ... (et il cite les ordonnances de 1344, 1446, 1453 ...).

23 Cf. Ordonnance 58–1270 du 22 décembre 1958 portant loi organique relative au statut de la magistrature, chapitre 1: *Dispositions générales:* «*Tout magistrat, lors de sa nomination à son premier poste, et avant d'entrer en fonctions, prête serment en ces termes: Je jure de bien et fidèlement remplir mes fonctions, de garder religieusement le secret des délibérations et de me conduire en tout comme un digne et loyal magistrat*». La formulation a de quoi surprendre dans un régime fondé sur la séparation de l'Eglise et de l'Etat!

1337. Ce *Style* est aussi le premier texte proclamant, plusieurs années avant la législation royale, le principe du secret des délibérés. Son auteur distingue cependant très clairement les deux notions. Lorsqu'il vise les secrets de la Cour, il emploie le terme «*secreta*» alors que quand il s'intéresse aux motifs, il parle de «*causa*». Et s'il interdit expressément aux membres du Parlement de violer le secret des délibération[24], il leur conseille simplement de ne pas révéler les motifs de leurs décisions[25]. Mais la manière dont il justifie le principe du secret des délibérés est pour le moins ambiguë. Si ce secret s'impose au Parlement – dit-il – c'est parce que son pouvoir vient de Dieu ou, tout au moins, parce qu'il est dépositaire de l'autorité du Prince, lui-même désigné par Dieu, et qu'il lui appartient donc de décider selon sa conscience, en s'écartant au besoin de la rigueur du droit pour se conformer à l'équité[26]. La tentation est grande, à partir de là, d'établir une équation entre le secret des délibérés et la non-motivation[27]. L'ambiguïté a sans aucun doute été soigneusement entretenue par le Parlement qui en a profité pour imposer une conception extensive du secret aboutissant à interdire indirectement toute forme de motivation. De fait, la motivation des arrêts, de plus en plus rare depuis les années 1320, disparaît définitivement à la suite de la publication du *Style*[28]. La principale raison de cette disparition est assurément d'ordre politique. Si le Parlement dissimule désormais les raisons de ses décisions, c'est avant tout pour s'assurer «*un pouvoir pratiquement sans contrôle*»[29], dans «*le souci d'éviter tout contrôle de ses actes*»[30], parce qu'il sait que cette absence de motivation le «*dispense ... de rendre des comptes aux plaideurs et au roi*»[31]. En bref, la non-motivation com-

24 *P. Guilhiermoz*, op. cit., p. 221, n° 166: «*Nec debent cuilibet apperere secreta curie supreme*».

25 *P. Guilhiermoz*, op. cit., p. 219, n° 162: «*Cavere etiam habet reportator quod in conclusione arresti non ponat aliquam causam*» ... (le texte propose ensuite des exemples de formules susceptibles d'être employées par les juges). Pour une analyse détaillée du *Style* du Parlement, voir notre article à la *R.H.D.F.E.* précité.

26 *P. Guilhiermoz*, op. cit., n° 166, p. 221 – 222. Lorsqu'il statue en équité, le Parlement est censé agir par délégation du pouvoir royal, qui n'est pas lié par les lois. Cette thèse – qui sera reprise par l'ensemble des parlements – est clairement exposée par *B. de la Roche Flavin*, Treize livres des Parlemens de France, Genève 1621, livre 13, ch. XI: «*La puissance des magistrats venir de Dieu originairement et du Prince immédiatement*» (p. 689 – 690). Sur le pouvoir des parlements de statuer en équité, voir *Guilhiermoz*, op. cit., p. XVII-XIX, p. 152 et 154 et *Cl.-J. De Ferrière*, Dictionnaire de droit et de pratique, Paris 1769, 2 vol., t. 1 au mot *Droit étroit*, p. 504. Voir aussi *Ph. Godding*, art. cit., p. 52; *J. Hilaire*, art. cit., p. 184; *S. Dauchy*, art. cit., p. 244.

27 C'est ce que fait *P. Guilhiermoz*, op. cit., p. XIX: «... *dès lors*, (la cour) *ne saurait admettre que les parties ou le public puissent à leur tour juger ses actes, et elle doit éviter de leur fournir aucun moyen de se rendre compte des raisons qui la déterminent. Cette théorie du secret empêchait notamment de motiver les arrêts* ... ».

28 T. Sauvel souligne, à fort juste titre, que l'ancienne formule explicative «*a été écartée de façon progressive et certainement volontaire entre 1320 et 1336*» (art. cit., p. 21).

29 *J. Poumarède*, Les arrêtistes toulousains, in: Les parlements de province, Pouvoirs, justice et société du XVIIe au XVIIIe siècles, Toulouse 1996, p. 369 – 391 (p. 371).

30 *Ph. Godding*, art. cit., p. 52.

porte de nombreux avantages pour les parlementaires auxquels elle assure une totale indépendance et une grande liberté d'appréciation[32]. On comprend dans ces conditions qu'elle se soit imposée dans la pratique, au point de devenir un véritable «usage», par la volonté des parlements qui y ont vu un moyen de renforcer leur position[33]. C'est donc à juste titre quÁrlette Lebigre présente l'absence de motivation comme *«un privilège que les cours se sont octroyé»*[34]. Ce privilège ne leur a cependant pas été unanimement reconnu par la doctrine.

31 *C. Blery,* L'obligation de motiver les décisions de justice était-elle révolutionnaire en 1790?, in: Revue d'Histoire de la Justice, 4 (1991), p. 79–97 (p. 81). La formule du *Style de la chambre des enquêtes* – qui affirme qu'il n'est pas bon qu'on puisse juger du contenu d'un arrêt – est révélatrice (*op. cit.,* n° 164, p. 121: *«nec est bonum quod quilibet possit judicare de contentis in arresto»* ...).

32 Non seulement le Parlement peut juger en équité mais il n'est pas lié par ses propres précédents: pour plus de détails sur ces points, voir notre article à la *R.H.D.F.E.* précité.

33 Les autres cours de justice ont rapidement suivi l'exemple du Parlement de Paris (Cf. *T. Sauvel*, art. cit., p. 21). Certains parlements de province se sont efforcés de renforcer le secret des délibérés. C'est ainsi que, par un arrêt de règlement de 1505, le parlement de Toulouse interdit *«l'entrée de quiconque, même gens du roi, au greffe et aux salles d'audience pendant le délibéré» (Cf. J. Poumarède,* loc. cit.). Quant au parlement de Flandre, il réaffirme la nécessité du secret par une résolution particulière du 29 juillet 1692 (Cf. *G.M.L. Pillot,* op. cit., t. 1, p. 11). En revanche, la référence au secret des cours disparaît brusquement de la législation royale dans la seconde moitié du XVIe siècle: les ordonnances de réformation promulguées en 1560, 1566, 1579 et 1629 n'y font plus aucune allusion (*Isambert,* t. 14, p. 63 sq.: Ordonnance d'Orléans de 1560, art. 30 à 104: *de la justice et de la police;* p. 189 sq.: Ordonnance de Moulins de 1566 *«sur la réforme de la justice»;* p. 380 sq.: Ordonnance de Blois de 1579, art. 89 à 209 *«relatifs à l'administration de la justice et à tout ce qui s'y rattache»*; t. 16, p. 223 sq.: Ordonnance de 1629 dite *«code Michaud»*, art. 53 à 123: *Administration de la justice*). L'ordonnance civile de 1667 est elle aussi silencieuse sur ce point et ses commentateurs le sont tout autant (Voir, par exemple, *Bornier,* Conférences des ordonnances de Louis XIV, roi de France et de Navarre, avec les anciennes ordonnances du royaume, le droit écrit et les arrêts, t. 1, Paris 1737 et *D. Jousse,* Nouveau commentaire sur l'ordonnance civile du mois d'avril 1667, nouv. éd., Paris 1757). Ce silence n'est pas vraiment surprenant: l'obligation de respecter le secret des délibérés, telle qu'elle est conçue par les cours, ménage, nous l'avons vu, la possibilité pour les parlements de statuer en équité or cette possibilité leur est contestée par l'ordonnance de 1667 (*Isambert,* t. 18, p. 103 sq: *Ordonnance civile touchant la réformation de la justice,* tit. 1, art. 6. Cet article vise à limiter les pouvoirs des cours tout comme l'article 7 qui leur interdit d'interpréter la loi. En pratique cependant, ces interdictions sont restées lettre morte: sur ce point, voir *J.-M. Carbasse,* Introduction historique au droit, P.U.F., coll. Droit fondamental, Paris 1998, p. 243, n° 143).

34 Art. cit., p. 24. Le terme «privilège» est également employé par *Ph. Godding,* art. cit., p. 65 et par *C. Blery* art. cit., p. 80. Quant à *T. Sauvel,* Les demandes de motifs adressées par le conseil du roi aux cours souveraines, in: Revue Historique de Droit Français et Etranger (1957), p. 529–548 (p. 530), il classe la possibilité de statuer sans motifs parmi les *«droits des cours souveraines».*

2. Les hésitations de la doctrine

Si un courant majoritairement hostile à la motivation se dessine en doctrine dès le Moyen-Age, certains auteurs adoptent cependant une position nuancée, en réservant le cas des sentences pénales, et un courant dissident, favorable à la motivation, voit même le jour au XVIe siècle.

Le courant défavorable à la motivation trouve sa première expression chez les canonistes médiévaux. Leur réflexion s'appuie sur la décrétale *Sicut nobis* (1199) dans laquelle le pape Innocent III constate qu'il n'est pas d'usage que les juges expriment dans leur sentence les considérations qui les ont amenés à statuer dans tel ou tel sens[35]. Sans s'opposer formellement à l'idée d'une motivation ou, plus simplement, d'une justification des décisions judiciaires, les décrétalistes conseillent au juge la plus grande prudence en la matière. C'est ainsi qu'Hostiensis († 1271) affirme qu'il serait imprudent de la part du juge d'indiquer ses motifs car les erreurs susceptibles de s'y glisser risquent de fournir l'occasion de critiquer sa décision. Cette analyse est partagée par tous les auteurs postérieurs, du XIIIe au XVe siècle: aucun d'entre eux ne prétend qu'il est interdit au juge de motiver mais tous conviennent qu'il est préférable qu'il ne le fasse pas[36]. La prise de position des canonistes n'est certainement pas étrangère à l'évolution de la pratique du parlement de Paris. Il ne faut pas oublier qu'au XIVe siècle de nombreux conseillers reçoivent une formation universitaire et on peut légitimement penser que c'est sous l'influence des droits savants et, plus particulièrement, du droit canonique, que la Cour a fini par opter pour l'absence de motivation[37]. La même influence transparaît encore, au XVIe siècle, dans les écrits des juristes flamands Philippe Wielant et Josse de Damhouder. Le premier, après avoir rappelé que «dans les affaires civiles, le juge n'est pas tenu d'expliciter la cause ou les raisons pour lesquelles il statue dans tel ou tel sens, mais qu'il suffit qu'il condamne ou absolve, qu'il confirme ou infirme», s'empresse de taxer de «fou» le juge qui motive son jugement. Certes le juge est en droit de fournir des explications, précise Wielant, mais il ne serait pas «sage» de le faire[38]. Quant au second, il est encore plus incisif lorsqu'il déclare que seuls les juges «sots ou désinvoltes» se hasarderont à proposer, en matière civile, une motivation qui n'est pas nécessaire et qui risque d'amener plus d'inconvénients que d'avantages[39]. Il convient toutefois de remarquer que

---

35 X 2, 27, 6.

36 La décrétale *Sicut nobis* et la position des canonistes sont analysées de manière approfondie dans notre article paru à la *R.H.D.F.E.*, auquel nous renvoyons le lecteur. Sur la doctrine canonique voir aussi *Ph. Godding*, La jurisprudence, Typologie des sources du Moyen Age occidental, fascicule 6, Turnhout 1973, p. 20 et la note 14; *id.*, art. cit., p. 47 sq.

37 Le droit romain ne semble pas avoir imposé la motivation contre laquelle, nous l'avons vu, les canonistes ont nettement pris position dès la seconde moitié du XIIIe siècle. Pour *T. Sauvel*, art. cit., p. 22: «*l'influence exercée alors sur l'esprit de bien des légistes par les règles du droit canonique ne pouvait que contribuer à faire écarter les motifs*».

38 *Ph. Wielant*, Practijcke civile, Anvers 1573, section IX, cap. VI: *Van te stellen de cause inde sententie*, sect. 9, p. 282.

Wielant, comme Damhouder, réservent expressément cette non-motivation aux affaires civiles et affirment à l'inverse tout aussi expressément que, s'agissant des sentences criminelles, la motivation est obligatoire[40].

La doctrine semble effectivement réserver un sort particulier aux décisions rendues en matière pénale. Dès le XIVe siècle, cette question a retenu l'attention des romanistes[41] qui l'ont envisagée parallèlement à celle de l'arbitraire des peines. Il faut rappeler ici que le mot *arbitraire* n'avait pas, dans notre ancien droit, le sens péjoratif actuel: il désignait le droit pour les magistrats d'arbitrer les peines, c'est-à-dire de choisir, dans chaque affaire, la sanction la plus adaptée, en tenant compte des circonstances du délit et de la personnalité du coupable[42]. Le principe de l'arbitraire ne l'a définitivement emporté qu'au XVIe siècle – comme en témoigne la maxime fameuse à l'époque, en France comme à l'étranger: «*Toutes peines sont arbitraires*» – mais il trouve son origine dans la pensée des glossateurs médiévaux. Cynus de Pistoie († 1336) est le premier à admettre, en s'appuyant sur la loi *Hodie*, que le juge peut augmenter ou diminuer la peine légale ou coutumière, à condition qu'il soit «mû par de bonnes raisons» (*certis rationibus motus*). Après lui, Bartole et Balde s'interrogeront plus précisément sur la question de savoir si le juge doit alors exprimer dans sa sentence «la cause» de l'atténuation ou de l'aggravation de la peine (*in sententia exprimere causam*)[43],

---

39 *J. de Damhouder*, Practijcke in civile saken, La Haye 1626, cap. CCXXI: *Van reden in de sententie te stellen*, p. 570.

40 Le principe, posé a contrario dans la *Pratique civile* de ces deux auteurs (cf. *Wielant*, loc. cit., n 4; *Damhouder*, loc. cit., n° 1 et 4), est réaffirmé, toujours a contrario (mais en sens inverse), dans leur «Pratique criminelle». Cf. *Wielant*, Corte instructie in materie criminele, éd. *J. Montballyu*, Bruxelles 1975, cap. 42, n° 6, p. 75: «*Alle sentencien criminele moeten inhouden de causen van der condempnatie, twelcke gheenen noot en es in materie civile*»; *Damhouder*, La practique et enchiridion des causes criminelles, Louvain 1555, chap. LV: *De iuger, condemner, et punir en criminel*, n° 9 et 10, p. 94: «*Et en toutes condemnations criminelles, faut-il mectre la cause de la sentence, ce que n'est besoing d'observer en deffinitive civile*».

41 Comme l'a fort justement souligné *B. Schnapper*, Les peines arbitraires du XIIIe au XVIIIe siècle (doctrines savantes et usages français), in: Tijdschrift voor Rechtsgeschiedenis / Legal History Review, XLI (1973), p. 237–277 et XLII (1974), p. 81–112, voir t. XLI, p. 238, le droit savant restera longtemps (c'est encore vrai au XVIIIe siècle) «*la référence privilégiée des criminalistes*». On notera qu'alors que les romanistes ne se sont apparemment pas intéressés au problème de la motivation des sentences civiles, ils se sont très vite interrogés sur celle des sentences criminelles. Le droit romain n'ayant formulé aucune règle expresse en la matière, il leur a fallu trouver des textes pouvant servir de prétexte à leurs gloses. Ils se sont principalement appuyés sur trois textes relatifs à l'infamie: un texte du *Code* (C. 2, 12, 13: loi *Et si severior*) et deux fragments d'Ulpien repris au *Digeste* (D. 3, 2, 13, 7: loi *Quid ergo, § Poena gravior* et D. 3, 2, 2, 2: loi *Quod ait praetor*); ils ont également utilisé un autre fragment d'Ulpien (D. 48, 19, 13: loi *Hodie*) autorisant le juge à moduler la peine pour les crimes extraordinaires.

42 Sur la question de l'arbitraire des peines voir *B. Schnapper*, art. cit. Voir aussi *A. Laingui / A. Lebigre*, Histoire du droit pénal, I – Le droit pénal, Paris 1979, p. 129 sq. et *J.-M. Carbasse*, op. cit., p. 133 sq.

autrement dit s'il doit motiver sa décision. Leur argumentation sera reprise par les pénalistes du XVIe siècle. C'est ainsi que, dans la *Préface* de son *De poenis temperandis,* Tiraqueau († 1558) pose clairement la question des pouvoirs des juges mais, malheureusement, la réponse qu'il propose est très embrouillée. Fidèle à la méthode scolastique du *sic et non,* il commence en effet par affirmer une chose puis soutient son contraire. A la question «le juge est-il lié par les peines fixées par les lois ou les statuts?», il répond d'abord par l'affirmative et soutient que le juge ne saurait augmenter ou diminuer ces peines sans être lui-même puni (n° 1 à 15), mais aussitôt après il déclare qu'il peut les modifier impunément «s'il existe une cause» (n° 16 à 49)[44]. Il s'interroge alors sur le point de savoir si, dans ce cas, le juge est tenu d'inscrire dans sa sentence la cause qui l'a porté à augmenter ou à diminuer la peine. Là encore, il commence par soutenir l'affirmative (n° 52 à 69)[45] mais il retire ensuite tout contenu à cette prétendue obligation de motiver en faisant valoir (au n° 70) qu'il ne s'agit pas là d'une «formalité substantielle ou nécessaire à la validité de la sentence». En pratique, il suffit donc au juge de s'abriter derrière «... cette clause courante ‹Pour certaines causes et considérations à nous mouvant›, ou encore ‹Et pour cause›». Cette opinion est partagée par Julius Clarus († 1575)[46]. Le célèbre jurisconsulte italien va même plus loin en affirmant, de manière très générale, qu'en pratique, la révélation des motifs n'est pas obligatoire en matière criminelle et que le juge peut se réfugier derrière la formule «vu le procès, nous condamnons et absolvons»[47]. En définitive, les auteurs s'accordent donc pour reconnaître que l'obligation de motiver les décisions pénales est largement formelle. Dans ces conditions, la situation du juge statuant en matière répres-

---

43 Leur opinion est rapportée par *Tiraqueau* dans son De poenis temperandis, 1559, traduction *A. Laingui,* 1986, *Préface,* n° 52 p. 34 et n° 70 p. 36. Voir aussi le commentaire d'A. Laingui (note 1, p. 37).

44 *Tiraqueau,* op. cit. Au n° 23, il parle d'une «*minoration motivée*».

45 Voir, en particulier, le n° 52: « ... *alors que normalement, il n'est pas nécessaire de rapporter la cause de la sentence, ... dans ce cas cependant, dis-je, le juge doit exprimer dans sa sentence la cause de l'atténuation ou de l'aggravation de la peine*». Au n° 54, Tiraqueau affirme que la même solution prévaut, de manière plus générale, dans tous les cas où le juge «*pour quelque cause, s'écarte du droit commun*» (alors, «*il doit spécifier cette cause*»).

46 *J. Clarus,* Receptarum sententiarum, Opera omnia, Francfort 1590. Lib. V: *Practica criminalis,* Quaestio LXXXV, n° 10, p. 381 et p. 384–385. S'interrogeant, lui aussi, sur la possibilité pour le juge de moduler la peine, Clarus suit la même démarche que Tiraqueau: il commence par affirmer que le juge serait infâme s'il modifiait la peine sans «juste cause» (*iusta causa*) et qu'il lui faut donc indiquer cette cause dans sa sentence (*exprimere causam in sententia*) mais aussitôt après il déclare qu'à son avis il suffit que le juge dise qu'il a agi «pour de justes causes» sans devoir préciser ces causes: «*Puto tamen sufficere, quod iudex dicat ex iustis causis animum suum moventib. id facere, absq. eo, quod in specie causam ipsam exprimat* ... ».

47 *J. Clarus,* op. cit., Lib. V, Quaestio XCIII, n° 2, p. 399: à la question «*Et an in sententiis criminalibus iudex teneatur exprimere causam?*», Clarus répond: «*Apud nos ... non dicitur nisi viso processu, condemnamus, vel absolvimus, et sententia valet, et tenet*».

sive n'est pas fondamentalement différente de celle du magistrat qui se prononce en matière civile.

Le consensus doctrinal n'est pourtant pas total: dans la seconde moitié du XVIe siècle, un courant dissident voit le jour. Il est représenté par un auteur fantasque et visionnaire: Raoul Spifame. Cet homme singulier, que l'égarement de son esprit avait fait interdire des fonctions d'avocat, passa une partie de sa vie à imaginer de fausses ordonnances qu'il attribua à Henri II et qu'il rassembla dans un ouvrage publié en 1556. Si Spifame a produit «*une foule d'idée absurdes et chimériques*», il «*en a eu plusieurs aussi ingénieuses qu'utiles*» qui finiront par être «*exécutées en tout ou partie*»[48]. C'est sans aucun doute à cette seconde catégorie qu'il faut rattacher le texte qui aurait, d'après lui, imposé la motivation des décisions judiciaires: «*Le Roy* – écrit-il – *voulant que les proces et differendz de ses subjects et regnicoles soyent iugez par les loix de sa couronne royalle & imperiale, & non par les loix des Empereurs rois des Romains anciens et modernes qu'il n'entend recognoistre pour superieurs, a ordonné & ordonne que desormais tous iuges royaux & subalternes souverains et inferieurs exprimerons aux dictons de leurs sentences & iugemenz la cause expresse & speciale d'iceux, pour en faire une loy generalle & donner forme au iugemens des proces futurs fondez sur mesmes raisons & differens comme portans l'interpretation de ses statuts & ordonnances* ...»[49]. Certes, Spifame justifie sa proposition de manière très traditionnelle en invoquant le souci d'assurer le triomphe des lois royales sur le droit romain, mais cette proposition n'en présente pas moins un caractère très moderne dans la mesure où il affirme la nécessité d'une jurisprudence investie d'une mission d'interprétation de la loi et où il annonce qu'une telle jurisprudence ne saurait exister en l'absence de motivation. Ce nouveau courant de pensée semble rencontrer un certain écho dans l'opinion qui s'exprime à travers les doléances des états généraux. En 1560, aux états d'Orléans, la noblesse demande que les arrêts soient motivés: elle voudrait qu'il soit désormais interdit aux juges de se réfugier derrière des formules aussi vagues que «*pour ces causes et autres semblables*» et souhaite qu'ils indiquent «*les points péremptoires de la décision des causes*». Ce faisant, elle cherche, elle aussi, à favoriser la formation d'une jurisprudence censée permettre une meilleure administration de la justice. Elle se montre en effet persuadée que «*Ce faisant, les juges s'étu-*

---

48 Voir *Prost de Royer*, Dictionnaire de jurisprudence et des arrêts, Lyon 1781 – 1787, 6 t., t. 6, au mot *Arrêt*, p. 731 et *Michaud*, Biographie universelle, t. 39 – 40, p. 53 – 54.

49 *R. Spifame*, Dicaearchiae Henrici regis christianissimi progymnasmata, s. l. n. d., Arrest LXV, p. 93 (Cet ouvrage est assez rare. L'exemplaire que nous avons consulté est conservé à la Bibliothèque Sainte-Geneviève à Paris; il ne mentionne ni lieu ni date d'édition). Ce texte est intégralement reproduit par *P.-J. Brillon* qui le qualifie «*d'arrêt du roi Henri II en 1552*» (Dictionnaire des arrêts ou jurisprudence universelle des parlemens de France et autres tribunaux ..., Paris 1727, 6 vol., t. 3, p. 926, n° 68, au mot *Jugement*). Mieux informé, *Prost de Royer*, loc. cit., signale que Spifame a «*supposé*» cet arrêt qu'il ne peut cependant s'empêcher de rapporter car il est conforme à ses opinions (cf. *infra:* Prost de Royer est un des rares auteurs de la fin de l'Ancien Régime qui se prononce ouvertement pour la motivation des décisions).

dieront à juger mieux, et lesdits arrêts et jugements serviront d'instruction à tous en semblables causes et y aura moins d'appellations»[50]. Mais le pouvoir fait la sourde oreille: le Conseil du roi se contente de répondre «*qu'il ne se pouvoit rien ordonner sur cet article et qu'il falloit le laisser à la religion des juges*». Cette réponse confirme que la question de la motivation, loin d'être régie par un principe rigide, relève essentiellement de la pratique. En 1614, les états de Paris rouvrent le débat. C'est le troisième ordre qui réclame cette fois la motivation des arrêts, tout au moins de ceux «*donnés sur l'interprétation des coutumes ou poincts de droit*», parce qu'en ce cas les motifs «*serviroient eux-mêmes de loy*»[51]. Ces revendications resteront également sans suite: en pratique, la non-motivation se maintient et on peut même dire qu'elle triomphe définitivement, au XVIe siècle, à titre d'usage. Ainsi s'explique le constat de La Roche Flavin: «*Anciennement, les juges souloyent insérer en leurs iugemens, sentences, et Arrests, la cause ou motif de la condamnation ou absolution ... Mais aujourd'huy cela n'est en usage et les arrests et iugemens ne contiennent que ce qui est ordonné simplement, sans autre raisonnement, soit en civil ou en criminel*»[52]. Pourtant les juges ne vont pas tarder à s'apercevoir des inconvénients de l'usage qu'ils ont contribué à faire prévaloir et ils seront eux-mêmes à l'origine d'un certain nombre de dérogations qui vont s'imposer entre le XVIe et le XVIIIe siècle.

II. Les nécessaires dérogations à l'usage

Sous lÁncien Régime, la non-motivation les décisions de justice n'a pas toujours été respectée. Elle a été formellement remise en cause dans un certain nombre de cas qu'on peut considérer comme autant d'exceptions à l'usage établi (II.1). Par ailleurs, cet usage a été très habilement contourné grâce à l'intervention des arrêtistes (II.2).

---

50 *G. Picot,* Histoire des états généraux, 2e éd., Paris 1888, 5 t., t. 2, p. 303. Notons que la motivation semble conçue tant en fait qu'en droit; il est en effet précisé que ces motifs doivent contenir «*les points péremptoires de la décision des causes, soit par titre, témoins ou confession des parties, articles de coutume et lois*».

51 *G. Picot,* op. cit., t. 4, p. 466. Comme l'a fort justement remarqué Picot, cette revendication s'inscrit dans la droite ligne de la lutte menée par les états pour obtenir des lois écrites encadrant les pouvoirs des juges (op. cit., t. 5, p. 20).

52 *B. de la Roche Flavin,* op. cit., livre 13, ch. LXI, n° XXVIII, p. 1084. Signalons que La Roche Flavin a manifestement été plagié par Guenois dans sa nouvelle édition des «Lois abrogées» de *Bugnyon*: cf. *Philiberti Bugnyon legum abrogatarum ...*, 3e éd., Bruxelles 1702, lib. 2, art. CXCIII, p. 315: «*Les juges souloient anciennement inserer en leurs jugemens et sentences, la cause et le motif de la condemnation ou absolution des parties litigeantes ... Mais telle manière de faire ne s'use plus aujourd'huy et les Magistrats ne sont pas obligés de faire mention de ce qui les emeus et incitéz à juger, ou absoudre les personnes, soit en matière civile ou criminele ...*». Comme l'a noté *J. Poumarede,* art. cit., p. 371, cet usage ne soulève guère d'objections: Géraud de Maynard est le seul à laisser «*percer une critique ironique*» contre cette pratique.

1. Les exceptions à l'usage

Certaines de ces exceptions ont été officiellement reconnues alors que d'autres ne se sont imposées que dans la pratique des cours. Toutes présentent cependant un point commun: elles constituent des entorses plus que de véritables atteintes à la *«règle du jugement sans motifs»*[53].

La première exception «officielle» à l'absence de motivation intervient en cas de recours contre une décision souveraine: suite à l'apparition du système de la cassation[54], l'habitude de réclamer aux procureurs généraux les motifs des arrêts dont la cassation est demandée s'est introduite dans la pratique[55] avant d'être officiellement consacrée par le règlement du 28 juin 1738. Il convient de souligner que, d'une part, cette demande de motifs n'est pas automatique[56] et que, d'autre part, le secret est préservé par rapport aux greffiers et aux parties[57]. L'exception reste donc limitée. Une seconde exception concerne les décisions rendues sur les questions de compétence. Pour ces décisions, la motivation est non seulement possible mais même nécessaire comme le constate Wielant qui affirme de manière péremptoire que «la cause doit être explicitée en cas de conflit entre cours»[58];

---

53 Selon l'expression de *T. Sauvel,* Histoire, p. 33. Cette expression paraît justifiée par les propos de *Merlin,* Répertoire ..., t. 11, p. 287, v° *Motifs des jugemens,* qui rappelle que *«sous l'ancien régime, et suivant une règle générale ..., les jugemens n'étaient et ne pouvaient être motivés».*

54 D'après *T. Sauvel,* Les demandes de motifs, p. 533, *«la demande de cassation s'est ... développée lentement par la pratique plus que par les textes»*; son existence a cependant été rappelée par l'ordonnance de Blois de 1579 (*Isambert,* op. cit., t. 14, p. 380 sq., art. 92, p. 404) et par l'édit de Rouen de 1597 *sur l'administration de la justice, les évocations, etc...* (*Isambert,* op. cit., t. 15, p. 120 sq., art. 18, p. 124).

55 Cf. *T. Sauvel,* Les demandes de motifs, p. 534. L'existence de cette pratique est attestée, au début du XVIIIe siècle, par *Brillon,* op. cit., t. 3, p. 926, n° 68, au mot *Jugement: «quand on porte au Conseil du Roy, des demandes en cassation des arrêts rendus dans les tribunaux différens, l'usage s'est introduit d'en demander les motifs aux procureurs généraux».* Voir aussi *P. Dawson,* op. cit., p. 303.

56 Cf. *Isambert,* op. cit., t. 22, p. 42 sq., *Règlement concernant la procédure du conseil* (28 juin 1738), titre IV: *Des demandes en cassation d'arrêts ou de jugements rendus en dernier ressort,* article 26, p. 49: *«Lorsque, sur le rapport fait au conseil, de la requête en cassation, il aura été jugé à propos de demander les motifs ... ».* D'après *T. Sauvel,* Les demandes de motifs, p. 536, cette demande de motifs est assez rare.

57 *Isambert,* loc. cit., article 27: *«Les motifs seront envoyés cachetés, et remis en cet état au sieur rapporteur de la requête en cassation. Défenses sont faites aux greffiers du conseil de les décacheter, et ce, sous telles peines qu'il appartiendra».* Voir aussi *T. Sauvel,* Les demandes de motifs, p. 537–538 (par ailleurs, comme le souligne Sauvel, les arrêts du conseil ne révèlent jamais le contenu de ces motifs).

58 *Wielant,* loc. cit.: *«de cause geerpressert moet siin ... in oorlof van hove»* (dans le même sens voir *Damhouder,* Practijcke civile, ch. 221, n° 3, p. 570). Ph. Godding rapporte effectivement une décision motivée rendue par le Conseil de Brabant dans un procès de ce type (cf. *Ph. Godding,* Le Conseil de Brabant sous le règne de Philippe le Bon (1430–1467), Académie royale de Belgique, Mémoire de la Classe des Lettres, 3e série, t. XIX, Bruxelles

quant à Brillon, il soutient que la motivation est en principe exclue, «*si ce n'est dans le cas des sentences de compétence*»[59].

Les autres exceptions résultent de la seule volonté des cours souveraines. Celles-ci, prolongeant à leur manière le débat doctrinal, ont cherché à soumettre les sentences pénales à un régime spécifique. Au XVIe siècle, nous l'avons vu, la doctrine a définitivement renoncé à exiger des juges répressifs une véritable motivation de leurs décisions. Les parlements semblent s'être fort bien accommodés de ce laxisme dont ils ont apparemment refusé de faire profiter les juges inférieurs. Tandis que la célèbre formule «*Pour les cas résultant du procès*» devenait une sorte de clause de style dans leurs arrêts[60], ils ont contraint les tribunaux de leurs ressorts à justifier leurs décisions. Ce régime discriminatoire n'a d'autre objet que de ménager les pouvoirs des parlements, comme le laisse fort bien entendre Jean-Charles-Nicolas Dumont dans son *Nouveau style criminel* paru en 1770. Après avoir rappelé que «*Les jugemens des premiers juges doivent contenir la cause de la condamnation*», il souligne que ces juges «*sont astreints à juger selon la rigueur de la Loi*» et qu'«*il est réservé aux juges supérieurs de juger ex æquo et bono*»[61]. L'absence de motivation est donc, une fois de plus, pressentie comme un moyen de préserver la liberté d'appréciation des parlements, voire leur pouvoir de statuer en équité. Mais peut-on affirmer pour autant que les parlements imposaient aux juges inférieurs une véritable motivation? Pour répondre à cette question, il convient de cerner ce que recouvre exactement l'expression «*la cause de la condamnation*»[62]. S'agit-il vraiment, comme le prétend Dumont, du «*motif qui détermine* [les juges]»[63]? Cela ne semble pas être le cas. Au XVIe siècle, Jean Imbert

1999, note 501 p. 439: la décision d'appointement motivée rendue par le Conseil le 13 mars 1456 tranche un conflit de compétence entre des échevins et le juge ecclésiastique).

59 Loc. cit.

60 Sur la généralisation de cette formule, voir *A. Laingui/A. Lebigre,* Histoire du droit pénal, p. 104. D'après B. Schnapper, cette «*désinvolture judiciaire*» remonte, à Bordeaux, au premier quart du XVIe siècle (cf. *B. Schnapper,* La répression pénale au XVIe siècle. L'exemple du parlement de Bordeaux (1510–1565), in: Voies nouvelles en histoire du droit, Paris 1991, p. 53–105; p. 56). Les parlements utilisent d'autant plus volontiers cette formule qu'elle leur permet de couvrir les nouvelles prérogatives qu'ils se sont attribuées à partir du XVIe siècle. Prenant des libertés de plus en plus grandes avec le système des preuves légales, ils ont adopté la torture avec réserve des preuves (à laquelle l'ordonnance de 1670 donnera une existence légale) et ils admettent la condamnation à une peine inférieure à la peine ordinaire en cas de preuve incomplète. Sur ce point, voir les remarques d'A. Laingui sur la cause 27 du «De poenis temperandis» de *Tiraqueau,* op. cit., p. 147 ainsi que *Y. Bongert,* Le *pro modo probationum*: intime conviction avant la lettre?, in: R.H.D.F.E., 78.1 (2000), p. 13–39.

61 *J.-Ch.-N. Dumont,* Nouveau style criminel, Paris 1778, 1re partie, chap. XXIII, p. 86.

62 Cette expression, employée par Dumont est également utilisée par Jousse: cf. *D. Jousse,* Nouveau commentaire sur l'ordonnance criminelle de 1670..., Paris 1763, tit. XXV, art. XIV, p. 447, note 2.

63 Loc. cit.: «*Les bons juges ne se décident jamais sans avoir un motif qui les détermine et ils s'empressent de l'expliquer pour leur justification*».

affirmait déjà «*qu'en sentence criminelle il faut spécialement dire pour quel crime on condamne l'accusé*»[64]. Quant aux commentateurs de l'ordonnance de 1670, lorsqu'ils évoquent cette question, ils sont unanimes à considérer que «*Les premiers juges ... doivent exprimer dans leurs jugemens la nature du crime qui donne lieu à la condamnation*»[65]. Ainsi s'explique l'injonction adressée par le parlement de Flandre aux échevins de Valenciennes: par son arrêt du 2 août 1687, il leur défend «*de prononcer en cette forme 'pour les cas résultans du procès', leur ordonnant à l'advenir d'exprimer les cas dont les accusés seront atteints et convaincus ou suspectéz*»[66]. En réalité, l'obligation des juges inférieurs se borne donc à qualifier les faits ou, au moins, à les décrire, parfois avec force détails[67]. Tout cela ne constitue nullement une motivation de la décision, comme le constate Antoine Bruneau: «*Aucuns magistrats* – écrit-il – *ne sont obligéz de faire mention dans leurs sentences de ce qui les a mûs ou incitéz à condamner ou absoudre les personnes accusées ... Toutefois aux condamnations il faut ajouter la cause généralle de 'duëment atteint et convaincu d'avoir etc ...', sans pour autant spécifier par tant de témoins ou par confessions ...*»[68]. On ne saurait donc affirmer que les obligations imposées aux premiers juges par les cours souveraines impliquent une véritable exception à l'absence de motivation. En revanche, il semble bien que, dans leurs propres décisions, les parlements aient parfois pris quelques libertés avec l'usage établi. C'est du moins ce que laisse penser le discours de nos anciens

---

64 *J. Imbert,* Practique judiciaire ..., 2e éd., Paris 1604, liv. 3, ch. XX, n° 6, p. 761. Mais il s'empresse d'ajouter: «*toutefois les juges royaux ne le gardent point, ains mettent par leurs sentences cette clause: ‹pour la punition et réparation des cas dont il est trouvé atteint et convaincu par le procès›*».

65 A L'inverse, comme le précise aussitôt Salle, «*les cours ne sont point astreintes à cette formalité: elle se contentent seulement d'insérer dans leurs Arrêts cette clause générale, ‹pour les cas résultans du procès›*»: *M. Salle,* L'esprit des ordonnances de Louis XIV, 2 t., Paris, 1755 – 1758, t. 2, p. 303 (commentaire sur l'art. XIV du titre XXV). Dans le même sens voir *Ph. Bornier,* Conférences des ordonnances de Louis XIV, Paris 1744, 2 t., t. 2, p. 348: le juge doit indiquer «*le crime dont* [l'accusé] *est convaincu*».

66 Archives départementales du Nord, 8 B 2e série n° 763, folio 150.

67 Sur ce point, voir *Y. Bongert,* art. cit., p. 25. Par ailleurs, comme le souligne le parlement de Flandre, les premiers juges peuvent eux aussi utiliser des formules traduisant le degré de conviction auquel ils sont parvenus: si l'expression la plus courante est «*duement atteint et convaincu*», qui correspond à la pleine conviction, il leur arrive aussi d'avouer leur doute sur la culpabilité de l'accusé en le déclarant seulement «*fortement*» ou «*véhémentement suspecté*». Sur la pratique suivie dans le ressort du parlement de Flandre, voir *T. Le Marc'hadour,* La question préparatoire dans les Pays-Bas français: législation française et usages flamands (1679 – 1790), dans *B. Durand* (éd.), La torture judiciaire, approches historiques et juridiques, Lille 2002, 2 vol., t. 2, p. 743 – 800 (p. 766 sq.). Comme le note T. Le Marc'hadour (p. 766), «*le Parlement qui n'est pourtant pas tenu de motiver ses arrêts, énonce parfois ses doutes par les mêmes formules*» mais, à l'inverse (cf. p. 771), il «*ne prend pas toujours la peine d'appliquer la formule ‹pour les cas résultant du procès›*» qui est censée tenir lieu de motivation à ses arrêts.

68 *A. Bruneau,* Observations et maximes sur les matières criminelles, Paris 1715, liv. 1, tit. 27, n° XXX, p. 269.

auteurs qui établissent une hiérarchie entre ces décisions (arrêts de règlement, arrêts en robes rouges, préjugés) selon «*la plus ou moins grande difficulté d'en retrouver les motifs*»[69]. L'autorité des arrêts de règlement s'expliquerait ainsi par le fait que «*les motifs en sont apparents*»[70] et celle des «*arrêts dits 'de robe rouge', prononcés dans quelques affaires jugées importantes*» parce que, dans ce cas, «*le premier président, après avoir lu l'arrêt, donnait oralement quelques explications publiques*»[71]. Mais, en réalité, les arrêts de règlement ne sont pas à proprement parler plus motivés que les autres et la «conférence explicative» du premier président, lors des «*arrêts solennels de robe rouge*», renferme moins «*une formulation des motifs*» qu'«*une dissertation qui offrait à certains l'occasion de faire étalage de leur érudition juridique et plus souvent littéraire*»[72]. En définitive, si ces deux types d'arrêts se voient traditionnellement reconnaître une valeur spécifique, c'est avant tout «*parce qu'ils ont force de loi*»[73], parce qu'ils «*servent de loy*»[74], parce que la Cour entend qu'ils «*soient tenus pour règles, loix et maximes au Palais*»[75]. Le classement opéré par les auteurs n'en est pas moins très intéressant car il

---

69 *J. Hilaire*, Questions autour de la jurisprudence des arrêts, in: *S. Dauchy* et *V. Demars-Sion* (édd.), Les recueils d'arrêts et dictionnaires de jurisprudence (XVIe-XVIIIe siècles), Paris 2005, p. 21–39.

70 *J. Hilaire*, loc. cit. En ce sens, voir *C.-J. de Ferriere*, op. cit., t. 2, au mot *Jurisprudence*, p. 91: «*Dans les arrêts qui se rendent à l'ordinaire sur les raisons alléguées par les parties, on ne voit point les motifs de leurs décisions, comme on le voit dans les arrêts de règlement*».

71 *J. Poumarède*, art. cit., p. 371. *J. de Montholon*, Arrests de la cour prononcez en robbes rouges, dernière édition, Paris 1695, *Advis au lecteur*, cite le nom de plusieurs magistrats – parmi lesquels le président de Harlay, pourtant célèbre pour sa formule «*Un arrêt est bon pour celui qui l'a obtenu*» (*cf. infra* note 82) – qui n'hésitent pas à donner des conférences explicatives pour ces arrêts. D'après l'*Encyclopédie* (*Diderot* et *d'Alembert*, Encyclopédie ou Dictionnaire raisonné des sciences, des arts et des métiers..., Paris 1751, 17 t., t. 1, p. 707, au mot *Arrêt*), les arrêts en robes rouges interviennent «*sur des questions de droit dépouillées de circonstances*» et visent à «*fixer la jurisprudence sur ces questions*»; comme les arrêts de règlement, ils sont prononcés de manière solennelle et doivent «*faire loy*» dans le ressort de la cour qui les a rendus (*J. de Montholon*, loc. cit.; c'est sans doute pour cette raison que Montholon ou la Roche Flavin les qualifient d' «*arrêts généraux*»). Ces deux sortes d'arrêts semblent donc assez proches et Denisart les identifie purement et simplement en présentant les arrêts en robes rouges comme une forme ancienne des arrêts de règlement (*Denisart*, Collection de décisions nouvelles ..., Paris 1757, 2 t., t. 1, p. 79, au mot *Arrêt*).

72 *J. Poumarède*, loc. cit.

73 *J. Hilaire*, loc. cit. C'est ainsi que d'après *Guyot*, op. cit., t. 1, p. 627, au mot *Arrêt*, les arrêts de règlement «*doivent tenir lieu de loi ... dans les tribunaux ... du ressort du Parlement*». Pour *Denisart*, loc. cit., ces arrêts doivent «*être observés comme des lois dans le ressort des cours qui les ont rendus*».

74 *B. de la Roche Flavin*, op. cit., liv. 13, ch. LXI, n° XIV, p. 1081, oppose, de manière très significative, les arrêts «ordinaires» qui n'ont qu'une autorité relative (ils «*ne servent point de loy, qu'entre les parties nommées*») aux «*arrests généraux et solennels, prononcez en robes rouges, donnés sur les pures questions de droict, lesquels en pareilles questions servent de loy*».

75 *J. de Montholon*, loc. cit.

prouve qu'ils ont perçu l'existence d'un lien nécessaire entre la motivation des décisions et l'autorité qui leur est reconnue. Ce lien, déjà pressenti par Spifame[76], est mis en évidence par La Roche Flavin lorsqu'il souligne la portée particulière des «*arrests donnez et prononcez en lÁudience*». D'après lui, si ces arrêts «*ont beaucoup plus d'éclat, d'efficace, d'exemple et de profit pour le public, que ceux qui se donnent au Bureau* (et) *s'enregistrent au Greffe seulement*», c'est «*parce que non seulement les Advocats et procureurs, mais aussi les parties, et tous les assistans entendent la playdoirie des Advocats, et les motifs desdits Arrests, pour s'en servir de preiugez aux faicts et cas semblables et les enregistrent et perpétuent en leur mémoire audit effect ... Là où les motifs des autres donnés sur le Bureau est incognu* (sic)». C'est pourquoi, dit-il, les arrêts ordinaires «*peuvent estre nommés Arrests muets*» alors que les arrêts d'audience sont des «*Arrests parlans*»[77]. Au siècle suivant, Lucien Soefve adopte la même démarche: il oppose lui aussi les «*arrests d'audiance*» aux «*arrests donnés sur procès par écrit dont pour l'ordinaire on ne peut sçavoir les motifs*»[78]. Mais ces arrêts d'audience présentent un caractère exceptionnel. Dans l'immense majorité des cas, les arrêts ne doivent donc être considérés que comme des décisions d'espèce ne pouvant avoir d'effet qu'entre les parties concernées. La doctrine ne manque pas une occasion de rappeler cette vérité élémentaire en invoquant le droit romain et, plus particulièrement, la règle selon laquelle «*non exemplis sed legibus iudicandum*»[79]. Les auteurs soulignent aussi que la plupart des décisions sont dictées par les circonstances particulières de la cause. C'est ainsi que, pour la Roche Flavin, l'autorité relative de la chose jugée s'explique par le fait «*qu'il se trouve fort peu de procez de tous poincts semblables*» or «*les circonstances* (font) *varier les jugemens*»[80]. Quant à Charles Du Moulin, il relève que «*la moindre différence dans le fait produit une grande différence dans le droit*»[81]. Dans ces conditions, on ne saurait tirer une

---

76 Cf. *supra*, p. 97.

77 Op. cit., liv. 13, ch. LXI, n° IV, p. 1078.

78 *L. Soefve,* Nouveau recueil de plusieurs questions notables tant de droit que de coutumes jugées par arrests d'audiances du parlement de Paris depuis 1640 jusques à présent, Paris 1682, 2 t., *Préface.*

79 Ce principe est tiré du Code de Justinien (C. 7, 45, 13): «*Nemo iudex vel arbiter existimet, neque consultationes, quas non rite iudicatas esse putaverit, sequendum, et multo magis sententias eminentissimorum praefectorum vel aliorum procerum. Non enim si quid non bene dirimatur, hoc et in aliorum iudicum vitium extendi oportet: cum non exemplis, sed legibus iudicandum sit, neque si cognitionales sint amplissimae praefecturae, vel alicuius maximi magistratus praelatae sententiae: sed omnes iudices nostros veritatem et legum et iustitiae sequi vestigia sancimus*». Ce texte affirme avant tout la supériorité de la loi à laquelle le juge se trouve nécessairement subordonné, mais il ne s'oppose pas à l'autorité des décisions de justice rendues conformément à la loi; c'est donc de manière quelque peu tendancieuse que nos anciens auteurs s'en prévalent pour dénier toute autorité à ces décisions.

80 Op. cit., liv. 13, ch. LXI, n° XIV, p. 1081: c'est pourquoi, conclut-il, «*il est dit que non exemplis sed legibus iudicandum*».

81 *C. du Moulin,* Opera, 5 vol., t. 1, Paris 1681, *Commentariorum in consuetudines Parienses,* gloss. 1, tit. 2: *Des censives et droits seigneuriaux,* § LXXVIII, n° 164, p. 755:

«*autorité valable*» de «*la jurisprudence des arrêts*»[82]. Certains auteurs semblent toutefois déplorer cette situation. Tel est le cas de Coquille. Confronté à la question de savoir si une donation d'un de ses acquêts faite par un tiers à l'un des époux tombe ou non en communauté, il relève que deux arrêts du parlement de Paris de 1517 et 1536 ont considéré une telle donation comme conquêt mais l'absence de motivation l'oblige à écarter ces deux décisions «*parce que nous ne sçavons pas les circonstances particulières des procez, ny en quelle Coûtume c'étoit*»[83]. Ainsi, comme le laisse fort justement entendre Coquille, la connaissance des motifs, tant en fait qu'en droit, constitue une condition indispensable à la naissance d'une jurisprudence. A contrario, l'absence de motivation fait obstacle à la formation de cette jurisprudence. Il y a là un véritable handicap pour les cours souveraines qui vont cependant parvenir à remédier à cette situation grâce à l'intervention des arrêtistes.

2. Le contournement de l'usage: l'œuvre des arrêtistes

L'invention de l'imprimerie ne suffit certainement pas à expliquer la multiplication des recueils d'arrêts à partir du XVIe siècle. Si cette littérature se met alors à prospérer, c'est avant tout en raison du changement d'attitude des parlements. Pendant longtemps – pratiquement pendant tout le Moyen Age – ils se sont montrés hostiles au développement d'une jurisprudence au sens moderne du terme. A une époque où la coutume, principale source du droit, était encore orale et donc mal

---

«*Modica enim circumstantia facti iudicit magnam diversitatem iuris ...*». Cette opinion reste partagée par de nombreux auteurs des XVIIe et XVIIIe siècles. Voir par exemple *C. Loyseau,* Œuvres, Paris 1701, «Traité du déguerpissement ...», liv. 2, ch. 7, n° 15, p. 46: il déclare avoir renoncé à alléguer des arrêts «*parce que le plus souvent il y a tant de particularitez et tant de circonstances aux faits sur lesquels ils interviennent, qu'il est malaisé sur le simple récit d'iceux, d'y pouvoir reconnoistre l'intention de la Cour*»; il cite ensuite la maxime de Du Moulin. Dans le même sans, voir *Guyot,* op. cit., t. 1, p. 627 au mot *Arrêt* («*il n'arrive pas souvent que les circonstances des faits soient les mêmes*»). Quant à *Camus,* Lettres sur la profession d'avocat et bibliothèque choisie des livres de droit qu'il est le plus utile de connaître, 2 t., 4e éd. par M. Dupin, Paris 1818, t. 1, 4e lettre, p. 72, il affirme que citer des arrêts constitue «*un abus*» car les arrêts ayant simplement «*pour objet ... de prononcer ce qui doit avoir lieu dans des circonstances particulières, sont susceptibles de variation à l'infini*».

82 *De Ferrière,* op. cit., t. 2, p. 90, au mot *Jurisprudence.* A l'appui de cette affirmation, Ferrière reprend la proposition de du Moulin en faisant le lien avec le principe selon lequel «*non exemplis sed legibus iudicandum*». Il invoque aussi l'opinion «*d'un grand magistrat*» qui a dit «*en parlant des Arrêts, qu'ils étoient très bons pour ceux au profit de qui étoient rendu*». Cette boutade est traditionnellement attribuée au président de Harlay: cf. *Prost de Royer,* op. cit., t. 1, *Discours préliminaire,* p. XXVII.

83 *G. Coquille,* Les coustumes du Nivernois ..., in: Œuvres, t. 2, p. 266 (nous tenons à remercier Nicolas Warembourg qui nous a communiqué cette référence et, pour plus de précisions sur la position de Coquille, nous renvoyons le lecteur à sa thèse: Guy Coquille et le droit français, Lille 2005).

connue, les cours contribuaient à «dire» le droit[84] et elles entendaient préserver leur pouvoir de juger en toute liberté. Elles ne voulaient donc pas être liées par leurs propres décisions dont elles refusaient de faire des précédents[85]. Mais les choses changent au XVIe siècle lorsque, du fait de la rédaction officielle des coutumes et de la multiplication des textes royaux, le pouvoir des cours diminue. Elles réalisent sans doute alors qu'elles se sont privées d'un moyen de devenir elles-aussi source de droit, à travers leur «jurisprudence», et elles révisent leur position: tandis qu'au Moyen Age elles avaient favorisé le triomphe de l'usage de non-motivation, sous lÁncien Régime elles vont accepter, voire encourager, les atteintes à cet usage par les arrêtistes. Si les moyens employés sont absolument opposés, l'objectif poursuivi est cependant le même: il s'agit toujours d'asseoir le pouvoir des cours[86].

Soucieux de défendre leur autorité, les parlements s'en sont donc fort habilement remis aux arrêtistes qui ont assuré à la fois la publicité des décisions et la révélation de leurs motifs. Faire connaître les motifs des décisions rapportées est en effet une des grandes préoccupations des arrêtistes[87] qui n'en font pas mystère comme en témoigne la lecture des *Préface, Avertissement, Avis au lecteur* ou *Discours préliminaire* placés en tête de leurs ouvrages. Certains d'entre eux y affichent leur volonté de rapporter à la fois les circonstances de la cause et les motifs de la décision. C'est ainsi que l'arrêtiste bourguignon Bouvot déclare qu'il présentera «*tant les faits sommaires et moyen des parties, que les raisons et motifs des juges*»[88] tandis que Brillon, plus prudent dans sa formulation, se targue seulement de faire «*entrevoir les motifs, aussi bien que les circonstances essentielles*»[89]. Ces deux auteurs font donc partie des «*jurisconsultes*» que Prost de Royer félicite d'avoir «*reconnu la nécessité de publier* (les arrêts), *avec les espèces et les motifs de décision*»[90]. La révélation des motifs est en effet pressentie comme constituant

84 Jusqu'au XVIe siècle, le rôle des cours consistait essentiellement à reconnaître la coutume, en lui accordant la consécration judiciaire: cf. *J. Hilaire/C. Bloch*, art. cit., p. 67 et *S. Dauchy*, art. cit., p. 237.

85 Ces raisons profondes de la position des parlements au Moyen Age ont été examinées de manière plus détaillée dans notre article précité paru à la R.H.D.F.E., auquel nous renvoyons le lecteur.

86 Les cours sont d'autant plus favorables à la publication des recueils d'arrêts qu'elles y voient un moyen d'affirmer leur pouvoir tout en préservant leur liberté d'appréciation et leur totale indépendance. Pour plus de détails sur ce point, voir *V. Demars-Sion*, Les recueils d'arrêts et les dictionnaires de jurisprudence à l'épreuve de la pratique: l'exemple des mariages à la Gaulmine, in: Les recueils d'arrêts ..., op. cit., p. 283–451.

87 Cette préoccupation s'est affirmée très tôt: dès la fin du XIVe siècle, Jean le Coq – premier arrêtiste du parlement de Paris – se livre à «*la recherche des motifs qui ont pu fonder la décision*» (*J. Hilaire/C. Bloch*, art. cit., p. 63–64); ce faisant, il s'efforce déjà de combler la lacune laissée par l'attitude de la Cour qui, à son époque, a cessé de motiver ses décisions (cf. *supra*, p. 88).

88 *J. Bouvot*, Nouveau recueil des arrests du parlement de Bourgogne, 2 t., Genève 1623–1628, t. 1, *Préface*.

89 Op. cit., *Préface*.

le principal intérêt de ces ouvrages et elle contribue à justifier leur édition, voire leur réédition. François Catellan, qui a assuré la publication du manuscrit de son oncle, Jean, ne manque pas de souligner que le «*génie*» de ce grand magistrat lui a permis de retrouver «*les véritables motifs et les raisons décisives des Arrests*»[91]. Quant à l'avocat Richer, il cherche à démontrer les mérites de sa nouvelle édition du recueil dÁugeard en faisant valoir que «*les motifs des décisions*» y sont «*plus développés*» que dans l'édition précédente[92]. Certains arrêtistes magistrats, retenus sans doute par un ultime scrupule au moment de violer le «secret» qui leur est traditionnellement imposé, prennent cependant des précautions oratoires, tel Pinault des Jaunaux, qui déclare qu'«*afin de rendre* [son recueil] *plus utile,* [il s'est] *étudié non seulement de rapporter les raisons principales des parties; mais particulièrement de prendre l'esprit des arrêts, et d'entrer dans le sens des juges qui ont pris la décision ...*»[93].

Mais pour faire connaître les motifs, il faut d'abord les retrouver et c'est assurément là «*le grand art de l'arrêtiste*»[94]. Or cet «art» s'avère souvent difficile, voire périlleux. Si les arrêtistes magistrats bénéficient d'une position privilégiée[95], la tâche des avocats – qui se sont rapidement fait une spécialité de ce genre de littérature[96] – est beaucoup plus délicate.

L'exemple des arrêtistes du parlement de Flandre – qui furent tous membres de la Cour[97] – illustre bien les facilités dont disposent les magistrats qui se consacrent

90 Op. cit., t. 1, *Discours préliminaire,* p. VII. Voir aussi p. XXXIX: Prost de Royer annonce son programme en ces termes: «*Assurons nous de l'espèce, et tâchons enfin d'en pénétrer les motifs*».

91 Arrests remarquables du parlement de Toulouse ... recueillis par *Messire Jean de Catellan* ... et donnez au public par les soins de Messire François de Catelan ..., 2 t., Toulouse 1705, t. 1, *Préface.*

92 *M. Augeard,* Arrests notables des différens tribunaux du royaume, nouv. éd. considérablement augmentée, 2 t., Paris, 1756, t. 1, *Avertissement sur cette nouvelle édition.* D'après *Camus,* op. cit., t. 2, p. 270, cette nouvelle édition doit être attribuée à Richer.

93 Certes, le terme «motifs» n'a pas été lâché mais la périphrase ne trompe pas! Cf. *Mathieu Pinault, seigneur des Jaunaux,* Recueil d'arrests notables du parlement de Tournay, 2 t. en 1 vol., Valenciennes 1702, t. 1, «*Au lecteur*», *in fine.*

94 Comme l'a souligné *C. Chêne,* L'arrestographie, science fort douteuse, in: Recueil de mémoires et travaux publiés par la Société d'Histoire du Droit et des Institutions des Anciens Pays de droit écrit, XIII (1985), p. 179–187 (p. 181).

95 Comme l'a justement remarqué *Ph. Godding,* Jurisprudence, p. 63, les recueils rédigés par des magistrats sont «*les plus sûrs*».

96 Les premiers arrêtistes étaient souvent magistrats mais, à partir du XVIIe siècle, ce sont de plus en plus souvent des avocats. A ce propos, voir les remarques de *V. Demars-Sion,* Les recueils d'arrêts ..., art.cit., p. 290, note 35.

97 Trois recueils d'arrêts du Parlement de Flandre ont été publiés: 1°) *J. Pollet,* Arrests du parlement de Flandre sur diverses questions de droit, de coutume, et de pratique, 1re éd. Lille 1716, 2e éd. Lille 1772; 2°) *M. Pinault, seigneur des Jaunaux,* Recueil d'arrests notables du Parlement de Tournay (précité) et Suite des arrests notables du parlement de Flandres, 2 t. en

à la rédaction de tels ouvrages: ils choisissent systématiquement des affaires dans lesquelles ils ont siégé et pour lesquelles ils disposent donc d'un maximum d'informations. C'est ainsi que, d'entrée de jeu, Pinault se flatte auprès de son lecteur d'avoir sélectionné à son intention *«les plus notables arrêts d'entre ceux à la résolution desquels* [il a] *eu l'honneur de présider ou d'assister»*. D'une manière générale, ces magistrats n'hésitent pas à prendre parti et, ce faisant, ils en arrivent nécessairement à faire connaître les motifs de la décision dès lors qu'elle est conforme à leur position[98]. Ils signalent systématiquement l'existence d'un partage d'opinions en résumant le contenu des thèses qui se sont affrontées et en indiquant le nombre de voix que chacune de ces thèses a recueilli. Certains d'entre eux vont même jusqu'à nommer les conseillers qui ont souscrit à telle ou telle opinion, au mépris des ordonnances sur le secret des délibérés[99]. Leur intervention est souvent précieuse, comme en témoigne l'exemple du procès de Marie-Joseph Hiet et Marie-Jeanne Dubois, poursuivies devant les échevins de Valenciennes, la première pour vol domestique et la seconde pour complicité et recel. L'affaire est portée au parlement de Flandre à la suite de la sentence condamnant Marie-Jeanne Dubois à la question. Par son arrêt du 8 octobre 1692, la Cour infirme cette sentence et statue sur le sort des deux femmes: Marie-Jeanne Dubois est condamnée à la fustigation, à la marque et au bannissement perpétuel; quant à Marie-Joseph Hiet, son procès est évoqué et elle est condamnée, *«pour les cas en résultans»*, à douze coups de fouet et au bannissement pour trois ans. Rien dans l'arrêt ne permet de se faire une idée de la portée de la décision rendue ni des motifs qui l'ont inspirée. A

---

1 vol., Douai 1715; 3°) Recueil d'arrêts du parlement de Flandres, par *MM. Dubois d'Hermaville, de Baralle, de Blye* et *de Flines*, 2 vol., Lille 1773.

Jacques Pollet († 1713) fut conseiller à la Cour; Mathieu Pinault des Jaunaux († 1734) et Antoine-Augustin Dubois d'Hermaville furent présidents à mortier; Ladislas de Baralle († 1714) fut Procureur général du roi; Jean-Baptiste de Blye († 1699) fut Premier président et Robert de Flines († 1673) conseiller.

98 De Baralle va plus loin: il est parfois expressément mentionné dans son Recueil que *«Les motifs de l'Arrêt sont les raisons suivantes»* (voir, par exemple, op. cit., vol. 2, Arrêt L, p. 105–108, p. 107). Nous proposerons une analyse approfondie de son œuvre dans la communication que nous avons présentée au colloque *«Juristische Argumentation – Argumente der Juristen»*, organisé par le *Gesellschaft für Reichskammergerichtsforschung* (Wetzlar, 8–10 octobre 2004), sous le titre: «Argumentation et motivation dans les recueils d'arrêts des cours souveraines de France. L'exemple du parlement de Flandre (fin XVIIe – début XVIIIe siècle)», in: *A. Cordes* (dir.), Juristische Argumentation – Argumente der Juristen, Wetzlar 2006, p. 127–151.

99 Cf. Recueil d'arrêts du parlement de Flandres, t. 2, deuxième partie contenant les arrêts recueillis par *M. De Flines*. Voir par exemple p. 292, n° 4, arrêt du 20 juillet 1690: *«Il fut jugé de commun consentement, excepté de celui de Mr de Buissy»*; p. 358, n° 63, arrêt du 6 juin 1699: *«De cet avis furent Mrs de Roubaix, Desnaux, de Flines, Lescaillet et Desjaunaux; contradicentibus Mrs Couvreur, de Maffles, de la Place et de Forest»*. Il faut signaler, à la décharge de l'intéressé, que son recueil n'avait été rédigé que pour son usage personnel (il n'a été publié que longtemps après sa mort). Sur la méthode suivie par les arrêtistes du parlement de Flandre, voir *J. Lorgnier*, Les droits de la femme en ‹questions›, apport des arrêtistes au parlement de Tournai à la science du droit, in: S. Dauchy / V. Demars-Sion (édd.), Les recueils d'arre"ts... op. cit., p. 147–218, en particulier, les pages 157–161.

vrai dire, si on ne disposait que du texte de cet arrêt, on ne saurait même pas pour quel crime ces deux femmes ont été jugées![100] Mais c'est là qu'intervient l'arrêtiste: cette affaire est en effet rapportée par Dubois d'Hermaville – alors conseiller au Parlement[101] – qui, en une trentaine de lignes, fournit une excellente analyse de la décision dont il expose clairement les motifs[102].

La tâche des arrêtistes avocats est beaucoup plus délicate. Le plus sûr pour eux *«est bien entendu de tenir les motifs du magistrat concerné»*[103] et, de fait, certains ont bénéficié de *«l'indiscrétion des magistrats»*[104]. Cette *«indiscrétion»* est susceptible de revêtir des degrés différents. Elle résulte parfois de l'intervention d'un juge qui, tel le président de Harlay dans un procès jugé en 1700, vient exposer publiquement la raison ayant emporté la décision de la Cour[105]. Il arrive aussi que

---

100 Cet arrêt est conservé aux Archives départementales du Nord: VIII B 2e série n° 767, folio 4 v°. L'arrêt suit le schéma traditionnel: il rappelle les différentes étapes de la procédure et prononce la condamnation. A aucun moment il ne précise la nature des faits reprochés; c'est ainsi qu'il indique simplement que les échevins ont condamné M.-J. Dubois à *«estre appliquée à la question ordinaire et extraordinaire pour apprendre par sa bouche la vérité d'aucuns faits résultans du procès, manentibus indiciis»*.

101 Cf. Notes historiques relatives aux offices et aux officiers de la cour de parlement de Flandre, Douai, 1809, p. 35, art. 45: Antoine-Augustin Dubois d'Hermaville fut reçu conseiller à la cour le 31 octobre 1689 puis président à mortier le 7 février 1695. Cet office fut supprimé par l'édit de septembre 1703. Dubois d'Hermaville reçut alors le remboursement de la finance qu'il avait payée et se retira apparemment de la vie judiciaire (ce qui lui laissa peut-être le temps de rédiger son recueil d'arrêts, beaucoup plus volumineux que celui de ses collègues restés en activité: ses arrêts occupent tout le premier volume du *Recueil d'arrêts du parlement de Flandres* paru à Lille en 1773 alors que les arrêts consignés par de Baralle, de Blye et de Flines tiennent en un seul volume).

102 Cf. Recueil d'arrêts du parlement de Flandres, par *MM. Dubois d'Hermaville, de Baralle* ..., op. cit., t. 1, Arrêt C, p. 399–400. Dubois d'Hermaville souligne la portée de principe de cet arrêt qui a jugé *«que le recéleur pouvoit en certains cas être puni plus rigoureusement que le voleur même»* et, surtout, il en révèle très précisément les motifs: *«La Cour* – écrit-il – *ne confirma pas cette sentence, parce que le vol étoit de peu de valeur, les preuves n'étoient pas considérables, la fille qui avoit commis le vol en la maison où elle étoit domestique, n'étoit âgée que de 16 ans, elle avoit l'esprit foible, & c'étoit le seul témoin qui chargeoit cette femme du recélé du vol & d'y avoir coopéré; elle s'étoit trouvée garnie d'une partie du vol. Par ces considérations, ces deux femmes ont été l'une et l'autre condamnées à...»*. Voir, dans le même sens, l'arrêt du parlement de Paris du 22 janvier 1658 refusant de condamner à mort un bigame. Les motifs de cette décision, qui consacre un «revirement de jurisprudence» (au XVIe siècle le parlement de Paris avait opté pour la peine de mort dans cette hypothèse: cf. *B. Schnapper,* Les peines arbitraires ..., art. cit., p. 95), ne nous sont connus que grâce à une dissertation de Blondeau et Guéret, insérée dans leur *Journal du Palais*. Cf. *C. Blondeau* et *G. Guéret,* Journal du Palais, 4e éd., 2 t, Paris 1755, t. 2, p. 972: si la Tournelle a décidé, après de longues discussions, qu'il était impossible d'imposer cette peine à un bigame, c'est *«parce qu'il n'y avoit point d'Ordonnance ni de Loi civile qui imposât cette peine à la bigamie»*.

103 *C. Chêne,* art. cit., p. 181.

104 *T. Sauvel,* Histoire ..., p. 33.

105 A la suite de l'arrêt rendu par la Grand'Chambre du parlement de Paris le 22 juin 1700, *M. Augeard,* op. cit., t. 1, p. 551, indique: *«Après la prononciation de l'arrêt, M. le 1er*

des magistrats acceptent de fournir, de manière sans doute non officielle, des explications à l'arrêtiste. Matthieu Augeard *«a demandé les éclaircissements dont il a eu besoin, à messieurs les rapporteurs et messieurs les gens du roi, qui lui ont communiqué les moyens sur lesquels ils se sont déterminés»* et les auteurs du *Journal du Palais* ont travaillé *«quelquefois sur les instructions des juges eux-mêmes»*[106]. Enfin, certains arrêtistes ont pu bénéficier de révélations faites à titre purement privé, tel l'avocat Perrier qui *«a largement profité des confidences que lui faisait le Premier Président du Parlement, Nicolas Brulard, chez qui* (il) *logeait»*[107]. De telles indiscrétions restent cependant exceptionnelles: dans la grande majorité des cas, les arrêtistes sont donc *«livrés à leurs propres forces»* et ne peuvent que *«supposer les motifs de l'arrêt»*, en procédant *«par déduction»*[108]. En pratique, ils induisent souvent les raisons du juge de l'exposé des arguments des parties ou des réquisitions du ministère public[109]. Si l'on en croit Lucien Soefve, dès l'instant où l'on dispose de ces éléments *«on sçait les raisons et motifs qui peuvent avoir servy de fondement»* à la décision[110]. Les auteurs de recueils d'arrêts accordent une attention toute particulière aux affaires pour lesquelles ils disposent des conclusions des gens du roi, surtout quand l'arrêt est conforme à ces conclusions. Dans ce cas, ils peuvent sans grands risques affirmer connaître les raisons de la décision et ils insistent sur le fait qu'elle a été rendue *«conformément*

---

président de Harlay dit au barreau que la probité reconnue de François Pillon, et le désintéressement avec lequel il avoit toujours fait sa profession, avoit principalement déterminé le legs fait en sa faveur» (il s'agissait en l'occurrence de décider de la validité d'un legs fait à un procureur par sa cliente). *G. du Rousseaud de la Combe*, Recueil de jurisprudence civile, Paris 1769, p. 452, arrêt du 21 février 1732, mentionne également une affaire dans laquelle le 1er président Portail a *«averti le barreau»* des raisons pour laquelle la Cour *«s'est déterminée»*.

106 *M. Augeard*, op. cit., *Avertissement sur cette nouvelle édition. Journal du Palais*, t. 1, *Avertissement sur l'édition de 1701 de ce livre.* Cette collaboration des magistrats conduit à penser que certains arrêtistes étaient en quelque sorte accrédités par la juridiction dont ils rapportaient les décision (à ce propos, voir *V. Demars-Sion*, art. cit., p. 292).

107 *M. Petitjean*, Regards sur l'arrestographie bourguignonne, in: Les recueils d'arre"ts ..., op. cit., p. 91–104 (p. 98).

108 *E. Meynial*, Les recueils d'arrêts et les arrêtistes, in: Le code civil, livre du centenaire, t. 1, Paris 1904, réédition 1969, p. 173–204, p. 182; *Ph. Godding*, Jurisprudence, p. 51 et p 64; *J. Hilaire*, Question autour de la jurisprudence des arrêts, p. 27; *J. Poumarède*, Les arrestographes toulousains, in: Les recueils d'arre"ts ..., op. cit., p. 69–89 (p. 85): «*C'est par déduction* [que l'avocat Albert] *tente de percer les motivations de la Cour*».

109 L'apport des arrêtistes est d'autant plus important qu'à partir du XVIe siècle la manière de rédiger les arrêts évolue: désormais, ces arrêts ne font plus systématiquement mention des arguments des parties ni des conclusions du ministère public. Sur ce point cf. *S. Dauchy*, Les recueils d'arrêts et dictionnaires de jurisprudence, op. cit., *Préface*, p. 18. Sur l'évolution du contenu des arrêts aux XVIIe-XVIIIe siècles, voir les observations de *V. Demars-Sion*, ibidem, p. 298. Comme l'a fort justement remarqué *Ph. Godding*, Jurisprudence et motivation, p. 64, cet apport est cependant susceptible de varier considérablement selon «*le genre adopté par l'auteur*»: les recueils qui rapportent les cas jugés «*de façon circonstanciée*» sont évidemment beaucoup plus instructifs.

110 Op. cit., *Préface*.

à ces conclusions» ou que ces conclusions ont été *«suivies par la Cour»*[111]. A défaut, il leur arrive souvent de rapporter les arguments des parties en laissant entendre, de manière plus ou moins explicite[112], que ceux de la partie gagnante ont emporté l'adhésion de la Cour à sa cause. Cette technique consistant à déduire les motifs de l'arrêt de l'argumentation des parties semble particulièrement hasardeuse; elle a pourtant la faveur de nombreux arrêtistes: Camus n'hésite pas à affirmer qu'*«on ne sauroit connaître plus surement* [la jurisprudence] *qu'... en s'instruisant, par la lecture des mémoires, des moyens qui ont été capables de faire pencher la balance»*[113]. Certains arrêtistes, magistrats de leur état, prennent cependant soin de souligner les limites d'un tel procédé. Forts, sans aucun doute, de leur propre expérience, ils dénoncent sans ménagement la démarche de *«biens des compilateurs»* qui *«présument* (les questions) *jugées dans le sens, et suivant la prétention de la partie qui gagne»*. Or, comme le rappelle François de Catellan, il arrive que les juges se soient *«déterminez par des motifs singuliers et des raisons imprévues»*[114] et, si l'on en croit Jacques de Montholon, les raisons d'un arrêt *«sont bien souvent toutes autres que celles déduites par les parties»*[115]. La Cour peut effectivement avoir donné gain de cause à la partie gagnante pour des motifs différents de ceux qu'elle faisait valoir; elle peut aussi n'avoir retenu que partiellement son argumentation. Les juges ne se sont pas nécessairement tous décidés sur les mêmes raisons, et il peut arriver que leur décision ait été emportée par des considérations d'équité et non par l'argumentation des plaideurs[116]. Ainsi, on ne saurait nier que les différents moyens employés par les arrêtistes pour essayer de faire connaître les motifs des décisions rapportées constituent *«autant de procédés qui ne donnent jamais une certitude»*[117].

---

[111] Voir les exemples tirés du *Journal du Palais* rapportés par *V. Demars-Sion,* art. cit., p. 311 (notes 148 et 149). Ce genre de formule se rencontre très souvent chez les arrêtistes: voir, par exemple *Soefve,* op. cit., t. 1, p. 137; *Augeard,* op. cit., t. 1, p. 549 , 567, 625, 649, 670, 702, 719, 759, 872, 895..., t. 2, p. 33, 52, 211, 244, 254, 277....

[112] La formulation adoptée est plus ou moins tranchante: tantôt l'arrêtiste se contente de rapporter l'argumentation des deux parties en laissant simplement supposer que celle de la partie gagnante était la bonne; tantôt il n'hésite pas à montrer sa préférence pour la thèse qui, d'après lui, a emporté la conviction des juges en utilisant les formules *«voici quelles furent les raisons de douter» et «voici les raisons de décider»* (sur ces différents points voir les exemples rapportés par *V. Demars-Sion,* art. cit., p. 311. Voir aussi *Augeard,* op. cit., t. 1, p. 856. Augeard rapporte d'abord la thèse de l'appelant, puis celle de l'intimé et conclut: *«par ces motifs, l'arrêt rendu le 6 mars 1706 confirma la sentence ...»*; l'argumentation de la partie gagnante est donc identifiée aux motifs. Voir encore t. 2, p. 61 et p. 513 où Augeard s'en tient aux formules plus vagues *«sur ces raisons» ou «sur ces derniers moyens, la cour a confirmé la sentence»).*

[113] Op. cit., t. 1, *Quatrième lettre sur l'étude du droit français,* p. 62.

[114] Op. cit., *Préface.*

[115] Op. cit., *Advis au lecteur.*

[116] Sur ce point cf. *Ph. Godding,* Jurisprudence et motivation, p. 64; *J. Hilaire,* Questions autour de la jurisprudence des arrêts, p. 28; *M. Petitjean,* Les recueils d'arrêts bourguignons, in: A. Wijffels (éd.), Case-Law in the Making, op. cit., vol.1: Essays, p. 267 – 276, p. 273.

[117] *T. Sauvel,* Histoire, p. 32.

L'«arrestographie» constitue donc de toute évidence une *«science fort douteuse»*[118]. Certains arrêtistes reconnaissent d'ailleurs eux-mêmes, plus ou moins explicitement, les limites de leur art, comme en témoigne la formule très révélatrice occasionnellement employée par l'un des premiers d'entre eux, Jean Le Coq: *«et je crois que les raisons de décider furent...»*[119]. On pourrait encore citer Prost de Royer qui déclare: *«Nous tâcherons ... d'énoncer les motifs des arrêts quand il seront parvenus jusqu'à nous ou de les rechercher à travers les probabilités»*[120]. De fait, la révélation des motifs s'avère très aléatoire: les arrêts rapportés n'ont qu'une *«valeur subjective, empruntée tout autant à la perspicacité, à l'ingéniosité et au discernement de l'arrêtiste qu'à la propre autorité de la décision»*[121] et, dans ces conditions, la littérature arrêtiste risque de devenir *«un miroir déformant de la jurisprudence»*[122]. L'avenir de la «jurisprudence» semble bien incertain tant que sa révélation restera tributaire d'une telle science: on voit mal comment, dans de telles conditions, elle pourrait devenir une source, même indirecte, de droit et les chances de succès de ceux qui invoquent son autorité sont donc bien minces. Le débat qui oppose, en 1679, les avocats des sieurs Colon et Le Blan devant le parlement de Paris est significatif à cet égard: au premier, qui invoque *«la jurisprudence des arrêts»*[123], le second rétorque, avec succès, qu'on ne saurait s'appuyer sur des décisions dont ceux-là même qui les rapportent *«ignorent souvent les véritables motifs»*[124].

Malgré les entorses qu'il a subies, l'usage de ne pas motiver les décisions a résisté jusqu'à la fin de lÁncien Régime et le moins qu'on puisse dire est que la doctrine ne s'est pas mobilisée contre cette pratique. Au XVIIIe siècle, certains auteurs – comme Jousse – continuent à penser que puisque les juges sont libres de motiver ou non leurs décisions il est préférable qu'ils ne le fassent pas[125]. D'autres

118 Selon l'expression de *C. Chêne*, art. cit.

119 *J. Hilaire/C. Bloch*, art. cit., p. 67 note 96.

120 Et il s'empresse d'ajouter que cela suppose un *«soin délicat et pénible»*: *op. cit.*, t. 1, *Discours préliminaire*, p. XC. Voir aussi p. XXIX: *«tâchons de pénétrer les motifs* (de l'arrêt)*»*.

121 *E. Meynial*, art. cit., p. 182.

122 *J. Hilaire/C. Bloch*, art. cit., p. 67; *J. Hilaire*, Jugement et jurisprudence, p. 186.

123 Il s'appuie plus précisément sur un arrêt du 19 décembre 1600 ainsi qu'une décision rendue *«environ deux ans auparavant»* (cf. arrêt du 13 juin 1679 – rendu dans un procès relatif à une rente constituée – rapporté dans le Journal du Palais, précité, t. 2, p. 53 sq., voir p. 56).

124 *Ibidem*: *«il ne suffit pas d'alléguer des Arrêts sur la foi des Auteurs qui les rapportent, parce qu'encore qu'ils ayent assisté à la plaidoirie des causes ou même qu'ils ayent écrit dans les procès sur lesquels ils sont intervenus; il est néanmoins certain qu'ils en ignorent souvent les véritables motifs»*; il cite ensuite, à l'appui de son argumentation, la doctrine hostile à l'autorité des arrêts (étudiée *supra*). Son argumentation a apparemment convaincu la Cour qui a confirmé la décision incriminée.

125 *D. Jousse*, Traité de l'administration de la justice, 2 t., Paris 1771, t. 2, partie 3, titre 1, section 2, art. 4, p. 34, n° 74: *«Il n'est pas nécessaire que les Juges expriment les motifs de*

ont pourtant compris les inconvénients d'un tel usage qui empêche «*l'existence d'une jurisprudence cohérente, disposant d'une réelle autorité*»[126]. «*Dans les Arrêts qui se rendent à l'ordinaire*», écrit Claude-Joseph de Ferrière, «*on ne voit point les motifs de leurs décisions... Cela fait qu'on n'en peut faire avec certitude une juste application à d'autres espèces, quoiqu'elles paroissent semblables; car le motif étant l'âme d'un Jugement, se servir d'un arrêt sans en rapporter le motif, c'est se servir d'un corps sans âme*»[127]. Tous ces auteurs s'accordent pour reconnaître le rôle nécessaire de la jurisprudence, à laquelle ils attribuent une valeur supplétive ou interprétative, et pour déplorer les faiblesses de la «jurisprudence des arrêts», qu'ils envisagent comme une conséquence de l'absence de motivation. Toutefois, ils ne vont pas jusqu'à proposer ce qui apparaît pourtant comme la seule véritable solution: obliger les juges à révéler eux-mêmes les motifs de leurs décisions. Les propos des auteurs de *l'Encyclopédie* illustrent bien cette position majoritaire: «*dans les matières sur lesquelles il n'y a point de loi précise*», écrivent-ils, «*on a recours à la jurisprudence des arrêts; et il n'y auroit point de meilleur guide si l'on étoit toujours bien instruit des véritables circonstances dans lesquelles les arrêts sont intervenus, et des motifs qui ont déterminé les juges*»[128]. Seul Prost de Royer fait exception à la règle. Certes, comme la plupart de ses contemporains, il commence par dresser la liste des infirmités de la jurisprudence inhérentes à l'absence de motivation des décisions[129] mais il propose, lui, un remède et ce remède, c'est la motivation: «*Pour que l'autorité des arrêts fut vraiment irréfragable, pour que les recueils d'arrêts fussent essentiellement* utiles», affirme-t-il, «*il seroit nécessaire que les juges rendissent toujours compte des motifs de leurs décisions; il faudroit que les arrêtistes développassent les faits principaux qui ont servi de base aux juges pour prendre leur parti*»[130]. Pour lui, c'est à

---

leurs jugemens ... Mais s'ils le veulent faire, cela dépend d'eux. Neanmoins il vaut mieux ne point exprimer ces motifs, afin de ne pas donner lieu à des chicanes de la part de celui qui auroit perdu sa cause».

126 *C. Blery*, art. cit., p. 82.

127 Op. cit., t. 2, p. 91, au mot *Jurisprudence*.

128 Op. cit., t. 9, p. 82, au mot *Jurisprudence des arrêts*. Voir aussi *Guyot*, op. cit., t. 1, au mot *Arrêt*, p. 627: il est «*rare* (que les arrêts) *puissent absolument être regardés comme des motifs de décision, parce qu'on ... ignore ordinairement les raisons de la décision*»; Guyot reconnaît pourtant ensuite le rôle interprétatif de la jurisprudence (*loc. cit.*: «*Cependant il faut convenir...* (qu') *une suite de jugemens uniformes fait un usage qui est le meilleur interprète des loix*»).

129 «*Les oracles de la justice n'expliquant point les causes de leurs dispositions, les arrêts offrent aux prétentions les plus opposées, des titres que la prévention fait toujours valoir. Souvent des préjugés contraires fournissent des armes pour et contre dans la même affaire; espèce de contradiction qui ne surprendra point, si on considère que par la différence des circonstances, deux arrêts qui ont des dispositions conformes peuvent avoir des motifs différents, tandis que deux arrêts différents peuvent être fondés sur le même principe*» (op. cit., t. 6, au mot *Arrêt*, n° 45, p. 725).

130 Op. cit., t. 6, au mot *Arrêt*, n° 46, p. 730. Notons que la formulation laisse entendre que les juges donnent parfois les motifs de leurs décisions; notons aussi l'intéressante distinction

cette condition, et à cette condition seulement, que la jurisprudence pourra jouer son indispensable rôle, à la fois supplétif et interprétatif[131], conduisant à faire des arrêts «*les ancres des loix*»[132]. Mais cette prise de position de Prost de Royer – qui écrit dans la dernière décennie de lÁncien Régime – est isolée et ses propositions resteront lettre morte: aucune véritable réforme n'interviendra avant la Révolution. Car il ne faut pas se méprendre sur la portée de la déclaration royale de 1788[133]. Certes ce texte condamne l'usage de la formule «*Pour les cas résultant du procès*» mais, contrairement à ce qu'on a trop souvent écrit[134], à notre sens il n'introduit pas pour autant une obligation de motiver les jugements en matière criminelle. En réalité, en exigeant que, désormais, «*tout arrêt ou jugement énonce et qualifie expressément les crimes et délits sont l'accusé aura été convaincu et pour lesquels il sera condamné*», le roi ne fait qu'étendre aux cours l'obligation qu'elles avaient réservée jusque-là aux tribunaux inférieurs et qui, comme nous l'avons démontré, n'aboutissait qu'à une simple qualification des faits[135].

établie entre la mission du juge et celle de l'arrêtiste (qui reflète, en quelque sorte, la distinction du droit et du fait). Signalons encore que dans la suite de ses développements (p. 732), Prost de Royer établit un parallèle également très intéressant avec la motivation des textes législatifs.

131 Une phrase du *Discours préliminaire* résume bien les multiples missions que Prost de Royer assigne à la jurisprudence: «*la législation moderne s'établit, se modifie, s'interprète et se supplée par des Arrêts*» (op. cit., p. XXVIII). Voir aussi p. XXIX où il défend le rôle supplétif de la jurisprudence: «*lorsqu'il n'y a point de loi précise, pourquoi ne citerait-on pas l'Arrêt rendu sur la même question?*» et t. 6, au mot *Arrêt*, n° 45 p. 725, où il évoque implicitement le rôle interprétatif de la jurisprudence: «*la disposition des loix étant claire et générale, il faut religieusement s'y arrêter sans avoir égard* (aux) *arrêts*» ... (a contrario, si la loi n'est pas claire, il appartient au juge de l'interpréter).

132 *Prost de Royer*, op. cit., t. 6, au mot *Arrêt*, n° 46 p. 730 et 732, utilise deux fois cette expression qu'il a empruntée à Bacon.

133 Déclaration relative à l'ordonnance criminelle, 1er mai 1788: *Isambert*, op. cit., t. 28, p. 526 sq.

134 Voir, par exemple, *E. Seligman*, La justice en France pendant la Révolution (1789–1792), Paris 1901, p. 114: à partir de cette déclaration, «*les cours supérieures devront motiver leurs jugements*»; *J.-M. Carbasse*, op. cit., p. 312, n° 86: par ce texte, le roi «*obligeait* [ses juges] *à motiver précisément leurs jugements et arrêts*». J.-P. Royer, plus nuancé, écrit que ce texte a introduit une «*première motivation partielle*» (*op. cit.*, p. 64, n° 30 *in fine*). On notera – ce qui peut contribuer à expliquer la position de ces auteurs – que les promoteurs de cette loi l'ont eux-mêmes présentée comme une remise en cause de l'usage de non-motivation: dans son *Discours pour annoncer la déclaration* ..., rapporté par *Ph.-J.-B. Buchez/P.-C. Roux*, Histoire parlementaire de la Révolution française, 40 vol., Paris 1834–1838, t. 1, p. 239 sq. (p. 241), Lamoignon déclare en effet: «*La dignité de vos jugemens exige l'énonciation expresse des délits. Quel tribunal pourrait être jaloux de la prérogative d'infliger des peines capitales sans motiver ses arrêts?*».

135 Article 3 de la déclaration, *Isambert*, op. cit., t. 28, p. 531: «*Ne pourront nos juges, même nos cours, prononcer en matière criminelle, pour les cas résultants du procés; voulons que tout arrêt ou jugement énonce et qualifie expressément les crimes et délits dont l'accusé aura été convaincu, et pour lesquels il sera condamné* ...». Comme le souligne à juste titre *T. Sauvel*, Histoire, p. 42, ce texte «*exige la qualification du crime plutôt qu'un véritable raisonnement et ne demande pas une argumentation de fait et de droit démontrant l'existence*

Il faudra donc attendre la Révolution pour que tous les juges se voient obligés à fournir une véritable motivation de tous leurs jugements. La législation révolutionnaire[136] comporte pourtant encore quelques ambiguïés. Certes, dès la grande loi sur l'organisation judiciaire de 1790, le principe de la nécessaire motivation des décisions de justice est posé de manière très claire et très générale[137] mais les textes postérieurs ne sont pas tous aussi explicites. Certains restent silencieux sur ce point: tel est la cas de la constitution de 1791[138]. Quant à la constitution de 1793, elle semble limiter l'application du nouveau principe en proposant une distinction entre «*la justice civile*» rendue par des «*arbitres publics*» qui «*motivent leurs décisions*», et «*la justice criminelle*» dans laquelle «*le fait et l'intention sont déclarés par un jury de jugement*»[139]. La constitution de 1795 reviendra toutefois à une formulation plus claire en énonçant que, de manière générale, «*les jugements ... sont motivés, et on y énonce les termes de la loi appliquée*»[140]. Ce principe, consacré par la législation de l'Empire[141], ne sera plus remis en cause par la suite.

---

de ce crime»; il n'exige donc pas encore de motivation au sens actuel du terme. *A. Laingui*, dans son introduction au *De poenis* ... de Tiraqueau, op. cit., p. 26, soutient cependant qu'il «*serait erroné ... d'affirmer que dans l'ancien droit pénal les décisions judiciaires n'étaient pas motivées*», mais comme il le constate lui-même, «*le texte même de la déclaration royale de 1788 montre les limites de cette motivation*».

136 Cette législation répond aux vœux exprimés dans les cahiers de doléances (sur ce point, voir *C. Blery*, art. cit., p. 82–84).

137 *Duvergier*, Collection complète des lois, t. 1, Paris 1834, Décret des 16–24 août 1790, Titre V, p. 324: l'article 15 *in fine* dispose que «*Dans la troisième* (partie de la décision) *les motifs qui auront déterminé le jugement seront exprimés*».

138 Cette constitution ne renferme aucune allusion à la motivation des décisions: cf. *Duvergier*, t. 3, p. 239 sq. (voir en particulier le titre III: *Des pouvoirs publics*, chapitre V: *Du pouvoir judiciaire*).

139 *Duvergier*, t. 5, p. 356–357 (*De la justice civile*, article 94 et *De la justice criminelle*, article 96). L'obligation de motiver *stricto sensu* ne s'appliquerait donc qu'aux procès civils.

140 *Duvergier*, t. 8, p. 223 sq. (Titre VIII: *Pouvoir judiciaire*, article 208 *in fine*). Cette règle est à nouveau conçue comme une règle générale: l'article 208 figure en effet parmi les «*Dispositions générales*» exposées au début du titre VIII; ce titre comporte ensuite des rubriques particulières: *De la justice civile* (art. 210 à 221), *De la justice correctionnelle et criminelle* (art. 222 à 253), *Tribunal de cassation* (art. 254 à 264), *Haute cour de justice* (art. 265 à 273). Ce texte annonce notre système moderne qui distingue le *visa* et les motifs. L'obligation du *visa* était inconnue sous l'Ancien Régime, ce qui s'explique très certainement par la diversité et l'imprécision des sources du droit à cette époque (sur ce point cf. *T. Sauvel*, Histoire, p. 15; *B. Schnapper*, Les peines, p. 238).

141 *Duvergier*, t. 17, p. 66 sq: *Loi sur l'organisation de l'ordre judiciaire et l'administration de la justice* (20 avril 1810), ch. 1: *Des cours impériales*, art. 7, p. 66–69: «*La justice est rendue souverainement par les cours impériales; leurs arrêts ... qui ne contiennent pas les motifs, sont déclarés nuls*». On notera que cette obligation de motiver n'est formulée que pour les cours d'appel (tout comme, nous l'avons vu, sous l'Ancien Régime, l'interdiction de révéler le secret ne visait que les parlements) mais cette disposition s'est vu reconnaître une portée générale comme en témoignent les décisions de la cour de cassation rapportées sous le texte (*Duvergier*, loc. cit., p. 69 note 1: ces décisions concernent tant les motifs des arrêts que ceux des jugements).

Il contribuera, avec le temps[142], à asseoir l'autorité des décisions judiciaires. Ainsi, en définitive, «*c'est ... la Révolution qui, en rendant obligatoire la motivation des jugements et des arrêts, a facilité le développement de la jurisprudence et décidé de son importance depuis deux siècles*»[143]. Ce résultat peut paraître quelque peu paradoxal dans la mesure où les révolutionnaires contestaient l'existence de la jurisprudence[144] et voyaient avant tout dans la nécessaire motivation des décisions un moyen de limiter le pouvoir des juges en les subordonnant à la loi[145]. S'ils ont été les artisans du triomphe de la jurisprudence, ils ne l'ont donc été que d'une manière tout à fait involontaire. La nouvelle conception de la loi (adoptée par la représentation nationale) et le principe de l'unité du droit civil ont également contribué au triomphe de cette jurisprudence qu'on considère généralement aujourd'hui comme une source de droit, tout au moins indirecte[146].

Summary

The absence of reasons given for judicial decisions, which is one of the main characteristics of justice in Ancien Regime France, is generally inferred from the interdiction made by royal decrees since the fourteenth century to „disclose the secrets of deliberations". But there is in fact no causal link between them. No royal decree or other normative prescription explicitly forbade the judges of *Parlement* to give the reasons for their judgements. The „style" of the *Parlement de Paris* only advised the judges against the practice of disclosing the *rationes decidendi* and the judges indeed adopted the warnings repeated by the Decretalists since the early years of the thirteenth century. Therefore, not revealing the *rationes decidendi* appears to be a common use rather than a firm principle of ancient French law. That use soon became commonly adopted by the *Parlements* because it was a guarantee of the independence of its members and also because it ensured the sovereign courts great liberty. Nevertheless, there were some exceptions to that common use, for instance when cassation appeared, public prosecutors got used to ask the reasons of the judgements against which cassation was claimed.

142 Sur l'évolution qui a conduit à reconnaître à la jurisprudence «*le droit à l'existence*» voir *J. Hilaire*, Jugement et jurisprudence, p. 187.

143 *J. Hilaire*, Jugement et jurisprudence, p. 182.

144 Pour le Chapelier, par exemple, «*Si cette jurisprudence des tribunaux... existait, il faudrait la détruire*» (Sur ce point et, de manière plus générale, sur l'hostilité affichée par les révolutionnaires à l'égard de la jurisprudence voir *J. Hilaire*, Jugement et jurisprudence, article précité, p. 186).

145 Cette préoccupation se déduit de l'esprit général des réformes opérées en la matière: le législateur révolutionnaire entend à tout prix réduire les pouvoirs du juge qu'il considère comme un mal nécessaire et dont il entend faire une sorte de machine à appliquer la loi. Sur ce point voir, notamment, *J.-P. Royer*, op. cit., p. 274 sq. Pour plus de précisions sur la question de la motivation pendant la Révolution et au XIXe siècle voir la contribution de J.-L. Halperin dans ce volume.

146 Cette solution ne fait cependant pas l'unanimité: comme le rappelle *J. Hilaire*, Jugement et jurisprudence, p. 181, on discute toujours sur le point de savoir si la jurisprudence est «*simplement une autorité ou une véritable source de droit*».

Those exceptions were rather scarce and it is more through the printed reports, the so-called *recueils d'arrêts*, that the reasons of judgments became known to lawyers and professors and that jurisprudence could develop. Disclosing the *rationes decidendi* was presented by the authors of those *recueils* as the main interest of their work and it indeed largely contributed to the success of that kind of legal literature.

JOHN FINLAY

Ratio Decidendi in Scotland 1650 to 1800

In order to understand when and why the practice of giving *rationes decidendi* emerged in Scotland it is necessary briefly to review some of the relevant institutional background.[1] In comparison to England, Scotland has always been a small jurisdiction with a relatively limited case law. The resultant lack of domestic decisions, either encapsulating indigenous customary rules of law or confirming the adoption of rules from *ius commune* sources, encouraged Scottish jurists and judges occasionally to take notice of the decisions of foreign courts.[2] Advocates, many of whom had some foreign legal education, cited cases from foreign courts with which they were familiar, or from printed collections of decisions which were available to them either privately or, after its foundation in 1689, in the Advocates' Library.[3] Where domestic decisions did exist, their meaning was rarely beyond doubt, and in the eighteenth century decisions were cited that were often old and inadequately reported.

Such law reporting as there was in Scotland developed from the 1540s following the endowment of the Court of Session as a College of Justice in Edinburgh in

---

1 The author is very grateful to the Keeper and staff of the Advocates' Library, Edinburgh, for permission to access the Session Papers held in Faculty's collection. He also wishes to record his gratitude to his research assistant, Fiona MacDonald, and to Professor Hector MacQueen for his comments on a draft of this paper. The author remains responsible for any errors.

2 See *Thomas Craig,* Jus Feudale I.9.15 (a text written c. 1600); The Petition of John Stirling, Esq., Miscellany VII (1785–1786), Advocates Library, Session Papers [ALSP], p. 17: "The petitioner has not been able to find any case in the law of Scotland where the point has been brought to trial. Indeed it is a rare thing for any person in a narrow country like this to venture to assume a title to which he has no right, or for a certain person accidentally to design himself wrong, that such cases can seldom occur. On looking, however, into the English law-books, the petitioner finds that this matter is well understood ... The petitioner does not propose to state English cases to your Lordships as amounting to precedents in this Court: at the same time, in a matter of this kind, which seems to depend on that reasonable degree of form, which is the life and soul of judicial proceedings, and without which business cannot go on, the practice of other countries must have weight ...".

3 An example of a collection frequently cited is *Johannes Sande,* Decisions of the Court of Friesland, see *J. Blackie,* "History, historiography and comparative law" in L. Farmer & S. Veitch, eds., The State of Scots Law (Edinburgh, 2001), p. 77; on the large proportion of foreign law books in the library's collection, see *A. M. Cain,* "Foreign books in the 18th century Advocates' Library" in P. Cadell & A. Mathieson, eds., For the Encouragement of Learning (Edinburgh, 1989), p. 111.

1532 with fifteen salaried and professional judges. This new court was built on a pre-existing conciliar structure and the judges appointed in 1532 reflect strong continuity with judges who had been sitting prior to that year. A court of both law and equity, the collegiate nature of the Court of Session has been an important factor in the development of case law. The noted judge Lord Kames, in discussing the make-up of the court, believed that the multiplicity of judges in the court explained why jury trial was not used as it was in England. He referred to the maxim that "though questions in law may be trusted to a single judge, matters of proof are safest in the hands of a plurality."[4] For him, the Court of Session had both the powers of the judge and the jury and as such it was "the grand jury of the nation in *civilibus*".

Reports of what went on in the Court of Session initially took the form of works known as *practicks.*[5] Two types of such works have been identified: decision *practicks,* such as those by Lord President Sinclair (covering 1540–9), which simply recorded short notes of cases and rules of practice; and digest *practicks,* which were longer works setting out the law under titles arranged alphabetically, mixing reference to decided cases with references to treatises and statutes. Although manuscript collections of decisions circulated, the first decisions to be printed did not appear until 1683, when there appeared those collected by Lord Stair, lord president of the Court of Session and the most important writer on Scots law of the early modern period. Further printed decisions became available in the eighteenth century and William Forbes, the first professional law reporter employed by the Faculty of Advocates in 1705, published case reports in his *Journal of the Session* (1714) during his first full year as professor of Civil law at the university of Glasgow.

The appearance of printed decisions broadly coincided with the print publication of important legal treatises. Writers such as Sir James Dalrymple, viscount Stair, Sir George Mackenzie, Lord Bankton, Professor John Erskine and Professor George Joseph Bell, span a period of important development in Scots law and their works provide important evidence of what the attitude towards decided cases actually was.[6] In addition to such writers, the eighteenth century saw discussion of the

---

4 *Henry Home / Lord Kames,* Historical law Tracts (Edinburgh, 1761), pp. 271–272.

5 On this form of literature, see *D. B. Smith,* "Practicks", in The Sources and Literature of Scots Law (Stair Society, 1934); *A. L. Murray,* "Sinclair's Practicks", in Law Making and Law-makers in British History ed. A. Harding (London, 1980); *G. Dolezalek,* "The Court of Session as a *ius commune* court – witnessed by Sinclair's Practicks, 1540–1549" in H. L. MacQueen, ed., Miscellany IV, (Stair Society, 2001), p. 51; *S. Brooks,* "The Decision Practicks of Sir Thomas Hamilton, first earl of Haddington" (2004) in Edinburgh Law Review, p. 206; *P. G. B. McNeill,* Balfour's Practicks, 2 vols. (Stair Society, 1962–1963).

6 *Sir James Dalrymple, viscount Stair* (1619–95), Institutions of the Law of Scotland (1681; 2nd ed. 1693); *Sir George Mackenzie* (1636–91), Matters Criminal (1678), Institutions of the Law of Scotland (1684); *Andrew Macdouall, Lord Bankton* (1685–1760), An Institute of the Law of Scotland (1751); *John Erskine* (1695–1768), Principles of the Law of Scotland (1754), Institutes of *the Law of Scotland* (1773); *G. J. Bell* (1770–1843), Commentaries on the Municipal and Mercantile Law of Scotland (1804).

importance of case law in the writings of such influential Enlightenment empiricists as Adam Smith and Henry Home, Lord Kames.[7]

A fundamental feature of the period was the parliamentary union with England in 1707 following which the House of Lords quickly assumed jurisdiction as the imperial court of last resort in all British civil cases. Although the House of Lords, for various reasons, heard a disproportionately high number of appeals from Scotland in the eighteenth century, the Westminster parliament in general had limited interest in the development of Scots private law. It was largely left to the domestic judges to develop the law against a background of unprecedented social and industrial transformation.[8]

The Theoretical Importance of *Rationes*

Lord Stair, author of the first published set of law reports in Scotland, claimed that he "did seldom eat or drink, and scarcely ever slept" before each evening setting down in his collection the decisions of the court.[9] Such enthusiasm may be explained by the fact that for Stair the publication of decisions reflected his view that immemorial custom was the primary source of law, and that decisions worked out by the courts over time tended to produce mature rules that had passed the test of time. This idea of case law, however, was predicated not on the importance of a single decision, however sound its reasoning, but on consistency and the evidence of a number of decisions confirming the utility of any given rule and conferring the force of custom upon it. Such a manner of legal development was superior to statute in Stair's view because statute was the product of the moment, which might, in an expressive phrase, prove "abortive in the womb of time".

A more traditional Scottish approach was that of Sir George Mackenzie of Rosehaugh, a man of a significantly different political stamp. To Mackenzie, statutes were the "Chief Pillars of our Law", a fact underlined by his publication of the much-used *Observations on the Statutes* in 1686. But even Mackenzie recognised the importance of decided cases: "Our unwritten law comprehends the constant tract of decisions past by the Lords of Session *which is considered as law,* the Lords respecting very much their own decisions, and though

---

7 See *John W. Cairns,* "Adam Smith and the role of the courts in securing justice and liberty" in R. P. Malloy & J. Evensky, Adam Smith and the Philosophy of Law and Economics, (Kluwer, 1994), p. 3; *D. Lieberman,* The Province of Jurisprudence Determined (Cambridge, 1989).

8 Indeed, there was no formal requirement for the House of Lords to contain a judge trained in Scots law until as late as the Appellate Jurisdiction Act, 1876: see, most recently, *K. Goodall,* "Ideas of 'Representation' in UK Court Structures" in A. Le Sueur, ed., Building the UK's New Supreme Court (Oxford, 2004), p. 75.

9 *Stair,* Apology (1690).

they may, they use not to recede from them except upon grave considerations."[10]

As for Stair, a single decision carried little weight. Mackenzie had explained his wider view in his earlier work on Scots criminal law although the reasons he gives there appear to have general applicability.

> The Decisions of our criminal Court, as of all other, do bind the same or succeeding Judges, rather out of Decency than Necessity; for nothing ties Judges but Laws, and none can make Laws but the parliament, which is very suitable to *L. nemo, C. de dent. & inter.* where Justinian doth expressly command, *ne ullorum judicum sententia pro jure reputentur.* The Reason whereof given in that Law, is *quod non exemplis, sed legibus est judicandum,* and the other Reason *L. ult. C. de legibus, quia imperator est solus legum conditior.* And if we consider how much Circumstances influence particular Cases, how Judges may fail where Parties are nam'd, and that Decisions pass necessarily upon less Premeditation than is necessary to Laws, it will be found reasonable, not to trust Decisions too much ... And so frail and fallible a Thing are Mens Judgments, especially where Votes are numbred, and not weighed, or where Experience may discover the Errors, which the sharpest Reason could not foresee, that therefore Judges should no more be tied from altering their Decisions, than Philosophers to continue in the Errors of their Youth ....[11]

For reasons already discussed it is not surprising that Mackenzie should make such liberal reference to Roman law which was an influential source in developing the attitude of Scots lawyers to the authority of practick. According to the advocate and jurist Thomas Craig (1538–1608), practice furnished the best means of interpreting ambiguities in native written law.[12] The same sentiment is found later in the case of *Craw v. Craw* where the report described the "constant practice of the kingdom" as "the best interpreter of the laws".[13]

This reflects the Roman idea of a consistent line of similar decisions enjoying statutory force.[14] For the Scots, a consistent line of decisions clearly had considerable importance. But there was reason for caution in the light of another idea in Roman law mentioned by Mackenzie and expressed in Justinian's Codex, that *non exemplis sed legibus iudicandum est* (decisions ought to be based not on prior cases but on laws).[15] For the later writer Lord Bankton, a tract of "precedents uniform upon the same point, is justly esteemed as law, and ought to be followed in all time thereafter in parallel cases; but otherwise the rule is, that non exemplis sed legibus judicandum. Not one or two precedents, but the prescription of the law is

10 *Mackenzie,* Institutions of the Law of Scotland (Edinburgh, 1684), I, i, 10 (emphasis added).

11 Matters Criminal (1678) in Works, ii, 54.

12 Jus Feudale, 1. 8. 14. Craig did not directly use citation here; a later editor, however, not unreasonably cited D, 1. 3. 37–8 in regard to this passage.

13 25 Feb. 1680, *Morrison,* Dictionary, 13829.

14 D, 1. 3. 38.

15 C, 7. 45. 13.

to govern the decisions of the courts of justice."[16] John Erskine takes a similar approach though he reaches a different conclusion by distinguishing the antiquity of the line of decisions in question. For him older decisions may be cited as proof of custom, provided the custom is still maintained, and this had the force of law. More recent decisions, though entitled to "great weight" when uniform and consistent "for a reasonable time", were not law and lacked proper authority because they did not have that tacit consent of the people which gave custom its binding force. Given time, they might develop this. Thus he concluded that recent decisions:

> ... though they bind the parties litigating, create no obligation on the judges to follow in the same tract, if it shall appear to them contrary to law. It is, however, certain that they are frequently the occasion of establishing usages, which, after they have gathered force by a sufficient length of time, must, from the tacit consent of the state, make part of our unwritten law.[17]

Faced with conflicting evidence, the advocate Robert Bell, in his *Dictionary of Scots Law* (1815), took the view that:

> all that can safely be said seems to be, that, although those decisions are not to be held as equal in authority to our customary or unwritten law, yet they serve to explain the law, and to ascertain ancient usages; and a series of them, uniform upon the same point, is held to have the force of law, more especially where the practice or the conveyancing of the country has been regulated by such precedents.[18]

Scottish legal writers do not therefore present a consistent approach to the theory which underlay the role of judicial decisions in legal development. Some writers, themselves collectors of decisions, not unnaturally took a strong view of the value of such decisions although even they did not allow a single decision too much weight. All writers ascribed more value to a principle to be inferred from a tract of decisions than from a single decision, and this reflects the attitude among practitioners revealed in the eighteenth-century session papers.

The Preservation and Presentation of *Rationes*

Despite a reasonably lengthy pedigree, law reporting in Scotland was inadequate. In the preface to his *Commentaries on the Law of Scotland,* Professor George Joseph Bell, referring to the important principles of Roman law which advocates had traditionally used to discuss difficult questions of mercantile law, complained that skeletal reporting had robbed his generation of the benefit of the arguments constructed on the basis of these principles. As he put it:

---

16 *Bankton,* I, i, 74. *Cf. Mackenzie,* cited at note 10.

17 *Erskine,* I.i.47.

18 *R. Bell,* A Dictionary of Scots Law (Edinburgh, 1815), *sub nom.* "Decisions".

> ... those learned and able arguments, so often delivered by the judges on questions of general jurisprudence and of Mercantile Law, had for a long time been known only to those who heard them delivered, or to others by an obscure tradition; and what might have enlightened the law, and done honour to the judicial establishment of Scotland, had been lost in the imperfect reports made of adjudged cases.[19]

Bell was correct in suggesting that arguments were known only to those who heard them delivered or who heard of them through some "obscure tradition". Knowledge of such decisions was part of the common legal learning at the bar and it can be seen clearly in Thomas Craig's work, *Jus Feudale* (written c. 1600, printed in 1655), where cases are cited by name but usually with no other means of identifying them. But Craig used cases to illustrate points he was making; he expected contemporaries to know about the case, either through having witnessed it or through having been told about it, presumably during their training for the bar, or possibly having read a short digested report of it. The important cases were remembered in tradition found in Craig's generation and in every generation. Moreover, cases that were of practical importance were taken into account by practitioners almost as one of the tools of their trade. Even a case that was pending and, as yet, undecided, was worth mentioning. In 1585, for example, Thomas Craig included such reference in *Agnes Auchinleck v. George Boswell,* a case involving simulation (a species of fraud) where a liferentrix, and alleged tenant, allegedly assigned a lease of land to her son whilst retaining possession of the land.[20] According to Craig's argument that a proof should be led, no less than five practicks, one of which was still lying "unconcludit" before the court, were cited in favour of the proposition that "simulaciounis ar admitit to probatioun in ordinar fraudis".[21] To the allegation that some of the cases he cited were "invisible", he responded that "thay ar all visiball and in retentis in the clarkis handis befoir the saidis lordis with infinite utheris that salbe allegeit at the bar Albeit all can nocht be drawin furth for the infallabill practik hes evir bene observit that quhare simulatioun is allegeit aganis ane assignatioun the samyn is ay admittit to probatioun."[22]

---

19 Preface, x. Stair makes a similar point about transmission, though he uses it to comment on the inconsistencies resulting from the use of cases in a manuscript culture; see *infra.*

20 Stair said that circumstances of this kind were so common with liferenters that simulation was to be presumed: I.9.12. *Hope,* Major Practicks, does not mention anything beyond a reference to *Balfour,* Practicks. According to Balfour (Practicks, 170) a number of cases from the 1550s and 1560s demonstrated the rule that assignations of land were ineffective if the maker remained in possession of the land. The circumstances in *Auchinleck v. Boswell* were not quite straightforward, but none of these cases, all of which probably pre-dated Craig's attendance at the bar, were mentioned.

21 CS 7 / 101 fos 204r-v.

22 "They are all visible and *in retentis* in the clerk [sc. of court's] hands before the lords, with an infinite number of others that may be alleged at the bar, though they need not all be stated because the invariable *practick* has always been observed that where simulation is alleged against an assignation (*anglice* assignment), it is always admitted to proof."

A good practitioner acquired great benefit from keeping up to date with recent cases which raised potentially useful points of law, and maintaining familiarity with the practick of the court meant listening to the argument and trying to discern the reasoning which moved the court. Thomas Craig in his writings refers several times to cases which he had heard argued but in which he does not seem to have actively participated. Citation in oral debate of earlier decisions based purely on the memory of the pleader or the judge was already so common by 1585 that the court had to regulate it: "The lords ordaines that quhatsomever procurator proponed ane practique he should produce the same instantlie at the bar".[23]

In his major work, *Jus Feudale* (written c. 1600 but printed posthumously in 1655), Craig gives his opinion of the use of cases.

> However in regard to custom it must always be observed whether the custom was established at any time in a contested judgment; for a custom takes greater or lesser authority depending upon the frequency with which the matter has been judicially decided. Moreover the lack of attention, or negligence, or lack of skill or even the fraud of advocates will provide an opportunity for disputing custom, and one case that is carried on negligently will, as I have myself sometimes seen, prejudice subsequent cases. In written law and in custom it should be observed that where law, or express custom, is deficient, then we should go back to that law or custom which is nearest to it, especially if it is supported by the same reasoning (*ratio*). For anyone who has jurisdiction ought to make good any deficiency in native law or custom (*jus propium & consuetudo*), by bringing forth analogous cases, and [doing so] through their own jurisdiction or authority; particularly if this is consonant with reason and tends towards utility.[24]

Craig also refers to opinions expressed to him sometimes many years before.[25] The retention of such knowledge had practical application not only for Craig but for all advocates in every generation. After all, it was part of Stair's declared purpose in publishing his Reports to minimise the uncertainty that resort to memory invariably had through transmission by "uncertain Tradition from the memory of

---

23 *Thomas Hope,* Major Practicks, V.iv.69 [this is based on Act of Sederunt (i.e. a rule of court) of 10 Mar. 1585 (National Archives of Scotland, CS1 / 3 fo. 256)]. The sense is: "The lords ordain that any procurator whatever who presents a practique in argument should immediately produce written evidence of it at the bar."

24 Jus Feudale, 1. 8. 15: "In consuetudine tamen hoc semper observandum, si contradictorio aliquando judicio sit fermata: nam ex frequenta rerum eo modo judicatarum majorem aut minorem auctoritatem consuetude capit. Preaterea animadvertendum, ne vel negligentia, vel imperitia, aut fortasse dolus Advocatorum controvertentium occasionem consuetudini praebuerit, dum unam causam remissius agunt, ut majori praejudicetur, ut aliquando dactum vidi. In jure tamen scripto & consuetudine hoc observandum, ut sive jus, sive expressa consuetudini, sit recurrendum, praecipue si eadem ratione nitatur. Nam is qui jurisdictioni praeest, si jus proprium & consuetudo defecerint, ad similia producere, & vel jurisdicitione, vel auctoritate, supplere debet; praecipue si ad eandem utilitatem tendat, eademque concomitetur ratio." The translation is my own, the text is taken form the *editio tertia* of 1732 edited by James Baillie and published by Thomas Ruddiman in Edinburgh.

25 *J. Finlay,* "The early career of Thomas Craig, advocate" (2004) in Edinburgh Law Review.

Judges or Advocats, where a constant Custom was not introduced; but in circumstantiat Cases, all the points of Fact, could not be so preserved, but Pleaders would differ about them".[26]

But as Bell makes clear, neither Stair, nor his eighteenth-century successors, managed to achieve this purpose and Mackenze's wish in his oration at the opening of the Advocates' library, to see "the arguments and *rationes decidendi* set out at length, the reporters thus assuming the function now of advocate, now of judge", long remained unfulfilled.[27] Even in Bell's day, appeal to memory was still made in the courts. In 1824 Lord President Hope, in a case concerning the ranking of securities, made reference to a decision by Lord Braxfield (d. 1799), a noted expert on commercial matters.[28] Hope, who as counsel had debated the case, which had never been reported, not only discussed it but accepted Braxfield's reasoning and made it the basis of his own opinion in the case before him.

In Hope's day, as a requirement of the Act of Union, judges had to have practised as advocates; but that is the only essential difference from the same phenomenon witnessed in Craig's day more than two centuries before. The lack of adequate reporting at both junctures had precisely the potential disadvantages for future generations to which Bell adverted.

Reliance on memory led to the need for an aide-memoire and some of the early *practick* literature and manuscript digests of decisions may be seen as written in part to fulfil this purpose even though they ultimately enjoyed wide dissemination. The 1585 requirement that written practicks be produced at the bar suggests that the retrieval of such information was a reasonable possibility. But there was a severe limitation: judicial reasoning was not recorded. The records made by the clerks of court, principally the *acta* and the minute books of the Lords of Council and Session (the formal title of the judges in the Court of Session), form a procedural record which very rarely mentions legal argument and which was not ordinarily accessible to practitioners. Even if it had been accessible, sight of an old court process was of limited value. As William Forbes said in the preface to his *Journal of the Session:*

> I have followed the Faith only of my own Eyes and Ears, which contains much more relating to Cases therein determined, than can be learned from any Record, *viz.* Arguments and Reasoning of the Judges, that had escaped the Observation of the Lawyers; with their Resolutions and Judgments in Cases not a few, upon verbal Reports whereof nothing did enter into Record.[29]

---

26 *Sir James Dalrymple / Viscount Stair,* The Decisions of the Lords of Council & Session, (Edinburgh, 1683), Epistle Dedicatory.

27 *Mackenzie,* Oratio Inauguralis, March 1689.

28 *Rowland v. Campbells* (1824 – 1825) 3 S 134. In another case from the same year, *Gordon v. Cheyne* (1824 – 1825) 3 S 566, an extract from the Lord President's notebook was laid before the court containing a note of an earlier case, that of Maccombie, which the Lord Ordinary at first instance had made the basis of his interlocutor.

As well as the digest practicks, manuscripts of which appear to have been copied out by generations of aspiring advocates, there survive short digests of cases and it is known that other digests, some quite lengthy, once existed. In the sixteenth century Balfour cites in his *Practicks* cases by reference to a register of cases, which is now lost; in the eighteenth century, Lord Hermand made a dictionary of decisions from consistorial cases dating between 1664 and 1777 which he had drawn from an "Abridgement" which no longer survives.[30] The Advocates' Library and the National Archives have, in manuscript, collections of decisions some (but by no means all) of which have appeared in later printed collections, primarily Morison's *Dictionary of Decisions* (1811). Morison's *Dictionary,* which conveniently sets out under alphabetical headings by subject a large number of cases from all printed and most manuscript collections up to its date of publication, allows the easy comparison of earlier sets of reports particularly where the same case is reported in different collections. Such comparison demonstrates the unevenness of style and inconsistency of detail in these reports.

Morison's declared purpose in compiling his *Dictionary* was to remedy problems caused by the inaccessibility of early reports such as those by Lord Durie and Stair which by the early eighteenth century were "not likely to be soon reprinted; therefore must daily become scarcer and more expensive".[31] Of course Morison, no less than Stair in the advertisement to his Decisions or Forbes in the preface to his *Journal,* had a particular view of the importance of publishing judicial decisions and his comments must be read accordingly.

The Importance of *Rationes* in Legal Practice

The Court of Session invites obvious parallels with other European central courts, not only in terms of its early history and the chronology by which its basic procedural rules were developed and then confirmed under authority of an act of parliament, but also in the spirit and operation of those rules, drawn as they largely were from the Romano-canonical tradition. Like many continental courts, its decision-making process, at least between the later sixteenth century and the later seventeenth century, was not open to public scrutiny. After the Revolution and the

---

29 *Forbes,* Journal of the Session (1714), preface. *Cf. Henry Home, Lord Kames,* in the preface to his Remarkable Decisions of the Court of Session from the year 1730 to the year 1752 (Edinburgh, 1766) [henceforth *Kames,* Remarkable Decisions 1730–1752]: "And as to the arguments, which were borrowed from the bench not less frequently than from the bar, every reader will judge for himself whether they be properly adapted to the facts stated".

30 *W. M. Gordon,* 'Balfour's *Registrum*' in H. L. MacQueen, ed., Miscellany Four (Stair Society, 2002), pp. 127–38; *F. P. Walton,* ed., Lord Hermand's Consistorial Decisions 1684–1777 (Stair Society, 1940), p. xv.

31 *W. M. Morison,* The Decisions of the Court of Session from Its Institutions until the separation of the Court into two Divisions in the Year 1808, Digested under Proper Heads, In the Form of a Dictionary (Edinburgh, 1811), I, Advertisment.

Claim of Right (1689), an act of sederunt (*anglice* rule of court) in 1693 made it normal for the court to advise (i.e. to deliberate) and vote in public, although this process might still take place privately for cause shown in appropriate cases.

It is clear from notations by judges on their copies of pleadings that preliminary discussion of cases by the whole court was carried on by each judge in order, ending with the lord president and the lord ordinary who reported the case to his colleagues.[32] These preliminary views were then followed by open discussion, and summing up by the lord president followed by a vote. Advocates, in subsequent reclaiming petitions, regularly justify bringing further procedure by making much of the fact that the discussion was closely balanced and that the vote was a narrow one.[33] Not only was the process of advising by the judges conducted publicly, it evidently had an audience eager to hear which arguments had proved persuasive.[34] Moreover, it meant that the interlocutor drafted by the clerk of court could be challenged if it failed to reflect accurately the tenor of the judges' decisions.[35] In practical terms, the openness of proceedings required that judges explain their decision to vote in a particular way by reference to legal rules.

There was a clear recognition that some degree of reasoning be presented by the court in support of an interlocutor. The word "precedent" was used in a very specific sense to denote, not a reasoned judgement, but a judicially-determined outcome. The relevant feature was not the reasoning, it was the outcome as expressed in the interlocutor (and sometimes cumulatively in a series of interlocutors). The outcome was clearly the product of a process of reasoning leading to a majority vote on the bench, but normally that process had to be reconstructed because actual reasoning of the judges did not have to appear within the text of the interlo-

32 The Arniston collection in the Advocates' Library contains several glosses which record some of the discussion which took place during advising, but it is difficult to be sure the extent to which these glosses reflect the whole discussion.

33 E.g. The Petition of The Magistrates and Town-council of the Burgh of Paisley, and of Robert Fulton, Baillie and Delegate for the said Burgh, ALSP, (1760) Arniston Collection, vol. 50, pp. 1–2: "As your Lordships were much divided in your Opinion upon this Question, and the last Interlocutor was carried by the narrowest Majority, the Petitioners, as Administrators of this Burgh, think it their Duty, once more, to submit the Case to your Lordships Review ...".

34 The Petition of the Moderator and General Kirk-Session of Glasgow, and Matthew Bogle Clerk to the said Session, ALSP, (1756) Arniston Collection, vol. 41: "... as the last Decision of the Court was upon a Division of six to five, and as the second Topic in the Cause seemed to have much Influence on the Judgments of some of your Lordships, the Petitioners hope they will be excused, if they state, in this Petition, with Precision, those Things, which, in point of Fact, regard that second Branch of the Cause ..."

35 E.g. The Petition of Patrick Heron younger of Heron, ALSP, (1760) Arniston Collection, vol. 47, p. 3: "But the Interlocutor, as wrote out, by Mistake, is rather adapted to the Plan of the Lord Ordinary's Interlocutor, though in fewer Words, notwithstanding the Court were of Opinion it could not be adhered to in these Particulars. For nothing dropped from the Bench pointing at what is mentioned in the Interlocutor ..." The phrase "dropped from the Bench" is particularly expressive.

cutor, and generally it did not. This could lead to some difficulty for later interpreters of the court's decision. If fortunate, it would be possible to read from an interlocutor, or reconstruct from a series of interlocutors, the reasoning which underpinned the disposal of the case, though such reasoning was often more likely to emanate from the lord ordinary in the Outer House than collectively from the judges of the Inner House.[36] Where the case was recent, the *ratio* might be drawn from the reasoning expressed by the judges as they advised prior to voting, provided the party putting his interpretation on the discussion was of course present to hear it or had had it reliably relayed to him.[37] Moreover, the pleader in such a case, in stating what he "apprehended" the judges *rationes decidendi* to be, was clearly interpreting the court's reasoning in the manner that best suited his client's case and might construct them in such a way as to invite their instant retraction.[38] Judges, whether voting with the majority or the minority, were not regarded as bound by their vote and were free to change their mind.[39]

It was even easier for an advocate to define a *ratio* in regard to an old case and leave it to an opposing counsel to attempt to develop an alternative *ratio*.[40] Advocates certainly saw themselves as having a major input into the court's reasoning process, with the quality of pleading being regarded, ultimately, as affecting the juristic quality of the *ratio* itself.[41] This was one reason why the procurators of the Scottish Admiralty court saw clearly that admitting too many numbers to their

---

36 E.g. Answers for John Lumisden, late in Langley, now in Keith, Suspender, and Raiser of the Reduction to the Petition of John Gordon of Craig, Advocate in Aberdeen, Charger, ALSP, (1758) Arniston Collection, vol. 47, p. 7: "The Respondent hopes he will be forgiven for having stated these several Particulars to your Lordships, as introductory to the Answers to the Petition; which he apprehends may be extremely short, in respect the Lord Ordinary has, by the several Interlocutors of which the Petitioner complains, so particularly stated the *ratio decidendi*, that it is hardly believed the Petitioner or his Counsel, have any Hopes to prevail against them."

37 E.g. The Petition of Mr Charles MacDoual of Chrichen, Advocate, ALSP, (1741), Kilkerran Collection, vol. 7, no. 19, p. 1: "The *ratio decidendi*, so far as it occurs to your Petitioner, from the Reasoning among your Lordships, upon advising these Petitions and Answers, tho' not express in the Interlocutor, was ...".

38 The Petition of Robert Cockburn, Staymaker in Canongate, ALSP, (1741) Elchies Papers, vol. 14, p. 1.

39 Dirleton's Doubts and Questions in the Law of Scotland, Resolved and Answered by Sir James Steuart of Goodtrees (Edinburgh, 1715), 17; see also *Erskine*, cited at n. 17 above.

40 Thus, for example, in the Answers for the younger Children of the deceased Robert Scott Merchant in Glasgow to the Petition of John Watson of Muirhouse, and other creditors of Andrew Scott his Son, ALSP, (1759) Arniston Collection, vol. 50, counsel opposed the view which Mackenzie adopted to the case of *Creditors of Tarpersie contra the Laird of Kinfawns* (1673), and which had been cited in the petition, the view of Stair in his report of the case to draft a different *ratio*, allowing him to conclude that "It is apparent this Decision has no Connection with the present Case."

41 An indication that they were right to do so may be gleaned from jottings which (presumably) Lord Arniston made on memorials preserved in his collection, indicating the points made by counsel to which particular weight was to be given.

ranks, and reducing the quality of pleading, might directly produce ill consequences for the judge in their court.[42] But even advocates sometimes simply had to admit defeat since the pleadings might serve to obfuscate rather than enlighten and the standard form of interlocutor provided no help in deciphering the meaning of the court.[43]

The reasoning revealed in the surviving papers, therefore, is largely the ingenious reasoning of advocates, not judges; it does not tell us how cases were decided, but how the decisions in decided cases could be interpreted in a way consonant with particular principles contended for in later cases. In short, advocates were often interested less in the reasoning that an earlier case might bring to their argument, than in what argument they themselves might bring to earlier cases particularly when the earlier case was susceptible to interpretation.[44] Proof of this is easy to find in the session papers. Not only did earlier cases often not provide a clear *ratio,* the case itself might be mentioned in court with no citation whatsoever. Provision of the merest outline of the facts, however, was sometimes enough to elicit a response from the opposing party even where that party had no opportunity to find a report of the case.[45] It was the quality of argument put forward, rather than the bare authority of a decided case, or even a series of decided cases, that persuaded the judges.

---

42 Their (clearly not unbiased) view, was that more procurators fighting for the limited business ultimately meant less specialisation and would mean "every decision will be carried to review, and the court of session will disregard the opinion of his Lordship [i.e. the Admiralty judge] when they begin to suspect that his judgements are pronounced upon partial & inaccurate pleadings drawn up by men who pay no attention to their business & cannot even afford to pay attention to it from the scanty profit it affords them ...": National Archives of Scotland [NAS], Court book of Hodson Cay, judge admiral, AC 15/6/A, ff. 44–45, June, 1830.

43 E.g. Information for Robert Menzies, Writer in Edinburgh, ALSP, (1741) Elchies Papers, vol. 14, p. 19: "And, as to the Decision quoted for the Defender, the Pursuer must own, he cannot with certainty state either the Fact, or the *ratio decidendi* in that Case, after perusing two Petitions and Answers, reclaiming against and in support of the Interlocutor."

44 It may be as well here to quote the celebrated comment of James Boswell, the advocate and famous biographer: "When the Court were divided in opinion, they deliberated but very little; but when it happened that they were unanimous, they deliberated not at all", cited by *N. Phillipson,* The Scottish Whigs and the Reform of the Court of Session (Stair Society, 1990), p. 55.

45 E.g., Answers for James Young of Netherfield, and John Miller portioner of Hazledean, To the petition of Joseph Allan, ALSP, (1757) Arniston Collection, p. 19: "The Respondents do not find that Case marked in any Collection of Decisions: But taking it as the Petitioner states it, it admits of an easy Answer ..."; Memorial for James Brewhouse Tacksman of the Mills of Kelso, Pursuer, Against David Robertson Merchant and Brewer in Kelso, Defender, ALSP, (1741) Kilkerran Collection, vol. 7, no. 84, p. 8: "The Pursuer has had no Access neither [sic] to see the Decreet nor the MS. Collection; and therefore he cannot give full Credit to a Decision that appears to be single, and where no Reason is mentioned for this new Decision; but he must submit it to your Lordships, how far this single Decision is sufficient to establish a Point of Law of so universal Influence".

This can be put another way. How constrained did judges feel to follow a precedent or series of precedents? Certainly they had to follow statutes, for statutes were the supreme source of legal rules. But statutes had to be interpreted, and they also had to remain in force (traditionally acts of the pre-union Scottish parliament, the very acts most commonly cited to the court in the eighteenth century, might fall into desuetude if their rationale ceased to have effect through the passage of time). Consequently even statutes did not necessarily impose an extreme limit to judicial manoeuvrability. In dealing with statutes or cases, much was made of reason, rationality, and underlying principle.[46] The authority of opinions by respected legal writers, and the authority of decided cases, was subordinate to the reason regarded as justifying the opinion or case. This is clear from an argument presented in a case in 1741:

> And as to the Authority of my Lord Stair, the Pursuer has all due Deference to his Opinions; but then when his Opinion differs from that of our more ancient Lawyers, from *Craig* and *Spotiswood,* and when he supports his Opinion neither by any Reason, nor by any Precedents, the Pursuer will be forgiven to object to his Authority, and to consider such Opinions as Inaccuracies, that cannot be avoided in so long a Treatise; and this in a particular Manner applies to the present Case... And the same Answer will serve to the Authority of Sir *George Mackenzie,* with this Addition, that in this, as well as in many other Instances, Sir *George* servilely copies from my Lord *Stair.*[47]

This reflects the expectation that the court was to determine cases *legibus quam exemplis.* Whether the decision was justified in principle was usually the central issue rather than adherence to authority.[48] In one of his printed reports, Lord Kilkerran summed up the majority view (7 to 5) of the judges, who were "very sanguine against" the idea that a wife should give evidence against her husband in a civil case, stating that "abstracting from precedents, the rules of humanity were by the plurality thought to justify the judgment given, which prevents the endangering the peace of families".[49] Consistency of principle was seen as desirable, rather

46 Answers for Sir James Fergusson of Kilkerran, one of Senators of the College of Justice to the Petition of Alexander Coupar in Bayne, ALSP, (1737) Kilkerran Collection, vol. 1, no. 121, p. 3: "Many other Decisions have been given upon the same Principle, 28th November 2628 [sic for 1628], *Borthwick contra Clark;* 3d December 1664, *Clarkenton contra Corsbie:* But as the Principle itself is so strongly founded in Reason that it does not need any further Confirmation, it is unnecessary to enlarge upon particular Case ..."; see also *A. Stewart,* "The session papers in the Advocates Library" in *H. L. MacQueen,* ed., Miscellany Four (Stair Society, 2002), p. 206, n.

47 Memorial for James Brewhouse Tacksman of the Mills of Kelso, Pursuer, against David Robertson Merchant and Brewer in Kelso, Defender, ALSP, (1741) Kilkerran Collection, vol. 7, no. 84, p. 7.

48 A twentieth century commentator, writing in 1952, could still detect this attitude in contemporary Scottish case law: *T. B. Smith,* Judicial Precedent in Scots Law (Edinburgh, 1952), pp. 14, 83.

49 *Campbel contra Crawfurd,* Jan. 31. 1744, Decisions of the Court of Session from the year 1738 to the year 1752, Collected and Digested in the Form of a Dictionary, by Sir James

than precise congruence of factual circumstances.[50] Lord Kames, in his *Remarkable Decisions,* indicated that cases were not selected for print publication without "being resolvable into some principle, [which] may serve as a rule for cases of the same kind."[51]

In another case it was argued that while it was just to pay some regard to "a Chain of Decisions", the court was not bound *"ex necessitate* to judge according to former Precedents" and it was worth pointing out "that our Law not only consists of Statute, but of known Customs, *Quod de praxi quotidiana obtinet:* More especially when the very Nature of the Thing demonstrates the Justice of the Decision".[52]

The following memorial, drafted by George Joseph Bell when still a practising advocate, touches on these issues and is worth quoting:

> ... your Lordships, although you respect the opinions of your predecessors, owe them no *obedience,* unless they have been embodied into a decision which has or may have influenced the country. There is no such thing as *authority* in reason. Your Lordships care nothing for the private opinion of the most eminent lawyer that ever studied, further than as it is accompanied by reasons which have weight upon your own minds, or as implying, from your knowledge of his method of investigation, a deduction which, although the steps of it do not appear, you are convinced must be found.[53]

Bell went on to suggest that it was not improper for the court in the context of the case, which concerned another stage in the lengthy and litigious history of the literary property debate between Scotland and England, to consider how the House of Lords might treat the question.[54] The commercial confidence to be drawn from "uniformity of decision", he argued, was desirable, and the fact that the House of Lords would certainly be influenced by English precedents should encourage the Court of Session to "anticipate the principles of decision, which would influence the court of last resort, sitting as a court for the whole kingdom, in interpreting a British statute." Such an argument, while interesting, should not

---

Fergusson of Kilkerran, Baronet, One of the Senators of the College of Justice (Edinburgh, 1775), p. 597.

50 E.g., Answers for Mrs Helen Marshall Relict of the deceased Mr Alexander Farquharson Writer to the Signet, to the Petition of George Ross Writer in Edinburgh, ALSP, (1738) Kilkerran Collection, vol. 3, no. 80, p. 2: "A Difference in a Circumstance does not hinder a Decision to be a good Precedent, if the Principle established by the Decision is precisely the same with that pled in the present Case".

51 *Kames,* Remarkable Decisions 1730–1752, preface.

52 Answers for William Christie Cordiner in Glasgow to the Petition of Thomas Dunsmuir Merchant in Glasgow, and Robert Finlay Tanner there, ALSP, (1745) Elchies Papers, p. 3.

53 Information for Mess. Cadell and Davies, Booksellers in London, Thomas Manners, Writer to the Signet, their Mandatory, and William Creech, Bookseller in Edinburgh; against James Robertson, Printer in Edinburgh, ALSP, (1803) Blair Collection, vol. 65, p. 24.

54 The history of this litigation has attracted considerable literature; see recently *M. Rose,* Authors and Owners: The Invention of Copyright (Harvard, 1993).

be too readily accepted as indicative of any judicial attitude at the time or subsequently.[55]

Despite increasing reference to English practice, particularly in commercial cases, *stare decisis* did not take root in Scotland.[56] In particular, the idea that a single decision could bind any court was alien. If a reasonable argument, based on a single precedent, was put forward and had to be countered, the typical response was to attack the very singularity of the precedent case. The mere fact that it stood alone made it weak, if not suspect.[57] The attack would typically be buttressed by an appeal to sound legal principle.[58] At the same time, it was recognised that even a single precedent could be dangerous because it was not to be overturned lightly.[59] William Forbes alleged that the court's reluctance to overturn earlier decisions had been increased by the practice of printing decisions.[60] A single decision could not by itself overturn the authority of a series of prior similar decisions, but it might be the foundation of a future change in direction.[61] An example of this

---

55 Cf. the, perhaps more indicative, rebuke to counsel by Lord President Hope, following a "sweeping attempt to call upon us to make a general and unreasoning surrender to English cases, pressed upon us in a way which I am sure no Judge in the House of Lords would sanction," in *McCowan v. Wright* (1852–53) SC 229 at p. 232.

56 On the resort to "eminent English council", see *A. D. M. Forte,* "Opinions by 'Eminent English Counsel': their use in insurance cases before the Court of Session in the late eighteenth and early nineteenth centuries" (1995) Juridical Review, p. 345.

57 E.g. The Petition of The Creditors of the deceas'd William Baillie of Littlegil, ALSP, (1747) Elchies Papers, vol. 14, p. 11: "No instance appears to the contrary, but the Case 1711; which seems to be inaccurately observed; and cannot of itself overturn a whole Series of Decisions that occur on the other Side."

58 E.g. The petition of the Creditors of Sir William Gordon of Park, ALSP, (1760) Arniston Collection, vol. 48, p. 15: "The Case of *Buchan* is but a single Decision, which your Lordships never consider as sufficient to establish any Point"; Answers for the Creditors of Cairns of Garrioch, ALSP, (1742) Elchies Papers, vol. 14: "The other Decision, *Livingston contra Menzies,* is, no doubt, an Authority to the Case in Hand: But then it is evidently an erroneous Decision, and is against Principles. The Decision is single, and has never been followed; and your Lordships, in your later Practice, have been in Use of determining very differently, and according to the solid Principles of Law."

59 E.g., The Petition of Robert Cockburn, Staymaker in Canongate, ALSP, (1741) Elchies Papers, vol. 14, p. 2: "As for the formal Decision of *Scougal,* in the like Case, the Petitioner must admit, that it is parallel; but it is a single Decision, and, as he humbly conceives, a very dangerous one."

60 *Forbes,* Journal of the Session, preface: "[Judges] have always approved themselves very tender to alter printed Decisions; especially in determining Cases happening after such Precedents were published, upon the Faith wherof the Lieges might have probably transacted their Rights, or contracted, and settled their Interests"; cf. The Petition of James Jack, son to the deceast Alexander Jack in Glamis, ALSP, (1740) Elchies Papers, vol. 14 F-Y, p. 3: "Your Lordships have always been tender of overturning what has been settled in our Law, even by a single Decision, especially when it is supported by the concurrent Opinion of our Lawyers ...".

61 E.g. The Petition of Margaret and Agnes Ogilvies, Daughters to the deceast Robert Ogilvy of Coul, and Margaret Garden his Relict, ALSP, (1735) Kilkerran Collection, vol. 3,

process being recognised can be seen in an opinion dating from 1736, probably written by Lord Kilkerran. The opinion related to what in modern Scots property law is often referred to as "the off-side goals rule".[62] This principle applies where party A, infeft in land, grants a disposition of that land to B and (fraudulently) a second disposition of the same land to C. C is preferred to B provided he completes his real right first and does so in good faith (that, is, in ignorance of B's purely personal right under the disposition). Simply put, A is not denuded of his right in the property, and remains its owner, until C acquires the *jus in rem;* B, having not taken his opportunity to acquire a real right, has merely a contractual remedy against A. Kilkerran, in a critical re-examination which argued strongly in favour of this principle, denounced a supposed rule that had entered the law by which A, merely by granting his disposition, was thereby denuded of all right in the land.

> ... It comes out then that the first Decision upon this head which was no earlier than the [*sc.* year] 1710, was founded upon an absolute mistake. And the later Decisions have gone upon the authority of this Precedent without much opposition or investigation of the dreadfull [sic] consequences of such a Principle. At the same time, it must appear of great weight that from the first traces we have of our Law, down to the [*sc.* year] 1710 we can find no support to this Doctrine from any sort of Precedent or Authority. On the Contrary as Cases that fell to be regulated by this Principle must have been frequent, that no man has been found putting in his claim upon it, is a strong Demonstration of the opinion our Judges and Lawiers had of it at all Times.

Thus it was argued that the court had subsequently been wrong to follow the case of *Rule v. Purdie* (1710) which had been poorly decided. This case is instructive because it demonstrates not only how central reasoning was to notions of authority, but also how relatively easy it was for practice to change and change again.

Despite John Erskine's argument about the age of a series of cases enhancing their authority through the implied tacit consent of the people, the age of a precedent or series of precedents was not always seen that way in practice. An old case might be inaccessible or impossible to find, in which event it might be answered on general principles or simply ignored;[63] or, if the case was found, it might be inadequately reported. Indeed the record of a case cited as a precedent might con-

---

p. 4: "... where a Rule in Law has been established immemorially by the Opinion of our Lawyers; and an uniform Tract of repeated Decisions, it would require somewhat more than a single decision to infer an Alteration of our Law."

62 This terminology follows from the comments of Lord Justice Clerk Thomson in the leading modern case of *Rodger Builders, Ltd. v. Fawdry* 1954 SC.

63 "As to the Decision of the Court of Session mentioned; as the Pursuer has not thought fit to give us the particular Case, and the Decision is not mentioned in any of the printed Collections, it can have no particular Answer ... "; cf. Answers for James Young of Netherfield, and John Miller portioner of Hazledean, to the petition of Joseph Allan, ALSP, Arniston Collection, 1757, p. 19: "The Respondents do not find that Case marked in any Collection of Decisions: But taking it as the Petitioner states it, it admits of an easy Answer ...".

sist solely of the surviving process and this would often be in a state that did not reveal the final *ratio decidendi.*[64] Even as law reporting developed in the eighteenth century, and the Faculty of Advocates spread the work amongst several of its members, the reporters acknowledged in the advertisement to the first edition of the Faculty Collection in 1756 that the printed papers were lodged in the Advocates' library; they did not presume that their reports were capable of standing alone.[65] Practitioners still from time to time had to go behind the published report and consult the session papers.[66] To advocates the collection of Session Papers was a practical necessity; they constituted the main contemporary reservoir of legal argument containing precedents and reasoning upon which practitioners could, and often did, readily found.[67] Reports were of limited availability and of limited use as sources of legal argument; the session papers were not afflicted with either problem, although there was much chaff to wade through and, even in cases found relevant, teasing out the *ratio decidendi* from arguments presented by counsel was not easy. As Lord Kames somewhat wearily put it, in the context of selecting cases for publication, "To pester the world with circumstantiate cases that admit not any precise or single *ratio decidendi,* is a heavy tax."[68]

Despite difficulties, there were sometimes positive reasons in favour of the citation of older cases, even where the case did not establish a rule that was followed subsequently in a clear series of decisions, because the principle behind the decision appeared to have been enunciated in a particular way.[69] Having said that, recent cases had the advantage (or, perhaps, the challenge) of judges who might have had direct familiarity with them, although it is a peculiarity of eighteenth-century pleading that counsel tended to refer to earlier decisions, even ones centuries old, as though they had been decided by the same set of judges presently being addressed in argument.

---

64 See note 27 above.

65 Decisions of the Court of Session from the beginning of February 1752, to the end of the year 1756 (2[ed]., Edinburgh, 1787), Advertisement. Their aim, "to state with precision, the facts necessary to be known, the principal arguments used by each party, and the final judgment of the court", was only imperfectly carried out.

66 E.g., Robert Dundas of Arniston is quoted directly from the papers of an earlier case in The Petition of Mrs Rebecca Hog, spouse of Thomas Lashley, Esq.; and of the said Thomas Lashley, for his Interest, ALSP (1792), Abercromby Collection, vol. 15, p. 14, where the drafter of the petition goes on to say: "Numberless passages to the same effect might be quoted from the papers in that case now deposited in the Advocates Library ...".

67 *Stewart,* "The session papers in the Advocates Library", pp. 205–206; see also, in the same volume, *K. Campbell,* "The Session Papers in four early cases of damages for personal injuries", ibid., pp. 225–232.

68 *Kames,* Remarkable Decisions 1730–1752, preface.

69 E.g., Answers for Marion Wilson &c. to the Petition of John Smith, &c., ALSP, (1791), Abercomby Collection, vol. 15, p. 6: "This case [sc. *Hathorn v. Gordon,* 1696] is reported by Lord Fountainhall, and is not the less worthy of attention that it is an old decision, and pronounced at a time when the principles of the feudal law were more strictly interpreted, and more rigidly adhered to, than is agreeable to the genius of modern times."

Precedent and Natural Law

Pleadings indicate that appeal to natural law was made with great regularity, often articulated in terms of right reason, equity, and Roman law. An argument based on the law of nature could be constructed in the most unpromising circumstances, reflecting the potential for application of natural law to a case supported by little or no positive law. An example is the case of William Gordon, whose neighbour built an outhouse some two feet from his kitchen window. The Lord Ordinary took the view that an outhouse was not, and could not be, a nuisance; indeed the law regarded outhouses as a positive benefit by removing from public exposure matter that might otherwise have been a nuisance. Gordon's advocate, therefore, had to develop an alternative argument. He did so using the language of natural law reinforced by rules drawn from Roman law:

> [B]y the Laws of Nature, the putting a Necessary-house upon some particular Spots, may be a Nusance [sic]. One of the most respectable of the ancient Philosophers, arguing upon the Topick of the animal Oeconomy, takes Notice, that Nature has put behind Backs, those parts of the human Body, which may be offensive to the Senses...
>
> In Imitation therefore of this Law of Nature, Necessary-houses are not planted by our Doors or Windows, or Firesides, but are generally placed in some secret Place, and at a distance from Sight and Smell, to both which Senses their Contents are equally offensive. The Suspender relies upon this Maxim, that *dominus potest facere quodlibet in suo;*[70] but the Answer in point of Law will readily occur, that this Maxim is not without Limitation, for a Proprietor cannot do every thing upon his own Ground, he cannot do those things that are *in aemulationem vicini,* or against publik Decorum, and which may be otherwise done with equal Advantage to himself. As for Instance, it is a Case put in the Civil Law, that a Person cannot hew Stones or Wood near the March,[71] lest Splinters and Dust should fly over the March, and fall upon his Neighbour's Area. But is not this a much stronger Case? Can Splinters or Dust be said to be half so offensive as the Sight and Smell of a Little-house? Or can I be said to have the free Use and Exercise of my House, when I frequently cannot come near my Window without holding my Nose or shutting my Eyes?[72]

Advocates sometimes equated Roman law, "as the great Fountain of Principles of Justice and Equity", with natural law.[73] But ultimately the law of reason provided an independent and superior source of law which, though it might draw confirmation from the views of civilian writers, did not need their authority.[74] So fun-

70 An owner may do as he pleases in regard to his own property.

71 March, i.e. a border, a line of division between neighbouring properties.

72 The Petition of William Gordon of Campbelton, Charger against James Clerk, Surgeon in Kirkcudbright, Suspender, ALSP, Arniston Collection (1758) vol. 47, p. 7.

73 Answers for Alexander Grant writer in Edinburgh, ALSP, Arniston Collection, (1756) vol. 41.

74 E.g. "This, in a pretty parallel Case, is the Authority of an eminent Civilian; tho' without such Authority it would have been as indubitably true, as that the Law of Reason is paramount to the Law of Property." Cf. Robert Dundas, "But 'tis hoped Authorities are unneces-

damental was natural law argument to Scots advocates that their pleadings do much to suggest it simply by the form of language adopted. There are many examples of a particular interpretation of the facts being said to lead obviously and directly, using a favoured phrase "from the nature of the thing", to a desired conclusion. The flexibility of natural law complemented the ingenuity of the pleaders providing examples, in the phrase of Lord Kames, of reasoning "free from the shackles of authority".[75]

---

sary, where the Reason is so strong", cited by *I. S. Ross,* Lord Kames and the Scotland of his Day (Oxford, 1972), p. 38.

[75] *Henry Home, Lord Kames,* Elucidations Respecting the Common and Statute Law of Scotland (1777), p. xiii

JAMES OLDHAM

Lord Mansfield, *Stare Decisis*, and the *Ratio Decidendi* 1756 to 1788

Despite his Scottish heritage and family ties to the Stuart pretenders, Attorney General William Murray in 1756 became William Lord Mansfield and assumed office as Chief Justice of England's dominant common law court, the Court of King's Bench. Mansfield is the man of whom Dr. Johnson remarked, "Much can be made of a Scot, if caught young." Mansfield served actively and influentially as Chief Justice for over thirty years, and his achievements are well-known. The long shadow he cast across the centuries since his time was due to a potent combination of factors. He was extraordinarily able, classically educated, in office a very long time, and a successful man of business who understood the workings and needs of the mercantile world.

Upon what sources of law did Lord Mansfield depend, and by what was he restrained? The concept of the authoritative legal treatise had not emerged by the late eighteenth century.[1] William Blackstone's *Commentaries* were not much relied upon in judicial opinions until after Mansfield's time, and the earlier eighteenth century treatise, Thomas Wood's *Institutes*, was not much respected. Edward Coke's *Institutes* were quoted from frequently by judges, along with early works such as Bracton and Glanvill, but these were references of convenience, or in response to arguments of counsel. Although the works were referred to as "authorities," this was not with any idea of their being binding.

The horizontal structure of the English central courts, moreover, inhibited the growth of the notion of binding precedent. Each of the three common law courts (King's Bench, Common Pleas, and Exchequer), each with four judges, operated largely independently of the other two. Past authorities from the same court were taken seriously and could be sufficiently on point or could acquire sufficient cumulative weight to restrict a later court, though this was infrequent. Decisions from another court would be looked to only as advisory, or as a means of persuasion.

---

1 See generally, *A. W. B. Simpson*, The Rise and Fall of the Legal Treatise: Legal Principles and the Forms of Legal Literature, University of Chicago Law Review, vol. 48 (1981): pp. 632, 651, 662–663; *M. Lobban*, The English Legal Treatise and English Law in the Eighteenth Century, in S. Dauchy / J. Monballyu, & A. Wijffels, Juris Scripta Historica XIII: Auctoritates Xenia R. C. Van Caenegem Oblata (1997), pp. 69–88.

Nevertheless, by Mansfield's day precedent had become the principal source of law for the central court judges.[2] As I will illustrate, Mansfield ordinarily insisted that he be fully informed about past authorities and endorsed, in principle, the doctrine of stare decisis. At the same time, he responded to precedent in ways that would be expected of a strong-minded, able judge. There was considerable maneuvering room.

Stare Decisis

As hardly needs stating, stare decisis is a fundamental doctrine intended to foster certainty and stability in the common law. Once a procedure has been established or a substantive issue decided, the case in which that step was taken becomes a precedent that should be honored in subsequent cases involving the same procedure or issue. Applications of the doctrine could occur in several ways. First, and strongest, would be a decision by higher authority. For the Court of King's Bench, this would mean a decision by Exchequer Chamber or by the House of Lords. A second form could be a consensus of a majority of the common law judges by means other than a formal appeal, as was customary in criminal cases from the assizes on questions reserved by the assize judges.[3] Third, and most common, would be the pattern earlier noted, past decisions by the same court or by more than one court.

This gradation could be refined further, as was attempted by eighteenth-century barrister Francis Maseres in an obscure work published in 1776, *The Canadian Freeholder.* Maseres wrote mainly about the Quebec Act, but he inserted a criticism of Lord Mansfield's 1774 decision in *Campbell v. Hall*[4] dealing with the extension of English law to Grenada after the island was captured during war with France. Maseres's format was that of a dialogue between a Frenchman and an Englishman, and at one point the Frenchman asked whether, "by the rules observed by English courts of justice," a question decided by the same or other courts "ought to be considered as having been decided for ever."[5] The Englishman thought the

2 Holdsworth argued that the system of precedent was stronger by mid-century than was commonly believed, quoting Lord Hardwicke, among others. *W. S. Holdsworth,* A History of English Law, vol. 12 (1938), pp. 146–49.

3 For example in Rex v. Pedley, Caldecott 218 (1782), Lord Mansfield yielded against his inclination to the consensus of the other common law judges that it was not a felony for a tenant "for a year, a month, or a day, to set fire to a house of which he is in possession." Mansfield thought this rule "based on wretched reasoning," but he lamented that "the question has been submitted to the consideration of the judges, and nine of them (all who attended) were unanimous ... The legislature alone can now supply the remedy." Id. at 227. See generally *D. R. Bentley,* Select Cases from the Twelve Judges' Notebooks (1997), pp. 8 – 24.

4 1 Cowper 208, Lofft 655 (1774), 20 State Trials 239.

5 20 State Trials 349 (portions of Maseres's work were reprinted in State Trials after Campbell v. Hall).

inquiry "very proper", since there was "no express law, nor even constant usage, that ascertains, in all cases, the degree of deference which is to be paid by courts of justice to the former judicial decisions of the same or other courts of justice."[6] The Englishman then identified four classes of precedents. The first class, of course, was the decision by the highest authority, the House of Lords.[7] Second was a solemn determination of a point of law "by one of the great courts of Westminster-hall" that was acquiesced in by the loser, even though, very infrequently, this could be "overturned by subsequent determinations of the same or other courts."[8] Third was a solemn determination by one of the courts on multiple points of law, acquiesced in by the loser, and fourth was an unappealed split decision, part for plaintiff and part for defendant.[9]

In only a handful of cases during his thirty active years in office was Lord Mansfield reversed by higher authority. The best-known of these were *Pillans v. Van Mierop*,[10] *Millar v. Taylor*,[11] and *Perrin v. Blake*.[12] In all three cases, Mansfield and his junior judges took bold steps that would have shaken established principles – in *Pillans*, making the doctrine of consideration unessential for mercantile contracts; in *Millar*, affirming the continuation of authors' common law copyrights independent of the copyright Statute of Queen Anne[13]; and in *Perrin*, refusing to invoke the Rule in Shelly's Case where the testator's intent clearly called for another result. *Perrin* was reversed by direct appeal to the Exchequer Chamber, in an opinion by Mr. Justice Blackstone,[14] whereas *Pillans* and *Millar* each stood for a number of years until overruled by the House of Lords in different cases.[15]

Appeals to Exchequer Chamber or the House of Lords were uncommon. In the flow of cases in the Court of King's Bench, however, the search for and discussion of precedent was constant. Further, the term "precedent" was used both procedurally and substantively. When an unfamiliar procedure was attempted, the court

---

6 Id. at 350.

7 Maseres omitted the Exchequer Chamber.

8 Id. at 350–51.

9 According to Maseres, Campbell v. Hall fell into this fourth class. Id. at 352.

10 3 Burrow 1663 (1765).

11 4 Burrow 2303 (1769).

12 Perrin v. Blake was reported, in its various phases, at 1 W. Blackstone 672 and 4 Burrow 2579 (1770); *F. Hargrave*, Collectanea Juridica, vol. 1 (1791), p. 283; *F. Hargrave*, A Collection of Tracts Relative to the Law of England (1797), p. 487.

13 Statute of 8 Anne, c. 21 [c. 19 in some statute editions] (1709).

14 Astonishingly, Lord Campbell asserted that "Mr. Justice Blackstone's argument on this occasion was so inimitably exquisite, that his reputation as a lawyer depends upon it still more than upon his Commentaries". *J. Campbell*, The Lives of the Chief Justices of England, vol. 2 (1857), p. 433, note.

15 Pillans was overturned in Rann v. Hughes, 4 Brown P.C. 27, 7 Term Reports 350 (1778), and Millar was disposed of in Donaldson v. Becket, 2 Brown P.C. 129, 4 Burrow 2408 (1774).

would customarily ask, "do you have any precedent"? If none could be produced, the procedural ploy would likely be rejected. In *Rex v. Skinner,*[16] a justice of the peace had been indicted for declaring to a grand jury, "You have not done your duty, you have disobeyed my commands; you are a ... scandalous, corrupt, and perjured jury." In moving to quash, counsel for the defendant called the indictment of a sitting judge for words spoken in office "a very new and singular proceeding." Lord Mansfield remarked that the indictment "would be subversive of all ideas of a constitution." He proposed to quash the indictment if no precedent could be found, but stated, "I am willing, as neither Serjeant Davy nor Mr. Buller [counsel for the prosecution] find any precedent in the history of England, for an indictment of this kind, to give them time till next term to find any."[17]

Substantively, the stare decisis doctrine arose whenever the barristers or judges relied on prior decisions that they claimed were authoritative. The common law judges often said they believed in and adhered to the doctrine. In *Hanslap v. Cater,*[18] Chief Justice Matthew Hale followed precedents against his inclination, "for he said it was his rule, stare decisis." Nearly a century later, in the settlement case of *Rex v. Inhabitants of Underbarrow and Bradleyfield,*[19] Lord Mansfield stated, "For several reasons...we should not depart from the adjudged cases; but chiefly from the inconvenience of altering and overturning settled determinations. It is best, stare decisis." And in *Keiley v. Fowler,*[20] Mansfield's colleague, Sir Eardley Wilmot, Chief Justice of the Court of Common Pleas, adhered to prior decisions in giving a tortured interpretation to words in a will, "because 'stare decisis' is a first principle in the administration of justice, and this is not from any fear of bringing appeals or writs of error in particular cases ... but because these cases have furnished the light by which conveyancers have been directed in settling and transferring property from one man to another."[21]

There were, nonetheless, limits. Stare decisis was not adhered to slavishly, as Mansfield's predecessor, Sir Dudley Ryder, pointed out in *Rex v. Inhabitants of St. Botolph Bishopsgate.*[22] There the court held that a woman's settlement was not suspended during coverture by her marriage to a man who had no settlement in England, and on being presented with conflicting precedents, Ryder observed, "The maxim stare decisis is a good general maxim; but it is not always to be adhered to; and it must be allowed that the Court is as well warranted in the present case to depart from what was holden in the case of *Rex v. The Inhabitants of*

16 Lofft 54 (1772).

17 Id. at 55. For another example of a procedure refused in the absence of any precedent, see Rex v. Stratton, 1 Douglas 239 (1779).

18 1 Ventris 243 (1673).

19 2 Burrow Settlement Cases 545, 548 (1766).

20 Wilmot 298 (1768).

21 Id. at 312.

22 Sayer 198 (1755).

Norton, as the Court was, in that case, to depart from what had been holden in the four or five antecedent cases."[23]

If Lord Mansfield agreed with a principle established in prior cases that appeared to be applicable to the facts of the case before him, he might find it convenient to declare those cases controlling. If he disagreed, however, there were several ways around adverse precedents. Declarations in prior cases could be dismissed as "mere dicta." The accuracy of the printed report of a prior case could be questioned, which was an especially attractive method if a reporter was not well respected. And regardless of a reporter's reputation, it was frequently possible to produce a manuscript version of a prior case with content that varied from the printed report. Or close analysis of a report could almost always produce factual differences that would permit a prior case to be distinguished.

In the interesting case of *Rex v. Cowle*,[24] the Court of King's Bench had to decide whether the king's writs ran to the territory of Berwick, a borough that had belonged to Scotland but had metamorphosed in various stages into an English corporate entity. Mansfield and his court held that the writs did run – that even though Berwick "was to be deemed a dominion of the Crown, and no part of the realm of England, it may be under the control and superintendence of the King in this Court."[25] Yet, as Mansfield noted, "Two great authorities are indeed urged, in opposition to this; they are no less than those of Lord Chief Justice Coke and Lord Chief Justice Hale. Lord Coke, in *Calvin's case*, says 'that Berwick is no part of England, nor governed by the laws of England.' And Ld. Ch. Justice Hale follows him."[26] Lord Mansfield said that both Coke and Hale were clearly mistaken, as he demonstrated by bringing out details of Berwick's history. He also pointed out that, "In *Calvin's case*, there was no question concerning the constitution of Berwick" and "What was dropped about it in *Calvin's case*, was a mere obiter opinion, thrown out by way of argument and example. My Lord Coke was very fond of multiplying precedents and authorities; and, in order to illustrate his subject, was apt, besides such authorities as were strictly applicable, to cite other cases which were not applicable to the particular question under his judicial consideration."[27]

Another approach, as noted, was to discount a printed case report because the reporter was young, inexperienced, incompetent, or because the notes of cases had never been intended for publication. In a case decided during his first term on the bench,[28] Mansfield was urged to follow a decision by Chief Justice John Holt that was reported by Lord Raymond, to which Mansfield responded: "These Notes

23 Id. at 199–200.

24 2 Burrow 834 (1759).

25 Id. at 853–54.

26 Id. at 858.

27 Id.

28 Cooper v. Chitty, 1 Burrow 20 (1756).

were taken in 10 W.3. [1698] when Lord Raymond was young, as short Hints for his own Use: But they are too incorrect and inaccurate, to be relied on as Authorities."[29] Similarly, when puisne Justice Francis Buller remarked on a case in William Blackstone's reports, observing that subsequent to the phase of the case reported by Blackstone, the court had decided "quite the other way," Mansfield exclaimed, "What a terrible thing it is that such loose notes are published!"[30]

Even if the reporter's reputation was sound and his case reports were published as he intended, manuscript versions of printed cases constantly circulated, and if these were more detailed than what was in print, they could trump the printed versions. In *Chilton v. Cromwel,*[31] for example, a case in Strange's Reports was cited for the defendant, and Chief Justice Wilmot, after observing that it was the only case that clashed with other authorities, said that "he had looked into his own note of this case, taken by himself at the bar ... and that he, and the other gentlemen his contemporaries at the bar, used to confer and compare their notes together; and that therefore his note of the case was probably more accurate and full than Sir John Strange's report of it."[32]

The technique of studying an adverse precedent closely and discovering factual differences that permit the case to be distinguished from the case at bar is familiar to any law student. It is also a familiar recourse taken by judges, and Lord Mansfield was no exception. An example is *Hawkes v. Saunders,*[33] a case that seemingly should have been controlled by the House of Lords' decision in *Rann v. Hughes.*[34] The *Rann* case was the occasion when the Lords disapproved of Mansfield's sabotage of the doctrine of consideration in *Pillans v. Van Mierop.* The facts of *Rann* were simple; the defendant, administratrix of an estate, had acknowledged the testator's obligation to pay a specified sum to plaintiff, and defendant personally promised to pay the debt when requested. It turned out that the assets of the estate were insufficient to cover the debt, and plaintiff brought suit in assumpsit on defendant's personal promise. Chief Baron John Skynner, speaking for the House of Lords, said that "here no sufficient consideration occurs to support this demand against her in her personal capacity; for she derives no advantage or convenience from the promise here made."

Later, in *Hawkes v. Saunders,* the Court of King's Bench faced an almost identical situation. A testator had bequeathed a legacy of £50 to plaintiff, and the executrix, defendant, promised to pay it. Suit was brought on that personal promise, and

---

29 Id. at 36.

30 Rex v. Atkinson, "Copy (from Mr. Gurney's short hand Notes) of the proceedings on a motion for arresting the judgment in the Court of King's Bench April 29, 1784," Public Record Office, TS 11 / 927, fol. 11.

31 2 Wilson 13 (C.B. 1768).

32 Id. at 16 – 17.

33 1 Cowper 289 (1782).

34 4 Brown P.C. 27, 7 Term Reports 350 (1778).

in oft-quoted words, Lord Mansfield ruled that, "Where a man is under a moral obligation, which no court of law or equity can inforce, and promises, the honesty and rectitude of the thing is a consideration" – "as the promise is only to do what an honest man ought to do, the ties of conscience upon an upright mind are a sufficient consideration."[35] He added: "It is not like the case of *Rann* versus *Hughes;* for there, there were no assets, nor any averment of assets stated in the declaration. But in this case there was a full fund; and therefore she was bound in law, justice, and conscience, to pay the plaintiff his legacy."[36] This is a perfect example of what law teachers call "a distinction without a difference." What Mansfield wholly glossed over was the fact that the executrix in Hawkes was in exactly the same position as the administratrix in *Rann* – in both cases, as Chief Baron Skynner said in *Rann,* the personal promise brought no benefit to the promisor.

The truth is that Lord Mansfield was much more interested in establishing and applying sensible, fundamental principles than he was in adhering to past decisions. At times he "talked the talk" of stare decisis, but at other times, he was more candid. In *Jones v. Randall,*[37] for example, suit was brought on a wagering promise that a decree given in the Court of Chancery would be reversed in the House of Lords. Lord Mansfield said that there was no applicable positive law, nor was there any case in the books on point, and then observed: "The law would be a strange science if it rested solely upon cases: and if after so large an increase of commerce, arts and circumstances accruing, we must go to the time of Rich[ard] 1 to find a case, and see what is law. Precedent indeed may serve to fix principles, which for certainty's sake are not suffered to be shaken, whatever might be the weight of the principle, independent of precedent. But precedent, though it be evidence of law, is not law in itself, much less the whole of the law."[38]

There were, nevertheless, occasions when the weight of precedent would be too great to overcome, as is shown by the case of *Bishop of London v. Fytche.*[39] At issue there was the legality of what was called a "resignation bond," a penal bond given by a clerk appointed to a living in a rectory that the clerk would resign at any time at the request of his patron. Such penal bonds were open to many objections,[40] but as Lord Mansfield stated in the *Fytche* case, ever since the time of Elizabeth I and James I, "all the Courts of Westminster Hall have uniformly holden it to be a lawful bond, and to such a degree that in some of the last cases the

---

35 1 Cowper at 290.

36 Id. at 291.

37 1 Cowper 37, Lofft 383 (1774).

38 Lofft at 385.

39 1 Brown C.C. 96 (1781); 3 Douglas 142, 1 East 487 (1782); 2 Brown P.C. 211 (1783).

40 See, e.g., the enumeration by Lord Eldon in Lord Kircudbright v. Lady Kircudbright, 8 Vesey Jr. 51, 61 (1802). On penal bonds generally, see *A. W. B. Simpson,* The Penal Bond with Conditional Defeasance, Law Quarterly Review, vol. 82 (1966), p. 392.

Court would not even suffer the point to be argued."[41] Thus, he said, the court "was not permitted to go into the question," not even "if all the authorities be wrong."[42] Justice Buller added, according to East's report: "The rule stare decisis is one of the most sacred in the law: but if not adhered to in such a case as this, it would be very difficult to say that it ought to weigh in any."[43] Douglas's version of Buller's remarks was more succinct: "The decisions are uniform, and unless we support them, the rule of stare decisis must be blotted out of the books."[44]

The *Fytche* case was appealed to the House of Lords, and it is interesting to consider the role of the judges in such a context. According to Brown's report of the appeal, the judges were asked twelve questions, the last of which was "Whether the bond stated in either of the pleas, is good and valid, or corrupt or void in law?"[45] Eight judges (not including Mansfield) responded, and all of them said the bond was good and valid. Naturally the judges would not be free to urge a reversal by the House of Lords of their decision below, but possibly they could do so by innuendo or subtle suggestion. This might have been Justice Buller's tactic, since according to East's report of the case, Buller gave the following opinion to the House of Lords: "I have taken no small pains to find out on what principle those decisions were founded; but without much effect: for after all the labour I have bestowed upon the subject, it does seem to me that they are destitute of all sense, reason, or principle."[46] He added that for two hundred years the judges had been so uniformly of the same opinion and the law "so universally acted upon ... that I think it would be very dangerous to overturn or even to shake it."[47] Nonetheless, after listening to full argument, the Lords took the hint and by a one-vote margin, 19 to 18, voted to reverse.[48]

Legislation

In 1767 there was a prosecution at the Surrey assizes of an Irish priest, John Baptiste Maloney, who was convicted and sentenced to life imprisonment "for unlawfully exercising the functions of a Popish Priest."[49] This conviction galva-

41 1 East at 493.

42 Id. at 494.

43 Id. at 495.

44 3 Douglas at 147.

45 2 Brown P.C. at 217.

46 1 East at 495.

47 Id.

48 Id. at 496.

49 *P. Hughes,* The Catholic Question, 1688–1829 (1929), p. 137. On 19 June 1771, Maloney was pardoned, conditional upon his undertaking to transport himself for life (PRO / KB 21 / 40, fol. 250; PRO / SP 46 / 151 / fol. 63). It would appear from the warrant of Secretary of State Rochford that Maloney was tried before Mansfield at Croydon on 19 August 1767 (PRO / SP 44 / 90, fol. 293).

nized Mansfield into what appears to the modern eye to be extraordinary judicial activism. A meeting of all the central court judges was called and, according to a modern scholar, "The fruit of this conference was an agreement that all henceforth would insist on so rigorous an interpretation of the law that convictions would be impossible to secure."[50] Reportedly, Mansfield described this conference himself, stating: "As for the meaning of those statutes, I own before that affair happened in Surrey I had not thoroughly examined them. But since that time, all the twelve Judges have consulted upon them, and we have all agreed in opinion that the Statutes are so worded that in order to convict a man upon those Statutes, it is necessary that he first be proved to be a priest: and secondly that it be proved he has said Mass."[51]

Catholics were also legislatively restricted from taking land by devise, and in *Foone v. Blount,*[52] this restriction was invoked to prevent a Catholic creditor from collecting from the debtor's estate because the assets of the estate derived from the sale of land. The statutory language relied on by the estate in resisting payment declared that "any. . .interests or profits whatsoever out of lands, for the use, or in trust for the benefit or relief of [Roman Catholics] should be utterly null and void."[53] Lord Mansfield's opinion in the case is interesting in terms of both statutory interpretation and stare decisis. He said that, "The statutes against Papists were thought, when they were passed, necessary to the safety of the State: upon no other ground can they be defended."[54] He acknowledged that, "The Legislature only can vary or alter the law: but from the nature of these laws, they are not to be carried by inference, beyond what the political reasons, which gave rise to them, require." And, "The political objective the Legislature had in view, was, to take off from the Roman Catholics that weight and influence, which is naturally connected with landed property."[55]

Having laid this groundwork, it was easy for Mansfield to conclude that the Catholic creditor should prevail. To him it was not a close case – "The creditor has no interest in the land"; he "can have nothing till the land is turned into money," and his claim is only "to be paid out of legal assets."[56] There was, however, one

---

50 *J. Innes,* William Payne of Bell Yard, Carpenter 1718 – 1782: The Life and Times of a London Informing Constable (1980), p. 61 (unpublished paper cited and quoted with permission).

51 *E. H. Burton,* The Life and Times of Bishop Challoner, 1691 – 1781, vol. 2 (1909), p. 94, quoting *J. Barnard,* The Life of the Venerable and Right Reverend Richard Challoner (1784), p. 167.

52 2 Cowper 464 (1776).

53 Statute of 12 William III, c. 4.

54 2 Cowper at 466.

55 Id.

56 Id. at 468. Interestingly, and unusually, Mansfield supported these conclusions with a passage from *M. Bacon,* Abridgment, said to have been taken from Lord Chief Baron Gilbert's notes.

precedent in the way, the case of *Roper v. Radcliffe*,[57] in which the House of Lords held that a devise to a Roman Catholic of the surplus of money arising from the sale of lands was an interest within the statute of 12 Will. III. Lord Mansfield admitted that, since this was a decision of the House of Lords, his court would be bound by it if the circumstances were parallel; "But though it must govern parallel cases, yet being so little satisfactory, it ought not to be carried further."[58] Mansfield noted that in the proceedings below in the *Roper* case, four of the judges thought that the devisees might take the surplus money, though Chief Justice Thomas Parker of the Court of King's Bench disagreed. Mansfield explained why he thought that Parker's argument "is very able, but I cannot say convincing to me."[59] Thus despite the reversal of the judges' majority opinion by the House of Lords in favor of Parker's opinion, the precedent was brushed aside as not precisely parallel to the case at bar.

While at the bar, Lord Mansfield had an extensive equity practice and was a great admirer of Lord Chancellor Hardwicke. Even after becoming England's dominant common law judge, Mansfield remained attentive to the equities of each case. Indeed, according to William Holdsworth, Blackstone's treatment of equity in his *Commentaries* "is, in substance, a literary summary of Mansfield's views," especially concerning "the essential unity of the rules of law and equity."[60]

As is shown by his narrow reading of the anti-Catholic statutes, Mansfield strove mightily to avoid inequitable applications of what he regarded as vindictive or hateful legislation. Another well-known example is the case of *Atcheson v. Everitt*,[61] which posed the question of whether a jury verdict that depended on a Quaker's testimony should be overturned because the Quaker testified under affirmation, not under oath. Parliament had previously authorized Quaker testimony by affirmation, but witnesses in criminal cases were excepted. The issue in *Atcheson* was whether the case was within the statutory exception. The action was for debt based on bribery, as authorized by another statute. After much analysis of hybrid cases with both criminal and civil features, the court decided that the testimony by affirmation was valid.[62] Since Mansfield considered the issue "very important,

---

57 9 Modern 167 (1714).

58 2 Cowper at 467.

59 Id. The *Roper* case was initially heard by Lord Keeper Simon Harcourt, who requested an opinion of fellow judges before issuing an opinion. In favor of the devises were Common Pleas Chief Justice Thomas Trevor, King's Bench Justice John Powell, and the Master of the Rolls, Sir John Trevor. Chief Justice Thomas Parker was alone in dissent; accordingly, Lord Keeper Harcourt's decree authorized the sale of the real estate and ordered that the Roman Catholic devisee (an heir at law) should be among those receiving the distribution of surplus proceeds.

60 *W. S. Holdsworth,* Some Aspects of Blackstone and his Commentaries, Cambridge Law Journal, vol. 4 (1932) pp. 261, 272.

61 1 Cowper 382 (1775).

62 The case was later affirmed by the House of Lords. 1 Cowper at 395.

both as to all the Quakers in the Kingdom, and to the general administration of justice," he inquired into the case with great care. He instructed puisne justice Richard Aston and court reporter Sir James Burrow to search diligently for precedents, and Mansfield said he believed they had "furnished all the cases that are to be found."[63] No case was found where a Quaker's affirmation was refused "where the action, though in form a criminal action, in substance is a mere action between party and party."[64] And as to the statute itself, Lord Mansfield personally "looked into the debates" and found "that every step and clause of the Act was fought hard in the House of Commons, and carried by small majorities."[65] It was originally only a temporary statute, but somehow it was made perpetual many years later. Mansfield could not discover why the exception for criminal cases was made, but under all the circumstances, he said that "it is an exception not to be extended by equity."[66] He concluded that, "The Legislature, when they excepted to the evidence of Quakers in criminal causes, must be understood to mean causes technically criminal"; any "different construction would not only be injurious to Quakers, but prejudicial to the rest of the King's subjects who may want their testimony."[67]

Another well-known case in which Mansfield dodged precedent and wrenched a statute to give it what he considered a sensible meaning was *Wyndham v. Chetwynd.*[68] The statute in question was part of the famous Statute of Frauds of 1677, said by some to have a special pedigree because of having been drafted by Sir Matthew Hale.[69] The case involved whether creditors who were holders of a mortgage on real estate of a testator were good witnesses to the testator's will. Among other things, Fletcher Norton argued for the defendant that the applicable provision of the Statute of Frauds calling for "credible" witnesses meant something more than "competent," since the law before the Statute of Frauds already required witnesses to be competent, and "it is not to be imagined, that the learned compiler of this statute, Lord Hale, would put in a word, which at best, was superfluous."[70]

---

63 Id. at 382–83.

64 Id. at 383.

65 Id. at 390.

66 Id. at 391.

67 Id.

68 1 W. Blackstone 95 (1757).

69 For example, in Wain v. Wartlers, 5 East 10, 17 (1804), Lord Ellenborough construed a word in the Statute of Frauds and said that the court (King's Bench) was "bound to give its proper effect; the more so when it is considered by whom that statute is said to have been drawn, by Lord Hale, one of the greatest Judges who ever sat in Westminster Hall, who was as competent to express as he was able to conceive the provisions best calculated for carrying into effect the purposes of that law."

70 1 W. Blackstone at 97. Holdsworth found no evidence to support the claim that Hale had a part in drafting the statute; he attributed the authorship mainly to Lord Nottingham and Chief Justice North. *W. S. Holdsworth,* History of English Law, vol. 6 (1924), pp. 383–84.

Lord Mansfield observed that since Hale died in 1676, he was probably not the author of the Statute of Frauds "any farther than by perhaps leaving some loose notes behind him, which were afterwards unskillfully digested."[71] Mansfield said that for the word "credible" to mean something more than "competent" would be "absurd." He noted that, "There have been perpetual doubts...upon every clause of this statute, not only among the unlearned, for whom it ought to have been calculated, but even among the learned also." He concluded that the word "credible" could fairly be disregarded; "In so inaccurate a statute, I therefore think the word credible might accidentally slip in, and ought not to be attended to, as if it carried any special legal meaning."[72] Finally, he demolished a contrary precedent by talking to one of the surviving puisne justices to confirm that the case had turned on particular circumstances, not general doctrine, and by explaining why Chief Justice William Lee's reliance on Roman law in the prior case was misplaced because the Roman law "was not sufficiently considered."[73]

On rare occasions, nevertheless, Lord Mansfield found no interpretative escape route and was constrained by statutory mandate to reach an inequitable result. For example, the Marriage Act of 1753[74] recognized only marriages solemnized at places where banns had usually been published, so that marriages conducted at chapels constructed subsequent to the passage of the Marriage Act could not qualify. In *Crigan v. Maddock,*[75] Mansfield rejected proof of marriage at such a chapel, thus denying a settlement to a married couple, but according to a newspaper report of the case, he "hinted at the propriety of Parliamentary interposition, to rectify the many marriages, which have been had, in chapels so circumstanced."[76] In this instance, Parliament responded with a corrective statute.[77]

One more point about Mansfield and legislation should be mentioned, that sometimes statutes proved useful in unexpected ways. In 1777, two cases came before Mansfield in which the plaintiffs sought to collect on wagering contracts that had been entered into on whether the cross-dressing French Ambassador to England, the Chevalier D'Eon, was male or female. Naturally in order to prove one sex or the other, eyewitness or other unsavory testimony would be required. The wagering bargain in the first of the two cases, *Da Costa v. Jones,*[78] was struck in 1771, and Mansfield's opinion in the case came to stand for the proposition that indecent evidence was inadmissible unless it was essential to evaluate a claim that

---

71 Id. at 99.

72 Id.

73 Id. at 101. The precedent in question was Anstey v. Dowsing, 2 Strange 1253 (1746).

74 Statute of 26 George II, c. 33.

75 Dampier MSS, BPB Bundle 113–42, Lincoln's Inn Library, London (unreported). See *J. Oldham*, English Common Law in the Age of Mansfield (2004), p. 32.

76 Morning Chronicle, 24 May 1781.

77 Statute of 21 George III, c. 53.

78 2 Cowper 729 (1777).

legitimate rights had been unlawfully invaded. In the second case, *Roebuck v. Hammerton,*[79] the wagering contract was entered into in 1776, and this enabled the court to strike it down by invoking a 1774 statute requiring parties to insurance contracts to have an interest in the subject of the insurance. The title of the statute suggested that the statute was specifically about life insurance, but the text of the statute covered "all insurances upon lives, or any other event or events, without interest in the parties."[80]

Secondary Authorities

As has been noted, the use of legal treatises, abridgements, or compilations was in Mansfield's time a matter for argument and persuasion. The authoritativeness of the work will have depended on the reputation of the author, as was only natural. The treatises of Hale and Coke had the benefit of age, whereas Blackstone's *Commentaries* were deserving of less weight, both because they were directed to a popular readership and because they were the work of a contemporary. Indeed when Blackstone was on the Court of King's Bench with Mansfield, Mansfield refused to allow counsel to cite the *Commentaries*. According to *Lloyd's Evening Post* for 18 May 1770:

> A few days ago, as *Sir William Blackstone* was on the Bench, in the Court of King's Bench, Counselor Impey availed himself of applying to that Gentleman's Commentaries on the Laws of England, and was entering into some observations upon that head, when Lord Chief Justice Mansfield stopped him short, and said, "he would suffer no such references in that Court; for though the work alluded to was of much utility to the public, and would be remembered and applied to when the Author was no more, yet, while living, he thought it unnecessary, as well as improper."

Later, after Blackstone had moved to Common Pleas, even Mansfield occasionally invoked the *Commentaries*. In *Atcheson v. Everitt,*[81] for example, Mansfield observed that "Mr. Justice Blackstone, and all modern and ancient writers upon the subject distinguish between [criminal prosecutions and civil actions]."[82] This reference and occasional others like it were, nonetheless, merely shoring for outcomes based on principle and precedent.

---

79 2 Cowper 737 (1777).

80 Statute of 14 George III, c. 48 (1774).

81 1 Cowper 382 (1775), discussed above.

82 Id. at 391.

Conclusion

The sketch that I have given of Lord Mansfield and his approach to decision-making is of an extremely intelligent and skillful manipulator of precedent and statute, one who sought to advance and apply reasoned principles that would achieve equitable results within the framework of the common law. Mansfield was not invariably successful, and he had his critics, but he usually carried the day with the junior justices, and his powerful influence reverberates down to the present. One more feature of his ratio decidendi should be mentioned before concluding, the importance of custom and usage. As is well-known, Mansfield perceived how to work with merchant juries to fold mercantile customs into the common law, and he accomplished this remarkably effectively. But that, as we say, is another story.

J. THOMAS WREN

The Common Law of England in Virginia 1776 to 1830

The Virginia Court of Appeals embraced, on the whole, the English legal heritage, despite the violent separation from Great Britain in 1776. This loyalty to English precedents was an illustration of the conservative tenor of the Revolution in Virginia. The English common law continued to be revered because it was perceived to be a bulwark of English, and hence American, liberty. Adherence to English precedent also maintained stable rules of law, which in turn protected existing property rights. At the same time, however, the Court of Appeals was not slavishly devoted to the common law, and the court's departures from accepted precedent illustrate the nature of Virginia's revolutionary settlement.

The instances of judicial deviation from English rules of law during the Commonwealth's first decades were infrequent but illuminating. One example of the Virginia court's departure from English precedents occurred when the English rules clearly contravened republican principles. The Court of Appeals also consistently supported the will of the Virginia legislature, as expressed through statute, over traditional rules of law. This demonstrated a respect for manifest policy choices by Virginians over English traditions and was also an early indication of the court's perception of its limited role in the making of policy. Another instance where the Court of Appeals refused to blindly follow the English rules was when they did not comport with local conditions in Virginia. Likewise, the court refused to stand on technicality when to do so prevented the execution of an individual's obvious intent. Finally, the court also stepped in when the common law or statute provided no clear guidelines. In such cases, the Court of Appeals articulated a policy based upon principles of "reason."

Largely through the contributions of the Court of Appeals, then, the English legal heritage was adapted to the Virginia experiment. On the whole, traditional legal rules went unchallenged, evidencing a conservative respect for stability and property rights. Where the court did depart from English legal precedents, it was for the purpose of implementing legislative policy, or adapting the common law to Virginia's situation. The result was a legal system which was tradition-laden, but not tradition-bound; a conservative yet pragmatic jurisprudence which was to define Virginia's approach to the new order.

Theoretically, at any rate, once the Virginia colony slashed its ties with the mother country, the source and authority of the British legal system were extinguished. In this veritable "state of nature," it was the duty of the new sovereign and independent state to fill the vacuum by establishing a new legal order.[1] One of the first orders of business for the Virginia Convention in May 1776 was to address the matter of the continued validity in Virginia of the British statutes and the English common law, that amalgam of rights, duties, and liabilities built up through centuries of judicial decisions in the English courts which formed the basis for the vast majority of the substantive law that governed the rights and obligations of all English subjects. The Virginia Convention did not hesitate and immediately embraced the English system. In order "to enable the present magistrates and officers to continue the administration of justice ... till the same can be amply provided for," the Convention specifically adopted the English common law, and all applicable English statutes passed before 1607, "until the same shall be altered by the legislative power of this colony."[2] The end result was, as St. George Tucker described it, "That the common law of England, and every statute of that kingdom, made for the security of the life, liberty, or property of the subject, before the settlement of the British colonies, respectively, so far as the same were applicable to the nature of their nature and circumstances, respectively, were brought over to America ...".[3]

The hasty adoption of the essence of the English legal system at the very moment the Virginians were engaged in a violent revolt against that government is not the contradiction that it would at first appear. In many ways the Virginians, taking their cue from the British "Opposition" writers of the early eighteenth century, believed that their revolution was not a revolution at all but merely a last, desperate attempt to recover the traditional English liberties that had been lost at the hands of a "corrupt" English government.[4] One of the bulwarks of those traditional English liberties was the substance and procedure of the English common law. Accordingly, the common law was claimed as the "birthright of American citizens."[5] The Virginia Court of Appeals was fully aware of the libertarian nature of the common law inheritance. As Judge Tucker phrased it, "No man I trust would be more jealous than I of the danger of preserving any part of the theory of monarchy in our Commonwealth; but the rights of individuals, upon whatever theory originally founded, after having settled into the known law of the land for six centuries, in England, and after being considered in a similar light in this country,

---

1 *St. George Tucker,* Blackstone's Commentaries (1803), vol. 1, app. E, p. 430.

2 Stat. of May 1776, c. 5, § 6, *W. W. Hening,* Statutes at Large of Virginia, vol. 9, p. 126 [hereinafter Hening].

3 *St. George Tucker,* Blackstone's Commentaries, vol. 1, app. E, p. 432. See generally *W. H. Bryson,* English Common Law in Virginia in Journal of Legal History, vol. 6, pp. 249–56 (1985); *W. H. Bryson,* Virginia Civil Procedure (2005), § 2.02.

4 See generally *Bernard Bailyn,* The Ideological Origins of the American Revolution (1967).

5 *J. R. Pole,* Equality in the Founding of the American Republic, in *G. S. Wood/J. R. Pole,* edd., Social Radicalism and the Idea of Equality in the American Revolution (1976), p. 18; *P. Miller,* The Life of the Mind in America: From the Revolution to the Civil War (1965), p. 122.

from its first foundation, ought not to be shaken, unless the imperative voice of the constitution, or of the legislature, shall compel it to be done."[6]

There was also a more pragmatic reason for adhering to the known rules and procedures of the common law which the Court frequently articulated. That was the idea that it was important that the law remain predictable. Nowhere was the rationale for this position more cogently arrayed than in the early case of *Commonwealth v. Posey,* which dealt with a 200-year old precedent which had been definitive in construing the English statute regarding the benefit of clergy. (The "benefit of clergy" was a privilege of exemption from execution in a capital crime granted originally to clergymen but later expanded to include many others.) In *Posey,* Judge William Fleming gave the essential rule: "precedents, so long acquiesced in, cannot be overturned, without more danger than benefit, as no point will ever be settled."[7] But it was Judge Peter Lyons who expressed the underlying rationale: "The security of men's lives and property require that [the earlier cases] should be adhered to: for precedents serve to regulate our conduct, and there is more danger to be apprehended from uncertainty, than from any exposition, because, when the rule is settled, men know how to conform to it; but when all is uncertain, they are left in the dark, and constantly liable to error . . .".[8] The importance of this holding did not go unrecognized. Nearly fifty years later, in 1833, Daniel Call, in publishing his edition of this case, added a postscript that "No cause decided, since the revolution, is more important than this, as it fixes, by the opinion of a large majority of the judges, distinguished for their patriotism, independence, and ability, a principle necessary for the tranquillity of society and the safety of the general transactions of mankind, namely, that a settled construction of a statute forms a precedent, which should be adhered to as part of the law itself; and ought, upon no criticism of words, to be departed from. Accordingly, the decisions of the court [of appeals], since that period, abound with instances of the same kind, but none of them state the ground and reason of it with so much force . . .".[9]

Call was correct about the Court of Appeals' continued respect for the rules of property as established by the English cases. The reports teem with similar professions of allegiance to the accepted common-law interpretations of legal doctrines. In 1827, the Court refused to overrule a longstanding interpretation of the effect of language creating a "future interest" in property, even though the legislature had shown a clear dissatisfaction with the judicial reasoning in such cases. The Court, normally deferential to legislative wishes, here refused to change its position (in a case that arose prior to the enactment of the corrective statute). Judge Dabney Carr articulated the Court's reasoning. While a statute was prospective, and gave everyone notice of the new rule, a judicial decision was by its very nature retrospective.

---

6 *Read v. Read,* 5 Call 160, 173 (1804).

7 *Commonwealth v. Posey,* 4 Call 109, 119 – 120 (1787).

8 *Id.* at 120.

9 *Id.* at 124.

"If we say that these decisions [that the Court has held to over the years] are wrong," asserted Carr, "all the estates which have been settled, all the contracts which have been made, all the titles which rest on the foundation of their [i.e., the former cases'] correctness, are uprooted."[10] Nor did Carr stop there. If all those decisions were overturned, it would be impossible to foresee "the extent of the mischief." "But, only open the door," concluded Carr, "[and] proclaim to the world that all which has heretofore been done is wrong; and then we shall see the wild uproar and confusion among titles, which will follow. Is it not better to prevent this, by holding on in the course we have so long run?"[11]

So strong was the loyalty to precedent that the Court was willing to follow a common-law rule even when the rationale underlying that rule had been lost in the mists of time. As late as 1829, we find Judge William Cabell intoning: "It cannot be admitted, that a law ceases to exist, merely because the reason which gave rise to its adoption has ceased. If this were admitted, we should demolish at once much of the venerable fabric of the common law."[12] And Judge John Green, searching in 1830 for the reasoning behind the doctrine that all judgments "relate back" to the first day of the judicial term, finally threw up his hands in despair. "This general principle of the common law, like many others, is of such remote antiquity and so long recognized without dispute that the reasons and policy are, in great degree, left to conjecture."[13] Even more revealing are the cases where the judges followed the common-law even in the face of their own sense of justice. Throughout the first five decades of the new republic, judges subsumed their own views to the interest of upholding precedent.[14] Perhaps Spencer Roane summed it up best in the case of *Claiborne v. Henderson* in 1809. Roane noted that there are "innumerable instances to be found in the books of a reverence for decisions and rules of property which have been established by the concurrent decisions of successive judges and acted under for a long series of time. They ought to be adhered to as the sine qua non of all certainty and stability in the law, the private opinion of any single judge to the contrary notwithstanding."[15]

Given this reverence for common-law precedent, both in terms of its protections of individual liberties and because of the fear of disruption from an overturning of established rules, it should come as no surprise that the Virginia reports abound

---

10 See, e.g., *Bells v. Gillespie,* 5 Randolph 274 (1827); *Minnis v. Aylett,* 1 Washington 300 (1794); *Boswell and Johnson v. Jones,* 1 Washington 322 (1794); *Jiggets v. Davis,* 1 Leigh 368 (1829); *Blow v. Maynard,* 2 Leigh 29 (1830); *Coutts v. Walker;* 2 Leigh 268 (1830); *Cole v. Scott,* 2 Washington 141 (1795); *Claiborne v. Henderson,* 3 Hening & Munford 322 (1809).

11 *Bells v. Gillespie,* 5 Randolph 274, 285 (1827).

12 *Jiggets v. Davis,* 1 Leigh 368, 426 (1829).

13 *Coutts v. Walker,* 2 Leigh 268, 276 (1830).

14 See, e.g., *Cole v. Scott,* 2 Washington 141 (1795); *Claiborne v. Henderson,* 3 Hening & Munford 322 (1809).

15 *Claiborne v. Henderson,* 3 Hening & Munford 322, 376 (1809).

with professions of allegiance to the common law.[16] Indeed it is logical that this should be so. As one commentator has put it, "English precedents had been for two centuries the ways and woof of the Virginia system, and it was neither possible nor desirable to cast them aside."[17]

Perhaps the most telling indicator of the continuing role of the English common law in Virginia's system came in the early 1830s, when Henry St. George Tucker advised practicing attorneys concerning the matter of rent payments when the lessor died before the rent payment was due. Under English law, the death of the lessor absolved the renter from liability to pay rent, unless the lease specifically provided otherwise. Although common sense dictated that this should not be the outcome, Tucker warned lawyers that "until... some adjudication shall justify us in department in practice from English authority, it will be always safest in practice to make reservations of rent in conformity with their decisions ...".[18]

Given the clear commitment in Virginia to English precedent, what becomes most interesting and informative are the exceptions to this common-law allegiance. It is manifest that only a deeply-held belief in some countervailing value or circumstance could induce the Virginia Court of Appeals to depart from its respectful attitude toward the common law.

Interestingly, one rationale for deviating from the common law is expressed specifically in terms of republicanism. In the 1806 case of *Baring v. Reeder,* Judge Roane acknowledged that "I consider myself bound to pare down the governmental part of the common-law of England to the standard of our free republican constitution ....[19] St. George Tucker elaborated in his annotation to Blackstone's Commentaries: "every rule of the common law, and every statute of England, founded on the nature of regal government, in derogation of the natural and unalienable rights of mankind or inconsistent with the nature and principles of democratic governments were absolutely abrogated, repealed, and annulled by the establishment of such a form of government in the states, respectively. This is a natural and necessary consequence of the revolution and the correspondent changes in the nature of the governments ....[20]

A further subtlety was inherent in this perception of the common law in light of republican principles. Even when the Virginia courts were at the height of their "homage-paying" to the English precedents, there was a subtle but very important distinction between *reliance* upon English decisions and their *authority.* The Revo-

---

16 *C. F. Hobson,* ed., The Papers of John Marshall, vol. 5, Selected Law Cases (1987), pp. 458, 462 [hereinafter *Hobson,* Selected Law Cases]; *D. J. Mays,* Edmund Pendleton (1952), vol. 2, p. 301.

17 *Mays,* Edmund Pendleton, vol. 2, p. 300.

18 *Henry St. George Tucker,* Commentaries on the Laws of Virginia (1831), vol. 1, bk. 2, p. 25.

19 *Baring v. Reeder,* 1 Hening & Munford 154, 161 (1806).

20 *St. George Tucker,* Blackstone's Commentaries, vol. 1, app. E, pp. 405–406.

lution, argued St. George Tucker, "by separating us from Great Britain forever, put an end to the *authority* of any future decisions or opinions of her judges and sages of the law in the courts of this Commonwealth; those decisions and opinions, I make no doubt, will long continue to be respected in Virginia, as the decisions of the wisest and most upright foreign judges; but from the moment that Virginia became an independent Commonwealth, neither the laws, nor the judgments of any other country, or its courts, can claim any *authority* whatsoever in our courts...".[21] This, in the end, was exactly the point Roane was making in *Baring v. Reeder:* "On such rules of the common law ... as are neither affected by a change in the form of government, nor by a variation in the circumstances of character of the nation, I am free to avail myself of the testimony of able judges and lawyers of that country ... I am not willing that an appeal to my pride, as a citizen of independent America, should prevail over the best convictions of my understanding ... I wish it, however, to be clearly understood that I ... would not receive even them, as binding authority. I would receive them merely as affording evidence of the opinions of eminent judges as to the doctrines in question ...".[22]

A more obvious exception to the preeminence of the English common law in the court decisions of Virginia occurred when the English precedents were displaced by statutory provisions. The superiority of enactments of the Virginia General Assembly to any common-law doctrine was a commonplace. This was made express in the statute adopting English common law and statute in May 1776, when it was declared that the English law was to remain "in full force, until the same shall be altered by the legislative power of this colony."[23] The Court of Appeals was assiduous in upholding this doctrine of legislative supremacy where there was a direct conflict between statute and common law. *Whittington v. Christian* is a typical example. That case, decided in 1824, had to do with a technical error in an action of ejectment. When the defendant sought to have the case dismissed under the common-law rule, the Court looked to the more lenient provision of the Virginia statute. "It is true," admitted Judge Green, "that this construction of the statute and the rule of the common law referred to cannot exist together. The consequence is, that the statute abrogates the rule of the common law in toto ...".[24] Similarly, in *Templeman v. Steptoe,* Judge Tucker noted in 1810 that under the 1785 statute of descents, it was "too plain to require proof, that ... all former rules and canons of inheritance and succession to estates within this Commonwealth, whether established by common law, or by statute, were rescinded, abrogated, and annulled, and that they cannot be revived in any manner but by some express legislative provision for that purpose."[25]

---

21 *Ibid.*, vol. 5, p. 436, n. 1.

22 *Baring v. Reeder,* 1 Hening & Munford 154, 162 (1806).

23 Stat. of May 1776, c. 5, § 6, Hening, vol. 9, p. 127.

24 *Whittington v. Christian,* 2 Randolph 353 (1824).

25 *Templeman v. Steptoe,* 1 Munford 339 (1810). For similar examples, see *White v. Jones,* 4 Call 253 (1792); *Bennet v. Commonwealth,* 2 Washington 154 (1795); *Shaw v. Clements,* 1

Within the parameters of absolute statutory superiority in areas of actual conflict, however, there was still room for a considerable amount of reliance upon common-law principles and remedies. Oftentimes Virginia statutes were exact copies of or derivative from English predecessors. In such cases, the relevant common-law doctrines were often used to inform and illuminate the statutory provisions.[26] The Court of Appeals was also quite careful when a new statutory remedy was enacted that deviated from traditional common-law rights. In such cases, the Court acknowledged the statute, but took special care that the common-law remedies were also available, unless the statute clearly abrogated those rights.[27] Thus, in 1798, when a debtor sought to stave off a creditor because he had not complied with the statutory requirements on a bond, Judge Pendleton for the Court held that it was "immaterial whether the creditor had or had not a remedy by motion, under the Act of Assembly, since the act having no negative words, the creditor had his election to pursue the statutory mode, or his common-law remedy on the bond."[28] Ten years later, Judge Roane commented with respect to an alleged fraudulent transfer that "the statutes in question are merely superogatory in relation to the common law ...".[29] And, in 1825, the Court held that the statute regarding proof of a will "is only cumulative, and does not deprive any party of remedy at common law."[30] Similarly, the Court held that "when a statute gives a remedy without prescribing a particular mode of proceeding, the mode of the common law is to be pursued."[31]

Another situation in which the Court of Appeals was willing to overcome its predilection for common-law precedent was when the local conditions did not favor its application.[32] As a contemporary commentator noted in 1821, "The common law of England is, at this day, the law of Virginia, except so far as it has altered by statute, or so far as its principles are inapplicable to the state of the country. It adopts itself to the situation of society, being liberalized by the courts according to the circumstances of the country and the manner and genius of the people."[33] Judge Roane added that "in applying ... [the common law] we must

---

Call 429 (1798); *Fleming v. Bolling*, 3 Call 75 (1801); *Branch v. Bowman*, 2 Leigh 170 (1830); *Peasley v. Boatwright*, 2 Leigh 195 (1830); see also, e.g., *Henry St. George Tucker*, Commentaries, vol. 1, bk. 2, p. 86.

26 *Jackson v. Sanders*, 2 Leigh 109, 114–115 (1830).

27 *Braxton v. Winslow*, 1 Washington 31 (1791); *Asbury v. Calloway*, 1 Washington 72, 74 (1792); *Gordon admrs. v. Justices of Frederick*, 1 Munford 1 (1810).

28 *Booker's exrs. v. M'Roberts*, 1 Call 243, 244 (1798).

29 *Fitzhugh v. Anderson*, 2 Hening & Munford 289, 303 (1808).

30 *Smith v. Carter*, 3 Randolph 167 (1825). See also *Johnston v. Meriwether*, 3 Call 523 (1790); *Beale v. Downman*, 1 Call 249 (1798); *Hooe v. Tebbs*, 1 Munford 501 (1810); *Henry St. George Tucker*, Commentaries, vol. 2, pp. 13, 372. But see *Taylor v. Beck*, 3 Randolph 316 (1825).

31 *Braxton v. Winslow*, 4 Call 308, 318 (1791).

32 *Miller*, Life of the Mind, pp. 125–127; *O.* and *M. F. Handlin*, Commonwealth (1947), pp. 134–135.

adapt [it] to the circumstances of the case ... so as to effect a reasonable and substantial compliance therewith, rather than a literal one."[34]

One distinguishing circumstance in the new commonwealth was the variation in the court structure between Virginia and England. Judge Pendleton addressed the issue in 1792 in *Thornton v. Smith* when he held that the requirement of asserting a court's jurisdiction in the pleadings was not necessary in Virginia. Pendleton argued that the English rule "grew out of the local situation of the inferior courts in that country, and was grounded upon considerations in which ours totally differ from theirs." After discussing the confusing mishmash of jurisdictions in England and the straightforward statutory scheme in Virginia, Pendleton concluded that in this case "the [English] precedents cannot bind us."[35] A similar situation confronted Judge Tucker in the 1809 case of *Nimmo's exr. v. Commonwealth.* The question there was whether a decedent's executor was presumed to know of pending judgments which might bind the estate. Tucker acknowledged that presumption applied in England. "But," he interjected, "it is not every common-law rule, founded upon the judicial system of that country, that can be deemed, in strictness, applicable to the circumstances and situation of this." After noting that there were only four courts of record in England compared to over two hundred in Virginia, Tucker concluded: "Can it be supposed, that under such circumstances ... an executor must at his peril take notice of all judgments against the testator in his lifetime, in what court, or part of the state soever, the same may be entered? I conceive not ... ".[36] Similarly, the dispersed nature of Virginia courts forced some departures from traditional requirements. Often pleading requirements were relaxed. "Considering the circumstances in this country," noted the Court, "and the dispersed situation of the attorneys and their clients who can seldom communicate with each other but at court, justice seems to require a relaxation in these rules of practice."[37]

The demands of settling a new country also affected the substantive rules of the common law. In England, a mere tenant on the land was limited as to his utilization of permanent resources of the land such as timber. If he were to cut more trees than was reasonably necessary for fencing and the like, he was liable to the owner of the land for "waste." But in Virginia, where there was a more compelling need to tame and make productive the land, the rule was different. In *Findlay v. Smith,* a life tenant was permitted, in 1818, to extract unlimited quantities of salt, and to use

---

33 William Munford in *Findlay v. Smith,* 6 Munford 134, note (1818).

34 *Coleman, exr. v. Moody,* 4 Hening & Munford 1, 20 (1809).

35 *Thornton v. Smith,* 1 Washington 81, 83 – 84 (1792).

36 *Nimmo's exr. v. Commonwealth,* 4 Hening & Munford 57, 66 (1809).

37 *Downman v. Downman's exrs.*, 1 Washington 26, 28 (1791), *W. H. Bryson,* Virginia Law Reports and Records, 1776 – 1800, in *A. Wijffels,* ed., Case Law in the Making (Comparative Studies in Continental and Anglo-American Legal History, Band 17/II, 1997), p. 101; see also *Tabb v. Gregory,* 4 Call 225, 229 (1792).

all of the woodland, if necessary, to supply fuel for the operation. As Judge William Cabell explained, "the law of waste, in its application here, varies and accommodates itself to the situation of our new and unsettled country."[38] Similarly the common-law right of a purchaser of the land to the tenant's growing crops was questioned in Virginia, "where lands are seldom let out upon leases ...".[39]

In sum, the Virginia Court of Appeals was willing to change common-law rules and procedures to conform to the requirements of Virginia experience.[40] On the other hand, such deviations were relatively infrequent and always accompanied by an explanation of the circumstances which demanded the variance.

Another exception to the tradition of common-law preeminence in the Virginia courts was broad in concept but rather strictly limited in practice. It arose because there were inevitably times when the common-law precedents gave no guidance, or provided conflicting rules of law. In such cases, by default, the Court had to step in and make a policy decision with little guidance from the precedents. Such was the case of the interpretation of an insurance contract in *Bourke v. Granberry* in 1820. There, the precedents were diverse and conflicting, forcing Judge Roane to finally conclude, "We are to judge for ourselves in this chaos of judgments, and we submit the result of our best deliberations."[41] Judge Coalter faced a similar situation in 1829 regarding the admissibility of proof of handwriting in a forgery case. "The decisions, so far as I have examined them, are not, I think, very consistent with the general rules of evidence, or with each other, or with the principles by which they profess to be governed; nor, indeed, have I as yet been fully able to comprehend those principles."[42] In such cases, the Court had no alternative but to strike out on its own without solid guidance from the precedents. On the whole, however, the Virginia Court of Appeals was very circumspect in availing itself of the opportunity to claim a lack of positive direction from prior cases, thus justifying the creation of a new policy initiative by judicial fiat.[43]

Despite the tradition of respect for precedent, there was at least one particular area where the Court of Appeals did evince a resistance to the pattern of adherence to common-law rules, in the interpretation of wills. Cases involving wills provided much of the grist for the mills of justice in the late eighteenth and early nineteenth

---

38 *Findlay v. Smith*, 6 Munford 134, 142 (1818); see *Henry St. George Tucker*, Commentaries, vol. 1, bk. 2, pp. 4, 50.

39 *Crews v. Pendleton*, 1 Leigh 297, 302 (1829). See also *Ross v. Poythress*, 1 Washington 120 (1792) [regarding lack of hard money in Virginia].

40 *G. R. Wood*, Creation of the American Republic (1969), p. 296.

41 *Bourke v. Granberry*, Gilmer 16, 26 (1820).

42 *Rowt's admr. v. Kile's admr.*, 1 Leigh 216, 224–225 (1829).

43 In only two cases does the Court intimate that it was primarily "result-oriented." In *Martin v. Lindsay's admr.*, Judge Brooke said, "It is of more importance to decide causes in this court, than to settle or unsettle the law." 1 Leigh 499, 513 (1829). And in *Coleman exr. v. Moody*, Judge Roane noted: "We do not sit here to lay down mere abstract propositions, but to administer justice." 4 Hening & Munford 1, 20–21 (1809).

centuries. And in most will cases, the standard deference to English precedent was evident. Indeed, one commentator has noted that "owing to their great complexity, will construction cases came before the appellate court in disproportionate numbers. They afforded numerous occasions for the bar and bench to display their mastery of the abstruse doctrines of property law and the technical rules for construing wills that had evolved with ever greater refinement in a multitude of cases. Not surprisingly, the string of English citations was longest in will cases."[44]

One aspect of will construction, however, provided an exception to this rule. This occurred in the cases involving the interpretation of the intent of the testator (the writer of a will) in the application of the provisions of the will. The resistance to common-law rules in such cases was partially justified in the familiar terms of a lack of clear guidance from the common-law precedents. In a 1792 case, the court expressed its willingness to follow the traditional rules of will construction if it could find them. "If we could discover those settled rules of construction," lamented the Court, "we would pursue them. But, after all our researches, we are much inclined to affirm ... 'that cases on wills serve rather to obscure, than illuminate questions of this sort'."[45] Two years later Judge Edmund Pendleton reiterated this argument. "In disputes upon wills ... which depend ... on the intention of the testator ... adjudged cases have more frequently been produced to disappoint, than to illustrate intention." As a result, Pendleton concluded that the proper way to decide such cases was not to rely upon precedent, but upon "the state and circumstances of each case."[46]

But this reliance upon the crutch of a lack of "settled rules of construction" was a bit disingenuous. For in the same case that Pendleton decried a lack of established precedent, he went on to reveal the real theory underlying his approach to such cases. "I am free to own," admitted Pendleton, "that where a testator's intention is apparent to me, cases must be strong, uniform, and apply pointedly before they will prevail to frustrate that intention."[47] In supporting the perceived intention of testators over technical rules of law, the Court of Appeals was not so much rejecting precedent as it was acknowledging and effectuating the clear aims of common men, unschooled in the law. Judge Carr in 1830 stated the reasoning of the Court simply and directly. "The enquiry is to the meaning of the bequest: it is a pure question of intention. There are no technical words or forms of expression used in the will. It is, evidently, the production of a plain man, who, though he understood very well what he meant to say, and was able to express himself quite intelligibly, knew nothing of legal forms and legal phrases. To ascertain his meaning, we must not look to treatises on wills, or to adjudged cases, but simply to the

---

44 *Hobson, ed.*, Selected Law Cases, p. 463. See e.g., *Roy v. Garnett,* 2 Washington 9 (1794).

45 *Kennon v. M'Roberts,* 1 Washington 96, 102 (1792).

46 *Shermer v. Shermer's exrs.*, 1 Washington 266, 271–272 (1794).

47 *Id.* at 272.

words he has used."[48] Carr's statement, although more eloquent, was really echoing the same point made by the Court in 1792. In that year, the Court in *Kennon v. M'Roberts* set up a simple rule of interpretation: "if the testator use legal phrases, his intention should be construed by legal rules. If he uses those that are common, his intention, according to the common understanding of the words he uses, shall be the rule."[49]

Perhaps the most illuminating cases where a testator's intent clashed with a legal rule came when there was a devise (i.e., a testamentary disposition of land) of real property to the testator's children. In 1797, for example, John Guthrie, an uneducated man, left land to his eldest son James. Everything about the will indicated Guthrie's intention to leave the land to James absolutely, without limitation or restriction. But Guthrie did not devise the land to James "and his heirs," and by leaving out those three key words, the common-law rule had it that James took the land only during his lifetime, and that at his death it went not to James' heirs or his own devisees, but to the "residuary legatee" of Guthrie's will. The Court of Appeals in this case concluded that "if we consult common sense and the reason of mankind, we shall be satisfied that where a man gives an estate in lands, without limitation or restraint, he means to give his whole interest."[50] And so the Court continued to hold until the problem was remedied by a statutory abrogation of the common law.[51]

Despite examples of the Virginia Court of Appeals effecting a testator's intent over technical rules of law, there were acknowledged limitations to this policy in both theory and practice. Although it was a familiar refrain throughout the period, Judge Carr perhaps articulated it best in 1825: "In the constructions of wills," said Carr, "the cardinal point, the polar star, is the intention of the testator; and this being clear, must be pursued, *unless it be in violation of some fixed and settled rule.*"[52] Just exactly what were the "fixed and settled" rules which no testator could abridge were never clear, and, indeed, seemed to vary. St. George Tucker thought them limited to such citadels of common-law construction as the rule

48 *Madden v. Madden's exrs.*, 2 Leigh 377, 380 (1830). See also *Wyatt v. Sadler's heirs*, 1 Munford 537 (1810); *Carnagy v. Woodcock and Mackey*, 2 Munford 234 (1811).

49 *Kennon v. M'Roberts*, 1 Washington 96, 100 (1792).

50 *Fairclaim v. Guthrie*, 1 Call 7, 15 (1797).

51 See also *Davies v. Miller*, 1 Call 127 (1797); *Kennon v. M'Roberts*, 1 Washington 96 (1792); *Johnson v. Johnson's widow*, 1 Munford 549 (1810); Stat. of Oct. 1785, c. 61, Hening, vol. 12, p. 140. For other cases where the testator's intent affected the application of a rule of law, see *Griffith v. Thomas*, 1 Leigh 321 (1829) [rule against perpetuities]; *Tabb v. Archer*, 3 Hening & Munford 399 (1809); *Lupton v. Tidball*, 1 Randolph 194 (1822); *Henry St. George Tucker*, Commentaries, vol. 1, bk. 2, pp. 140–142 [rule in Shelley's case]; *Harrison v. Allen*, 3 Call 289 (1802); *Hyer v. Shobe*, 2 Munford 200 (1811); *Henry St. George Tucker*, Commentaries, vol. 1, bk. 2, p. 146 [after-acquired lands, contingent interests].

52 *Goodrich v. Harding*, 3 Randolph 280, 282 (1825) (emphasis supplied). See also *Roy v. Garnett*, 2 Washington 9, 31 (1794); *Reno's exrs. v. Davis*, 4 Hening & Munford 283, 291–292 (1809).

against perpetuities (which forbade making property inalienable beyond a certain length of time) or the prohibition against devises in mortmain (that is, to religious institutions).[53] But in a series of cases adjudged between 1791 and 1803, we find the Court upholding rules of law against intention in a far wider variety of instances. Thus, despite the testator's apparent intention, the court strikes down the intended conveyance of after-acquired lands,[54] a 999-year lease,[55] and a remainder in land.[56]

The Court's struggles with the rule of law versus the intent of the testator is revealing regarding the prevailing attitude toward the common law. On the one hand, we see the Court willing to throw over the shackles of ancient law to give effect to the obvious desires of the individuals. In so doing, the Court was merely acknowledging a pragmatic reality of the Virginia countryside: unschooled men often made wills wherein their intent was clear, but whose language did not comport with all the legal niceties. The Court chose, where possible, to recognize that reality. On the other hand, the Court could not, *would* not, overthrow the familiar rules of common-law construction entirely. This was more than mere antiquarianism. Again, the Court of Appeals shied before the bugbear of unsettling property rights. As Judge Peter Lyons phrased the argument in 1803, "It is to no purpose to be arguing about the intention... for, mere intention cannot prevail against a settled rule of interpretation, which has fixed an appropriate sense to particular words; because, when the sense is once imposed, they become the indicia of the testator's mind, until the contrary is shown by countervailing expressions... It is better that it should be so, too, for the law ought to be certain; and, when the rule is once laid down, it should be adhered to. Otherwise, what is called liberality, at the bar, will degenerate into arbitrary discretion, and all must depend upon the will of the judge."[57] Once again we see that interesting mix of an abiding respect for the common law, leavened by the acknowledgment of the requirements of pragmatic reality. And through it all was woven the continuing support for fixed and settled rules of property.

Judge Lyons' concern that the law might "degenerate into arbitrary discretion, and all must depend upon the will of the judge,"[58] provides a key insight into why

---

53 *St. George Tucker,* Blackstone's Commentaries, vol. 3, p. 381, n. 12.

54 *Shelton v. Shelton,* 1 Washington 53 (1791).

55 *Minnis v. Aylett,* 1 Washington 300, 302 (1794).

56 *Hill v. Burrow,* 3 Call 342 (1803). This case involved a "remainder in tail" which was an ongoing matter of judicial attention. It should be noted that the examples of a common-law rule overriding individual intention fell chiefly in the early decades of the period. It would be hasty to immediately jump to any conclusion on this score, however, since Carr states as late as 1825 the principle that rules of property can overturn intent. *Goodrich v. Harding,* 3 Randolph 280, 282 (1825).

57 *Hill v. Burrow,* 3 Call 342, 353 (1803).

58 *Ibid.* See also *Young v. Gregory,* 3 Call 446 (1803); *St. George Tucker,* Blackstone's Commentaries, vol. 1, p. 53, n. 10; *ibid.*, app. C, p. 133.

a republican commonwealth like Virginia would unhesitatingly accept an antique system of judge-made law derived from an essentially monarchical system. For the judicial opinions collectively known as the "common law" were *not* perceived as the collective opinions of appointed judges, but as reflections of a "higher" entity, and it was the nature of this "higher law" to be protective of individual rights and property. Indeed, it was only when a court threatened to deviate from the accepted notions of the "common law" that individual liberties and property rights were endangered.[59] This conception of law had been suggested by Coke, propounded by Locke, and elevated to a commonplace by Blackstone.[60] In Virginia, Spencer Roane admitted in 1803, "I hold myself bound by well-established precedents, and disclaim any power to change the law."[61] Such a position espoused the familiar doctrine of predictability in law, but it also contained an undercurrent of republicanism. Thus, to Virginians, adhering to the common law was more than just a bow to accepted wisdom, more than a means to avoid unsettling existing property rights; it was an affirmative statement of their belief in natural law and natural right, which in turn was a fundamental basis of traditional English, and hence American, liberties.[62]

In sum, the Revolution did not mean the overthrow of English jurisprudence in Virginia. Rather, "the great body of English law... remained intact in post-Revolutionary Virginia. Its rules and principles were the predominant authority relied upon in arguing and deciding cases ...".[63] This is not to say that the common law was accepted unquestioningly. When the English cases did not suit the practical or ideological demands of Virginians, the Court did not hesitate to cast them aside. Henry St. George Tucker put it succinctly in 1831: "the common law of England is at this day the law of this commonwealth, except so far as it has been altered by statute, or so far as its principles are inapplicable to the state of the country, or have been abrogated by the revolution and the establishment of free institutions."[64] Through it all, the Virginia Court of Appeals incorporated the English common law into the emerging jurisprudence of Virginia in a manner consistent with republicanism. In the great majority of cases, the influence of the English precedents

59 *W. E. Nelson,* Americanization of the Common Law: The Impact of Legal Change in Massachusetts Society, 1760–1830 (1975), pp. 18–19; *Miller,* Life of the Mind, pp. 234–235; *Hobson,* ed., Selected Law Cases, p. lix.

60 *Miller,* Life of the Mind, pp. 130–131, 164–165.

61 *Young v. Gregory,* 3 Call 446 (1803).

62 When the Virginia court could find no appropriate precedent, it specifically looked to decide the matter "upon principle." See *Shelton v. Shelton,* 1 Washington 53, 64 (1791); *Kennon v. M'Roberts,* 1 Washington 96, 100 (1792); *Shaw v. Clements,* 1 Call 12, 429, 434, 436, 442 (1798); *Wilkinson v. Hendrick,* 5 Call 12–13 (1804); *Bourke v. Granberry,* Gilmer 16, 25 (1820); *Richards v. Brockenbrough's admr.,* 1 Randolph 449, 454 (1823); *Blow v. Maynard,* 2 Leigh 29, 62 (1830).

63 *Hobson,* ed., Selected Law Cases, p. 459.

64 *Henry St. George Tucker,* Commentaries, vol. 1, bk. 1, p. 9.

went unchallenged. When the English decisions were distinguished or overruled, the Court always articulated its reasoning for the exception. And, indeed, it is the exceptions that prove the rule. The willingness of the Virginia Court of Appeals to follow the common law when to do so protected individual liberties and predictability in social and economic relations, but to depart from English precedent when it seemed contrary to republican principles or to the circumstances of the new country, or, especially, to the will of the people voiced through statute, proved its commitment to a new order. For all this, however, there is a strain of conservatism in the attitude of the Court of Appeals toward the English heritage.[65] With the exception of occasional and necessary deviations, the commitment was to predictability and stability, which could best be achieved by conforming to the safe and familiar rules and procedures of the English common law.

Of course, as the decades progressed, an indigenous Virginia law also gradually developed, although, by 1830, the citations to Virginia cases were still outnumbered by those to their British counterparts.[66] It is an interesting study to review how the Virginia Court of Appeals treated Virginia precedent. Predictably, as a general rule, the ability to cite a Virginia decision as directly on point was a boon to any lawyer's argument.[67] But there appears an interesting dichotomy between the Court's treatment of the pre-Revolutionary General Court cases and the respect given the postwar decisions of the Court of Appeals. It was not uncommon for the Court of Appeals to disregard the decisions of the colonial (i.e. "royal") General Court. At one point the Court noted that "it has never been pretended that the decisions of the old General Court have been considered as conclusive."[68] Partially this was because, technically, the old General Court was not a court of last resort. It was left unstated, and therefore a matter of speculation, whether this disrespect had anything to do with that Court's close association with the hated colonial governors.[69]

The point about a willingness to overrule General Court cases should not be overstated. Consistent with our findings regarding the English common law, the stress was on continuity rather than change. Perhaps no case better displays the limited nature of the Revolution's impact on Virginia law than that of *Wallace v. Taliaferro,* decided in 1800. That adjudication brought into question the binding power of precedents from the old General Court regarding property in slaves. Judge Roane was aghast at the very thought of questioning that line of cases. "I

---

65 *Hobson,* ed., Selected Law Cases, p. 459.

66 *Ibid.*, pp. 458–459. In volume 1 of *B. W. Leigh,* Reports (1829), 151 English cases were cited, and 140 Virginia cases. For an example of Virginia precedent as determinative, see *Mickie v. Lawrence,* 5 Randolph 571, 573, 576 (1827); see also *Spencer v. Moore,* 4 Call 23 (1798).

67 *Hobson,* ed., Selected Law Cases, p. 462.

68 *Claiborne v. Henderson,* 3 Hening & Munford 322, 375 (1809).

69 *Wallace v. Taliaferro,* 2 Call 447, 469, 489 (1800). See also *Pickett v. Claiborne,* 4 Call 99 (1787); *White v. Johnson,* 1 Washington 159 (1793).

had supposed that no question would have been made of the competency of those decisions to fix rules of property in this country ... if we reject such rules of property as have been fixed by that court and under which our people have regulated their property through a long series of time, the mischief, which would ensue, is incalculable."[70] It was Judge Pendleton, however, who directly responded to any insinuation that the Revolution had engendered a change in the law of property in Virginia. Pendleton assumed that such cases had been brought "to discover if the Revolution had produced any change in the legal sentiment. Fortunately, for the peace of the country, the experiment failed, and the point was left at rest." The chief justice concluded: "I imagine some young gentleman of the bar, not old enough to know the practice of the country, nor acquainted with the former decisions, advised the suit ...".[71] Nowhere can one find a better illustration of a Revolution admittedly fought for "liberty," but one in which, all the while, *property* rights were conservatively protected.

In any event, the Justices appeared even less likely to overrule the decisions of their own predecessors on the Virginia Court of Appeals. In an early case, Judge Pendleton felt he must offer an explanation for an apparent deviation from a recent adjudication. In *Jollife v. Hite,* he admitted that "Uniformity in the decisions of this Court is all important. We have, however, progressed but little from the commencement of our existence; and, if, in any instance, we should recently discover a mistake in a former decision, we should surely correct it, and not let the error go forth to our citizens, as a governing rule of their conduct."[72] As the decades progressed, the rare instance of the Court overruling a previous decision was without exception accompanied by such protestations as Judge Carr's in 1830: "I believe there are few men less disposed than myself to disturb the decisions of this court made by the enlightened judges who have gone before us. Cases, however, do sometimes arise in which our respect for their decisions must yield to a more imperious duty."[73]

The discussion thus far has neglected the reception greeted pre-Revolutionary English statutes in Virginia. That story is more straightforward. The same ordinance of May 1776, which accepted the English common law also adopted "all statutes or acts of Parliament made in aid of the common law prior to ... [1607]."[74] Here, too, the Virginia Convention evinced a willingness to rely heavily upon the English legal heritage. But, it is interesting to note the English statutes that were *not* adopted by the Virginia Convention in May 1776. By the specific language of the ordinance, English statutes passed since 1607 were not included.

70 *Wallace v. Taliaferro,* 2 Call 447, 469 (1800).

71 *Id.* at 489.

72 *Jollife v. Hite,* 1 Call 301, 328 (1798).

73 *Commonwealth v. Lilly's admr.,* 1 Leigh 525 (1830). See also *Bolling v. Mayor,* 3 Randolph 563, 578 (1825).

74 Stat. of May 1776, c. 5, § 6, Hening, vol. 9, p. 127.

This had the disadvantage of eliminating salutary English laws passed since that date, but the theory was that most such statutes had already been adopted by the colonial legislatures or soon would be by the new General Assembly.[75] And this proved true enough. The new Virginia legislature did copy many prior English statutes, such as the statute of frauds,[76] making certain improvements where necessary.[77] The reception statute of 1776 also accepted only British statutes "which are of a general nature, not local to that kingdom ...".[78] As St. George Tucker phrased it, this meant that some English enactments did not transfer because they were considered "obsolete, or have been deemed inapplicable to our local circumstances and policy."[79] Finally, and most importantly, the acceptance of British statutes was only "until the same shall be altered by the legislative power of this colony."[80] It was here that the most significant activity occurred, as the Virginia General Assembly undertook between 1776 and 1792 a "revisal" of the laws of Virginia which significantly altered both the common law and statute law of England as they had been originally adopted in May of 1776.[81] With the completion of the revisal in 1791, the General Assembly was evidently satisfied with its comprehensive nature because, in that year, it moved to repeal the ordinance of 1776 adopting the British statutes, and that thenceforth, "no such statute or act of parliament shall have any force or authority within this commonwealth."[82] In repealing the British legislation, the General Assembly sought to come full circle and exercise, in St. George Tucker's phrase, "the undisputed right which every free state possesses, of being governed by its own laws."[83] In doing so, however, the legislature in no way intended that its constituents should be deprived of any of the liberties which had been enjoyed under British law. To ensure that such would be the case, a caveat was inserted in the 1792 legislation preserving "all rights arising under any

---

75 *C. T. Cullen,* St. George Tucker and Law in Virginia, 1772–1804 (1987), p. 97.

76 English Stat. of 28 Car. II, c. 3 (1677); Stat. of Oct. 1785, c. 66, Hening, vol. 12, pp. 160–162.

77 Compare, e.g., the English Statute of Jeofails, 21 Jac. I, c. 13 (1626), and the Virginia Statute of Oct. 1789, c. 28, Hening, vol. 13, pp. 36–38. See *Stephens v. White,* 2 Washington 203, 210 (1796); *Braxton v. Winslow,* 4 Call 308 (1791).

78 Stat. of May 1776, c. 5, § 6, Hening, vol. 9, p. 127.

79 *St. George Tucker,* Blackstone's Commentaries, vol. 1, p. xi.

80 Stat. of May 1776, c. 5, § 6, Hening, vol. 9, p. 127.

81 *C. T. Cullen,* Completing the Revisal of the Laws in Post-Revolutionary Virginia, in Virginia Magazine of History and Biography, vol. 82, pp. 84–99 (1974); *K. Preyer,* Crime, the Criminal Law, and Reform in Post-Revolutionary Virginia in Law and History Review, vol. 1, pp. 53–85 (1983), and *K. L. Hall,* ed. Crime and Criminal Law, pp. 653–685 (1987).

82 Va. Rev. Code (1803), c. 147, § 3. It should be noted that the English common law remained in effect. *St. George Tucker,* Blackstone's Commentaries, vol. 2, p. 467, n. 1; see *Southall v. Garner,* 2 Leigh 372, 376 (1830).

83 *St. George Tucker,* Blackstone's Commentaries, vol. 1, app. E, p. 406.

such statute or act ... and ... the right and benefit of all ... writs, remedial and judicial ...".[84]

In its application of the English legal heritage to Virginia's new order, the Virginia Court of Appeals went a long way toward enunciating and defining the nature of Virginia's Revolutionary settlement. The first and most important attribute of this judicial settlement was the traditional and conservative nature of the court's approach to change in the legal traditions inherited from England. The reliance upon existing rules of law maintained the libertarian aspects of the English common law, but also had the effect of protecting property rights and thereby sustaining the existing social order.

The Court of Appeals, however, was not slavish in its devotion to English law. The most important exception to the court's usual loyalty to traditional legal rules occurred when the Virginia General Assembly overruled English statute or common law by statutory enactment. The court at all times deferred to the legislature in such instances, displaying a respect for the more "popular" (i.e. democratically elected) branch of republican government and its policy determinations. At the same time, the court continued to support traditional rules of law and property unless they were directly and unequivocally overruled by the General Assembly.

Moreover, the Virginia Court of Appeals displayed a distinctly pragmatic vein when it came to the application of English precedents. For example, it refused to do so when the results did not comport with the realities of Virginia's situation, or when the technical rules of the common law yielded an unreasonable result.

In all of this, one fact emerges as particularly striking. Throughout the period stretching from the Revolution to 1830, the Court of Appeals displayed a remarkable consistency in its approach to the salient issues which arose. The court displayed a like respect for traditional rules of law in the 1790s as in the 1830s. Similarly, respect for statutory pronouncements spanned the decades under study, and the same continuity can be seen in the other topics discussed. Indeed, in all areas, examples of judicial attitudes can be drawn as easily from the early nineteenth-century reports as from those of the late eighteenth century. It is significant that, in 1830, the Court of Appeals was evincing a judicial approach nearly identical to that of forty and fifty years earlier. This doctrinal stability in the face of social and economic change in the Commonwealth would loom as important as many of the court's substantive pronouncements.

A corollary to these conclusions pertains to the evolving role of the Court of Appeals. In the decades between the Revolution and 1830, the court became a key player in the process of defining the nature of Virginia's adaptation to its new status as a republican commonwealth free from the dictates of English law and policy. Perhaps no other institution made a greater contribution to the complex task of

---

84 Va. Rev. Code (1803), c. 147, §§ 3, 5.

interweaving the threads of the English legal heritage into the fabric of a republican legal system. Thus, by 1830, not only had the Virginia Court of Appeals played a pivotal role in establishing and defining Virginia's new constitutional order, but it had also been instrumental in adapting the inherited English legal system to a republican commonwealth.

CHARLES F. HOBSON

Precedent, Statute, and Law in John Marshall's Jurisprudence 1801 to 1835

John Marshall (1755 – 1835) was the fourth chief justice of the United States, serving from 1801 to 1835.[1] At the time he took office, the government under the United States Constitution had been in operation twelve years. Before 1789 national concerns had been conducted by a congress of states, as provided in the Articles of Confederation adopted during the War of Independence. The guiding feature of the Confederation Congress was the absolute equality and sovereignty of the individual states. The Congress did not directly legislate but adopted "ordinances" that were to be carried into effect by the state governments. The Constitution, framed in 1787 and adopted in 1788, created a new central government of national jurisdiction, superimposed upon the existing thirteen state governments that had been formed at the outset of independence in 1776 and 1777. Consisting of legislative, executive, and judicial departments, the new national government operated directly on the people. It was vested with certain enumerated powers, most importantly the power to lay taxes and to regulate commerce. In one house of the national legislature representation was proportional to population; in the other the principle of state equality was preserved. The Constitution diminished state sovereignty by means of specific restrictions and prohibitions on the states and also by a general declaration that the Constitution, laws, and treaties of the United States were to be the "supreme law of the land." In time this compound system of overlapping general and state governments came to be classified as a federal system, though one embodying a new definition of "federalism" in contradistinction to the "confederalism" of the Articles of Confederation.

The Constitution provided only a brief outline for the judicial department, naming just one court, the Supreme Court. It left to Congress's discretion the establishment of inferior federal courts and conferred lifetime appointments on the judges of both the supreme and inferior courts. It prescribed the federal judiciary's jurisdiction as extending to "all cases, in Law and Equity, arising under" the Constitution, laws, and treaties of the United States; to cases affecting ambassadors and other diplomatic officers; to admiralty and maritime cases; and to controversies

---

1 See generally *C. F. Hobson,* The Great Chief Justice: John Marshall and the Rule of Law (1996), chaps. 6, 7.

between specified parties – between two or more states, between a state and citizens of another state, between citizens of different states, and between a state or its citizens and foreign states or citizens. It assigned limited original jurisdiction to the Supreme Court – cases involving diplomats and those in which a state was party – and gave appellate jurisdiction in all other cases "with such Exceptions, and under such Regulations as the Congress shall make."[2]

These provisions were fleshed out in an organic law adopted by the First Congress in 1789. The Judiciary Act provided for a Supreme Court composed of the chief justice and five associate justices. It divided the nation into judicial districts corresponding to the states, in each of which there was to be a United States District Court composed of a United States District Judge. The districts, in turn, were divided into three circuits, in each of which there was to be a United States Circuit Court composed of any two Supreme Court justices and the district judge of the district where the court was held. In general, the district courts were to serve as original courts for trying admiralty and maritime causes, including seizures made under the impost, navigation, and trade laws of the United States, and suits for penalties and forfeitures incurred under federal laws. The circuit courts were primarily to be original tribunals for trying civil suits at common law or in equity and for trying crimes cognizable under federal law. A provision of immense importance was section 25, providing for appeals to the United States Supreme Court from the highest state courts. Such appeals were restricted to cases involving a "federal" question, as for example when a losing party in a state court claimed a right set up under the federal Constitution, laws, or treaties.[3]

The federal court system established in 1789 remained essentially intact throughout Marshall's years as chief justice. In 1801 Congress enacted a new judiciary law, creating a host of new circuit court judges and relieving Supreme Court justices of circuit duty. However, in 1802, the new Congress elected with the accession of Thomas Jefferson to the presidency repealed this law and restored the former system with some slight modifications. There were now six circuits, with courts composed of one Supreme Court justice and the district judge. In 1807 Congress added a seventh circuit and a new associate justice of the Supreme Court, increasing the number of justices to seven. Chief Justice Marshall was assigned to the fifth circuit, comprising the districts of Virginia and North Carolina. His judicial year consisted of five court terms: a single Supreme Court term in Washington, commencing the first week in February (changed to the second week in January in 1827) and adjourning usually by mid-March. In mid-May he began his spring circuit, first in Raleigh, North Carolina, where he held court for about a week, then in Richmond, Virginia, his home, where he sat from late May to mid-June and later. In the fall he repeated this circuit, beginning in mid-November and

---

2 United States Constitution, art. 3.

3 The Public Statutes at Large of the United States of America, 1789–1873, vol. 1 (1845), pp. 72–93.

concluding by late December. When sitting on the United States Circuit Court, Marshall was primarily a trial judge, though that court did have some appellate jurisdiction over district court cases. On the Supreme Court, he was almost exclusively an appellate judge, hearing cases originating in the federal circuit courts and in the state courts. On both courts he wore two hats: as a judge of common law and as a chancellor of equity.

Marshall was commissioned chief justice at the age of forty-five, having acquired broad experience as a statesman and lawyer. After serving as an officer the continental army in the War of Independence, he established a successful law practice in his native state of Virginia, sat in the state legislature, and held a seat on the state's executive council. In 1788 he helped secure Virginia's ratification of the new federal Constitution, notably in defending the judiciary article. During the 1790s, he publicly defended the measures of the government under George Washington, the first president of the United States. In 1797 and 1798 he served on an important diplomatic mission to France that earned him high praise for his defense of American honor. That assignment launched Marshall on a rapid ascent to the inner circle of the administration of John Adams, Washington's successor as president. He was secretary of state when President Adams nominated him to the bench. Marshall held the office of chief justice for thirty-five years, a tenure that so far has not been exceeded. Even before his death in 1835, he had earned a reputation as a jurist of great eminence, a peer of the most renowned English judges. In 1825, Adams wrote that it was "the pride of my life that I have given to this nation a Chief Justice equal to Coke or Hale, Holt or Mansfield."[4]

Unlike his English counterparts, Marshall won fame not as a common law interpreter or expositor of equity jurisprudence but for his achievements in the novel field of constitutional law, an area closed to the English lawyer. In an early case, *Marbury v. Madison* (1803), the Supreme Court voided a portion of a legislative act on the ground that it was contrary to the Constitution.[5] In this and in subsequent cases, the Marshall Court successfully asserted its claim to be the guardian of the Constitution and the arbiter of conflicts arising from the clash of federal and state sovereignties. This claim embraced the "duty" to consider the Constitution as paramount law in its ordinary function of adjudicating cases and to invalidate acts held to be repugnant to that law. The Marshall Court did not invent "judicial review" (a term coined in the twentieth century), but developed and refined the practice by employing the traditional methods of common law and statutory interpretation to expound the Constitution. The core of its constitutional law consisted of a "nationalist" reading of the Constitution that gave effect to the enumerated and implied powers of the federal government and to the restrictions and prohibitions on the state governments.

---

4 John Adams to Marshall, 17 Aug. 1825, in *C. F. Hobson* et al., eds., The Papers of John Marshall, vol. 10 (2000), p. 197 (hereafter cited as Marshall Papers).

5 1 Cranch 137.

Situated in the historical context of early nineteenth-century America, when the experiment of a compound federal republic had scarcely yet begun, when the role of the judicial department in particular was still largely undefined, when constitutional law was mostly uncharted territory, the Marshall Court had a unique opportunity to be creative, to write on a virtually clean slate, to make the precedents that would be the starting point for subsequent judicial inquiry. The Marshall era was "foundational" in making the national judiciary an important player in the American federal scheme of government, in making enforcement of the Constitution primarily if not exclusively a judicial responsibility, and in virtually creating the field of constitutional law and laying down enduring principles of that law. Yet for all its acclaim as a tribunal that declared the law of the Constitution, the Marshall Court was first and foremost a court of law for adjudicating the legal rights of private parties. In this respect, it was a far cry from the Supreme Court the twenty-first century, which only in matters of form bears any resemblance to an ordinary court of law. Having virtually complete control over its docket, the modern Supreme Court no longer decides routine private lawsuits but acts rather "as a roving commission seeking out important constitutional questions."[6] By definition, it takes on only the weightiest public causes, the decision of which involves it in policy-making in ways scarcely distinguishable from legislating. The Marshall Court, by contrast, remained essentially a legal institution, an appellate court for deciding ordinary cases at law. Constitutional adjudication remained an infrequent if not extraordinary exercise of judicial power. There were periodic bursts of activity, to be sure, but the Marshall Court was not "activist" in the modern sense. Most of the time it quietly pursued its strictly legal business, far removed from the controversies that agitated the public arena. Of course, it was during these long periods of quiescence that the Court solidified its institutional identity and authority in a way that conditioned Americans to accept its role in making constitutional law.

In a career of more than three decades, Marshall delivered some five hundred reported opinions on the Supreme Court and another hundred on the United States Circuit Courts for Virginia and North Carolina.[7] The Supreme Court opinions were published contemporaneously by William Cranch, Henry Wheaton, and Richard Peters, the three Supreme Court reporters of the Marshall period. Their reports were later embodied in the official series of Supreme Court reports known as *United States Reports*. Marshall's circuit opinions were first published in 1837 in a two-volume edition by John Brockenbrough, a Virginia lawyer to whom Marshall had entrusted his manuscripts. These were later incorporated in *Federal Cases*, a multivolume series of circuit court reports organized alphabetically by case title.[8] This vast corpus of judicial writings furnishes ample evidence of how

---

6 *S. M. Griffin*, American Constitutionalism: From Theory to Politics (1996), p. 129.

7 Only about thirty of Marshall's opinions can be classified as "constitutional." All but a handful of his reported circuit opinions were given in the Virginia court.

Marshall plied the craft of judging, in particular the ways in which he performed the distinct but similar enterprises of common law interpretation and statutory construction.

I. Precedent

John Marshall's understanding of the nature of law and of the theory of precedent was founded in eighteenth-century English jurisprudence, as embodied most prominently in William Blackstone's *Commentaries on the Laws of England* (1765–1769) and in the judicial opinions of Lord Mansfield, chief judge of the English Court of King's Bench (1756–1788).[9] The *Commentaries* was Marshall's student law text, and Mansfield inspired the future American chief justice as the very model of a modern common law judge.[10] As conceived by Blackstone and Mansfield, law was a body of principles and rules existing independently of particular decisions. Judicial opinions and law were not, as Blackstone put it, "convertible terms." According to Mansfield, English law "would be a strange science indeed if it were decided upon precedents only. Precedents serve to illustrate principles and give them a fixed certainty." Judicial opinions were evidence of the law, not the law itself, which (said Mansfield) consisted not "in particular cases, but in general principles, which run through the cases and govern the decision of them."[11] During the nineteenth century, the English doctrine of precedent became more rigid, reflecting a conceptual change in which judicial decisions came to be regarded not merely as evidence of the law but as the very material of the law itself.[12] No indications of such an intellectual shift were evident in the United States during the Marshall period, however, and well into the nineteenth century American lawyers continued to inhabit an eighteenth-century legal universe that not only posited a sharp distinction between principle and precedent but also gave primacy to the former over the latter.

---

8 The Marshall Papers edition is publishing only a fraction of the Supreme Court opinions (mainly, the constitutional opinions) but all of the circuit opinions.

9 For Lord Mansfield, see the essay by James Oldham, which is printed above.

10 Marshall's father Thomas Marshall was a subscriber to the first American edition of the Commentaries, published in 1772. As a student, Marshall copied extracts from Blackstone into his legal commonplace book. *W. F. Swindler,* "John Marshall's Preparation for the Bar – Some Observations on His Law Notes," in American Journal of Legal History, vol. 11 (1967), pp. 207–213; Marshall Papers, vol. 1 (1974), pp. 37–87. On Marshall's admiration for Mansfield, see *Hobson,* Great Chief Justice, 37.

11 *W. Blackstone,* Commentaries on the Laws of England, vol. 1 (1765), p. 71; *C. H. S. Fifoot,* Lord Mansfield (1936), pp. 220–221 (quoting Jones v. Randall (1774) and Rust v. Cooper (1777)).

12 *J. Evans,* "Change in the Doctrine of Precedent During the Nineteenth Century," in *L. Goldstein,* ed., Precedent in Law (1987), pp. 35–36.

A Pennsylvania judge writing in 1814, for example, urged upon his fellow American judges the duty to examine past decisions, "which are only evidence of law; and supposes a law of which they are the evidence." He went so far as to assert that a law student's "first lesson" should be "to distrust authority. A mere automaton of decision, is little better than the machine that plays chess by springs." Although he agreed that *stare decisis* was "a salutary maxim," he believed it had "been carried sufficiently far in this country."[13] James Kent, a distinguished New York jurist, endorsed a pragmatic view of judicial discretion in the first volume of his *Commentaries on American Law,* published in 1826. Precedents, he wrote, should be "duly regarded and implicitly followed" in order to give certainty and stability to legal rules, so that lawyers could give sound advice to their clients, and so that "people in general can venture with confidence to buy and trust, and to deal with each other." While noting that the "inviolability of precedents" was a principle instilled early in the history of common law adjudication, Kent would not "press too strongly the doctrine of *stare decisis*" in recollecting that the books of reports contained "more than a thousand cases" that had "been overruled, doubted, or limited in their application." The doctrine should be less rigidly adhered to in America, he suggested, where it was probable the many courts were "replete with hasty and crude decisions." These cases should "be examined without fear, and revised without reluctance."[14]

A persistent myth about John Marshall is that he was indifferent to, even disdainful of, precedent. For example, the author of a Supreme Court textbook writes that Marshall "saw issues with a vision unencumbered by reverence for precedent and not confined within the calfskin covers of the English reporters."[15] Such a remark misunderstands Marshall in bestowing too much heroic individuality on the great chief and failing to see the extent to which his jurisprudence was grounded in the Anglo-American legal tradition. Although it is true that his constitutional opinions contain relatively few citations to authorities, this omission bespoke not inattention to or disregard for precedent but rather a belief that an appeal to such authority was largely irrelevant or inappropriate in deciding this particular kind of case. "A question growing out of the constitution of the United States," Marshall explained, "requires rather an attentive consideration of the words of that instrument, than of the decisions of analogous questions by Courts of any other country."[16] In many other kinds of cases, however, such as those arising upon contracts and commercial law and those dealing with wills, trusts, and estates, he engaged in a full, sometimes exhaustive, discussion of adjudged cases. The degree of this engagement depended on the nature of the case.

---

13 *H. H. Brackenridge,* Law Miscellanies (1814), pp. 52, 54.

14 *J. Kent,* Commentaries on American Law, vol. 1 (12 ed. 1873), pp. 476–477.

15 *W. M. Wiecek,* Liberty Under Law: The Supreme Court in American Life (1988), pp. 32–33. See also *D. P. Currie,* The Constitution in the Supreme Court: The First Hundred Years, 1789–1888 (1985), pp. 89, 196.

16 Osborn v. Bank of the United States, 9 Wheaton 851 (1824).

A commentator writing in 1824 "observed with pleasure that the opinions of Mr. Chief Justice Marshall, are more generally founded upon principle than upon authority."[17] The polarity of principle and authority provides a useful analytical framework to examine Marshall's voluminous judicial opinions for evidence of the role of precedent in his jurisprudence.[18] Time and again he reiterated this distinction, typically reaching a tentative conclusion "upon principle" or "in reason" and then reviewing the relevant authorities to determine how they bore on the point at issue.[19] The differentiation between law as a body of fixed principles and the application of those principles to particular cases invited if it did not compel judges to hold up every precedent to the standard of reason. Marshall, however, resisted the temptation to stretch or exceed the limits of judicial discretion as sanctioned by the common law tradition. Examination discloses a moderate, circumspect attitude toward case law. Deeply respectful of the wisdom and learning contained in centuries of common law adjudications, Marshall was sufficiently confident in his own mastery of the law to undertake the task of engaging precedent with great independence of mind. His discussion of authorities often had the character of a running dialogue with his fellow jurists, past and present, "as if the very minds of the judges themselves stood disembodied before him."[20]

The books of English reports, together with treatises, abridgments, and digests, amounted to some 650 published volumes in 1826, to which could be added another 200 volumes of American materials – an immense repository of case law that provided illumination and guidance in resolving the myriad and often intricate disputes that came before Marshall.[21] In Marshall's court, English precedents continued to be the most frequently cited authorities. Modern English decisions, to be sure, did not have the appellate authority of those made before independence and could now "only be considered as the opinions of men distinguished for their talents & learning expounding a rule by which this country as well as theirs pro-

---

17 *P. S. Du Ponceau,* A Dissertation on the Nature and Extent of the Jurisdiction of the Courts of the United States (1824), p. xxiv.

18 *Fifoot* employed it to great effect in Lord Mansfield, chap. 7: "Principle and Precedent," pp. 198–229.

19 For examples of the distinction in Supreme Court opinions, see United States v. Grundy and Thornburgh, 3 Cranch 351 (1806); Rose v. Himely, 4 Cranch 269–270 (1808); Alexander v. Baltimore Insurance Co., 4 Cranch 376 (1808); Schooner Exchange v. McFadon, 7 Cranch 136 (1812); The Venus, 8 Cranch 298 (1814); The Commercen, 1 Wheaton 404 (1816); Hughes v. Union Insurance Co., 3 Wheaton 164 (1818); Blight's Lessee v. Rochester, 7 Wheaton 550 (1822). See also the following circuit opinions: Blane v. Drummond (U.S. Cir. Ct., Va., 1803), in Marshal Papers, vol. 6 (1990), p. 216; United States v. Burr (U.S. Cir. Ct., Va., May 28, 1807, *ibid.*, vol. 7 (1993), p. 29; Mutter's Executors v. Munford, (U.S. Cir. Ct., Va., 1814), *ibid.*, vol. 8 (1995), p. 56.

20 *J. Story,* "A Discourse upon the Life, Character, and Services of the Honorable John Marshall," in *J. F. Dillon,* ed., John Marshall: Life, Character, and Judicial Services, vol. 3 (1903), p. 377.

21 *Kent,* Commentaries, vol. 1 (12 ed. 1873), p. 474, note.

fesses to be governed," said Marshall, adding: "When however they are reasonable, are conformable to general principles, and do not change a rule previously established such decisions cannot be entirely disregarded."[22] Over time, the chief justice heard an increasing number of citations of American state and federal court decisions, which on questions of general law supplemented those contained in the English books. In seeking guidance on such questions, Marshall did not distinguish between English and American case law. The authoritativeness of a precedent depended on whether it expressed the correct legal principle, not, except in special circumstances, on the jurisdiction of the court making the decision. On circuit in Virginia, for example, he once had to choose between a decision of the Virginia Court of Appeals and a modern English decision in a case concerning principal and agent. In this instance he followed the English precedent because it laid down the general rule and appeared "to be directly in point."[23]

Marshall, like other eighteenth-century Anglo-American judges, fully recognized the dominant and often binding authority of adjudged cases. He acknowledged his duty to submit to authority even if it did not seem to conform strictly to reason and justice. He did not consider himself free to break the chain of precedents when his own opinion leaned another way. In a circuit opinion of 1822, for example, he said, if this were a case of "first impression," he would incline strongly to the opinion that a tenant by elegit could be considered a tenant for years and that therefore an action of waste could be maintained against him – he could not clearly perceive the distinction between the two. However, the question was "as completely settled as a question of law can be settled by authority. Lord Coke in his commentary on the statute of Gloster says that tenant by elegit is not within it, because he is not tenant for years. All the books concur in this opinion." Likewise, in an 1824 circuit case, Marshall abandoned his original opinion that a simple contract creditor in a court of law would retain the same rank in a court of equity. Examination showed that the "the decisions are otherwise, and I must acquiesce in those decisions."[24] Personal inclination also gave way in a celebrated case of 1811, when Edward Livingston sued Thomas Jefferson in the United States Circuit Court of Virginia for evicting him from the "batture" at New Orleans during the latter's presidency. Taking advantage of the venerable distinction between local and transitory actions, Jefferson pleaded to the jurisdiction, contending that this court could not hear the case because the alleged trespass took place outside the district of Virginia. Marshall upheld this plea, not having the "hardihood" to

---

22 Murdock v. Hunter (U.S. Cir. Ct., Va., 1809), in Marshall Papers, vol. 7 (1993), pp. 209–210, 211. See also Livingston v. Jefferson (U.S. Cir. Ct., Va., 1811), *ibid.*, p. 284.

23 Short v. Skipwith (U.S. Cir. Ct., Va., 1806), Marshall Papers, vol. 6 (1990), pp. 458–459. For another circuit case in which he adhered to a line of English decisions, this time in preference to a decision of the United States Supreme Court, see United States v. Nelson and Myers (U.S. Cir. Ct., Va., 1822), *ibid.*, vol. 9 (1998), pp. 267–268.

24 Scott and Lyle v. Lenox (U.S. Cir. Ct., Va., 1822) ; Lidderdale v. Robinson (U.S. Cir. Ct., Va., 1824, *ibid.*, vol. 9 (1998), pp. 251–252; vol. 10 (2000), p. 130.

challenge a distinction so encrusted in the common law that not even the great Mansfield had been able to dislodge it. Even though this rule produced "the inconvenience of a clear right without a remedy," the chief justice reluctantly concluded he "must submit to it."[25]

Marshall assumed that an authority or chain of authorities was more or less binding, depending on circumstances. An inferior court was of course absolutely bound by the decisions of the highest appellate court of its jurisdiction. Lower federal court judges, including Supreme Court justices sitting on circuit, were not free to depart from points decided by the Supreme Court. This was also true of state court judges in cases that presented federal questions, though the Supreme Court's appellate jurisdiction over the state courts under section 25 of the Judiciary Act encountered sporadic resistance during the Marshall era. On one notable occasion the Virginia Supreme Court refused to acknowledge the Supreme Court's mandate and presumed to declare section 25 unconstitutional.[26] Without actually employing the term, the Supreme Court acknowledged the force of the doctrine of *stare decisis* with respect to its own decisions, while at the same time presumed its competence to revise and reverse those precedents. The Court may have felt a greater obligation to reopen cases that presented great constitutional questions, as when it revisited in 1824 a case decided in 1819 voiding a state tax on the Bank of the United States. "This point." said Marshall, "was argued with great ability, and decided by this court, after mature and deliberate consideration, in the case of [*McCulloch v. Maryland*]. A revision of that opinion has been requested; and many considerations combine to induce a review of it."[27]

The notion of "binding authority" perhaps operated most strictly in cases where courts expounded the legislative acts of their government. No court, said Marshall, could presume that the courts of another jurisdiction "had misunderstood their own statutes, and therefore erect itself into a tribunal which should correct such misunderstanding." Thus federal judges were "no more at liberty to depart" from the construction of a state law given by the courts of that state "than to depart from the words of the statute." In a circuit case of 1821 Marshall declared that, if the Virginia Court of Appeals had decided a particular point under the state's statute of frauds, he would "have followed that precedent, however erroneous" he believed it to be. To submit to the authority in this instance was not to abandon principle but rather to abide by a higher principle, namely, "that the judicial department of every government ... is the appropriate organ for construing the legislative acts of that government." On the same principle, said Marshall, the Supreme Court's construction of federal law should prevail in the state courts independent of its appellate jurisdiction over those courts.[28]

---

25 Livingston v. Jefferson (U.S. Cir. Ct., Va., 1811), *ibid.*, vol. 7 (1993), pp. 284, 285.

26 Martin v. Hunter's Lessee, 1 Wheaton 304 (1816), reversing 18 Virginia (4 Munford) 1.

27 Osborn v. Bank of the United States, 9 Wheaton 859 (1824).

Bowing to the authority of precedents was easiest when they laid "down the positive rule in strict conformity with principle." On the other hand, the easiest and least controversial means of deeming a case to be an unsatisfactory authority was that it was too "imperfectly," "vaguely," "obscurely," "loosely," or "carelessly" reported.[29] Denying the authority of adjudged cases was also relatively easy to do when the question turned on practice rather than principle. Thus, Lord Mansfield's reasons for adhering to a rule concerning pleading did "not apply in the United States, where costs are not affected by the length of the declaration." Similarly, after noting the "different practice" prevailing in Virginia concerning sales under a decree of a court of equity, Marshall stated "after mature consideration" that he could not be influenced by the course of English decisions on this subject. On another occasion, he replied to counsel's citation of English authorities by observing "that the law which governs the practice [of pleading] in England, is different from that which governs the practice in Virginia."[30]

More often than not, adjudication was an arduous intellectual exercise in reconciling principle and precedent. Assuming the reasonable accuracy of the report, Chief Justice Marshall employed a variety of time-honored lawyerly techniques to prevent a troublesome case from being drawn into the magnetic field of precedential authority. Rather than directly impugn the reasoning or correctness of a previous decision, he preferred to parry or deflate its significance for the case at hand. A common means of weakening if not exploding precedents was to distinguish them on "points of dissimilitude" so "striking" or "material" as to impair their authority for the point under consideration. Other alleged precedents either were not expressly in point or had not clearly decided a particular question. Or they might be pertinent but their application should not be extended to cases not "precisely similar."[31]

---

28 Elmendorf v. Taylor, 10 Wheaton 159–160 (1825); Backhouse's Administrator v. Jett's Administrator, (U.S. Cir. Ct., Va., 1821), in Marshall Papers, vol. 9 (1998), p. 163; Marshall to James M. Marshall, 9 July 1822, *ibid.*, vol. 9 (1998), p. 240. For other cases affirming the rule that federal courts must adopt state judicial constructions of local law, see M'Keen v. DeLancy's Lessee, 5 Cranch 32 (1809); Polk's Lessee v. Wendell, 9 Cranch 98 (1815); Thatcher v. Powell, 6 Wheaton 127 (1821).

29 Mutter's Executors v. Munford (U.S. Cir. Ct., Va., 1814), in Marshall Papers, vol. 8 (1995), p. 57; Graves & Barnewall v. Boston Marine Insurance Co., 2 Cranch 442 (1805); United States v. Feely (U.S. Cir. Ct., Va., 1813), in Marshall Papers, vol. 7 (1993), pp. 393, 394; Backhouse's Administrator v. Jett's Administrator, (U.S. Cir. Ct., Va., 1821), *ibid.*, vol. 9 (1998), pp. 161–162; Garnett v. Macon (U.S. Cir. Ct., Va., 1825), *ibid.*, vol. 10 (2000), p. 230; Hamilton Donaldson & Co. v. Cunningham (U.S. Cir. Ct., Va., 1828), *ibid.*, vol. 11 (2002), p. 122. See also Murdock v. Hunter (U.S. Cir. Ct., Va., 1809), *ibid.*, vol. 7 (1993), p. 210.

30 Wilson v. Codman's Executor, 3 Cranch 209 (1805); Bond v. Ross (U.S. Cir. Ct., Va., 1805), in Marshall Papers, vol. 6 (1990), pp. 418–419; Furniss v. Ellis & Allan (U.S. Cir. Ct., Va., 1822), *ibid.*, vol. 9 (1998), pp. 205–206.

31 For examples, see Calloway v. Dobson (U.S. Cir. Ct., Va., 1807), *ibid.*, vol. 7 (1993), pp. 34–35; Alexander v. Harris, 4 Cranch 302 (1808); Hughes v. Union Insurance Co., 3

Another common mode of blunting the force of precedent was to confine a judge's decision to the particular circumstances of the case decided. "Every opinion, to be correctly understood, ought to be considered with a view to the case in which it was delivered," said Marshall. Statements going "beyond the case ... may be respected, but ought not to control the judgment in a subsequent suit when the very point is presented for decision," he explained, adding: "The reason of this maxim is obvious. The question actually before the Court is investigated with care, and considered in its full extent. Other principles which may serve to illustrate it, are considered in their relation to the case decided, but their possible bearing on all other cases is seldom completely investigated." Marshall invariably resorted to this maxim whenever counsel seized upon a judge's "dicta" (statements not essential to the decision of a case) to support what he considered to be dubious legal conclusions. It proved particularly handy when the chief justice had to finesse his way around recalcitrant precedents of his own making, as for example when he attempted to reconcile *Ex parte Bollman* with *United States v. Burr* and *Marbury v. Madison* with *Cohens v. Virginia.*[32]

Marshall employed the maxim to repel the authority of an eminent jurist without implying that his illustrious fellow judge had committed error or reasoned falsely. The errors and false reasoning, on the contrary, were committed by others in drawing unwarranted inferences from a judicial opinion. "It is extremely dangerous," he cautioned, "to take general *dicta* upon supposed cases not considered in all their bearings, and, at best, inexplicitly stated, as establishing important law principles." Marshall issued this warning while limiting the application of certain dicta uttered by Lord Mansfield. In similar fashion, he dealt with some unguarded statements of his mentor, Judge Edmund Pendleton of the Virginia Court of Appeals: "To consider the judge, in such a case, as laying down a new and important principle, contrary to uniform decisions, on vague and general expressions, would be doing injustice both to the judge and to the subject."[33]

In relying on the maxim that a judge's opinions must be understood by reference to the particular case decided, Marshall was quick to exploit any special circumstances that could aid his project of bringing precedent, properly understood, in line with principle. For example, in the treason trial of Aaron Burr, the chief justice labored mightily to restrict the reach of certain dicta in Matthew Hale's treatise on English criminal law. Suggesting that the treatise was based on a flawed

Wheaton 166 (1818); Garnett v. Macon (U.S. Cir. Ct., Va., 1825), in Marshall Papers, vol. 10 (2000), p. 211; Alexander v. Baltimore Insurance Co., 4 Cranch 377 (1808); Scriba v. Deane (U.S. Cir. Ct., Va., 1810), in Marshall Papers, vol. 7 (1993), p. 264.

32 United States v. Burr (U.S. Cir. Ct., Va., August 31, 1807), *ibid.*, vol. 7 (1993), pp. 87–88; Cohens v. Virginia, 6 Wheaton 399–400 (1821).

33 Alexander v. Baltimore Insurance Co., 4 Cranch 379, 380 (1808); Scriba v. Deane (U.S. Cir. Ct., Va., 1810), in Marshall Papers, vol. 7 (1993), p. 266. See also United States v. Nelson and Myers (U.S. Cir. Ct., Va., 1822), *ibid.*, vol. 9 (1998), pp. 266–267; Brooks v. Marbury, 11 Wheaton 90–92 (1826).

manuscript, he went so far as to surmise that, if Hale's revised manuscript had served as the published text, the offending dicta "would, if not expunged, have been restrained in their application to cases of a particular description." In a dissenting opinion in an 1812 prize case, Marshall contended for a less rigid application of the principle that residence or domicile determines the national character of a merchant. In arguing this position, he confronted the imposing authority of Sir William Scott, the English admiralty judge, to whom he paid deference as a "truly great man" whose decisions he would not depart from "on light grounds." In justifying a restrictive reach of Scott's decisions, Marshall delicately suggested that Scott unconsciously adopted the English "national bias" in favor of the captors.[34]

Time and again Marshall undertook a critical examination of precedents to determine the precise extent and applicability of the rule said to be established by them. Typically, he would find that the rule had never been pressed to the extent urged in the case at bar. In a case arising on the statute of frauds, he exploited the distinction between a general principle and one "universal in its application." The numerous decisions expounding that statute, both in England and the United States, were "admitted to bind this Court," he said. They had established the sound general principle "that a voluntary gift is void as to creditors, whose debts existed at the time the gift was made." But had these decisions converted a general rule into one so universal and rigid as to make the statute "equivalent to an act annulling all gifts or voluntary conveyances, made by a person indebted at that time, however large his fortune, and however inconsiderable his debts or his gift"? Marshall's review showed that, in all the cases in which the principle was reiterated, the gift in question was "property to a considerable amount" conveyed by formal deed. In no case had a court expressly declared that "every gift, however trivial," was void as to creditors.[35] Marshall adverted to this distinction again in cautioning against undue reliance on the authority of treatises such as Joseph Chitty on the law concerning bills of exchange. "Elementary writers," he wrote, "sometimes state general rules as if they were universal; and do not always make those discriminations which a comparison of cases themselves shows ought to be made; nor trace results to the true principle which produces them."[36] Here Marshall succinctly expressed his own method of treating precedent and underscored his commitment to principles as standing apart from particular cases. The duty of a judge was not to give unquestioning deference to adjudged cases but to scrutinize them with a critical eye to nice discriminations found on a comparative review and to discover the "true principle" that governed them. From the voluminous mass of

---

34 United States v. Burr (U.S. Cir. Ct., Va., August 31, 1807), in Marshall Papers, vol. 7 (1993), pp. 104–106; The Venus, 8 Cranch 298–99, 314, 315 (1814).

35 Hopkirk v. Randolph (U.S. Cir. Ct., Va., 1824), in Marshall Papers, vol. 10 (2000), pp. 101, 105.

36 Hamilton, Donaldson & Co. v. Cunningham (U.S. Cir. Ct., Va., 1828), *ibid.*, vol. 11 (2002), p. 121.

centuries of common law adjudications, the judge was to extract the essence of law – the general principles running through and beyond particular cases.

In giving primary allegiance to principle rather than precedent, Marshall acted on the assumptions of eighteenth-century Anglo-American jurisprudence. Every technique he employed in dealing with precedent fell within the accepted canons of common law adjudication as passed down through generations of judges and solidified in the pages of Blackstone. Within the eighteenth-century understanding of judicial discretion, a recurrent debate about the nature of judging oscillated between strict submission to precedent and trust in individual judicial capacity to discern the true principles of law. Marshall's handling of precedent reflected the essential moderation and caution of his jurisprudence. He remained sensitive to the danger of pursuing principle to an extreme that risked turning a legal judgment into an act of legislation. Even as he felt the pull of principle, he acknowledged the constraints of authority. The primacy of principle did not confer a license to disregard the authority of adjudged cases but imposed a duty to reconcile the two. When they could not be harmonized, Marshall recognized that expediency or public policy might be a sufficient justification for preserving intact a chain of precedents whose basis in reason and principle had disappeared in the mists of time. In law, Marshall clearly understood, certainty was no less desirable than rationality and must often be the preferred choice of judicial wisdom.

II. Statutory Construction

Chief Justice Marshall exercised a like moderation and restraint in cases that depended on the interpretation of statute law. By the eighteenth century, statutes had become a voluminous source of English law, in contrast to the medieval period, when statutes were relatively few and confined mainly to declaring the common law. Such "legislation" was not distinguishable from adjudication, and both functions were shared by Parliament and the courts of law. In the absence of authoritative texts, judges had great freedom to interpret statutes equitably to cover cases within the spirit though not within the words of the law. Over time, legislature separated from judicature. Parliament became a self-consciously law-making institution, whose chief activity was the enactment of positive legislation to meet the demands of a modernizing society. Legislation was more carefully drafted and embodied in accurate texts. With the triumph of the doctrine of Parliamentary sovereignty, statutes as the express written will of the legislature became the supreme law of the land, having unquestioned and controlling authority in the courts of law. The judiciary's role changed accordingly, its discretion in applying statutes restricted by an elaborate set of rules designed to prevent judges from crossing the line between "interpretation" and "legislation." As judges became more closely constrained by the words of a statutory text, the principle of equitable interpretation became much attenuated.[37]

If no longer free to engage in the equitable interpretation of earlier times, judges nevertheless continued to play an essential role in expounding statutory texts, exercising an interpretive power founded on the imprecision, obscurity, and ambiguity of language that characterized even the most carefully drawn statute. Indeed, a veritable explosion of statutes in the eighteenth century created new opportunities for the judiciary to enhance its power and prestige. The swelling Parliamentary statute book produced a sustained critique of legislation as riddled with gross defects and inconsistences and a corresponding new respect for judicial interpretation as a means of rationalizing and reconciling legislation to accord with the principles of the common law and equity. Even in a system that recognized the doctrine of Parliamentary sovereignty, there was plenty of room for a robust conception of judicial power, as celebrated by Blackstone in his *Commentaries* and exemplified by Lord Mansfield on the Court of King's Bench.[38]

The same forces were at work in post-Revolutionary America and produced a similar critique of legislation, none more perceptive than that by James Madison. More quickly than anyone else, Madison recognized that the turbulent, faction-ridden, interested politics that characterized the new republican state governments was ill-suited to the task of making good laws. Instead, the assemblies enacted a profusion of ill-digested, inaccurate, confusing, and, worse, unjust laws that threatened the whole experiment in republican government. Madison understood the principal problem of reform to be the checking of legislative power, which he regarded as more than an overmatch for the executive and judiciary combined. "The legislative department," he wrote, "is everywhere extending the sphere of its activity and drawing all power into its impetuous vortex." With state legislatures each year producing an abundant harvest of new statutes requiring ever increasing adjudications, Madison and other constitutional reformers came to perceive the advantages of a knowledgeable and professionally-trained judiciary in bringing order and stability to popular government that at times threatened to careen out of control. Overcoming a widespread distrust of courts and judges at the time of independence, Americans in a remarkably short time came to the realization that courts were necessary to prevent or ameliorate mischiefs arising from the laws. An emerging distinction between "legislative will" and "justice," a growing perception that statutory law was not necessarily reasonable and just, became the foundation of a conception of judicial independence and discretion that was consistent with the republican belief in popular sovereignty. In brief, republicanism enhanced rather than constrained judicial discretion in the interpretation of written law. Indeed, so successful was the American judiciary in accommodating itself to a republican political order that Marshall and other judges were able to extend their traditional

---

37 *J. H. Baker,* An Introduction to English Legal History (3d ed. 1990), pp. 239–243; *W. D. Popkin,* Statutes in Court: The History and Theory of Statutory Interpretation (1999), pp. 9–29.

38 *D. Lieberman,* The Province of Legislation Determined: Legal Theory in Eighteenth-Century Britain (1989), pp. 13–20; *Popkin,* Statutes in Court, pp. 19–29.

power of statutory interpretation to the novel field of interpreting written constitutions.[39]

Because legislative enactments did not automatically gain the status of "law" and often required judicial intervention to clarify their meaning, statutory interpretation and common law interpretation were similar endeavors. "Law" was conceived of as something apart from either statute or precedent, In construing statutes, judges sought to rationalize legislation, to bring it into conformity with justice and reason, in the same way they attempted to reconcile principle and precedent. The governing principle of these cases was to read the statute so as to carry into effect the intention of the legislature. The authority relied on was the statutory text, but the "imperfection of all human language," its inability to express accurately for all times and circumstances the precise meaning of the text, created space for a judge to decide which interpretation of the words most faithfully conformed to legislative intent.[40]

Marshall frequently invoked the phrase "fair construction" to describe his pragmatic, common-sense approach to interpreting written law. Fair construction, as he described it, was "a medium between that restricted sense which confines the meaning of words to narrower limits than the common understanding of the world affixes to them, and that extended sense which would stretch them beyond their obvious import." It "gives to language the sense in which it is used, and interprets an instrument according to its true intention."[41] To the extent possible, fair construction should be minimal construction, departing in the smallest degree from the literal meaning of the words. He acknowledged that in earlier times courts exercised equitable interpretation, often going "far beyond the words" and supplying omissions. Modern practice, he observed, had "been a good deal restrained," though courts still construed "words liberally, to reach that intention the words themselves import."[42]

As a modern judge, Marshall was reluctant to take words beyond their natural import, to discard the literal meaning in favor of one supposedly more faithful to

---

39 *Madison* ("Publius"), The Federalist No. 48, in *C. Rossiter,* ed., The Federalist Papers (1961), p. 309. See *J. N. Rakove,* "The Origins of Judicial Review: A Plea for New Contexts," Stanford Law Review, vol. 49 (1996–1997), pp. 1051–1060; *G. S. Wood,* "The Origins of Judicial Review Revisited, or How the Marshall Court Made More Out of Less," Washington and Lee Law Review, vol. 56 (1999), pp. 799–801.

40 King v. Delaware Insurance Co., 6 Cranch 80 (1810). For other references to the imperfection of language, see United States v. Burr (U.S. Cir. Ct., Va., June 13, 1807), in Marshall Papers, vol. 7 (1993), p. 40; Shore's Executor v. Jones (U.S. Cir. Ct., Va., 1814), *ibid.*, vol. 8 (1995), p. 44.

41 Turner v. Fendall, 1 Cranch 131 (1801); United States v. Willing & Francis, 4 Cranch 56 (1807); United States v. Burr (U.S. Cir. Ct., Va., June 13, 1807), in Marshall Papers, vol. 7 (1993), p. 40; Peisch v. Ware, 4 Cranch 363 (1808); Rutherford v. Green's Heirs, 2 Wheaton 201 (1817); Chirac v. Chirac, 2 Wheaton 271 (1817); Postmaster General v. Early, 12 Wheaton 150 (1827); "A Friend to the Union," No. II, in Marshall Papers, vol. 8 (1995), p. 299.

42 Kirkpatrick v. Gibson (U.S. Cir. Ct., Va., 1828), *ibid.*, vol. 11 (2002), p. 182.

the spirit of the law. The "spirit of the law," he said, was simply "the intention of the legislature, to be collected from the general language of the act, the scope of its provisions, and the object to be attained." The burden of proof was always on the party seeking to vary the usual understanding of words or to infer an implication where there was no explicit provision.[43] A law, he said, "was the best expositor of itself," every part of which was "to be taken into view, for the purpose of discovering the mind of the legislature." Words could not be understood in isolation, detached from their context, or without reference to the subject, nature, and purpose of the legislation. In keeping the whole law in view, one part might be "expounded by any other, which may indicate the meaning annexed by the legislature itself to ambiguous phrases." It was also appropriate in certain circumstances to consider several acts on the same subject in reference to each other, using the provisions of one to expound those of another.[44]

In statutory construction cases, Marshall encountered numerous instances in which the words of a law, taken by themselves, were of doubtful or ambiguous meaning. The typical case required him to determine the sense in which general words or expressions were used. Here the rule was "that general phrases may be explained, and restrained or enlarged by other words which demonstrate the sense in which those general phrases were used." A related rule was "that general expressions may be restrained by subsequent particular words" that showed the legislature's intention to use those general expressions "in a particular sense."[45] As general words might have a more or less restrictive meaning, so words having "a direct and common meaning" might "also be used in a less common sense." But they were not to be so understood, Marshall cautioned, unless the context showed a "clear design" or "manifest intent" to give them "a less obvious meaning."[46]

If the construction to be given words did not emerge clearly from the context, a jurist might properly call in aid the subject of the legislation, the reasons for its enactment, and the effects and consequences of adopting one interpretation or

43 Schooner Patriot [Thompson] v. United States (U.S. Cir. Ct., Va., 1820), *ibid.*, vol. 9 (1998), p. 79; United States v. Fisher, 2 Cranch 386 (1805): "As the enacting clause in this case, would plainly give the United States the preference they claim, it is incumbent on those who oppose that preference, to shew an intent varying from that which the words import."

44 Pennington v. Coxe, 2 Cranch 52 (1804); Postmaster General v. Early, 12 Wheaton 152 (1827). See also similar statements in United States v. Fisher, 2 Cranch 386 (1805); Alexander v. Mayor and Commonalty of Alexandria, 5 Cranch 7 – 8 (1809); The Mary Ann, 8 Wheaton 387 (1823); United States v. Burr (U.S. Cir. Ct., Va., September 18, 1807); Strode v. Stafford Justices (U.S. Cir. Ct., Va., 1810); United States v. Twitty (U.S. Cir. Ct. N.C., 1811); Shore's Executor v. Jones (U.S. Cir. Ct., Va., 1814), in Marshall Papers, vol. 7 (1993), pp. 144, 260, 275; vol. 8 (1995), p. 44.

45 United States v. Burr (U.S. Cir. Ct., Va., September 18, 1807), *ibid.*, vol. 7 (1993), p. 144; Adams v. Woods, 2 Cranch 341 (1805). See also Alexander v. Mayor and Commonalty of Alexandria, 5 Cranch 7 – 8 (1809); The Mary Ann, 8 Wheaton 387 (1823).

46 The Brig Wilson v. United States (U.S. Cir. Ct., Va., 1820), in Marshall Papers, vol. 9 (1998), p. 35; Oneale v. Thornton, 6 Cranch 68 (1810).

another. It was not unusual for Marshall to combine close analysis of the words with extensive analysis of subject, purpose, and consequence. A notable example was his construction of a revenue law in an 1804 case, in which he exempted from payment a duty on sugar refined before the expiration of the law but not yet sent out.[47] Marshall read a statute, so to speak, inside out and outside in to gather evidence of the mind of the legislature. Depending on the nature and circumstances of the case, the results of his analysis confirmed or departed from a literal reading of words; gave a restrictive or an enlarged sense to words; or endorsed a "strict" or a "liberal" construction.

In a leading case, *United States v. Fisher* (1805), Chief Justice Marshall upheld a literal, nonrestrictive reading of a section of an act for settling the accounts of receivers of public money so as to give the United States priority of payment out of the estates not only of public officers and other receivers of public money but of any insolvent debtor to the government. This was a good example of relying on the "plain meaning" of words as the safer guide to intention than relying on deduction from the title and other sections of the statute that might imply a restrictive reading. A nonrestrictive construction was appropriate in this case because it produced only "inconvenience" and did not affect fundamental rights.[48] Similarly, he construed the patent laws to sustain the right of an inventor to sue for damages against a person who had built and used his machine before the patent had issued. Although "some injustice" might result from this construction, Marshall concluded that "the great fundamental principles of right & of property do not appear to be so vitally wounded as to induce the court to resist & struggle against the obvious meaning of words."[49]

When fundamental rights were implicated, however, Marshall was inclined to adopt strict construction, as when he restricted the operation and reach of criminal statutes, embargo and nonintercourse laws, and laws enacted during wartime. Thus he read a statute defining crimes against the United States restrictively to exclude foreigners from being tried for piracy under the act. He interpreted the same law in denying federal jurisdiction in a case of manslaughter committed by an American seaman on board an American vessel in a foreign river. Although the act prescribed punishment for murder committed on the "on the high seas" and "in any river, haven, basin, or bay, out of the jurisdiction of any particular State," the punishment for manslaughter included only "the high seas." Marshall refused to enlarge the construction of this phrase beyond its "plain meaning." No intention was to be implied from the probability that Congress might want to make manslaughter cognizable in the same places it prescribed for murder. "It would be dangerous, indeed," he warned, "to carry the principle, that a case which is within the

47 Pennington v. Coxe, 2 Cranch 51 – 64 (1804).

48 2 Cranch 386, 390.

49 Evans v. Jordan and Morehead (U.S. Cir. Ct., Va., 1813), in Marshall Papers, vol. 7 (1993), p. 407.

reason or mischief of a statute, is within its provisions, so far as to punish a crime not enumerated in the statute, because it is of equal atrocity, or of kindred character, with those which are enumerated." While invoking the standard canon that penal statutes were to be construed strictly, Marshall relied principally on intention as manifested by the words of the statute. A minute investigation of the language satisfied him that Congress had not prescribed punishment for manslaughter in any place other than on the "high seas" and that the Court could not "enlarge the statute."[50]

In similar fashion, Marshall restricted the reach of acts for prosecuting war, refusing to extend them to cases not explicitly embraced by the words of the law. In such cases, he called in aid another conventional rule of construction, namely, that legislative enactments were to be interpreted as being in harmony with the principles of natural law and the law of nations. Wartime laws, for example, should "never be construed to violate neutral rights, or to affect neutral commerce, further than is warranted by the law of nations as understood in this country." He further assumed that the United States had adopted the more civilized and humane understanding of that law that prevailed in the advanced commercial nations of Europe. Thus Congress in declaring war could not be presumed to have authorized confiscation, since the modern rule, "introduced by commerce in favor of moderation and humanity," was opposed to the idea that war automatically vested enemy property in the belligerent government. Because Congress had not by express legislation confiscated enemy property, Marshall applied the law of nations to restore seized property to its owner. In another case he refused to condemn property as prize of war because no statute for that purpose had been adopted. "Till such an act be passed," he said, "the Court is bound by the law of nations which is a part of the law of the land."[51]

The most difficult cases were those in which a court was asked to modify statutory language, supply omissions, draw implications – in short, to give a liberal construction to the legislature's words. Marshall justified liberal construction only to the extent necessary to reach an intention manifested positively by the language, subject, and purposes of the law and negatively by the absurd, repugnant, or meaningless consequences of a literal or strict construction. A "law requiring two repugnant and incompatible things," he said, "is incapable of receiving a literal construction, and must sustain some change of language to be rendered intelligible. This change, however, ought to be as small as possible, and with a view to the sense of the legislature, as manifested by themselves." Thus a simple change of a participle

---

50 United States v. Palmer, 3 Wheaton 630–631 (1818); United States v. Wiltberger, 5 Wheaton 93–105 (1820) (quotations at 96, 105). See also United States v. Bevans, 3 Wheaton 386–391 (1818).

51 The Venus, 8 Cranch 297 (1814). See also Talbot v. Seeman, 1 Cranch 44 (1801); Murray v. Schooner Charming Betsey, 2 Cranch 118 (1804); Meade v. Deputy Marshall of Virginia District (U.S. Cir. Ct., Va., 1815), in Marshall Papers, vol. 8 (1995), p. 88; Brown v. United States, 8 Cranch 125 (1814); The Nereide, 9 Cranch 423 (1815).

into the future tense of a verb could "destroy the repugnancy" contained in a particular passage of a law and "reconcile" it with another that "absolutely demonstrates" the legislature's intention. In certain situations, as when "the whole context of the law" showed a "particular intent ... to effect a certain object," a court could call in "some degree of implication ... to aid that intent." From Congress's affirmative declaration in the judiciary act that the Supreme Court's appellate power extended to circuit court judgments of a value exceeding 2,000 dollars, for example, the Court implied an intent to except from its jurisdiction judgments of less value.[52]

Among the rules of construction set down by Blackstone was that statutes against frauds "were to be liberally and beneficially expounded." Marshall applied this maxim, without expressly referring to it, in extending Virginia's law regulating conveyances to embrace deeds conveying personal as well as real property. The act voided as to creditors and subsequent purchasers all deeds of trust and mortgages unless acknowledged, proved, and recorded according to the directions of the act. This legislation appeared to give directions only for conveyances of land, however, omitting mortgages of personal property. Acknowledging that the statute was "very obscurely penned in this particular respect," the chief justice nevertheless concluded that it was sufficient to embrace deeds conveying personal property. "In a country where mortgages, of a particular kind of personal property [i.e., slaves], are frequent," he observed, "it can scarcely be supposed that no provision would be made for so important and interesting a subject." Since the legislature clearly intended to provide for mortgages of personal property and the "inconvenience resulting from the total want of such a provision would certainly be great," the Court was justified in liberally construing the law to effect that intention.[53] He construed the same law as also designating in which court mortgages of personal property were to be recorded, acknowledging that to effect this intention he had to read the statute as if certain phrases had been inserted. "There are few cases in which this freedom of construction can be justified," he admitted. "If any act will justify it, it is the act for regulating conveyances." Again, Marshall was not content with a mechanical application of a rule of construction but conducted a discriminating review of the act's language to discover the legislature's intention. Indeed, he confessed that he was "not sure" he would have given this opinion had it not been supported by a case decided in the state court of appeals.[54]

---

52 Huidekoper's Lessee v. Douglas, 3 Cranch 66 (1805); Durosseau v. United States, 6 Cranch 314 (1810).

53 *W. Blackstone,* Commentaries, vol. 1 (1765), p. 88; Hodgson v. Butts, 3 Cranch 156–158 (1805).

54 Bond v. Ross (U.S. Cir. Ct., Va., 1815), in Marshall Papers, vol. 8 (1995), pp. 101–106 (quotations at 103, 105, 106). For other examples of liberal construction, see Gallego v. United States (U.S. Cir. Ct., Va., 1820), *ibid.*, vol. 9 (1998), p. 41; Postmaster General v. Early, 12 Wheaton 150–152 (1827).

Whether employing strict or liberal construction, judges risked invading the legislative province, a danger to which Marshall remained alert. A "constrained interpretation" of the words in the act for settling the accounts of receivers of public money, for example, would have avoided "inconvenience." But this would involve the court in weighing the costs and benefits of the legislation, a calculation that Congress should be presumed to have undertaken and one wholly inappropriate for judicial consideration.[55] Likewise, to enlarge the meaning of statutory words, as in a penal law, would extend it "to cases to which the legislature had not extended it, and to punish, not by the authority of the legislature, but of the judge." Construction should not "be carried so far as to thwart the scheme of policy which the legislature has the power to adopt."[56] Nor should it on grounds of convenience presume to advance policy goals by curing defects or supplying omissions.

Marshall can be described as a "textualist" in the sense that he preferred to adhere as closely as possible to the letter of the statute and believed that the letter was the most reliable guide to its "spirit." At the same time he eschewed clause-bound textualism in favor of a broader approach to unlocking statutory meaning. No "legislative act, no instrument of any description," he said, "is construed without regard to the object and intent of its framers, as manifested by itself. Language is too imperfect to admit of such a rule. The same words, in different connexion have a different import. The intention, therefore, must be regarded; and to find that intention, whatever relates to the subject must be inspected."[57] Marshall conducted his inquiry into intention by means of reciprocal, overlapping arguments focusing on words, context, nature and objects, and consequences. Without adhering to a set formula or strict order of argumentation, his expositions of statutes exhibited a similar pattern of dialogue between text and intention, letter and spirit.

Chief Justice Marshall applied the same methods and techniques of interpreting statutes by "fair construction" to the United States Constitution. He fully recognized the difference between a statute and a written constitution but considered this difference to be one of degree, not kind. He assumed that the Constitution could be construed like any other written instrument. Although a discussion of Marshall's constitutional cases is beyond the scope of this essay, some observations about his mode of interpreting the Constitution may be in order. "In performing the delicate and important duty of construing clauses in the constitution of our country, which involve conflicting powers of the government of the Union, and of the respective States", the chief justice wrote, "it is proper to take a view of the literal meaning of the words to be expounded, of their connexion with other words, and of the general objects to be accomplished by the prohibitory clause, or by the

---

55 United States v. Fisher, 2 Cranch 390 (1805).

56 Ship Adventure (U.S. Cir. Ct., Va., 1812); Evans v. Jordan & Morehead (U.S. Cir. Ct., Va., 1813), in Marshall Papers, vol. 7 (1993), pp. 351, 406.

57 Shore's Executor v. Jones (U.S. Cir. Ct., Va., 1814), *ibid.*, vol. 8 (1995), p. 44.

grant of power."[58] Marshall characteristically read the Constitution in a liberal, nonrestrictive sense in construing both the grants of power to the federal government and the prohibitions and restrictions on the state governments. Liberal interpretation was the appropriate means to expound the Constitution, he insisted, because this instrument was not a prolix "legal code" but marked only the "great outlines" and designated only the "important objects." In considering the extent and scope of a delegated power, Marshall famously declared, "we must never forget, that is *a constitution* we are expounding."[59]

Marshall directed much of his constitutional interpretation against the "strict construction" advocated by proponents of state sovereignty. These critics complained that the chief justice virtually rewrote the Constitution by constructively enlarging federal powers while abridging state powers. He indignantly denied the charge as a gross misrepresentation of his efforts to expound the Constitution according to the accepted canons of legal interpretation. His quarrel with strict construction was not that it was an improper mode of explicating a legal text but that it was incorrectly applied to certain clauses of the Constitution to confine their meaning to narrower limits than the plain sense of the words imported, even when no restrictive intent could be shown. This rigid strict construction was bad law, said Marshall. Its labored attempts to prove an intent to depart from the "plain meaning" of words by some theory or evidence not grounded in the Constitution's text violated the received maxims of legal construction. States' rights advocates, he suggested, were guilty of the error of excessive constructionism, of ignoring the text of the Constitution and deducing intent from external sources. Perhaps his most effective reply to strict construction as applied to the Constitution was that it failed the test of consequences. It would leave the Constitution "a magnificent structure, indeed, to look at, but totally unfit for use." It "would essentially change the constitution, render the government of the Union incompetent to the objects for which it was instituted, and place all its powers under the control of the state legislatures. It would, in a great measure, reinstate the old confederation."[60]

More than anyone else, Marshall was responsible for assimilating constitutional exegesis to the principles and methods of adjudication sanctioned by centuries of Anglo-American law. He made judicial exposition of the constitutional text a more or less routine byproduct of adjudicating lawsuits. His broader significance may lie less in his particular interpretations of the Constitution than in his largely successful effort to infuse constitutional pronouncements with the qualities of an ordinary legal judgment. In this way he contributed immeasurably to the American people's ultimate acceptance of such pronouncements as so much *law*.

58 Brown v. Maryland, 12 Wheaton 437 (1827).

59 McCulloch v. Maryland, 4 Wheaton 406, 407 (1819).

60 Gibbons v. Ogden, 9 Wheaton 222 (1824); "A Friend to the Union," No. II, in Marshall Papers, vol. 8 (1995), p. 304.

JEAN-LOUIS HALPÉRIN

The Court of Cassation in Nineteenth-Century France and the Binding Effect of *Rationes Decidendi*

From the French Revolution, the relationships between the judicial power and the legislative power in France have been framed by two apparently contradictory evolutions. On the one hand, the legislative rule became the principal source of the law: a penal code was worked out by the Constituent Assembly; then, the napoleonic codification was carried out from 1804 to 1810. These codified laws were, in theory, to be strictly applied by the judges, according to Beccaria's principle of the legal syllogism. On the other hand, a law of 1790 established a *Tribunal de cassation* – it became the *Cour de cassation* in 1804 – empowered with controlling the respect of the laws by the lower courts. This was accomplished by quashing the judgments of the inferior courts that infringed the text of the law. In spite of the will expressed by some members of the Constituent Assembly to banish any jurisprudence, i.e. case law, this institution quickly developed a kind of binding jurisprudence.[1] The judicial experiment paralleled the contemporaneous legal experiment.

This double evolution, beginning at the same time, finds its origin in the obligation placed upon all the judges by the law of August 16–24, 1790, to express the reasons of their decision by quoting the text of the law they applied. In opposition to the practice of the Ancien Régime which had led the higher courts, the parlements, not to justify their decisions,[2] this legal obligation led the judges in the contrary direction. The purpose of this was to bring closer, in an argued reasoning, the facts of the case and the texts of the laws applied, knowing that in the majority of the cases it was necessary to combine several texts from different origins. Moreover, the Court of cassation was required to compare two texts, the text of the disputed judgment and the text of the quoted law. It was thus led to give the meaning of these texts, that is to clarify, explain, and imperceptibly interpret the law. Even in a civil law country, the Supreme Court had to declare the law in civil and criminal matters.

---

1 *Jean-Louis Halpérin*, Le Tribunal de cassation et les pouvoirs sous la Révolution française, Paris 1987.

2 See the essay by V. Demars-Sion and S. Dauchy, which is printed above.

My study of the holding of the decisions of the *Tribunal,* then the *Cour de cassation,* has for its purpose to see how the French writing style of judgments has been formed, which types of selection the judges had to operate between the sources of law, which are the arguments and the logical figures employed, how these instruments of legal reasoning were diffused in the lower courts, and how they were used to develop a jurisprudence, in some cases *praeter legem,* even *contra legem.* The French Revolution and the napoleonic era were the turning point of this history of the judicial style, and, during the nineteenth century, the change was more in publishing than in writing the judgments.

The law of November 27 – December 1, 1790, which created the *Tribunal de cassation,* only envisaged the insertion of the text of the law relied upon into the dispositive part of the judgment, a part in theory different from the reasons. In criminal matters, the law of September 16, 1791, evokes more clearly the "reason for the cassation". After a period of doubt about the general application of the holding to all the judgments of the *Tribunal de cassation,* including the decisions of rejection, two decrees of 1794 definitively impose this obligation, to give the reasons to any decision of the supreme court.[3]

Actually the writing-style of judgments of the Court of cassation changes quickly during the first years of the existence of the new institution. The first judgments, going back to 1791, are extremely laconic: the *Tribunal de cassation* quashes a decision "as contrary" to such article of such law which is quoted.[4] These first judgments, reduced to a few lines, are incomprehensible for the reader who does not know the arguments advanced by the plaintiff. As these requests were not wholly published with the judgments, no jurisprudence could be born from such a form of holding. The *Tribunal de cassation* undoubtedly understood this situation and tested, as of the end of 1791 and the beginning of 1792, other formulations. It clarified the contrariety between the judgment and the law by sentences beginning by "because" or exposed the requirements of the law in several points (introduced by the word *"attendu que"*, that is whereas) and the result (with the term "from which it results") of the infringement of these requirements.[5] Without giving up these various expressions, the *Tribunal de cassation* discovered in 1792 a more satisfactory formulation. It developed, in a long sentence beginning with *"considérant que"* (considering that), the list of the reasons for cassation by confronting the violated law and the decisions of the lower courts, using also the formula *"vu que"* (seeing that) to indicate a text of law or a procedural document. The judges started to develop the law by expressions as "it is obvious that the law" or "as a question of law, the Penal Code does not qualify offence", or "the law has

3 Decrees of 4 germinal and 9 messidor an II, *Halpérin,* op. cit., pp. 136–137.

4 *Jean-Baptiste Sirey,* Recueil général des lois et arrêts (1791–1830), revu et complété par Devilleneuve et Carette, Paris 1840, vol. I, p. 1: Cass. 26 August 1791 et 17 September 1791.

5 Cass. 2 March 1792, 30 March 1792, and 13 April 1792, Archives Nationales AD V 4 (20) 15, 31 and 73; *Sirey,* 2, 3, and 6, Cass. 25 November 1791 and Cass. 15 june 1792.

for purpose ..." (on the contrary, if the law were not executed, the rights of the defense would not be recognized).[6]

The origins of this formulation are revealing of the intentions of the judges. Whereas the Parlements and the Council of the king usually did not give the reasons of their decisions, they justified their *"arrêts de règlement"* (rulings with a general scope, more regulative as judicial precedents) by sentences beginning with *"vu que"* (seeing that) or *"considérant que"* (considering that).[7] This last formula appears in the preamble to the Declaration of the Rights of Man and of the Citizen and of several laws of the Constituent Assembly. The judges of the *Tribunal de cassation*, of which some were former legislators, thus wanted their court to speak as the legislator did, with a collective and imperative voice, that is not in principle an opinion.

At the end of the Revolution, the style of the decisions of the *Tribunal de cassation* is fixed, without becoming uniform; some judgments use again the term "considering that". The majority of the decisions begin with a view of the articles from the violated laws, then a list of *"attendus"* confronting, to oppose them, the sense of the laws concerned with the procedural documents or the judgments of the lower courts.[8] The cassation appears as the result of this contradiction: "by these reasons" the Court of cassation cancels the judgment following a reasoning of several lines. The logic of this argumentation must be manifest to determine not only the violation of the law, but its right or false application. The reasons of the judgment determine, initially, the applicable rule, which is a law, almost always quoted except in rare exceptions, for which the reference is in the conclusions of the *"commissaire du gouvernement"* (a kind of attorney general), or a text (constitution, royal decree, custom or rule of Roman law, or international treaty) which has the *"force"* of law. The *Tribunal de cassation* benefits thus from the revolutionary situation, in which coexist many rules of different origin, "to make the Law", by selecting the applicable rule, even by declaring "elementary principles". These elementary principles are always drawn from one or more texts of laws. The following stage consists in determining the signification of the law to reveal the infringement. This significance can be obvious (it does not leave any doubt, sometimes the judges say) or require an explanation on the scope of a word or a sentence.[9] The *Tribunal de cassation* shifts thus to a negative infringement, which results from a bad qualification, of a distortion of a legal fact or a legal act.[10]

---

6 *Sirey*, 12 and 13, Cass. 20 December 1792 and Cass. 11 January 1793.

7 *Fr.-A. Isambert*, Recueil général des anciennes lois françaises depuis l'an 420 jusqu'à la Révolution, Paris 1833, vol. XXVII, p. 457 (règlement concernant les capitaines de vaisseaux, 28 August 1784), vol. XXVIII, p. 67 (arrêt de règlement du Parlement de Paris), p. 354 (règlement pour le fonctionnement du Conseil des Finances, 5 June 1787), p. 578 (arrêt de règlement du Parlement de Paris, 31 May 1788).

8 *Sirey*, pp. 123 and 163, Cass. 11 Brumaire an VII and Cass. 22 Pluviôse an VII.

9 A stable is not a closed field: Cass. 25 October 1792, Archives Nationales AD V 4 (22), 23; a courtyard of a house is not a public place, Cass. 31 May 1792, AD V 4 (20), 57.

Allowed by law in criminal matters, this cassation for the false application of the law penetrates into civil matters,[11] widening the capacity of interpretation of the *Tribunal de cassation.*

In some cases, very few, it is possible to speak of "judge-made law", even though the *Tribunal de cassation* has always denied any judicial review of the laws. When the revolutionary laws were lacunar, the *Tribunal de cassation* had to refer to the Assembly about it, to ask the legislator what was the answer of the legal question. The *Tribunal de cassation* did it sometimes. But, when the questions remained without answer, it answered itself by decisions of principle giving its own interpretation of the law.[12]

Publication of these decisions (in official bulletins or private collections of reports), which resembled the interpretative decrees of the laws taken by the legislative assembly, and their influence on the lower courts are indubitable evidence of the power of jurisprudence at the end of the Revolution.

The *Tribunal de cassation* showed so much audacity under the Revolution – it had advanced so far – that a retreat was inevitable with the codification and the transformation of the *Cour de cassation* under the Empire. Several facts seem to indicate this retreat. Initially, a sorting is carried out among the decisions, of which only one part is published by the official *Bulletin.* This situation supports the private editors, but it needs some time so that the best publications, like that of Sirey, become efficient.[13] The role of Merlin de Douai, imperial prosecutor (*procureur imperial*) and at the same time editor of the *Repertory of jurisprudence,* is also a factor of disorder.[14] Merlin published, indeed, a great number of its conclusions. When they are taken again by the judgment, this one appears allusive and laconic, when the Court judged differently, it is almost a dissenting opinion!

---

10 *Sirey,* pp. 118 – 119, 203 – 204, and 209 – 210, Cass. 4 Brumaire, 6 Prairial and 19 Prairial an VII.

11 First example: Cass. 7 June 1793, AD V 6 (24), 7. These decisions were approved by *C. Lavaux,* Manuel du Tribunal de cassation, Paris 1797, pp. 40 – 41, and criticized by *Henrion de Pansey,* De l'autorité judiciaire dans les gouvernements monarchiques, Paris 1827, vol. II, p. 246.

12 *Halpérin,* op. cit., pp. 256 – 261.

13 Beginning in 1802, *Jean-Baptiste Sirey,* Jurisprudence du Tribunal de Cassation, is more and more developed during the Empire (every decision is preceded by an introduction indicating the legal question) and takes in 1808 the title *"Recueil général des lois et arrêts"* after a one-year collaboration with his concurrent Denevers' *Journal des audiences.* Other private reports of the judgments (of the Court of cassation and of the Courts of Appeals) failed during the Empire (as *Bavoux* and *Loiseau,* Jurisprudence du Code Napoléon). At the beginning of the Restoration (1814 – 1815), the *Journal du Palais* (created in 1801), and the two publications of Sirey and Denevers were the only surviving law reports.

14 *P.-A. Merlin de Douai,* Répertoire universel et raisonné de jurisprudence, continues the Repertory of Guyot (an alphabetical dictionary of law, published at the end of the Ancien Regime) with new editions in 1807 – 1808, 1812 – 1825, 1827 – 1828 including references to the Napoleonic Code and the judgments of the Court of cassation.

Perhaps the second cause of a more timid jurisprudence comes from a policy of self-restraint of the Court of cassation at the time when the napoleonic Codes came into effect. By restricting the cassations for false application of the law, openly criticized by certain lawyers, while refusing to cancel the decisions of the lower courts which had emasculated a contract, by recognizing a capacity of appreciation to the judges who examined the facts, the Court of cassation would have liked to stress the obvious violations of the new codes, but to be careful in their interpretation.

Sometimes the style of the decisions of the Supreme Court, always presented with *"attendus que"* or *"considérant que"*, seems to prove this reserve: several decisions are very short, like a report of the simplest reading of the articles of the Code. The briefness is sometimes one of a single sentence introduced by *"considérant que"*: *imperatoria brevitas!* However, beside decisions of cassation, or rejection, often emanated from the section of the requests with its role of filter, there are different ones lengthily justified (means of cassation after means), sometimes calling upon the intention of the legislature, with the opinions expressed during the discussion of the code, upon the old jurisprudence (but not the authors of law-books, that is not the style of the law), even with natural laws.[15]

After the fall of the Empire, under the constitutional monarchies (1814–1848), new factors were likely to lead to a less diffusion of the decisions of the Court of cassation. The desire to join again with the former tradition then justified the recourse to the sources of the Ancient Law, in particular to the Roman law, and the exaltation of the role of the Courts of Appeals. Those Courts were regarded as "sovereign", with the image of the Parlements of the Ancien Régime; before 1837, the Court of cassation could not force the Court of Appeals to accept its jurisprudence.[16] The power of the appreciation of the facts by the lower judges is confirmed. The collections of jurisprudence, then under full development,[17] granted a great place to the decisions of these Courts of Appeals.

15 Req. 27 August 1811, in *Désiré Dalloz*, Répertoire méthodique et alphabétique de législation, de doctrine, et de jurisprudence, Paris 1855, vol. 35, p. 352; Crim. 2 July 1813 in Bulletin des arrêts de la Cour de cassation en matière criminelle, Paris 1813, pp. 359–361.

16 After a law of the 30 July 1828, which gave it the last word to the Court of Appeal after a cassation (*Cour de renvoi*), the law of 1 April 1837 makes mandatory, after a second cassation, for the Court of Appeal to follow the legal solution of the Court of cassation.

17 The publication by Denevers is edited by the lawyer Désiré Dalloz (with the help of a clerk of the Court de Cassation) from 1822–1825 (with the title "Jurisprudence générale du royaume or Recueil Dalloz"). Dalloz had beforehand taken part in the review *Thémis*, influenced by the German Historical School, by writing in 1819–1820 an article about the "jurisprudence des arrêts" concerning the illegitimate children. Like Sirey, the *Recueil Dalloz* summarizes the solution in italics, generally presents the facts, then the decision itself of the Court of cassation or of a Court of appeal (very rarely of a lower court). Then Dalloz adds sometimes footnotes (without signature) quoting other judgments or writers of the doctrine in comparison. Sirey imitates this process, and the two concurrents publish Repertories of jurisprudence in relation with their law reports. The best composed is *Dalloz*.

But these same causes could have effects in a contrary direction. The Courts of Appeals, and even the lower courts (*"tribunaux de premire instance"*), in their turn, expressed their reasons with *"attendus que"* or *"considérant que"*, in judgments which sometimes are more developed than those of the Court of cassation. It is necessary to be careful about these published judgments – in small number for the lower courts – which are perhaps not representative of the whole of the caseload. In the public records, the judgments of the lower courts (*"tribunaux de premire instance"*) appear as simple decisions – a majority of small claims about debts which did not require the quotation of any article of the Napoleonic Code – with short and factual holdings.[18] However, some of them are remarkable by their length and indicate an acculturation of the motivation that came from the Court of cassation.[19] The decisions of the Courts of Appeals are useful to explain those of the Court of cassation and conversely.

The use of the sources of the Ancient Law, the analysis of the intent of the legislator, and the invocation of the principles of the natural law, far from weakening the range of the recall to the law, were means for the judges to develop their argumentation and to manage a place of discussion where it was possible to interpret freely the text of the Napoleonic Code. All the reasons contributed to the legal solution adopted by the judgment, as often the judges said themselves.[20]

Two examples, taken in the medium of the nineteenth century, illustrate the connection between the control, by the Court of cassation and the lower courts, of the technique of the holding and the rise of a jurisprudence interpreting the Civil Code *"praeter legem"*, even *"contra legem"*. The first relates to legitimation by marriage of the infants born from an incestuous relationship. Article 331 of the Napoleonic Code excludes these children from the benefit of legitimation. In an obvious way, this article does make sense if applied to the children of parents to a prohibited degree who could obtain from the Head of the State an exemption to marry. For the others, it is not question of marriage and thus of legitimation. In spite of this apparent clearness of the law, a doctrine had been developed by certain authors of the first third of the nineteenth century to utilize again a jurisprudence

---

18 For instance in the Archives Départementales de la Côte d'Or, for the *Tribunal de première instance* of Dijon, U IX Bc 62 (judgments of 1816) and U IX Bd 23 (judgments of 1828).

19 Tribunal du Havre 23 May 1858 with the study of the legislative intent and, that is uncommon, several writers of the Ancient Law quoted and Tribunal de Rennes 16 April 1844, *Dalloz* (above, note 15), Paris 1855, vol. 35, pp. 308 and 382; Cour de Rouen, 8 January 1827, *Dalloz* (above, note 15), Paris 1856, vol. 16, pp. 132–133.

20 *Bernard Beignier,* La conscience du juge dans l'application de la loi au début du XIXe siècle. La jurisprudence au temps de l'Exégèse, in: *Jean-Marie Carbasse* and *Laurence Depambour-Tarride,* La conscience du juge dans la tradition juridique européenne, Paris 1999, p. 284, quoting a decision of the Cour de Pau in 1835 using the different arguments of logic and the authority of Domat and Pothier, p. 289, an other decision of the Cour de Limoges in 1811 with natural law and the authors of the Ancient Law, and p. 290, a decision of the Court of Poitiers in 1811 about the natural law of the fathers' power.

of the Ancien Régime admitting the legitimation by marriage of the children born of an incestuous relationship whose parents have got an exemption. Several Courts of Appeals adopted these doctrines, without quoting the authors who had developed it, by affirming that the Civil Code had not innovated in this respect, that article 331 was only intended to reject incest and that reasons "drawn from morals, the peace and union of the families" contributed to reject any different interpretation from the law. The Court of cassation agreed with this jurisprudence, obviously contrary to the letter of the Civil Code, in 1867. The judgment contains six *"considérant que"*, taking as arguments the example of the Ancient Law, the refusal to take too many consequences of the principles of morality, and the warranty of the exemption given to the parents by the Government.[21] These arguments of judicial policy prevailed over a grammatical and logical interpretation of the Napoleonic Code.

The other example relates to the adoption of a natural child by one of his parents. The Civil Code did not say anything as to this possibility, which augmented considerably the succesoral rights of the natural child. It was, however, probable that the writers of the Code were unfavorable to this manner of improving the situation of natural children. Jurisprudence was all the more hesitant because legislative works on this subject were not known at the time and that the doctrine was divided. The Court of cassation validated this adoption in 1841, then refused it in 1843, before reversing again its jurisprudence in 1846. What were the reasons given by the judges? In 1841, there are five points (*"attendus que"*) in the holding: there is no prohibition of this kind of adoption in the Napoleonic Code (silence is equivalent to permission, which is a general principle of civil law based on liberty), there is no incompatibility between natural filiation and adoption (a logical argument), the lower courts are able to control the morality of these adoptions (which is an argument of judicial policy), the dispositions of the Code about the succession rights of the natural children do not concern the adoptive children (a grammatical argument), for all these reasons, the incompetence of the natural children to be adopted does not exist, neither in the letter of the law nor in its "virtual sense" (which is a repetitive argument with an allusive refusal of any historical interpretation, with recourse to preparatory works of the Code or to natural law).[22]

In contrast, the judgment of 1843 contains eight arguments, three about the procedure, and five *"attendus que"* about the question of interpretation. These latter arguments are focused on the strict separation between legitimate (or adopted) and illegitimate children, a separation based upon the fundamental principles of the law, that is the honor of the marriage, the notions of morality, and public order.

21 Civ. 22 janvier 1867, *Dalloz*, 1867, vol. 1, p. 5.

22 *Dalloz*, 1841, vol. 1, p. 37: the judgment, decided after due and long deliberation of the judges, is published with the contrary conclusions of the *avocat général* Gillon (in the preliminary examination of the case by the chamber of requests) and the confirmed conclusion of the *procureur général* Dupin.

The Court of cassation did not use the logical, grammatical, and historical arguments of the Courts of Appeals and of the writers opposed to the adoption of the natural children.[23] The majority of the Court preferred a more impressionist argumentation that did not dare to be purely textual.

Finally the last decision of 1846 contains only four arguments: the principle that any incompetence must result from a formal text (a more explicit interpretation of the silence of the Napoleonic Code than in 1841), the rejection of the argument about the rights of succession of the natural children (a reply to one of the arguments of the 1843 judgment), the legitimation interpreted as a proof of the possible change of a person's condition (a manner of overthrowing the argument of 1843 taking the legitimation as the only means to improve the situation of natural children), and the supposition that, without this adoption allowed, parents would not recognize their bastards in order to be able to adopt them as strangers (an argument of public policy with an hypothesis *a contrario*).[24]

How did the majority of French lawyers[25] accept this surprising overruling and consider the decision of the Court of cassation of 1846 as immutable? A first reason is the opinion in favor of this kind of adoption of the majority of the Courts of Appeals and of the writers. *"Optima legum intrepres consuetudo"* said the Court of Dijon in 1844 in this debate. The decisions of 1841 and 1843 take place in a majority stream, and this cluster of arguments, even not repeated by the Court of cassation, has sustained the final jurisprudence. Among these opinions in favor of the adoption, the conclusions of the *procureur général* Dupin in 1841 have given a great weight to the thesis supported by Dalloz and his law reports. Finally, the authority of the Court of cassation was so strong that any argument, or set of arguments, could justify a ruling of the Supreme Court.

These examples and this short history of the *rationes decidendi* of the French courts enlighten the importance of this period of approximately fifty years (1790–1840) in the formation of the judicial style in France in modern (or contemporary, in historical French parlance) times. In this short period, the judges of the Supreme Court adopted a specific style, copying the preamble of reasons at the beginning of some laws with the words *"attendu que"*, found a balance between the extreme laconicism of the first decisions and the risks of too long sentences in a text expressing a collective judgment without dissenting opinions, and succeeded in imposing this style made only to resolve questions of law to the lower courts. Up to today,

---

23 *Dalloz*, 1843, vol. 1, p. 97: the judgment, rejecting the review of a decision of the Court of Appeal of Angers against this kind of adoption, was decided against the conclusions of the avocat général, after a long deliberation and a partition of votes.

24 *Dalloz*, 1846, vol. 1, p. 81, with the contrary conclusions of the avocat général and a note of approbation of Dalloz, in favor of this kind of adoption since his article in *Themis* in 1819–1820.

25 But not all: the judge and legal writer *Pont* expressed his approbation of the judgement of 1843 and his criticisms of the judgment of 1846 in the Revue de législation et de jurisprudence (vol. 17, p. 750, and vol. 25, p. 475).

this style has hardly changed and judges were able to adapt it to very different situations, including for the inferior courts an abstract of the facts of the case.

Secondly, the early development of new law reports, the *Journal du Palais,* and, especially, the collected series of Sirey and Dalloz, gave a decisive aid to the acclimatization and the diffusion of this judicial style that seems so obscure outside the sphere of the French lawyers. These publications have furnished all the necessary materials to understand the more abstruse judgments of the Court of cassation: the abstracts, the indices, and, since the 1830s, many conclusions of the public attorney (*procureur général* or *avocat général*)[26] or of the judge speaking (reporting) for the court. In the same time, the use by Dalloz and Sirey of footnotes indicating the precedents and the links with other judgments or opinions permits one quickly to understand what is new or important in a decision of the Court of cassation. The legal reviews, expressing the opinions of the professors and of other lawyers (advocates and judges), have developed in their turn articles examining the jurisprudence of the Courts,[27] especially of the Court of cassation, that have globally reinforced the authority of the judiciary.

Thirdly, as the result of the parallel development of what we could call a "formal style" to use the words of Llewellyn and of modern legal publishing, the authority of the Court of cassation, legally consecrated in 1837 when the Supreme Court could impose interpretations of questions of law upon the inferior courts, became an absolute dogma of the doctrine, justifying even repetitive overrulings, as in the case of the adoption of natural children, in spite of criticisms from some lawyers and professors. The latter had some difficulty to explain the legal ground of what was really a "judge-made law". The lawyer Marcadé is perhaps the only one who understood that the law of 1 April 1837 gave to the Court of cassation the ability to deliver authoritative interpretations of the law, without being bound by its own precedents, this last point seeming abnormal to Marcadé.[28] Paradoxically,

---

26 For instance, *Dalloz,* 1833, vol. 1, p. 201; 1835, vol. 1, p. 225, 1837, vol. 1, pp. 6 and 145. In the same time, the procureur général *Dupin* has his conclusions published since 1836 in Réquisitoires, plaidoyers, et discours de rentrée prononcés par M. Dupin, 14 vols. to 1874. The editor (vol. I, p. XI) explains that the Court of cassation has often adopted the reasons of Dupin's conclusions and that, on the contrary, the dissenting conclusions of the *procureur général* could announce a future overruling by the Court. Even if this publication contains few conclusions in civil matters (like the question of the adoption of the natural child), it testifies to the influence of these conclusions of the public attorney and their utility to understand the overrulings of the Court of cassation.

27 The *Revue de législation et de jurisprudence* (often called *Revue Wolowski*) is the first to develop this "genre" of the "examen doctrinal of jurisprudence" since 1834–1835. Then, the *Revue critique* (created in 1851) and the *Revue pratique* (created in 1856) have tried, with many intermittencies, to make more regular this analysis of the leading cases. They do not succeed really in concurrencing the law reports by Dalloz and Sirey, but they complete them and participate in the blooming of the jurisprudence in nineteenth century France.

28 *Victor Marcadé,* Éléments du droit civil français, Paris 1844, vol. I, pp. 66–78.

the French style of *rationes decidendi* has created a powerful case law (*jurisprudence* in French), with an authority of the *Cour de cassation* not depending of the soundness and logical rigor of the reasons used by the supreme judges.[29]

[29] As we know, *Hortensius de Saint-Albin*, Logique judiciaire ou Traité des arguments légaux, Paris 1832, is the only – and very short – essay in nineteenth century France to present a study of judicial argumentation. Paradoxically Saint-Albin quoted no example of the case law of the Court of cassation.

GEORGES MARTYN

The Judge and the Formal Sources of Law in the Low Countries (19th – 20th Centuries): From 'Slave' to 'Master'?

I. The Legal Culture of the Low Countries in the Nineteenth Century: a French Heritage

The 1815 Vienna Congress created a new nation, the United Kingdom of the Netherlands, as had already been decided, in answer to an English suggestion, in the March 1814 peace treaty of Chaumont. In the Constitution (art. 163) of the newborn country it was stated that national codes should be elaborated. Although projects[1] were realized in a narrow co-operation of jurists from both the Northern and the Southern provinces, they never came into force before Belgium declared its independence in 1830. After this date, both states, the Southern longer than the Northern one, continued to use the Napoleonic codes. In the Netherlands a new civil code was introduced in 1838, but in Belgium jurists today still use, albeit with many subsequent textual changes, the *Code Civil,* the *Code de Commerce* and the *Code d'Instruction.*[2]

As a consequence, the development of the Belgian[3] legal culture[4] was very much influenced by the French one, in such a sense that some scholars[5] even won-

1 *John Gilissen,* Codification et projets de codification en Belgique au XIXe siècle (1804 – 1915), in: Belgisch tijdschrift voor nieuwste geschiedenis (1983), 219 – 229; *John Gilissen,* De Belgische commissie van 1816 tot herziening van het Ontwerp Burgerlijk Wetboek voor het Koninkrijk der Nederlanden, in: Legal History Review (1967), 383 – 443. On the codification projects in the Batavian Republic and the Kingdom of Holland, see recently *Alain Wijffels,* Balancing rationality and tradition: the French *Code civil* and the codification of civil law in the Netherlands, 1798 – 1838, in: Régine Beauthier/Isabelle Rorive (ed.), Le Code Napoléon, un ancêtre vénéré? Mélanges offerts à Jacques Vanderlinden, Brussels 2004, 285 – 318. Wijffels states (p. 316): 'The era of 19th-century legism had begun, and it would take some time before legal scholars could hope to regain control over legal doctrines'. We will deal with this 'legism' further in this text.

2 In 2004 the Belgian jurists commemorated the bicentennial in various ways, see o.a. *Dirk Heirbaut/Georges Martyn* (ed.), Napoleons nalatenschap. Un héritage Napoléonien. Tweehonderd jaar Burgerlijk Wetboek in België. Bicentenaire du Code civil en Belgique, Mechelen 2005; *Régine Beauthier/Isabelle Rorive* (ed.), Le Code Napoléon, un ancêtre vénéré? Mélanges offerts à Jacques Vanderlinden, Brussels 2004.

3 In this contribution we will especially focus on Belgium. The Dutch legal tradition did not follow extremely different ways of development, although the greater influence of the

der if one might speak of an autonomous 'Belgian' legal tradition. The rather short period of French occupation (1795 – 1815)[6] indeed seems to have been decisive for the Low Countries' legal history. The old customary and statutory law was entirely abandoned and five Napoleonic codes[7] were introduced. From this moment on it was strictly forbidden for judges to use any of the 'old sources' (Roman and canon law, local customs, old statutory law) in matters handled by the new codes. On the other hand, article 4 of the *Code Civil*[8] obliged the judge to decide each case, even if he thought the law was not clear or that there was no legislative rule at all that governed the problem at hand. Legal historians[9] have demonstrated that this prohibition, although not for the whole one hundred percent, was very well respected. The newly introduced and far more professional law courts (more professional than the aldermen and practitioners of the Ancien Régime system) indeed motivated, or justified, their decisions almost exclusively by referring to legislation. Towards the end and after the French period one can talk of a new generation of Belgian and Dutch law practitioners. They had never been confronted with the Ancien Régime legal system, but, in two decades, had got used to the French revolutionary and Napoleonic law and the whole French legal culture.[10]

German law, e.g. the open rules, cannot be denied. Important for the analogous developments after World War II is the construction of the Benelux, the Belgian-Dutch-Luxemburg-union, and the central role of these countries, first as three of the six founding states of the European Economic Community, now as member states of the European Union.

4 'Legal culture' is defined as 'a specific way in which values, practices, and concepts are integrated into the operation of legal institutions and the interpretation of legal texts', *John Bell,* Comparative law and legal theory, in: Werner Krawietz a.o. (ed.), Prescriptive formality and normative rationality in modern legal systems, Berlin 1994, 19 – 33.

5 *Dirk Heirbaut,* The Belgian legal tradition: does it exist?, in: *Hubert Bocken* and *Walter De Bondt* (ed.), Introduction to Belgian Law, Antwerp 2000, 1 – 22.

6 *Herman Van Goethem,* La Belgique sous l'annexion à la France, 1795 – 1813: l'acceptation des nouvelles institutions judiciaires et du droit français, in: Serge Dauchy / Jos Monballyu / Alain Wijffels (ed.), Auctoritates. Xenia R.C. van Caenegem oblata, Brussels 1997, 289 – 300.

7 The three mentioned above on the one hand and the *Code pénal* and the *Code de procédure civile,* both since replaced by Belgian codes of a still very French inspiration in the years 1867 and 1967 on the other.

8 Since 1967 this rule on denial of justice is placed in article 5 of the Belgian Judicial Code. Its history goes back to the French great ordinance of 1667.

9 For the Southern Netherlands: *Georges Macours,* De visie van de Belgische 19de-eeuwse rechtspraak op de subsidiaire rol van het oude Romeinse recht. Een verkennend onderzoek, in: Fred Stevens / Dirk Van den Auweele (ed.), 'Houd voet bij stuk.' Xenia iuris historiae G. van Dievoet oblata, Leuven 1990, 253 – 289. For the Northern Netherlands: *Henk Kooiker,* Lex scripta abrogata. De derde renaissance van het Romeinse recht. Een onderzoek naar de doorwerking van het oude recht na de invoering van de civielrechtelijke codificaties in het begin van de negentiende eeuw, Nijmegen 1996.

10 The separation between the French and the 'Belgian' or 'Dutch' proper legal history should not be overestimated. Also before 1795 the legal cultures of France and the Southern Netherlands were very alike, both regions having been part of the *pays coutumier* for ages and being influenced by roman and canon law and, at the end of the eighteenth century, by

One of the main features of this culture, as for judicial function concerns, was the obligation to motivate judicial decisions. Although it can be maintained that, besides the introduction of new legislative and judicial institutions and the unification of the legal norms, there is still a lot of continuity between the late eighteenth century 'Belgian' law and the Napoleonic one, the obligation to motivate judicial decisions was really unseen in the Low Countries. During the Ancien Régime the judge who explained the reasons of his decision was said to be a fool.[11] The desire to know more about the reasons of a judicial decision had frequently been expressed in the 1789 *Cahiers de doléances*, was answered by a *décret* of 1790, confirmed in the *Constitution de l'an III* and repeated in an 1810 statute.[12] It found also its way into the 1815 constitution of the United Kingdom of the Netherlands and it became article 97 (today article 149) of the Belgian fundamental law. In the discussions leading to this constitutional text, Montesquieu was quite often cited as an authority, and, in a system of separation of powers, very much inspired by this enlightened author, the judge was considered to be the *bouche de la loi*.

As already mentioned, no new judicial institutions were created under King William, and little legislation was enacted. In 1816 it was said that customary law was only to be admitted if a statute explicitly referred to it. The obligation to decide all cases, even if the statutory law was not clear, was confirmed in 1820.

Not much changed after the Belgian independence of 1830. Belgian legal culture was mainly (part of) French legal culture,[13] although about sixty percent of

---

the ideas of Enlightenment. It was especially for the 'Flemish' legal culture that the French period meant a sharp cutting off of the development of some historically grown institutions, customary rules and legal language. On the evolution of the Belgian legal culture in the nineteenth and twentieth centuries, see *Koen Raes*, Ontwikkelingen in de Belgische rechtscultuur. Een cultuurhistorische verkenning, in: Dirk Heirbaut / Xavier Rousseaux / Karel Velle (ed.), Politieke en sociale geschiedenis van justitie in België van 1830 tot heden, Bruges 2004, 345 – 356.

11 *Philippe Godding*, La jurisprudence, Turnhout 1973; *J.P.A. Coopmans*, Vrijheid en gebondenheid van de rechter vóór de codificatie, in: Rechtsvinding. Opstellen aangeboden aan Prof. Dr. J.M. Pieters, ter gelegenheid van zijn afscheid als hoogleraar aan de Katholieke Hogeschool te Tilburg, Deventer 1970, 71 – 109; *Tony Sauvel*, Histoire du jugement motivé, in: Revue du droit public et de la science politique en France et à l'étranger (1955), 5 – 53. On the ratio decidendi of the supreme court of the Netherlands, the Great Council of Malines, see *C. Verkerk*, Onderzoek naar de motivering in rechte bij de Grote Raad van Mechelen in de zestiende eeuw: de tienden van raapzaad en hennep in Snellerwaard, Hekendorp en Lange Linschoten, in Tom De Smidt (ed.), Miscellanea Consilii Magni, ter gelegenheid van twintig jaar Werkgroep Grote Raad van Mechelen, Amsterdam 1980, 97 – 120, also in: Verslagen en mededelingen van de Stichting tot uitgaaf der bronnen van het oud-vaderlandse recht, nieuwe reeks (1975), 295 – 354; *Philippe Godding*, La motivation des arrêts du Grand Conseil de Malines au 16e siècle. A propos d'un article récent, in: Legal History Review (1977), 155 – 157.

12 On what proceeded, see *Philippe Godding*, Jurisprudence et motivation des sentences, du moyen âge à la fin du 18e siècle, in: Chaim Perelman / Paul Foriers (ed.), La motivation des décisions de justice, Brussels 1978, 66 – 67.

13 *René Victor*, Een eeuw Vlaamsch rechtsleven, Antwerp 1953, 3.

the Belgian inhabitants are and were Dutch speaking. The reasons therefore were historical, scientific and social. Looking back into history, we see that it were the (French) Burgundian dukes who introduced in the fourteenth and fifteenth century new institutions and legislation, almost all of them inspired by French examples. These institutions continued to use the 'noble' French language during the Spanish and Austrian reign and also the enlightened and revolutionary ideas were propagated by French speaking citizens. In legal science the Latin texts of Roman and canon law were more easily accessible for French (a Romanic language) than for Flemish (a Germanic language) speaking legal practitioners. Books in Dutch on customary law were very scarce, while French law books were very well spread throughout the Low Countries. Most important although, is the social element, as the elites of the political, judicial and administrative institutions were all French speaking or, at least, were only using French in their professional and social relations,[14] before the French Revolution, certainly under French occupation, but also until far in the twentieth century.

Today, things have changed. Starting with the regulation of the use of the languages in criminal trials in the 1870's (after the scandal of two – not guilty! – Flemish men having been sentenced to death without having understood one word of their trial), other language laws followed on administrative matters, (primary, secondary and higher) education and civil justice. Since 1898 all statutes are published in both French and Dutch at the same time, both versions having the same force of law.[15] At the end of the nineteenth and in the first half of the twentieth centuries, law students started moot court exercises in Dutch, young barristers met in Flemish societies, Flemish reviews were published. An important consequence of this emancipation of the Flemish jurists is that many Walloon (Belgian French speaking) jurists today only keep on reading the French and francophone Belgian literature, while Flemish (Belgian Dutch speaking) jurists stick to their own Flem-

---

14 One of the fundamental 'Belgian' liberties of the 1831 Constitution is the freedom of the use of the languages. The French speaking elite used this liberty, disregarding the needs of the Flemish population in the Flemish part of Belgium, *Robert Senelle / R. Van De Velde,* Honderdvijftig jaar staatsrechtelijk denken in België, in: Egied Spanoghe / Robert Feenstra (ed.), Honderdvijftig jaar rechtsleven in België en Nederland 1830–1980. Preadviezen uitgebracht voor een colloquium georganiseerd door de juridische faculteiten van de universiteiten van Gent en Leiden, Gent, 5–7 November 1980, Leiden 1981, 309–340 (especially 314–315). It is for instance symptomatic that in a book on the great Belgian barristers ('advocaten / avocats'), only three out of the 36 lawyers were 'Flemish' (member of a bar in what today is the Flemish region), *Pierre Henri,* Grands avocats de Belgique, Brussels 1984. For many lawyers Dutch (or Flemish) could not be used as a legal language, *F. De Potter,* Het Nederlandsch geene rechtstaal?, in: Verslagen en Mededelingen van de Koninklijke Vlaamse Academie voor Taal- en Letterkunde (1897), 86–112.

15 More on the development of the Flemish legal language in *Georges Martyn,* Het Burgerlijk Wetboek en de evolutie van de 'Vlaamse' rechtstaal in België, in: Dirk Heirbaut / Georges Martyn (ed.), Napoleons nalatenschap. Un héritage Napoléonien. Tweehonderd jaar Burgerlijk Wetboek in België. Bicentenaire du Code civil en Belgique, Mechelen 2005, 271–300.

ish texts and, if they look over the wall, prefer Dutch[16] and more and more English or American[17] literature to the French or Belgian francophone literature. Belgian legal culture is getting split up. According to some authors,[18] Flemish jurists,[19] under Dutch, German and Anglo-American influence, are likely to think in a more problem-oriented way and are more creative in finding a solution, using different sources of law. Walloon jurists on the other hand seem to stick more to the literal text and its historical context. Although it cannot be denied that, indeed, there is a certain tendency in this sense, as is for instance made clear by the diverging case law of the Flemish and French speaking chambers of the supreme *Cour de Cassation* and the Council of State,[20] it is my personal opinion that the differences are still very small compared to the analogies. For the nineteenth and the largest part of the twentieth centuries the main line is that Belgian law, legislation, case law as well as jurisprudence, is very France-oriented. Let us now examine within this Belgian-French framework scientific research that has been done on how judges motivate their decisions or by what principles they are guided.

II. Scientific Research on Ratio Decidendi in the Low Countries: State of the Art

During the nineteenth century the judge's reasoning did not get any special attention. The application of the legal rule to the facts was considered to be a pure syllogism with a 'major' (the legal rule), a 'minor' (the facts) and one sole conclusion.[21] The answer to all possible situations was supposed to be found in the codi-

---

16 *Jacques Herbots*, Contract law in Belgium, Brussels 1995, 30.

17 The Anglo-American influence is for instance paramount in (international) commercial law, where in Dutch texts new terminology arises, like *factoring, leasing, sponsoring, ruling, franchising*, etc. Year after year more Flemish students study a year or more abroad, most of all in Great Britain or the United States.

18 *Yves Defoort*, The northern and southern legal culture in Belgium, (in the press); *Heirbaut*, The Belgian legal tradition, 16–19; *François Ost/Mark Van Hoecke*, La jurisprudence en Belgique, in: Revue interdisciplinaire d'études juridiques (1994), 107–137.

19 Very important for a further splitting up of the legal culture is the creation of distinct bar organisations. There is no longer a national order of 'advocaten/avocats', but an 'Orde van Vlaamse Balies' and an 'Ordre des Barreaux Francophones et Germanophone', *Georges Martyn*, Evoluties en revoluties in de Belgische advocatuur, in: Dirk Heirbaut/Xavier Rousseaux/Karel Velle (ed.), Politieke en sociale geschiedenis van justitie in België van 1830 tot heden, Bruges 2004, 227–255.

20 *Jérome Sohier*, Chambre flamandes et chambres francophones: divergences et dissonances, in: Bernard Bléro (ed.), Le Conseil d'Etat de Belgique. Cinquante ans après sa création, Brussels 1999, 699–731.

21 In 1925 *Henri De Page*, De l'interprétation des lois, Brussels 1925, wrote that, although many jurists condemn the pure logical interpretation, it was still the standard working style. By stressing the logical features of the judicial motivation, the judges tried to deny that they had to interpret the law. Half a century later the same view was confirmed: 'Les juges ne

fied law and the *Cour de Cassation*, more the handmaid of the legislature than an autonomous or creative court,[22] watched over the uniform interpretation of the law. To my knowledge, there has been no scientific research before 1900 on how judges actually really worked with the texts. In jurisprudence, the influence of the French Exegetic School was paramount, while the influence of the works of von Savigny or von Jhering was almost nil.[23]

German influences (especially by Esser) and American (by a.o. Hohfeld and Llewellyn) appear only in the twentieth century, first in the Netherlands, but soon after also in Belgium. In the first country scholars like Scholten, Meijers and Van Oven, before and around the Second World War, studied especially the historic influences on the legal evolution and so the sense in which judges should decide. After the war, people like Langemeijer, ter Heide and, most important, Wiarda paid also attention to the social influences.[24]

---

reconnaissent pas volontiers, du moins dans les motivations de leurs décisions, qu'ils ont procédé à une interprétation de la loi', *François Ost*, L'interprétation logique et systématique et le postulat de rationalité du législateur, in: Michel van de Kerchove (ed.), L'interprétation en droit. Approche pluridisciplinaire, Brussels 1978, 111 – 112.

22 *Jean-Pierre Nandrin*, La Cour de Cassation belge de 1832 et le pouvoir judiciaire. Héritage de la période française?, in: Justice et institutions françaises en Belgique (1795 – 1815). Traditions et innovations autour de l'annexion, Hellemmes 1996, 275 – 293. A study on the relations between the lowest tribunals of the Judges of the Peace and the supreme *Cour de Cassation* during the French period in the Low Countries, is *Vaast Van Herreweghe*, De Vrederechter en Cassatie. De verhouding tussen de wetsongebonden 'laagste' en de wetsbewakende 'hoogste' rechter, 1790 – 1813, Ghent 1993. On the history of the Belgian *Cour de Cassation*, see *Léon Cornil*, Het Hof van Verbreking: oorsprong en aard, Brussels 1948; *Sjoerd Faber*, Cassatierechtspraak in Nederland in civiele en strafzaken 1813 – 1838, in: Roel Pieterman a.o. (ed.), Bijdragen tot de rechtsgeschiedenis van de negentiende eeuw. Studiedag 1993, Rotterdam 1993, 43 – 52; *Charles Faider*, La première année de la Cour de cassation, in: La Belgique Judiciaire (1856), 65 – 75; *Raoul Hayoit de Termicourt*, Het hof van verbreking voor honderd jaar, in: Rechtskundig Weekblad (1953 – 54), 49 – 66; *Robert Janssens*, Het Hof van Cassatie van België. Enkele hoofdmomenten van zijn ontwikkeling, in: Legal History Review (1977), 95 – 116; *Matthieu Leclercq*, La Cour de cassation et son personnel (1832 – 1867), in: La Belgique Judiciaire (1867), 1217 – 1231; *Camille Scheyven*, Traité pratique des pourvois en cassation, de l'organisation et des attributions diverses de la Cour suprême, Brussels 1866. Especially on the law forming role of the supreme court: *Ernest Krings*, Aspecten van de bijdrage van het Hof van Cassatie tot de rechtsvorming, in: Rechtskundig Weekblad (1990 – 91), 313 – 325 and 345 – 359.

23 *Jan Van Den Broeck*, Het Burgerlijk Wetboek en de invloed van de Duitse rechtshistorische school in België tijdens de 19de eeuw, in: Jacques Vanderlinden a.o. (ed.), Liber amicorum John Gilissen. Wetboek en grondwet in historisch perspectief, Antwerp 1983, 417 – 425; *Emile Van Dievoet*, Het burgerlijk recht in België en in Nederland van 1800 tot 1940. De rechtsbronnen, Antwerp 1943, *passim*.

24 *G.E. Langemeijer*, Nieuwe Duitse theorieën over rechterlijke rechtsvinding, Brussels 1966; *J. Ter Heide*, Rechtsvinding, Zwolle 1965; *G. Wiarda*, Drie typen van rechtsvinding, has been very popular (first edition 1972, second and updated edition 1980), the 1999 (Deventer) edition by T. *Koopmans* is the fourth one. On the importance of Wiarda, but also Snijders, for the Dutch evolution, see recently *Paul Nève*, *Jan Smits*, H.C.F. Schoordijk, 'oerdom en ijzersterk': interview met een civilist pur sang, in: Pro Memorie (2004), 103 – 116,

In Belgium sociological arguments entered at first legal reasoning, still under French influence, viz. of Gény's school of the *libre recherche scientifique* around 1900. Vander Eycken[25] and a couple of decades later the great Henri De Page[26] could still be considered followers of Gény. They attributed an important role to equity in the solution finding process of the judge. More profound scientific studies on the judge's job were undertaken in the 1960's by Foriers and Perelman, especially in their Brussels' *Centre national de recherche de logique.* The proceedings of their congresses on the motivation of judgments, on lacunae and on antinomies in legislation or on the juridical rationality are still fundamental today.[27] Walter Van Gerven finally played an important part in the popularization of the scientific knowledge on how jurists think, bringing together the Belgian, but especially the foreign theories in his famous books 'Het beleid van de rechter' ('The policy of the judge') and '*Met recht en rede*' ('With law and reason').[28]

---

and in the same review the interview with Snijders, who stresses the important German influence on the way Dutch judges decide: *Matthias Storme/Mineke de Theije/Bram Delbecke,* Wouter Snijders: interview met de vader van het nieuwe vermogensrecht, in: Pro Memorie (2004), 117–143. See also *J.J.H. Bruggink,* Op zoek naar het recht. Rechtsvinding in rechtstheoretisch perspectief, Groningen 1987; *A. De Wild,* De rationaliteit van het rechterlijk oordeel, Deventer 1979; *R.J.P. Kottenhagen,* Van precedent tot precedent, over de plaats van het rechtersrecht in een gecodificeerd rechtsstelsel, Arnhem 1986; *Jimmy Polak,* Theorie en praktijk der rechtsvinding, Zwolle 1953; *J.A. Pontier,* Rechtsvinding, Nijmegen 1991; *Jan Ten Kate/Petrus Van Kopen,* Determinanten van privaatrechtelijke beslissingen, Arnhem 1984; *Jan Van Dunné,* De dialektiek van rechtsvinding en rechtsvorming, Arnhem 1984; *J.B.M. Vranken,* Kritiek en methode in de rechtsvinding, een onderzoek naar de betekenis van de hermeneutiek van H.G. Gadamer voor de analyse van het rechterlijk beslissingsgebeuren, Deventer 1978. One of the most recent views on ratio decidendi in the Netherlands, and especially the qualification and appreciation of the facts is the 1998 doctorate of *Carel Eduard Smith,* Feit en rechtsnorm: een methodologisch onderzoek naar de betekenis van de feiten voor de rechtsvinding en legitimatie van het rechtsoordeel, Leiden 1998. A recent Dutch view on ratio decidendi in a unifying European context is *Ewoud Hondius,* Nieuwe methoden van privaatrechtelijke rechtsvinding en rechtsvorming van een Verenigd Europa, Amsterdam 2001.

25 *Paul Vander Eycken,* Méthode positive de l'interprétation juridique, Brussels 1907.

26 *Henri De Page,* A propos du gouvernement des juges. L'équité en face du droit, Brussels 1931, 178 states: 'l'école de l'exégèse ne fut qu'un phénomène transitoire, une parenthèse'. The 'policy' of the judge, according to De Page, is on a higher level than politics: 'Les juges n'ont pas de désires qui puissent les menacer. Leur gouvernement est d'ordre bien supérieur. C'est celui des idées, des équilibres constitutionnels et moraux qui se trouvent audessus des lois, bien plus que dans les lois' (p. 189). On De Page: *Dirk Heirbaut,* Henri De Page. Een man in de schaduw van zijn werk (5 november 1894–27 augustus 1969), in: Tijdschrift voor Privaatrecht (2001), 111–121.

27 For this contribution we used: *Chaim Perelman* (ed.), Le problème des lacunes en droit, Brussels 1968; *Chaim Perelman/Paul Foriers* (ed.), La motivation des décisions de justice, Brussels 1978.

28 In 'Het beleid van de rechter' Van Gerven gives an overview of the most important German, American and Dutch ideas, from system thinking, over problem thinking to value-oriented thinking (not without mentioning the risks of a too value-oriented case law, like the French judge Magneaud; and thus pleading for a 'trans-subjective value-oriented judicial

How revealing these works of jurisprudence may have been, they still all were very theoretical, describing how judges think (or better: are thought to be thinking) and how they build up a reasoning from the bare facts to the final juridical decision. This was still about how a standard judge is handling law, not actually on what he really does and thinks. Very few researchers have gone further than the expressed reasons, but have also asked questions on the hidden values, the sociological[29] background and the psychological impulses leading to the decisions, but disappearing behind the formal justification of the decision taken.[30] How does a judge really act? How does he think as a man or woman of flesh and blood, not as an academically skilled jurist? The classic image of the judicial power is a conservative one, the judge only applying the rules and values offered by the legislature. In the 1970's, a research group led by Mark Van Hoecke[31] investigated in the decisions of the Ghent Court of Appeal. The research team revealed that in the jurisdiction, empirical enunciations are regularly considered as proved without any motivation or reference to sources, so that judges, although not expressing it, rely on their personal experiences. Judges also make rational errors and are guided by implicit values. Value judgements are rarely motivated, but they are formulated under the neutral form of a descriptive enunciation. Extra-judicial rules are often applied in decisions by juridical notions, such as fault or good faith. One should conclude from these investigations that the judge's personality plays – more than jurists would want to admit – an important part in the decision making process.

Ten Kate and Van Koppen, who did a comparable research in the Netherlands in the 1980's, on the contrary, stated that there was no great influence of the judge's personality.[32] All we can conclude from these research projects, is that investigat-

---

reasoning'). See also *Walter Van Gerven/J.C.M. Leyten,* Theorie en praktijk van de rechtsvinding, Zwolle 1977 and 1981. For a biographic interview with Van Gerven, professor, barrister, president of the Belgian Banking Commission and advocate-general of the European Court of Justice, see: *Herman Cousy/Wouter Devroe,* Met recht en rede, de reden van het recht: interview met Walter van Gerven, Pro Memorie (2004), 89 – 102.

29 *Anne Lagneau-Devillé,* Questions sociologiques à propos de l'interprétation en droit, in: Michel van de Kerchove (ed.), L'interprétation en droit. Approche pluridisciplinaire, Brussels 1978, 505 – 550.

30 Perelman talks of 'l'indication des raisons qui motivent le jugement', what Esser called the 'Begründung', the justification, and 'l'indication des mobiles psychologiques', *Chaim Perelman,* La motivation des décisions de justice, essai de synthèse, in: La motivation des décisions de justice, op. cit., 415 – 426.

31 *Mark Van Hoecke,* Mens- en maatschappijbeeld van de rechter, Ghent 1975, with an English summary (p. 110 – 111) on the judge's ideology.

32 *Jan Ten Kate/Peter van Koppen,* Determinanten van privaatrechtelijke beslissingen, Arnhem 1984, investigated on the determinants of private law decision-making, why judges often decide differently on the same civil cases. An experimental method was used to assess the relationship between personal characteristics of the judges and the variations found in decision-making (part I) and the elements of the cases which influence decision-making (part II). We quote from the summary (p. 95 – 97): 'judicial knowledge is of little importance for decision-making in these kinds of cases ... next to the minor influence of personal characte-

ing on the 'hidden' guiding principles is not an easy thing to do. That is why, in what follows, we will only concentrate on the explicitly expressed guiding principles and motivation.

III. The Judge's (Formal) Style

As already stated, the motivation of judicial decisions is a constitutional duty. It is based on the rights of defence. Each party should be able to know exactly why a decision was taken in order to, in case of errors, be able to appeal or introduce a request before the *Cour de Cassation* (in the Netherlands: the 'Hoge Raad'). The duty of motivation is a very formal duty, a bad motivation also being a motivation.[33] The form itself of the motivation is the classical (French) syllogism, as explicitly described in the standard work of Mimin, *Le style des jugements.*[34] The whole judgement is actually just one phrase, taking both facts and rules as objective elements. As critics have shown how the same facts can be understood in most divergent ways and how the same rules can be interpreted in all senses, judges have been taking more and more care to qualify the facts as precisely as possible and, as to the applicable rule, to interpret it in the most common sense, as proven by the preparatory works of the legislature, and, the last decades (see further), more and more by citing case law and legal scholars.[35] Still, also with this explanation on facts and rules, the judicial decision has always been and still is very formal and even formalistic, orchestrated by a very passive judge, who accepts the facts as proven by the parties, repeats or refutes the arguments presented by the parties (except in cases of public order where the bench can invoke exceptions in an active way) and takes care not to decide *ultra petita.*

Looking at this formal decision style, all being very logically built up, one has to admit that very often there are real guiding principles behind this formal style. The judge first makes up his mind on material grounds and only once the (materi-

---

ristics ... in practice so many other elements of the case influence the decision, that the influence of personal characteristics drowns in the error variance in individual decisions'.

33 *Robert Legros,* Considérations sur les motifs, in: La motivation des décisions de justice, op. cit., 7–8.

34 We used the fourth edition, *Pierre Mimin,* Le style des jugements (Vocabulaire – Construction – Dialectique – Formes juridiques), Paris 1962.

35 *Maurice Adams,* Het ongemakkelijk huwelijk tussen recht en politiek. Een essay over de rechter als evenwichtskunstenaar, in: Rechtskundig Weekblad (1996–97), 1209–1215; *Michel van de Kerchove* (ed.), L'interprétation en droit. Approche pluridisciplinaire, Brussels 1978; *Mark Van Hoecke,* De interpretatievrijheid van de rechter, Antwerp 1979, concludes: 'In order to restrict the conflicts and difficulties which may result from contradictions between the transmitter meaning and the receiver meaning of a statute, it is further argued that there should be closer co-operation between the courts and the legislature'. See also *Paul Foriers,* Les relations des sources écrites et non écrites du droit, in: Rapports belges au VIIIe Congrès international de droit comparé, Brussels 1970, 39–60.

al) decision is taken, he sets up the (formal) logical framework to justify his or her decision. Sometimes the guiding principles are not expressed at all; sometimes they are referred to with names like equity, reasonableness, rationality, (public) utility, common sense, the nature of things or even natural law. Sometimes these references to other 'guiding principles' than legislation are explicitly permitted by the statutory rule, as in the case of open texture norms,[36] sometimes they are not. In some branches their role is paramount (like the concept of good faith in contract law); in others it is restricted (as in criminal law[37]).

In the nineteenth century, judges were not supposed to express these material guiding principles. They were compelled to stick to a pure formal argumentation, only based on legislative texts. Today, judges feel a lot freer and refer without any problem also to case law and doctrine to justify the decision taken. The 'revolution' from a judge seen as the 'slave' of the legislature to a judge as the real 'master' of the formal sources of the law, even being a policy maker, is what will be described in the next section.

IV. The Use of the Formal Sources of Law

Still using the formal style of judgments as two hundred years ago,[38] the present day judge feels much more free to refer to other formal sources than statutory law

36 It is in this context that one can talk of 'judicial discretion', i.e. 'the power, granted to the judge, under specific conditions, to exercise his power of sentencing with a large degree of freedom. This freedom, however, can never result in arbitrary decisions. The judge remains bound by important legal bounds, such as: fundamental principles, basic constitutional guarantees, *Generalklauseln, Blanko-normen*), that are expressed by law or may be deduced from the whole legal system', *Karen Broeckx,* The discretionary power of the judge. Regional report: Belgium, France, Italy, Netherlands, in: Marcel Storme / Burkhard Hess (ed.), Discretionary power of the judge: limits and control, Mechelen 2003, 244. The new civil law of the Netherlands knows more 'open texture norms' than before, *Bas Kortmann,* Het Nederlands Burgerlijk Wetboek: het nut van de Nederlandse ervaringen voor België, in: Dirk Heirbaut / Georges Martyn (ed.), Napoleons nalatenschap. Un héritage Napoléonien, op. cit., 358–359.

37 A recent study on the guiding principles in the judging of criminal cases is *Erik Claes,* Legaliteit en rechtsvinding in het strafrecht: een grondslagentheoretische benadering, Leuven 2003.

38 The *Cour de Cassation* introduced a little bit more transparent style in 2003 (*Boudewijn Bouckaert / Bart De Moor,* Handleiding juridisch schrijven, Antwerp 2004, 41–43), but until the end of the twentieth century its style was harsh and short and therefore criticized by some scholars as elliptic and sibyllic (it is therefore recommended not only to read the decisions themselves, but also the advices of the proctor- or advocate-general), *Robert Janssens,* Het Hof van Cassatie van België. Enkele hoofdmomenten van zijn ontwikkeling, in: Legal History Review (1977), 108. On the motivation of the Belgian supreme court, see also *Ivan Verougstraete,* Het Hof van Cassatie en de motiveringsplicht, in: Mélanges offerts à Pierre van Ommeslaghe, Brussels 2000, 1061–1087, and the plea for better motivation by *Boudewijn Bouckaert,* Hoe gemotiveerd is Cassatie? Pleidooi voor een waarachtig precedentenhof en een hernieuwde motiveringscultuur, in: Thorbeckecolleges, XXI, Antwerp 1997.

than his colleagues of the nineteenth century. We compare the situation around 1900 and around 2000 for both parts of the Low Countries, for the Netherlands in a very short way, for Belgium more in detail.

1. The Netherlands

Just to cite one – important – scholar, we refer to Fockema-Andreae, who, around 1900, told the jurists to follow the written law, i.e. the legislative rule, even when it was wrong. Snijders[39] on the other hand, some seventy years later, although still admitting that the *Hoge Raad,* High Council, the Dutch supreme court, thought the legislation was the most important and first legal source, described how alternatives were possible, and, especially for the lower courts, he concluded that many judgments were very factual.

2. Belgium[40]

a) The Formal Sources of the Law in the Nineteenth Century

As referred to above, there was in Belgium no real theory or 'school' on how judges should motivate their decisions and no scientific research on how they actually did it. Looking at what the courts actually did in the nineteenth century and the beginning of the twentieth through the eyes of a legal historian, it becomes clear that the influence of the French Exegetic School, and its most important Bel-

39 *Henricus Snijders,* Rechtsvinding door de burgerlijke rechter. Een kwantitatief rechtspraakonderzoek bij de Hoge Raad en de gerechtshoven, Deventer 1978, tested at random decisions of the Dutch supreme court as well as of lower courts, during the period 1970–1974. As to the motivation of the High Council he found very few references to case law and just one to a scholarly text. It leads to his conclusion (p. 211) that the legislative text and legislative contextual factors like grammatical sense, history of the text, aims and system of the law are the main guiding principles for the supreme court. As to the 'factual' motivation of the lower courts, Snijders concludes (p. 217) that not the facts as such but the qualification or evaluation of the facts are the main issue. The case law, of which less than 10 percent is published, is of very little importance for the development of the legal landscape. Case law is very consistent with the legislation. Comparing however to the conclusions of the analogous research of Fockema-Adreae (1893–1903) and Polak (1936–1952) (p. 221), it is revealed that in the earlier period the judicial decisions stuck still more to the letter of the legislative text. Whereas for instance customary law *contra legem* was never accepted before (even if the lawgiver had made a mistake), case law did show some examples in the 1970s. In Fockema-Andreae's research arguments like utility and reasonableness never showed up, but they did according to Polak and Snijders. Only in the last period finally, judges dared to refer to the interests at stake.

40 This subject was elaborated more extensively in *Georges Martyn,* De verhouding tussen de formele bronnen van het Belgische recht in de twintigste eeuw: spiegels van de macht?, in: Dirk Heirbaut a.o. (ed.), De geschiedenis van het recht in de twintigste eeuw, Brussels 2006 (in the press).

gian representative François Laurent,[41] was paramount, propagating the exclusivity of the law, i.e. statutory law made by the legislature[42] and in the first place the Napoleonic codes (although this had not been the purpose of Portalis![43]). Making use of extensive interpretation, it should be possible to encompass every problem in the existing statutory rules.

Looking at what (especially the higher) courts actually did, this scholarly vision was also put in practice, as was shown by Bouckaert.[44] The court of cassation not only declared void judgments for having misinterpreted the law, but also for having based a decision on an extra-legal norm, i.e. on a guiding principle not literally expressed in an act of the lawgiver. There was no recognition at all of *desuetudo* or *consuetudo contra legem.* Costumary law was not recognised as an independent source of law, but could only play in a few small fields, like commerce, again explicitly defined by the legislature. In the courts' decisions no references were made to precedents or earlier decisions, neither to jurisprudence. It was this kind of judicial decision that was published in the (few) legal reviews, and in this sense they were an example for the other benches.

Although Van Dievoet[45] has demonstrated that many lower courts actually did not always follow Laurent's vision, it can be concluded that in general,[46] around

---

41 *Geert Baert,* François Laurent. Zijn leven, zijn tijd en zijn strijd (1810–1887), in: Liber Memorialis François Laurent, Brussels 1989, 54–57.

42 *Luc Wintgens* (ed.), Het wetsbegrip, in: Acta van het Centrum voor wetgeving, regulering en legisprudentie, I, Bruges 2003.

43 'Si l'on manque de loi, il faut consulter l'usage ou l'équité', *Charles Huberlant,* Les mécanismes institués pour combler les lacunes de la loi, in: Chaim Perelman (ed.), Le problème des lacunes en droit, Brussels 1968, 54.

44 *Boudewijn Bouckaert,* De exegetische school. Een kritische studie van de rechtsbronnen- en interpretatieleer bij de 19de eeuwse commentatoren van de Code Civil, Antwerp 1981. The author recapitulated the main conclusions and compared to the situation at the beginning of the third millennium in *Boudewijn Bouckaert,* Het Burgerlijk Wetboek en de andere rechtsbronnen, in: Dirk Heirbaut / Georges Martyn (ed.), Napoleons nalatenschap. Un héritage Napoléonien, op. cit., 253–269.

45 *Emile Van Dievoet,* Het burgerlijk recht in België en in Nederland van 1800 tot 1940. De rechtsbronnen, Antwerp 1943, investigates the evolution of legislation, jurisprudence, customary law and case law in civil matters. As to the Belgian case law he compares four periods: in 1814–1830 the judge has a difficult time trying to motivate (he does not refer very often to sources, but uses phrases as 'il est évident', 'cela est fondé sur le droit naturel autorisé par une loi positive'); in 1856–1860 the sentences are more extensively and better motivated, very often referring to the continuity with the old law or principles of Roman law; in the years 1886–1890 there is some influence of the Exegetic School and especially Laurent and if the rule is not clear, the French works of Pothier, Merlin or Dalloz are consulted; and only in 1931–1935 new ideas, fostered by jurisprudence, are dripping in, and precedents and jurisprudence are referred to.

46 An important exception is the Judge of the Peace (*Vrederechter / Juge de Paix*), an institution conceived by the French lawgiver as a tribunal close to the people, deciding civil matters *without* being forced to follow the legal rules. This magistrate was allowed to judge according to equity. Although this was not as such expressed in the law of August 16th-24th,

1900 in Belgium, there was a primacy of statutory law in judicial decision making. This legislation was the formal[47] law, as enacted by the two chambers of the Belgian national Parliament and escaping from any constitutional control.[48]

b) The Formal Sources of the Law Today

The sketched situation has changed radically. Statutory law is still, as well in legal education as in judicial handling, the cornerstone of the legal system, but it is no longer the one and only guide. Throughout the twentieth century, each of the three already mentioned formal sources of law, viz. statutory law, case law and jurisprudence, developed a lot, mainly as a consequence of internationalisation, specialisation and professionalisation. Secondly, a new formal source made its appearance on the legal theatre. Finally, the relations of mutual force or importance between the different sources altered.

What happened with legislation? Political evolutions led to the creation of new institutions. The Belgian Parliament is no longer the unique lawgiver. Since the 1970's, through a series of state reforms, Belgium became a federal state, existing of three communities and three regions, each of them having their own parliament, competent, in certain matters, to make decrees with the same force of law as federal legislation. Part of the national sovereignty was also transferred to the European Union, whose regulations have direct force of law in the member states. In the 'Le Ski' case of 1971[49] the Belgian Court of Cassation declared that European rules

---

1790, there could be no doubt about it according to the preparatory works. When four months later, by the law of November 17th-December 1st, 1790, the Cour de Cassation was established, introducing an explicitly legislation-bound control, this did not change. Complete juridical control over the Judge of the Peace (not only because of abuse of power but also because of infraction of the law) was not introduced in Belgium before 1876 and even then this change was only accidental and not at all well taken into consideration, *Vaast Van Herreweghe,* De Vrederechter en Cassatie. De verhouding tussen de wetsongebonden 'laagste' en de wetsbewakende 'hoogste' rechter, 1790–1813, Ghent 1993, 109–117.

47 The material legislation, being general rules enacted by the executive power, by the provinces or the municipalities, can be controlled by the judicial power using the exception of illegality.

48 Just like the American constitution, the Belgian (1831) one does not say a word on constitutional control of the legislature by the judicial power. Unlike the American Supreme Court in its famous decision Marbury v. Madison, the Belgian supreme court, the Court of Cassation, rejected the possibility of constitutional control by decision of 23 July 1849, in: Pasicrisie (1849), I, 443 (a.o. confirmed by decisions of 20 November 1962, in: Pasicrisie (1963), I, 362, and 21 October 1966, Pasicrisie (1967), I, 240); *M. Barzin,* Du contrôle de la constitutionnalité des lois, in: Académie Royale de Belgique. Bulletin de la Classe des Lettres (1966), 335–350; *Robert Janssens,* Het Hof van Cassatie van België. Enkele hoofdmomenten van zijn ontwikkeling, in: Legal History Review (1977), 111.

49 Cour de Cassation, 27 May 1971, in: Arresten van Cassatie (1971), 967. In the (5 February 1963, in: Jurisprudentie van het Hof van Justitie 1963, 3) Van Gend en Loos-case, the European Court of Justice had already decided that the European Community was a new

with direct action had priority over the national legislation. It was a small recognition of constitutional control (making it possible for judges to put binding national legislation aside), until that moment totally unseen in Belgium.

Case law, and especially published case law, also knew a kind of quantitative explosion. In books and reviews, and now online, one can find a multitude of decisions, not only of the 'old' benches of the judicial branch, but also of many arbitrational institutes and extra-judicial committees.[50] Although not enjoying the privileges of executive power by their decisions, it is important to stress the role these dispute-settling initiatives play for the interpretation of the written rules and the creation of guiding principles in specific domains of the law, such as consumer and environmental protection.

Case law indeed, today, is fully recognised as a formal source of law in the sense that judges indeed 'make' law and not only find and apply it.[51] In thousands of individual cases the legislative rules or interpreted, elucidated and balanced. General rules get a more precise content. The bench cannot change the formal law, but, interpreting it, it can adapt it to new circumstances, analyse it, modernize it, even fill in lacunae.[52] Interpretation of the statutory rule is indeed a task of, amongst others, the judicial branch. The lawgiver is not able to foresee all possible

---

legal order in international public law, for which in some fields of competence the national states had given up their sovereignty, and in which not only the member states but also the individual subjects had subjective rights.

50 *Luc Huyse/Hilde Sabbe,* De mensen van het recht, Leuven 1997, 174.

51 *Ivan Verougstraete,* De rechter en de macht, in Recht en macht, Turnhout 1990, 181–210; *id.*, Le juge, censeur de la loi, in: Le rôle du juge dans la cité, Brussels 2002, 47–61; *id.*, Rechtsheerschappij en sturing door de rechter. Ingrepen bij economische spanningen, in: Limburgs Rechtsleven (1995), 151–171. Illustrative for the fact that the recognition of case law as an important creator of law is an evolution of the post-War decades, is the comparison of two books by Rigaux: *François Rigaux,* La nature du contrôle de la Cour de Cassation, Brussels 1966 and La loi des juges, Paris 1997. Luc Huyse, the most important living legal sociologist of Belgium, states: 'In some matters, Parliament has become the notary, only formalising the new law created by precedent', *Dirk Luyten/Joggli Meihuizen,* Luc Huyse: interview met een multi-disciplinair grensbewoner, in: Pro Memorie (2004), 284. See also *Maurice Adams,* Government of laws, not of men? Over recht, macht en de democratische legitimiteit van rechtsvorming door de rechter. Een toepassing in de context van trias politica en vage normen, in: Chroniques de Droit Publique/Publiekrechtelijke Kronieken (1999), 173–201.

52 A crucial book in twentieth century Belgian law was, as already mentioned, *Walter Van Gerven,* Het beleid van de rechter, Antwerp 1973 (and many reprints), to be translated as 'the prudence or policy of the judge'. Although some scholars protested against the recognition of the judge's creative role, mainly on basis of the argument that judicial creation lacked the – in a system of separation of powers necessary – democratic control (*Robert Kruithof,* Naar een 'Gouvernement des juges' in het Belgische verbintenissenrecht?, in: Hulde aan Prof. Dr. R. Kruithof, Antwerp 1992, 27–79), it is today no longer doubted, *Maurice Adams,* Democratische rechtspraak: variaties op een ideaal, in: Maurice Adams/Patricia Popelier (ed.), Recht en democratie: de democratische verbeelding van het recht, Antwerp 2004, 337–380; *H.C.F. Schoordijk,* De methode van rechtsvinding en haar geschiedenis, in: Tijdschrift voor Privaatrecht (2003), 613–641.

cases and the judge, if he does not want to be guilty of denial of justice, is forced to be a modeler, adapting the rule to social evolution. In case of uncertainty, darkness or lacunae in the legislation, the judge is obliged to create law. Such creations, described, analyzed, compared to foreign developments and given a place in the legal system by jurisprudence, were for instance the theories of abuse of right and of neighbor nuisance. Also important has been the introduction of marginal control,[53] based on the principle of rationality, giving the judge the power to intervene in the balance of the contractual relations in private law or to leave the narrow control of pure legality in public law.

Certainly, the time of the strict Exegetic School has long gone. However, one should not exaggerate the break with the past. In the ways legislative texts are interpreted, there is a lot of continuity. What finally disappeared, are the extreme formalism and literalism. The 'new' visions of Gény in France ('la libre recherche scientifique'), of Vander Eycken (teleological interpretation in function of the social needs) and De Page ('l'induction sociale') are more theoretical than real.[54] Three changes are nevertheless important. The first is that, instead of referring to the words of a legislative text, judges today refer more and more to the consistency of their decision within the juridical system as such. A second alteration concerns the use of historical arguments. Whereas a century ago judges referred to the preparatory texts of legislation in order to understand the correct sense of it, they now make a quest for an 'intertemporal' lawgiver: what should the sense of a rule be today, taking in account the principles that guided the original lawgiver, but translated into the contemporary context. Finally, references to – a rather mystic – natural law changed to references to – an above all rational – legal science or system (see also further on the general principles of law).

Judge-made law was also influenced by other evolutions. Within the judicial branch the number of benches and courts increased and within these institutions also the number of chambers and magistrates. Moreover, these magistrates became more and more specialized and professional. In the area of labor (and social) law for instance, the nineteenth century *'Conseils de prud'hommes'*, composed of representatives of the working field, were replaced by labor tribunals, presided by a professional jurist.[55] A similar evolution occurred in the area of commercial law, where the old commercial tribunals only counted merchants as judges. From 1869 onwards, the clerk had to be an academically trained jurist; in 1910 he became a

---

53 *Jan Ronse*, Le contrôle marginal des décisions discrétionnaires en droit privé, in: Chaim Perelman / Paul Foriers (ed.), La motivation des décisions de justice, Brussels 1978, 403–414; *Robert Soetaert*, Rechtsbeginselen en marginale toetsing in cassatie, in: Liber amicorum Jan Ronse, Brussels 1986, 51–66.

54 *François Ost*, L'interprétation logique et systématique et le postulat de rationalité du législateur, in: Michel van de Kerchove (ed.), L'interprétation en droit. Approche pluridisciplinaire, Brussels 1978, 115–116.

55 *Luk Burgelman*, Geschiedenis van de Belgische magistratuur (1830–2002), in: Politieke en sociale geschiedenis van justitie in België van 1830 tot heden, op. cit., 187–215.

referendary; and finally, with the introduction of the 1967 Judicial Code, this referendary became the professional president of the commercial bench.

Another important enlargement of the public dispute-settling institutions was the creation in the middle of the twentieth century of the Council of State.[56] It judges the legality of governmental decisions, individual acts as well as general rules of any administrative authority.[57] What actually should be understood by 'administrative authority or service' is not explained in the 1946 legislation, nor in any later statute. This gap has been perfectly filled by the Council's (and the Court of Cassation's) case law, a beautiful example of the creative power of the judiciary. The lawgiver has even explicitly accepted this creation, as for the applicability of many statutes he simply refers to the term administrative authority 'as understood in the sense of article 14 of the coordinated statutes on the Council of State'.[58] The Council has been extremely busy. Whereas in the first years its activity was almost limited to disputes of public officers, under the influence of the ever growing public intervention in all kinds of matters, it is now dealing with environmental law, public ordering, economic ruling, asylum policy, etc. In these vast domains the Council interpreted in a very extensive way its grounds for nullification.[59]

The judiciary not only managed to get more control (the 1946 general nullification in addition to the old[60] exception of illegality in individual cases) over the executive branch, it also turned its critical eye to the legislative branch.[61] In the

---

56 The Council was created by the law of 23 December 1946 and it was solemnly installed 8 October 1948, *Gustaaf Baeteman*, De Raad van State op de drempel van de 21ste eeuw, in Gustaaf Baeteman / Geert Debersaques (ed.), 50 jaar Raad van State, Bruges 1998, 1–35; *André Alen*, Rechter en bestuur in het Belgische publiekrecht. De grondslagen van de rechterlijke wettigheidskontrole, Antwerp 1984; *Sabien Lust*, Raad van State. Afdeling Administratie. 6. Rechtsherstel door de Raad van State, Bruges 2000. The constitutional anchorage of the Council did not follow until 1994.

57 Jurists had already been asking for such an institution before the first World War, *R. Marcq*, La responsabilité de la puissance publique, Brussels 1911, and *M. Bourquin*, La protection des droits individuels contre les abus de pouvoir de l'autorité administrative en Belgique, Brussels 1912.

58 *Frederik Vandendriessche*, De invulling van het begrip administratieve overheid na de arresten Gimvindus en BATC van het Hof van Cassatie, in: Rechtskundig Weekblad (2000–01), 497–506.

59 *Baeteman*, De Raad van State, 21; see also further on the general principles of good governance.

60 The 'exception of illegality' (art. 107 of the 1831 Constitution, today art. 159) allows the judge to decide not to take a rule of the executive power or of the provincial or municipal level into account, when he considers it to be against a constitutional or formal legal rule. The introduction of this article is a reaction against the rather despotic government by King William, who, in the so-called 'conflict decree' of 5 October 1822, stated the judicial power was subjected to the executive one, *Vaast Van Herreweghe*, De Vrederechter en Cassatie, op. cit., 114; *J.-J. Thonissen*, La Constitution belge annotée offrant sous chaque article l'état de la doctrine, de la jurisprudence et de la législation, Brussels 1876, 326–335.

61 Whereas, as in Belgium, the judicial control over the executive branch exists also in the Netherlands (Council of State), the latter state still rejects the idea of constitutional control

last quarter of the twentieth century the Court of Arbitration was created.[62] It is a truly Belgian creation, composed of both legal scholars and former politicians (most of them in fact also jurists). Its first task was to decide conflicts of competence between the national state, the regions and the communities, but it could also declare decrees or national laws void, if these violated the principles of equality and non-discrimination (today articles 10 and 11 of the Constitution). The Court, very creatively, linked these articles of the Constitution to other constitutional fundamental rights and in this way managed to extend its control. In 2003 the lawgiver confirmed this case law by explicitly giving to the Court the competence to watch over all constitutional rights (as well as over some constitutional principles of tax law).

Case law finally also introduced state responsibility for the acts of the legislature, the executive power and the judiciary. In the nineteenth century public action enjoyed immunity.[63] A milestone was the 'Flandria judgment' of 1920, when the Court of Cassation decided the state was responsible for the damage caused by the imprudence of the executive power.[64] It was the starting point of a more and more extensive application of state responsibility, until also the lawgiver was deemed responsible for its actions, or better not-acting,[65] as had first been decided by the European Court of Justice in the Francovich case of 19 November 1991.[66] On a prejudicial question of an Italian judge, the Court decided that Italy could be held responsible for not having executed in time a European directive. Now that the Court of Arbitration, the European Human Rights Court and the European Court of Justice can declare legislation void on more and more grounds, more and more financial claims are being put before the civil courts.[67] If the judge is to be consid-

---

over the formal law, as legislation is seen as the democratic expression of the general will, 'omdat daardoor de trias politica en het vertegenwoordigingsprincipe onder druk komen te staan', *Hans Lindahl,* Rechtsvorming als politieke representatie: de kwestie van constitutionele toetsing, in: Bart Van Klink / Erik Broers (ed.), De rechter als rechtsvormer, The Hague 2001, 173 – 196.

62 Although not being an institution of the judicial order or branch, it cannot be denied that the Court does play a judicial role. The creation of this Court was announced in the 1980's constitutional reform and realized by the special majority law, 'special' referring to a political majority on both the Flemish and Walloon groups in Parliament, *Jan Velaers,* Van Arbitragehof tot grondwettelijk hof, Antwerp 1990.

63 *Paul Lewalle,* Les responsabilités des pouvoirs publics en droit belge. Antécédents et perspectives, in: L'administration face à ses juges, Liège 1987, and the same, Contentieux administratif, Brussels 2002.

64 Cour de Cassation, 5 November 1920, in: Pasicrisie 1920, I, 193.

65 *Michel Mahieu / Sébastien Van Droogenbroeck,* La responsabilité de l'état législateur, in: Journal des Tribunaux (1998), 825 – 846; *Gunter Maes,* Sancties bij een door het Arbitragehof vastgestelde ongrondwettige afwezigheid van wetgeving, in: Rechtskundig Weekblad (2003 – 04), 1201 – 1209 and the same, Algemene zorgvuldigheidsnorm en aansprakelijkheid voor de wetgevende macht, in: Nieuw Juridisch Weekblad (2004), 398 – 404.

66 *Dirk Arts,* Het Francovich-arrest en zijn toepassing in de Belgische rechtsorde, in: Tijdschrift voor Bestuurswetenschappen en Publiekrecht (1993), 495.

ered 'the mouth of the law', this mouth can bite seriously. The judicial power has today an enormous impact on the law, not only by interpreting, but also by creating and annihilating by way of legal and constitutional control and by adjudging responsibility claims.

And how did jurisprudence evolve during the twentieth century? Today, it is no longer discussed that the writings of legal scholars indeed form a source of law. These scholars no longer just summarize, explain or comment. They are critical and creative, as for instance in the case of the already mentioned theories of abuse of law or neighbor nuisances. Jurisprudence actually comments on what judges do and proposes new ideas, but only if the courts follow these ideas, they are to be considered effective.[68] A classic example is the rejection by the supreme Court of Cassation of the Dutch concept of 'rechtsverwerking' (holding, in short, that when a creditor acts as if he does not longer insist on the execution of a certain debt, but finally surprises his debtor anyway with a claim, his demand can be rejected), although propagated by several authors and adopted by several lower courts.[69]

What, on the other hand, is meanwhile totally accepted by jurisprudence *and* the judiciary, is the appearance of a new formal source of law on the legal theatre: the general principles of law. The basic idea of this is that there are some unwritten fundamental principles, true guiding principles of the law, having many applications in concrete legislative rules, but never having been expressed as such by the lawgiver, certainly not in an exhaustive way. The prohibition to take the law into one's own hands, for instance, is not expressed as such in a statute. The right of the suspected or the witness to remain silent in order not to incriminate oneself is another example. One of the first recognised[70] general principles was the right of defence, i.e. the obligation to give someone a rational chance to make his arguments or means of defence before the taking of a negative decision against him. These principles are not the kind of 'general principles of (a branch of) the law'

---

67 Finally the state has also been declared responsible for the wrong acts of the judicial power itself by the Anderlecht-Café-case, decided by the Court of Cassation 19 December 1991, *Alois Van Oevelen,* De aansprakelijkheid van de Staat voor ambtsfouten van magistraten en de orgaantheorie na het Anca-arrest van het Hof van Cassatie van 19 december 1991, in: Rechtskundig Weekblad (1992–93), 377–398 and the same, De overheidsaansprakelijkheid voor het optreden van de rechterlijke macht, Antwerp 1997.

68 *Ivan Verougstraete,* De invloed van de doctrine op de rechtspraak, in: Tijdschrift voor Privaatrecht (1984, extranummer Feestbundel 20 jaar Tijdschrift voor Privaatrecht), 65–88.

69 It is also an example of the above mentioned dividing legal cultures: 'rechtsverwerking' has Dutch origins and is well known by the Dutch speaking Flemish lawyers, but the word has not even got a French translation. The Court of Cassation, still thinking in the traditional French way, does not accept the creation, as it does not fit well in the existing codes, where for instance prescription has an analogous function.

70 *Walter Ganshof van der Meersch,* Le droit de défense, principe général de droit. Réflexions sur des arrêts récents, in: Mélanges en l'honneur de J. Dabin, II, Brussels 1963, 569–614.

one can already find in the old didactic books on law and legal education.[71] It has nothing to do with the gross lines of a branch of law. If one considers general principles as a formal source of the law, it is a rather concrete rule[72] that is meant, a rule a judicial decision is based on, although it is not a statutory rule, nor a precedent, nor doctrinal authority. The general principles of law are an autonomous formal source of law. The legislature, the judge or the scholar can find or formulate the principle, but it is pre-existing.[73] It is part of the unwritten[74] law of a society in a certain place at a certain time.[75] General principles stem from natural law, but are part of the positive legal system. Today, their binding character is entirely accepted. There are even general principles with constitutional value.[76] Just as in Belgium's surrounding countries, general principles only appeared after the Second World War.[77] In the 1970s their popularity grew in case law, while scholars tried to catalogue them.[78] Their biggest successes were harvested in the domain of administrative law, where principles were recognised (especially by the Council of State) such as the principle of confidence, of rationality, of proportionality, of fair play. They were labelled 'principles of decent or good governance or administration'.[79] Whereas in the first years of its existence the Council of State was very

---

71 *Sigrid Jacoby,* Allgemeine Rechtsgrundsätze: Begriffsentwicklung und Funktion in der Europäischen Rechtsgeschichte, in: Schriften zur europäischen Rechts- und Verfassungsgeschichte, XIX, Berlin 1997.

72 Although it is more a principle than an easily applied rule, it gives a clear indication in what sense the case at hand has to be decided. Important differences with equity are that there are several principles and not just one tempering idea on the one hand and, on then other hand, that it is not a moderation of another applicable rule, but that it can be applied autonomously and even against the text of an applicable rule.

73 'Ils ne sont pas créés par le juge...il en constate l'existence, *Walter Ganshof van der Meersch,* Propos sur le texte de la loi et les principes généraux du droit, in: Journal des Tribunaux (1970), 557–573 and 581–596.

74 Their unwritten character is a common feature with customary law, but contrary to customary law there is no need for repeated usage in order to become binding.

75 *Mark Van Hoecke,* De algemene rechtsbeginselen als rechtsbron: een inleiding, in: Mark Van Hoecke (ed.), Algemene rechtsbeginselen. Referaten van de lezingencyclus georganiseerd door de Interuniversitaire Kontaktgroep Rechtstheorie, november 1987-maart 1989, Antwerp 1991, 3; *Paul Van Orshoven,* Non scripta, sed nata lex, *eod.,* 69–70, and *Mark Van Hoecke,* Naar een theorie van de algemene rechtsbeginselen, *eod.,* 392–393.

76 *Johan Vande Lanotte/Geert Goedertier,* Overzicht publiek recht, Bruges 2001, 160–164.

77 According to *Van Hoecke,* De algemene rechtsbeginselen, 10, the maiden decision was taken by the Court of Cassation, January 10th 1950, in: Pasicrisie (1950), I, 302. It was the first time the supreme court accepted a general principle, viz. the continuity of public service, as a legitimate ground for reversal of a judgment, see also *Robert Soetaert,* Algemene rechtsbeginselen in Cassatie, in: Van Hoecke, Algemene rechtsbeginselen, 83–94.

78 *Van Hoecke,* De algemene rechtsbeginselen, 13; *P. Claeys Boúúaert,* Algemene beginselen van het recht. Vijftien jaar rechtspraak van het Hof van Cassatie, in: Rechtskundig Weekblad (1986–1987), 336. *Annelies Bossuyt/Ivan Verougstraete,* Algemene rechtsbeginselen, in: Jaarverslag van het Hof van Cassatie van België (2002–2003), Brussels 2003, 112–162.

much inspired by the case law of its French counterpart, the acceptance of the principles of good governance is an example of a growing Dutch influence.[80]

After having sketched the evolution of legislation, case law and jurisprudence and the appearance of the general principles, let us finally look at the changed relations between all of these formal sources of law. The primacy of the law of a century ago has been broken. Judicial institutions can nullify, or at least neglect, formal (European courts, Court of Arbitration) and material (Council of State and all courts using the exception of illegality) legislation. 'Illegality' does not any longer refer to the text of the statutory law, but in a more general way to the legitimate character of a rule and its standing with the general principles of law.[81] Case law, in an ongoing dialogue with scholarly jurisprudence, plays a paramount part in the creation of new law and the adaptation of the old. Whereas scholars look for new ideas abroad and can suggest many alterations, the (higher) courts finally decide on what is to be accepted or not. Instead of the primacy of the statutory law, which was legitimized by the democratic representation in Parliament, one can talk today of the primacy of the judiciary. Or in other words, far from still being the sole 'bouche de la loi', obliged to follow literally the legislative text, like a slave who follows his master, the judge has become the master himself.

---

79 *Jurgen De Staerke,* Algemene beginselen van behoorlijk bestuur en behoorlijk burgerschap. Beginselen van de openbare dienst, Bruges 2002 and *id.*, Algemene beginselen van behoorlijk bestuur, in: AdvocatenPraktijk. Administratief en Publiek Recht, IX, Mechelen 2004. Louis-Paul Baron Suetens was one of the most important pace-makers for the recognition of these principles as an autonomous formal source of law, *Louis-Paul Suetens,* Algemene rechtsbeginselen en algemene beginselen van behoorlijk bestuur in het Belgisch administratief recht, in: Tijdschrift voor Bestuurswetenschappen en Publiekrecht (1970), 379–396; Algemene beginselen van behoorlijk bestuur in de rechtspraak van de Raad van State, *eod.* 1981, 81–89; Algemene beginselen van behoorlijk bestuur: begrip en plaats in de hiërarchie der normen. Inleidende verkenning, in: Ingrid Opdebeek (ed.), Algemene beginselen van behoorlijk bestuur, Antwerp 1993, 1–26. Suetens refered to many decisions of the Council of State and drew up lists of principles in 1970, 1981 and 1993. The *Cour de Cassation* named the principles of good administration for the first time in a decision of 29 April 1960. After the publication of Suetens' 1970 contribution, the recognition as a formal source of law is no longer debated, as had been done before, *P. Maroy,* Application des principes généraux du droit dans la jurisprudence administrative. Rapport, Brussels 1961; *Charles Huberlant,* Le droit administratif belge comprend-il des principes généraux non écrits?, in: Mélanges en l'honneur de Jean Dabin, I, Brussels 1963, 661–690; *Marc Somerhausen,* Les principes généraux du droit administratif, in: Leon Cortinas-Pelaez (ed.), Perspectivas del derecho publico en la segunda mitad del siglo XX. Homenaje a Enrique Sayaqués-Laso, IV, Madrid 1969, 465–490.

80 *Baeteman,* De Raad van State, 17; *Suetens,* Algemene rechtsbeginselen, 379. The name "general principles of decent governance" has Dutch roots and has over there already been mentioned in legislation in 1954, *G.J. Wiarda,* Algemene beginselen van behoorlijk bestuur in het Nederlandse recht, in: Tijdschrift voor Bestuurswetenschappen en Publiekrecht (1970), 365–378.

81 *Karel Rimanque,* De grondwet toegelicht, gewikt en gewogen, Antwerp 1999, 318–319.

V. Evaluation by Way of Conclusion

At first sight, there is nothing wrong with the primacy of judge made law. It is certainly a step towards a more unified international legal context, where the contrast between the common law system based on precedents and the continental one based on statutory law was a hard steeple to take. Although officially Belgium does not recognize precedent as a binding source of law, one finds citations of and references to decisions of the (higher) courts hundredfold.[82]

And the fact that judges keep a watchful eye on what the legislature and the executive branch decide, is not that the ultimate realisation of the rule of law? (Or is it the 'rule of lawyers'?) Is it not the filling up of the missing checks and balances, needed by a system of true separation of powers?[83]

There is, however, also another side of the coin, at least in my personal opinion. Every control by a professional and academically trained judge is a technical control, obeying the rules of juridical logic. But let us not forget that law is not a guiding principle as such. Law is an instrument of social order. Rules and institutions are not true or good as such; they are only means to realize social aims, which are outside the legal system itself. The true guiding principles or the ultimate decision on good and bad are not juridical decisions. If our society entrusts the power of deciding to the jurists of the judicial power, one can only hope these men and women will be worthy of this confidence.

At least, it may be expected from the professional jurists that they do the best they can to make more use of explicit and extensive argumentation,[84] not only to convince the parties, but also to convince the public opinion. In the 1990s Belgian justice fell into a deep crisis, especially on the occasion of the 'Spaghetti decision'

---

82 *Maurice Adams*, De precedentenwerking van rechterlijke uitspraken, in: Jura Falconis (1996–97), 747–762 (summary of Adams' doctoral thesis, Leuven 1997). 'In de praktijk overtuigt men een rechter meer van de inhoud van het recht met een arrest van de hoogste rechtskolleges dan met hooggeleerde beschouwingen over de tekst van de wet. (In practice one convinces the judge more easily about the law by citing a decision of the higher courts than by giving scholarly explanations on the text of the statute)', *Van Orshoven*, Non scripta, sed nata lex, 78.

83 It was – not surprisingly – during the World War that the Belgian supreme court for the first time, by decision of the Cour de Cassation of 20 May 1916, declared void the decrees of the German occupier, 'la force ne créant pas le droit', *Burgelman*, Geschiedenis; *Janssens*, Het Hof van Cassatie, 102.

84 The above mentioned Van Gerven is pleading for more transparency and proposes to introduce in the argumentation of a judicial decision what Esser calls the 'Vorentscheidung', *Herman Cousy/Wouter Devroe*, Met recht en rede, de reden van het recht: interview met Walter van Gerven, Pro Memorie (2004), 92. More extensively on his 'creative justice': *Walter van Gerven*, Creatieve rechtspraak, in: Tijdschrift voor Privaatrecht (1997), 1–2, and on the position of the magistrates in this debate in the last decades: *Jan Loyens*, Het onbehagen van de magistratuur. Beschouwingen bij dertig jaar mercuriales, in: Rechtskundig Weekblad (2003–04), 1281–1293.

of the Belgian Court of Cassation in the Dutroux case, sentencing a man who had kidnapped and murdered several children. The supreme court removed a – in the public opinion's eyes 'good' – 'juge d'instruction' (a criminal investigation judge) because he had eaten a pasta at a benefit party offered to the family of the victims. Although the decision to remove the judge from the case was juridically correct (justice must also be seen to be done, a judge eating with one of the parties is not an impartial judge), it was not appreciated by the public. It made Belgian jurists aware of the broad gap between the citizen and the law. If the jurists, and especially the judges, want to legitimize the power and confidence put in their hands, they should be aware of the importance to be clear on their guiding principles.

MATTHEW C. MIROW

Case Law in Mexico 1861 to 1919: The Work of Ignacio Luis Vallarta

In a somewhat unusual development for a civil law country, Mexico permits the use of case decisions to provide binding rules of law in a particular class of cases.[1] Beginning in the nineteenth century, Mexico witnessed the development of *jurisprudencia,* the use of cases to provide binding rules of law, within *amparo* actions, a group of legislatively created actions to protect constitutional rights. Part one of this contribution describes the use of jurisprudencia today and how it relates to amparo actions. Part two examines the sources of jurisprudencia in nineteenth-century Mexico. This second part addresses the three important amparo acts of the mid to late nineteenth century and the works of the drafter of the Amparo Act of 1882, Ignacio Luis Vallarta. Part three then presents some of the contemporary criticisms of jurisprudencia. The final part examines Vallarta's uses of sources and concludes that his creation of jurisprudencia in Mexico was profoundly guided by United States law.

I. Jurisprudencia Today

Perhaps the first comment that must be made about jurisprudencia, or the use of case decisions to provide binding rules of law, is that it is an exception in Mexican law; it is an exception to the practitioner's general view that presently "appellate decisions have no binding effect in Mexico."[2] Furthermore, there is nothing to indicate that the situation was any different at earlier points in Mexican legal history.

Nonetheless, in some situations, judicial decisions determine applicable rules of law in Mexico. Although jurisprudencia operates within a limited context today, it is also a firmly established method of determining applicable rules of law.[3] Before

---

1 The author thanks Howard Wasserman for his helpful suggestions and Steven Harper for his research assistance.

2 *J. A. Vargas,* Mexican Law: A Treatise for Legal Practitioners and International Investors, vol. 1 (1998), p. 6.

3 There has even developed a practice of informal jurisprudencia in which Mexican court follow precedent not out of statutory obligation to do so, but to advance various policy con-

describing how the system of jurisprudencia works today in Mexico, it should be noted that the Mexican judiciary is a federal system containing both federal and state courts. Our examination of jurisprudencia is limited to the application of the doctrine within the federal courts.[4] These national courts are composed of a Supreme Court of Justice which may sit either *en banc* or in two *salas* or divisions. Below the Supreme Court are the Circuit Appellate Tribunals which may sit as either collegiate or unitary tribunals. There are presently about 80 collegiate circuit tribunals and about 50 unitary tribunals. Below these intermediate appellate courts are the District Courts, numbering about 180 throughout the country.[5] The similarity with the structure of the federal courts in the United States is no accident. Mexico, like many countries in Latin America, often looked directly to the Constitution of the United States and the structure of its judiciary when drafting Constitutions and creating judicial institutions.[6] This reflection of the United States Constitution can be observed in the Mexican Constitutions of 1824, of 1857, and even the revolutionary Constitution of 1917.

Jurisprudencia today in Mexico is the product of a statute entitled the *Ley de Amparo* or Amparo Act.[7] This act provides procedures for courts to protect constitutional rights and to review actions that may be unconstitutional. One portion of the current act states that five uninterrupted, consecutive decisions by the Supreme Court or Circuit Collegial Tribunal sharing the same legal opinion becomes obligatory.[8] This fifth decision becomes *jurisprudencia obligatoria* (obligatory jurisprudencia) and is obligatory authority in federal and state courts, in labor and administrative tribunals, and on other government actors.[9] Such a decision, however, may be overturned. The Supreme Court may change the established rule of law, although under Article 194 of the Amparo Act, the court must note the change and give reasons for the change.[10] Legislation also addresses other methods courts can use to overrule established jurisprudencia.[11]

---

siderations related to the judicial function. *S. Zamora* et al., Mexican Law (2004), pp. 87–88.

4 Jurisprudencia does exist at the state level and in administrative tribunals, but these manifestations appear to be later developments modeled after federal practice. *Zamora*, Mexican Law, p. 85.

5 *Vargas*, Mexican Law, pp. 51–56.

6 *M. C. Mirow*, Latin American Law: A History of Private Law and Institutions in Spanish America (2004), pp. 108, 167, 173.

7 Ley de Amparo, Diario Oficial, January 10, 1936 (and subsequent amendments).

8 Several other federal courts of special jurisdiction and administrative tribunals can establish jurisprudencia within their particular sphere as well. *Zamora*, Mexican Law, p. 86.

9 The precise nature of the binding effect of jusprudencia is slightly more complex. For example, jurisprudencia established by Circuit Tribunals only has obligatory effect on the courts and actors within the geographic region covered by the circuit. *Zamora*, Mexican Law, p. 86.

10 *Vargas*, Mexican Law, vol. 1, p. 59.

11 *Zamora*, Mexican Law, p. 86.

Since 1988, there has been a monthly gazette of every decision that may lead to obligatory jurisprudencia. Such a decision, called a *tesis aislada* ("an isolated ruling") is given a rank from one to five indicating the likelihood that the decision will become jurisprudencia. This development in publication of judicial decisions stems from a significantly long tradition in Mexico. Since the 1870s, an official journal, the *Semanario Judicial de la Federación,* has reported case decisions.[12]

Recalling that jurisprudencia is an exception to the general method of establishing rules of law in Mexican courts, the institution must be viewed in the context of Mexican constitutional, or amparo, actions. *Amparar* is a Spanish verb meaning "to protect, to shelter, or to provide refuge." Today an amparo action is a federal suit by an individual or legal person against any Mexican authority that by act or law has violated the constitutional rights of an individual (or legal person). The purpose of the action is to restore the rights of the individual. Amparo Acts have set out special procedures for these types of actions.[13]

As a general rule, even though jurisprudencia may establish a rule of law from a line of cases, a single case in an amparo action has no precedential value and no *stare decisis* effect. This limited value of amparo actions became encapsulated in the *Fórmula Otero,* or Otero Formula, which provides that the judgment in an amparo case is limited to providing the aggrieved party with the protection of federal justice in the particular case, *without making any general declaration with respect to the law or act* that produced the amparo judgment. Thus, the application of the judgment is only to the party, the particular aggrieved individual, and to no one else. Therefore, the next aggrieved individual, even under identical circumstances, must also file an amparo action. As a result, for some events or recurring situations, it not unusual to have thousands of individuals filing, with a concomitant overburdening effect on judiciary.[14]

With this problem in mind, President Zedillo in 1995 led the campaign to amend Article 105 of the Mexican Constitution. Following several European models, the amendment provides that the Supreme Court may determine that certain decisions have general, or *erga omnes,* application.[15]

---

12 *Zamora,* Mexican Law, p. 85; *Vargas,* Mexican Law, vol. 1, p. 59.

13 *Zamora,* Mexican Law, pp. 261–286. It should be noted that amparo actions are not only used as methods to protect individual rights, but also as instruments of political control and judicial review. It was this notion of constitutional control that led to the first use of the term "amparo" in a Mexican Constitution. The Constitution of Yucatán of 1840 by Manuel Cesencio Rejón employs the term in this sense. *Vargas,* Mexican Law, vol. 1, p. 62.

14 *Vargas,* Mexican Law, vol. 1, p. 61.

15 *Vargas,* Mexican Law, p. 62; This form of "single-ruling' jurisprudencia is very unusual in Mexico. "Only when the highest court in a judicial hierarch (such as the Mexican Supreme Court, or a state's highest court) decides a matter in plenary session will the rule of *jurisprudencia obligatoria* require subsequent courts to follow the single court decision." *Zamora,* Mexican Law, p. 84.

These paragraphs have sketched out the general structure of jurisprudencia and amparo and the relationship they have with each other. This structure goes back at least as far as the Mexican Constitution of 1917 and the first Amparo Act following that Constitution, the Amparo Act of 1919. The notion of jurisprudencia is not mentioned in the Constitution of 1917, but the Amparo Act of 1919 emphasizes jurisprudencia as a method of creating binding law. Thus, for our purposes, the first few decades of the twentieth century serve as a clear end point for the acceptance or assimilation of jurisprudencia in amparo actions.

II. Sources of Nineteenth-century Jurisprudencia

Determining the origins of jurisprudencia is complicated by the stature of jurisprudencia and amparo in the popular and even legal mind of the country. As the means of protecting constitutional liberties, amparo actions and their method of jurisprudencia are a subject of great pride among Mexican lawyers. Pride often leads to interesting historiographical challenges. For example, some scholarship about jurisprudencia asserts that the direct origins of Mexican jurisprudencia are found in Mexican developments of the mid-nineteenth century, rather than in temporally or geographically more distant places.

Referencing the binding quality of the praetorian edicts in Rome, Mexican writers assert that jurisprudencia is a "product of Mexican law" and appear to be uneasy with the possibility that foreign, and particularly United States, sources did anything more than whisper a suggestion to Mexican jurists who then transformed the notion so fundamentally that it became wholly Mexican.[16] Another study of jurisprudencia gives comparative discussions of constitutional actions and the use of cases without coming to conclusions about the source of the method.[17] Another study does not mention the possibility of United States influence and only quotes one section of a decision in which United States sources are used.[18] A few note that Vallarta used North American sources, but fall short of recognizing the impact of these works on the construction of jurisprudencia.[19] One Mexican state supreme

16 *M. Carbonell y Sánchez,* Una Aproximación al Surgimiento Histórico de la Jurisprudencia en México, Revista de la Facultad de Derecho de México, vol. 45 (1995), pp. 64–65. Divorcing amparo from North American influences is *R. Tamayo y Salmoran,* La formación de la doctrina del amparo. La contribución de Ignacio L. Vallarta. Una curiosa paradoja, in La Suprema Corte de Justicia a principios del Porfirismo (1877–1882), pp. 1093–1108 (ed. Suprema Corte de Justicia de la Nación, 1990).

17 *H. G. Zertuche García,* La Jurisprudencia en el sistema jurídico mexicano (1990), pp. 3–79.

18 *J. T. L. Cardenas,* Ignacio Luis Vallarta y Ogazón, precursor y arquetipo de la jurisprudencia, Revista Jurídica Jalisciense, vol. 7 (1993), pp. 21, 28–29.

19 *J. Barragán Barragán,* La Suprema Corte de Justicia de Ignacio L. Vallarta y el federalismo, in La Suprema Corte de Justicia a principios del Porfirismo (1877–1882), p. 1044 (ed. Suprema Corte de Justicia de la Nación, 1990); *L. Cabrera,* La Suprema Corte de Justicia en

court document notes correctly: "Through the influence of North American law, jurisprudencia finally passed to Mexico during the nineteenth century."

Furthermore, few writers approach the question of how jurisprudencia arose in Mexico or passed into Mexico. Nonetheless, it is possible to survey the standard explanation of the rise of jurisprudencia in amparo actions. This explanation finds the origins of jurisprudencia from before the Mexican Constitution of 1917 and the Amparo Act of 1919. Indeed, sources frequently note that jurisprudencia dates to the Amparo Act of 1882 drafted by one of Mexico's famous jurists, Ignacio Luis Vallarta. This idea of jurisprudencia was incorporated and expanded upon in the Federal Code of Civil Procedure of 1908.[20] Nonetheless, jurisprudencia as a method of determining rules of law was contested by some in Mexico's legal community, and there is not a direct unbroken development of jurisprudencia in amparo actions from the work of Vallarta to today. The story is more complex.

What happened in Mexican law during the nineteenth century that permitted the development of jurisprudencia in amparo actions? To explore the origins and sources of these actions and the method of jurisprudencia it is useful to think of the three nineteenth century amparo acts – of 1861, of 1869, and of 1882 – and of two important drafters of these acts, Ignacio Mariscal and Ignacio Luis Vallarta. These central pieces of legislation and drafters are important markers in tracing this development.

From the independence period to 1861, jurisprudencia only existed in scattered references, usually with the idea or goal of maintaining uniformity in decisions, as one document in 1840 uses the term in relation to the structure of one state's courts. Jurisprudencia is, of course, linked to the availability of published decisions of the courts, and this period also witnessed the unofficial publication of decisions of the Supreme Court.[21]

The notion of jurisprudencia as a means of establishing binding rules of law only appears to gain national recognition when Mexico considered the Amparo Act of 1861. When discussing the Amparo Act of 1861, Ignacio Mariscal, an important literary, political, diplomatic, and legal figure of nineteenth-century Mexico, asserted that judicial decisions may have the same force as statutes, later noting that only in the United States did there exist a similar idea to the Mexican Constitution.[22] Despite Mariscal's assertions concerning the force of judicial deci-

el primer periodo del Porfirismo (1877 – 1880), in La Suprema Corte de Justicia a principios del Porfirismo (1877 – 1882), pp. 43 – 48, 59 – 62 (ed. Suprema Corte de Justicia de la Nación, 1990); *H. Fix-Zamudio,* Ignacio Luis Vallarta. La incompetencia de origen y los derechos políticos, in A cien años de la muerte de Vallarta, p. 28 (ed. *M. López Ruiz,* 1994); *M. del Refugio González,* El derecho en la época de Ignacio L. Vallarta, in A cien años de la muerte de Vallarta, p. 64 (ed. *M. López Ruiz,* 1994).

20 *M. T. Lobo,* Algo sobre la jurisprudencia, Revista de Derecho Privado, vol. 1, p. 2 (2001).

21 *Zertuche,* p. 61.

sions, the Amparo Act of 1861 explicitly denied the precedential value of decisions. Tracking Article 102 of the Mexican Constitution of 1857, Article 30 of the Act states:

> Sentences pronounced in these types of cases only apply to the litigants. Consequently they may never be used as final judgments by others to avoid complying with the laws that motivated the case.

Although limiting the effect of judicial decisions to the litigants, the act made advances in the availability of these decisions. It required the publication of decisions in newspapers, but it was not clear which decisions were to be published or in what form. Thus, by 1861 and through the Amparo Act of the same date, there was no clear notion of jurisprudencia as binding authority.[23] Some commentators, however, were asserting that, in relation to amparo actions, case decisions might form binding law.

Only a few years later, Mariscal, as Minister of Justice, was able to move his view of amparo actions and jurisprudencia forward though his proposal of the Amparo Act of 1869.[24] This Act incorporated various elements that moved towards establishing jurisprudencia as a source of rules. First, the act made clear what type of decisions had to be published. The Act stated that "sentencias definidas dictadas en los recursos de amparo" or final decisions in amparo actions were subject to the publication requirement. The stated goal of this requirement was uniformity; publication of decisions avoided dispersion of and contradiction in federal decisions. Mariscal noted that the central idea of amparo actions was taken from the United States, but in practice there were many notable differences.[25] Published decisions of courts were not binding authority, but useful interpretative guides. They provided uniformity in constitutional law among all Mexican citizens within a federal system. Indeed, the United States model of precedent in federal courts was raised as a possibility, but rejected. Nonetheless, in analyzing amparo actions generally, Mariscal indicated that all decisions of the Supreme Court ought to serve as obligatory precedent on the Court as well as on inferior federal tribunals.[26]

---

22 *Carbonell y Sánchez*, pp. 66–67. Mariscal was viewed as "a very competent authority in constitutional law because of his long residence in the United States of America where he had frequent occasions to study, both theoretically and practically, American constitutional law, the origin of ours ...." This passage notes Mariscal's approval of Vallarta's Amparo Act of 1882. Ignacio L. Vallarta, El juicio del amparo y el writ de habeas corpus: Ensayo crítico-comparativo sobre esos recursos constitucionales, p. 19 (1881). For Mariscal and jurisprudencia see *L. Cabrera*, La Suprema Corte de Justicia en el primer periodo del Porfirismo (1877–1880), in La Suprema Corte de Justicia a principios del Porfirismo (1877–1882), pp. 47–48 (ed. Suprema Corte de Justicia de la Nación, 1990).

23 *Zertuche*, p. 63.

24 *Zertuche*, p. 64.

25 *Zertuche*, p. 65.

26 *Cabrera*, pp. 47–48, citing *I. Mariscal*, Algunas reflexiones sobre el juicio de amparo (1878).

The first act to establish expressly the obligatory nature of case decisions and to require their publication in an official journal was the Amparo Act of 1882 drafted by Ignacio Vallarta.[27] Several different sections of the act address the obligatory aspect. They are, as numbered in the act submitted by Vallarta:

> *Article 37.* Decisions pronounced by judges shall always be based on the applicable constitutional text. For its proper interpretation, attention shall be paid to the meaning given in the opinions of the Supreme Court and the writings [*doctrina*] of authors.
>
> *Article 44.* Decisions of the Supreme Court ought to state the reasons the tribunal considers sufficient for its interpretation of the constitutional texts and to resolve, by the application [of these reasons], the constitutional questions addressed. When the votes on decisions are not unanimous, the minority shall also set out in writing the reasons for its dissent.
>
> *Article 73.* The grant or denial of amparo against the text of the Constitution or against its fixed interpretation by the Supreme Court, by at least five uniform opinions, shall be punished with the loss of employment and imprisonment from six months to three years if the judge has acted fraudulently [*dolosamente*], and if by lack of instruction or care, with suspension of functions for one year.

Reviewing these provisions, one article states that tribunals must observe decisions that interpret the constitution. Another article, in requiring that opinions be based on the text of the applicable constitutional text, states that proper interpretation must be attentive of the meanings given in the opinions of the Supreme Court and of doctrinal sources. A third article sets out the numerical requirement in amparo cases. Five decisions create a jurisprudencia of repetition, *jurisprudencia por reiteración,* that must be followed by judges. A judge who does not follow such a rule created by past decisions is subject to punishment. The text justifies this invention by stating that the Constitution implicitly provides for this method of establishing rules through case decisions and that the Supreme Court is the supreme interpreter of the Constitution. We may ponder why five decisions were necessary. Vallarta's writings do not seem to indicate any reason for this particular number.[28] This threshold limit for sanction of a judge became a minimum for the creation of a binding series of cases.

The Federal Code of Civil Procedure of 1897 abandoned the concept of jurisprudencia, creating a dissonance between the Amparo Act and the rules of civil procedure. Then, the Federal Code of Civil Procedure of 1908 reintroduced the concept, noting the resulting judicial uncertainty after the 1897 Code and the utility of jurisprudencia in understanding the law. The most important provisions of the Federal Code of Civil Procedure of 1908 for our purposes are:

---

27 Vallarta's draft of the act and supporting statements are found in La Suprema Corte de Justicia a principios del Porfirismo (1877 – 1882), pp. 490 – 501 (ed. Suprema Corte de Justicia de la Nación, 1990).

28 *Carbonell y Sánchez,* pp. 70 – 71. There is nothing in Vallarta's *Votos* or his *El juicio del amparo* that indicates why he selected this number of cases.

> *Article 785.* Jurisprudencia established by the Supreme Court of Justice in its decisions of amparo shall refer only to the Constitution and other federal law.
>
> *Article 786.* The decisions of the Supreme Court of Justice, with votes of nine or more of its members, constitute jurisprudencia whenever the matter resolved is found in [a series of] five decisions not interrupted by another to the contrary.
>
> *Article 787.* The jurisprudencia of the Court in amparo trials is obligatory for district judges. The Supreme Court shall respect its own decisions. It may, however, contradict established jurisprudencia, but always expressing in this case, the reasons for deciding this way. These reasons ought to refer to those [reasons] that were present to establish the jurisprudencia that is contradicted.
>
> *Article 788.* When the parties in amparo trials invoke the jurisprudencia of the Court, they shall do so in writing, expressing its sense and designating precisely the decisions that have formed it; in this case the Court shall study the relative points of the jurisprudencia. In the discussion of the principal case and in the decision rendered, mention will be made of the motives or reasons for admitting or rejecting the mentioned jurisprudencia.

This code reflects the idea that jurisprudencia is an important tool to be brought in when there are omissions or interpretive doubts in the law. With this view of jurisprudencia in mind, commentators stated that it was a line of cases, rather than an individual case, that created the necessary material to construct a rule from opinions. The procedural code of 1908 also took into account the jurisprudencia requirement established by the Amparo Act of 1882. Thus under the Amparo Act of 1882 and the Federal Code of Civil Procedure of 1908, jurisprudencia was binding on inferior judges, but not the Supreme Court itself. The exposition of motives used to introduce the legislation notes: "to bind the court in any absolute manner to the precedents of its resolutions would be like imposing dogma in the way religions do; it would be to establish, like religions, absolute truths and give to jurisprudencia, even though it resulted erroneously, an immutability that neither any law or institutions may have."[29]

Furthermore, the code placed the burden of producing jurisprudencia to the court on the litigants to avoid an abuse of indiscriminately citing opinions. Litigants had to show how the opinions were applicable to the case and to state the number of opinions that establish the rule through jurisprudencia. From this point on, jurisprudencia in amparo actions was firmly established in Mexican law.[30]

---

29 *Carbonell y Sánchez*, p. 76.

30 For a noticeable decrease in jurisprudencia generally (and not within the particular context of amparo) around 1900 and then increasing in 1930 and more so by 1969 see *W. L. Butte*, Stare Decisis, Doctrine, and Jurisprudence in Mexico and Elsewhere in *J. Dainow*, The Role of Judicial Decisions and Doctrine in Civil Law and Mixed Jurisdicitions (1974) pp. 311–330.

III. Jurisprudencia Criticized

Between 1882 and 1908, jurisprudencia as a method of establishing constitutional doctrines through case decisions was subject to heated debate and criticism. The manner the concept was created in statutes and applied by judges was viewed by some as a negative development in the overall course of Mexican law. Even those who may not have objected to the application of jurisprudencia found fault with the quality and availability of published decisions from which to construct rules of law.

One example of contemporary criticism from a judge's perspective is found in a commentary by Fernando Vega on the Amparo Act of 1882. In an article in the newspaper *El Foro,* Vega addressed the problem of the requirement that judges provisionally suspend government actions pending actions of amparo, something akin to issuing a temporary restraining order. A related law, Ley 20 de enero, required that a judge "shall be able to declare suspension of the contested act whenever it is found in one of the cases that are found in Art. 1 of this law." Article 1 made reference to all types of amparo actions: violations of individual guaranties, attacks on the state's sovereignty by the federal authority, or invasion of federal authority by states. Judges complained about inconsistent situations when government action might be properly suspended. A heterogeneous jurisprudencia left no clear answer. Vega saw the answer in either legislative reform or more jurisprudencia. Legislative reform was politically impossible in Vega's view, and thus "for now at least, the remedy is only to hope for jurisprudencia, the power of interpretation belonging to the court, and a unity in rules [*doctrinas*]."[31] Nonetheless, jurisprudencia had done little in Vega's mind. Jurisprudencia had not clarified the application of the statute, but was as obscure as the statute; jurisprudencia was changeable, volatile, fleeting, turning, complex, and hence of little use. Jurisprudencia under such conditions was too vague for judges, who might face personal responsibility for wrong decisions.[32]

As mentioned earlier, the Federal Code of Civil Procedure of 1897 abandoned jurisprudencia as an obligatory source of law. An official explanation of the code spoke of maintaining separation of powers. It sought to limit the invasive tendencies of the judiciary and to return Mexican law to the principle that only the legislator may interpret, clarify, modify, or derogate the law; tribunals, in the tradition of the civil law, may only apply it.

The idea of jurisprudencia was sharply criticized even after its reintroduction to Mexican law in the Code of Federal Civil Procedure of 1908. Demetrio Sodi criticized the mechanics of jurisprudencia. In his view, there was no accessible register

31 *Ignacio L. Vallarta,* Archivo Inédito, Surprema Corte de Justicia de la Nación, p. 428 reprinting *El Foro,* Martes 8 de agosto de 1882, México.

32 *Ignacio L. Vallarta,* Archivo Inédito, Surprema Corte de Justicia de la Nación, pp. 427–436 reprinting *El Foro,* Martes 8 de agosto de 1882, México.

of decisions, and jurisprudencia was greatly hindered by the delay in publication of the *Semanario Judicial*. Beyond problems with the mechanical aspects of jurisprudencia, the very substance of the practice continued to be called into question. Emilio Rabas stated, "The Federal code, heir of all the bad one finds in the laws that preceded it, contains a section dedicated to jurisprudencia which in sum is so extravagant as trying to attempt a common law established by statute. It is a trick of the law" to give respectability to such decisions. He continued, "A complete submission to final judgments, despite the great advantages that it has produced in the Anglo-Saxon peoples, chokes the scientific spirit, because above the science of law one definitively places the opinion of the court. This destroys the stimulus of the judges to study juridical problems (that never are perfectly resolved) and cheapens the position of the lawyer, doing without him as an element in the investigation of principles and closing the door before hand to all expansion in the field of law."[33] Despite such criticisms, jurisprudencia survived.

IV. Vallarta and Jurisprudencia

Although nascent notions of jurisprudencia existed before Vallarta especially in the work of Mariscal, Vallarta was responsible for the language that legislatively fixed the doctrine in amparo actions. It appears that Vallarta's approach was strongly influenced by United States practices rather than purely Mexican juridical ways.

Vallarta indicated in his own works that he sought to follow United States practice. Vallarta was a member of the Supreme Court and served as its President from 1879 to 1883. During this period he not only drafted the Amparo Act, but also wrote substantial legal works leaving no doubt about the influences on his ideas of legal sources and judicial methods. These works include his *Cuestiones constitucionales o Votos* which provided annotated decisions in four volumes and a comparative treatise entitled *El juicio de amparo y el writ of habeas corpus: ensayo crítico-comparativo sobre esos recursos constitucionales*. These two works provide the practical and intellectual background to the Amparo Act of 1882. Let us first consider his *Votos* and then turn to the comparative work that is even more closely tied to his drafting of the Amparo Act of 1882.

The first volume of Vallarta's *Votos* was published in 1879, the last in 1882. The four volumes contain about 1,600 pages and report on 50 cases setting out many of the major areas of constitutional law. The entry for each case reported in the *Votos* consists of a title, followed by a legal question and sometimes the constitutional provision interpreted, then a brief recitation of the facts and procedural history. The next section is the largest, often running between 10 and, in one case, over 100 pages of text, with Vallarta setting out the reasoning for his decision. These

---

33 *Carbonell y Sánchez*, pp. 78–79.

read very much like United States Supreme Court opinions of the period. The last section is the official sentence or *ejecutoria* in the usual style of the civil law: "Taking note of and considering various facts and legal sources, the court decrees *x* and the judges subscribe the decree."

One illustration is sufficient. One report of ten pages is set out as follows. Under the title of "Amparo brought against the resolutions of a district judge," Vallarta states the issue addressed in the case as "can an action of amparo be brought against the acts of district judges? Interpretation of article 101, paragraph 1, of the Constitution." The description of the case provides:

> Mariano F. Medrano brought an amparo action before a judge of the first district of the Capital against the decision of a second judge that, following the requirement of a federal judge of Veracruz, he be imprisoned. The first judge declared the amparo improper, and remitted the decision to the Supreme Court. This case was discussed in the court on September 29, 1879, and Vallarta based his vote on these reasons:[34]

Vallarta's opinion begins, "This case which has just been considered neatly formulates this important question: Can an action of amparo be brought against the acts of district judges? And the court has the duty to face and resolve this question despite the difficulties that surround it to determine once and for all the constitutional jurisprudence on this point."[35] After noting that another district judge had admitted an amparo action in a similar situation, Vallarta presents the possibilities and consequences of either permitting or prohibiting such actions.

Vallarta gives several reasons for answering the question negatively for all federal courts in amparo actions and for all actions by the Supreme Court. Nonetheless, he decides that the action may be properly brought against lower federal courts in non-amparo actions. Vallarta's first source in addressing the question is an opinion (*ejecutoria*) dated November 6, 1874, in which the Supreme Court determined that an action for amparo could not be brought against the actions of the Supreme Court because the court is final arbiter of federal cases, and it would be improper to make the court a party to an action before it.[36] It is telling that the first source offered by Vallarta is another opinion of the Supreme Court. Vallarta's next source is language found at the beginning of an executive act concerning amparos from 1877. Here it was clear that amparos were not to be brought against federal courts hearing amparo actions, thus avoiding the possibility of endless appeals through further amparo actions: "This action shall not be brought against the acts or resolutions of federal tribunals and judges in actions of amparo."[37] The drafters added "nor against those [acts or resolutions] of the Supreme Court of

34 *Ignacio L. Vallarta,* Cuestiones constitucionales: Votos del Sr. Lic. D. Ignacio L. Vallarta Presidente que fue del la Suprema Corte de Justicia Nacional en los negocios más notables, Tomo I, p. 196 (1894) (hereinafter "Votos").

35 *Vallarta,* Votos, Tomo I, p. 196.

36 *Vallarta,* Votos, Tomo I, p. 198.

37 *Vallarta,* Votos, Tomo I, p. 198.

Justice in matters under its jurisdiction."[38] To support the view that the Mexican Supreme Court's actions were not subject to review by amparo, Vallarta emphasized that the Mexican Constitution provided no method for reviewing the decisions of the Supreme Court. At this point he analogized to the power of the United States Supreme Court. Translating Joseph Story's Commentaries on the Constitution and providing the English text in a footnote, Vallarta notes, "Congress is vested with ample authority to provide for the exercise by the Supreme Court of appellate jurisdiction from the decisions of all inferior tribunals... but no mode is provided by which any Superior Tribunal can reexamine what the Supreme Court has itself decided."[39]

Having established the important exemption from the action for the Supreme Court, Vallarta then turned to the question of whether the lower federal courts are subject to amparo actions, and here he reached an affirmative answer through his interpretation of the constitutional text that gives an amparo action against "the acts of *whatever authority* that violates individual guarantees."[40] Judges of the district courts and magistrates of the circuit courts are included in this term. To the expected objection that this might create problems in the judicial structural hierarchy because a district court judge may be faced with an amparo action against a circuit court magistrate, Vallarta reasserted the special nature of the Supreme Court. He stated:

> No one among us may use his rank to violate individual guarantees, not the Congress, not the Legislatures, not the President, not the Ministers, not the Governors. Only the Supreme Court, not by reason of rank, but because it is the supreme interpreter of the Constitution, because it is the one who ought to have the last word reviewing the judgments of judges, is the only authority that is excused from going before the district judge concerning its protested acts.[41]

Vallarta considers and counters several other structural arguments leading to an opposite conclusion.

The report of the case next presents the formal judgment of the court after the heading, "The Supreme Court pronounced the following judgment." This formal judgment sets out the factual and procedural history of the case followed by several paragraphs beginning with the word "considering." These paragraphs note the exclusion of the availability of amparo actions in amparo actions in federal courts and the exclusion of the Supreme Court from having its acts or judges subject to amparo actions. The third paragraph beginning with the word "considering" is unusual in the reports of judgments because it directly quotes Joseph Story to exclude

---

38 *Vallarta,* Votos, Tomo I, p. 198. Vallarta later notes in his opinion that this text with the additional exclusion of the Supreme Court was approved in the Cámara de Diputados in 1878 by a vote of 130 to 3. Vallarta, Votos, Tomo I, p. 203.

39 *Vallarta,* Votos, Tomo I, p. 199.

40 *Vallarta,* Votos, Tomo I, p. 200. (Vallarta's emphasis).

41 *Vallarta,* Votos, Tomo I, p. 201.

the Mexican Supreme Court from suit in amparo actions. The fourth paragraph states that other federal courts fall within the language of the constitutional text and are subject to amparo actions. The case was remanded to the district judge to consider the substance of the amparo action and the judgment is signed by the justices of the Supreme Court. The structure just described is used for the report of each case included in the *Votos*.

The breadth of constitutional topics addressed in the *Votos* is equally interesting. Because this study argues that Vallarta was profoundly influenced by United States law and practice in his creation of Mexican constitutional jurisprudence, it seems appropriate to list briefly the kinds of constitutional cases in which Vallarta called upon United States sources to help form his opinion.

Perhaps most important for the course Vallarta wished to chart for the Supreme Court are the cases addressing its jurisdiction and the jurisdiction of the federal courts in amparo actions. For example, in one opinion, quoting heavily from *Marbury v. Madison,*[42] Vallarta establishes the Mexican Supreme Court's power of judicial review.[43] Another case also addresses the courts' ability to review state legislative action.[44] Vallarta uses numerous United States sources to describe the scope of the Mexican admiralty jurisdiction and its differences from United States admiralty jurisdiction.[45]

Numerous cases attempt to shape the jurisprudence surrounding the amparo action itself. One case addresses the constitutionality of barring an amparo action because of the claimant's solvency.[46] The question of whether amparo actions are limited to constitutionally guaranteed rights or may be brought for other injustices is addressed at length in another.[47] Other cases discuss the appropriateness of using an amparo action to review a lower court decision that is merely claimed to be inconsistent with the applicable law.[48] As described above, another case determines the validity of bringing an amparo action against a lower court federal judge.[49]

Another important area the cases address is the nature and operation of a federal government and particularly the place of the federal judiciary within this structure. The constitutionality of a state law prohibiting the practice of medicine without a degree is considered in light of the Mexican Constitution's liberty provided to citi-

---

42 This leading constitutional case written by John Marshall is discussed in the essay by C. F. Hobson, which is printed above.

43 *Vallarta,* Votos, Tomo III, pp. 382–429.

44 *Vallarta,* Votos, Tomo I, pp. 56–80.

45 *Vallarta,* Votos, Tomo II, pp. 153–199.

46 *Vallarta,* Votos, Tomo IV, pp. 527–555.

47 *Vallarta,* Votos, Tomo III, pp. 1–55.

48 *Vallarta,* Votos, Tomo I, pp. 143–173; Tomo IV, pp. 494–510.

49 *Vallarta,* Votos, Tomo I, pp. 196–205.

zens to embrace any profession.[50] Conflict of laws, particularly as applied in a federal system, is another topic where Vallarta finds comparison to the United States helpful.[51] Vallarta considers President Abraham Lincoln's extra-legislative proclamations when discussing the confiscation of property from those involved with aiding the French during the invasion.[52] Local violations of election law are also addressed in the federal context.[53]

Another group of cases deals with constitutional protections for criminal defendants. Several cases address the rights of accused individuals, their apprehension, detention, extradition to other states and countries, and their right to asylum.[54] Another case sets out the right to counsel for criminal defendants.[55] Capital punishment and its constitutional application is addressed in several cases.[56]

Taxation and the constitutionality of various methods of taxation lead Vallarta to United States sources as well.[57] In one case, Vallarta describes the scope of the federal government's power to tax and how this power is situated within a federal bicamaral system.[58] Another case addresses the power of a state to tax gold and silver and the prohibition of states levying duties on imports and exports.[59] The constitutionality of a local tax provided Vallarta the opportunity, in an opinion of over 150 pages, to set out his theories of the federal structure and courts and the scope of judicial power, often making reference to United States sources.[60]

Related to taxation, property rights under the constitution are also extensively addressed. The constitutionality of mining legislation that created substantial deviations in ownership for mines, as opposed to other types of real property, is addressed on several occasions.[61] Vallarta reports a case concerning the status of a railroad concession that was not exercised quickly, the nature of the property

---

50 *Vallarta,* Votos, Tomo II, pp. 84 – 102.

51 *Vallarta,* Votos, Tomo I, pp. 18 – 26; Tomo I, pp. 100 – 104.

52 *Vallarta,* Votos, Tomo I, pp. 105 – 131.

53 *Vallarta,* Votos, Tomo II, pp. 200 – 216.

54 *Vallarta,* Votos, Tomo I, pp. 1 – 17; Tomo III, pp. 430 – 482; Tomo III, pp. 483 – 528; Tomo IV, pp. 88 – 187.

55 *Vallarta,* Votos, Tomo II, pp. 144 – 152.

56 *Vallarta,* Votos, Tomo III, pp. 56 – 103; Tomo IV, pp. 188 – 214.

57 *Vallarta,* Votos, Tomo I, pp. 132 – 142; Tomo III, pp. 104 – 137.

58 *Vallarta,* Votos, Tomo II, pp. 1 – 39.

59 *Vallarta,* Votos, Tomo II, pp. 48 – 83.

60 *Vallarta,* Votos, Tomo III, pp. 166 – 323.

61 *Vallarta,* Votos, Tomo II, pp. 103 – 143; Tomo IV, pp. 242 – 327. Cases dealing with the status of land held by indigenous populations and governmental actions to take such land are among those selected by Vallarta for publication, although these cases do not cite United States materials. *Vallarta,* Votos, Tomo IV, pp. 1 – 38; Tomo IV, pp. 49 – 87.

right created, and the constitutionality of withdrawing the concession.[62] The creation of a perpetual interest in a cemetery and land use regulations are also addressed.[63]

Another set of cases deals with the constitutionality of laws and their application. For example, one case discusses the retroactive application of laws and notes that Mexico follows the United States position.[64] Another case addresses a statement by the Minster of Foreign Relations that a Mexican woman who marries a foreigner became a national of her husband's country.[65] The Supreme Court's treatment of the jurisdictional battle between church and state over birth records and marriage ceremonies is also reported by Vallarta.[66] Yet others address freedom of the press, libel, and defamation.[67] Military conscription is also subjected to constitutional review.[68]

The use of United States sources is justified by Vallarta by the frequent textual similarities between the United States and Mexican Constitutions. For example, in one case Vallarta writes:

> The present article 16 was the 5th in the draft constitution, and reading this, it is now understood that the principal object of the commission was to implant in our fundamental law the precept contained in the fourth amendment of the United States Constitution. The similarity between the two texts is such that, saving certain traditional doctrines of our jurisprudence that were inserted into article 5, it is now seen that the one is nothing but a translation of the other. It is appropriate then first of all to understand the spirit of the law, to study its history, its rationale, its origin, figuring out, although very briefly, what meaning is given by our neighbor Republic to the precept that the commission wanted to copy.[69]

Similar comparative approaches are found throughout the *Votos,* and Vallarta often compares Mexican constitutional provisions to sections of the United States Constitution. Vallarta will even on occasion consider the state constitutional provisions from the United States.[70]

Numerous passages attest to this approach. In one case, Vallarta writes concerning United States law, "to consult its laws is for us almost a necessity when we want to make a study of comparative constitutional legislation, given the similarity of our institution with those of that country."[71] Again, Vallarta wrote, "It is not

---

62 *Vallarta,* Votos, Tomo I, pp. 174 – 190.

63 *Vallarta,* Votos, Tomo IV, pp. 393 – 439.

64 *Vallarta,* Votos, Tomo I, pp. 151 – 152.

65 *Vallarta,* Votos, Tomo III, pp. 138 – 165.

66 *Vallarta,* Votos, Tomo IV, pp. 440 – 493.

67 *Vallarta,* Votos, Tomo III, pp. 344 – 381; Tomo IV, pp. 328 – 360.

68 *Vallarta,* Votos, Tomo III, pp. 546 – 572.

69 *Vallarta,* Votos, Tomo I, p. 71.

70 *Vallarta,* Votos, Tomo III, p. 349.

71 *Vallarta,* Votos, Tomo I, p. 133.

necessary to advise that the reason and motives to the American constitutional texts are also the reason and motives of ours on this point. Keeping in mind the similarity that exists between them and between the institutions of the two Republics, this truth cannot be denied."[72] A bit later, Vallarta wrote in the same case, "I do not have to say that the theories that I defend are American, well-known by the commentators and sanctioned by the tribunals of that Republic."[73] Finally, Vallarta makes it clear that in the absence of Mexican authorities on constitutional law, United States sources are preferred:

> Without doctrine, without precedents, without opinions among us, these grave questions have at the same time a complete novelty and an indisputable importance. As delicate and difficult as the resolution is, I have not wanted to trust in my own reasoning, but I have gone to the source of our constitutional law, to the American jurisprudence, in search of the doctrines that illustrate my opinion, searching for the foundation of the vote that I shall give. And I ought to say once and for all I have found them so solid and robust that I think they will satisfy, as they satisfy me, whoever studies and mines these important materials. Here are the American ideas stated by their most respected authors:[74]

The textual similarity of the two constitutions led Vallarta to use a significantly broad range of sources to describe and to present United States constitutional law. For example, in a case addressing the ability of courts to review state legislative action, Vallarta, noting that the Mexican constitutional provision is a translation of the Fourth Amendment, rallies Joseph Story, the Federalist Papers, and Paschal's *Annotated Constitution* to find this power.[75] Many such examples are present in the *Votos*.

Vallarta regularly cites United States constitutional cases as authority. For example, when attempting to establish judicial review, Vallarta quotes *Marbury v. Madison* for several pages.[76] When discussing the taxing power of the federal government, Vallarta quotes John Marshall's opinion in *McCulloch v. Maryland.*[77] When the question of defining imports and exports comes up, Vallarta quotes extensively from *Brown v. Maryland.*[78] To decide whether Mexico's admiralty jurisdiction runs to inland navigable rivers, Vallarta considers Justice Campbell's opinion in *Jackson v. Steamboat "Magnolia"* and several other United States admiralty jurisdiction cases.[79] Vallarta even infrequently cites state court decisions from the United States. For example, in a case addressing takings, Vallarta uses the New York case of *People v. Smith.*[80]

---

72 *Vallarta,* Votos, Tomo II, p. 31.

73 *Vallarta,* Votos, Tomo II, p. 31.

74 *Vallarta,* Votos, Tomo II, p. 14.

75 *Vallarta,* Votos, Tomo I, pp. 59–60, 71.

76 *Vallarta,* Votos, Tomo III, pp. 399–402.

77 *Vallarta,* Votos, Tomo II, p. 14.

78 *Vallarta,* Votos, Tomo II, pp. 58–60.

79 *Vallarta,* Votos, Tomo II, pp. 167, 180–184, 193.

While Vallarta occasionally cites directly to decisions of the United States Supreme Court, he is more apt to rely on standard commentary works of the period. For English works from the United States, Vallarta almost always places the translated text of the work in his main text and the original in English in the footnotes.

Vallarta makes use of many secondary materials to support his arguments for moving Mexican constitutional law and jurisprudence along the lines of developments in the United States. For example, Vallarta often employs quotations from the Federalist Papers.[81] Story's *Commentaries on the Constitution* is a frequently used source for United States Constitutional law.[82] Vallarta also uses Cooley's *Constitutional Limitations* quite often.[83] Other, less-used, commentary sources on American constitutional law include Sedgwick,[84] Paschal,[85] and Bump.[86]

Vallarta's appropriation of United States law does not end with the expected sources of American constitutional law and secondary works. For general aspects of American law, Vallarta frequently turned to James Kent's *Commentaries on American Law.*[87] Specialized treatises from the United States also had their place in Vallarta's work. For example, in a case addressing the nature of railroad concessions, Vallarta turned to Pierce's *American Railroad Law,* Redfield's *The Law or Railways,* in addition to Kent's *Commentaries.*[88] In cases dealing with taxation, Vallarta cites passages from Burrough's *On Law of Taxation.*[89] For questions on habeas corpus, in addition to his own treatise, Vallarta uses Hurd's treatise on the topic.[90] For mining, Vallarta turns to Yale's *Legal Title to Mining Claims*[91] and Blanchard's *Law of Mines.*[92] For extradition, Clarke's *Law of Extradition,*[93] Whea-

80 21 New York Reports 597; *Vallarta,* Votos, Tomo IV, p. 414.

81 See, e.g., *Vallarta,*Votos, Tomo I, p. 140; Tomo II, pp. 28, 29, 30, 187, 197, 206; Tomo III, p. 397.

82 See, e.g., *Vallarta,* Votos, Tomo I, pp. 199, 205; Tomo II, pp. 7, 30, 31, 75, 98, 185, 191; Tomo III, pp. 13, 272–274, 402; Tomo IV, p. 466.

83 See, e.g., *Vallarta,* Votos, Tomo II, pp. 12, 13, 15, 18, 21, 64, 99, 100, 140, 147; Tomo III, pp. 14, 16, 17, 111, 119–122, 161, 211, 353; Tomo IV, pp. 212–214, 301, 303, 304, 339, 341, 343–345, 409, 466, 538, 542.

84 *Vallarta,* Votos, Tomo II, p. 16.

85 *Vallarta,* Votos, Tomo II, pp. 32, 206; Tomo III, pp. 255, 402.

86 *Vallarta,* Votos, Tomo III, p. 444.

87 *Vallarta,* Votos, Tomo II, pp. 111; Tomo III, pp. 209, 272, 396, 397, 402.

88 *Vallarta,* Votos, Tomo I, pp. 178–179.

89 *Vallarta,* Votos, Tomo II, pp. 15, 17, 64.

90 *Vallarta,* Votos, Tomo II, p. 100; Tomo III, pp. 43, 450, 471, 472, 474–476, 510, 520; Tomo IV, p. 129.

91 *Vallarta,* Votos, Tomo II, pp. 112, 113.

92 *Vallarta,* Votos, Tomo II, pp. 113, 114, 121, 122.

93 *Vallarta,* Votos, Tomo IV, p. 121.

ton's *Elements of International Law,*[94] and Wharton's *Conflict of Laws*[95] find place among Vallarta's sources.

Vallarta's opinions in the *Votos* directly and unapologetically rely on the constitutional jurisprudence of the United States. Of the 50 cases reported in the *Votos,* 32, or nearly two-thirds of the opinions mention, use, and analogize to United States constitutional law.

If determining Vallarta's approach to and reasons for writing these opinions were not clear enough from the texts themselves, we also have his statements about what he was trying to accomplish in the reports. Vallarta's introduction to the case reports makes clear that he believed he was doing something new for Mexico in copying the constitutional method of the United States. He wrote:

> The Constitution of Mexico is more complete, more perfect than the Constitution of the United States; the latter has more gaps than the former. The good sense of the American people, however, has never rejected the work of its elders, and instead of searching for novelties to change institutions, has not corrected the defects of its fundamental law until experience has strongly suggested reform. On the other hand, the constant work of publicists, the repeated and laborious decisions of the tribunals of the United States, not only have filled these gaps, leaving the work of Washington, Hamilton, Franklin, and Madison in tact, but also have formed the most complete constitutional jurisprudence of a free people. If this publication succeeds in sparking the desire to imitate this wise and patriotic conduct of our neighbors, if it serves to stimulate the study of constitutional law, even far from the heat of political battles, if it may be perhaps a grain of sand in the building the Mexican Republic is yet to construct, its constitutional jurisprudence, than all my hopes in producing this collection will be satisfied.[96]

Similarly, in the introduction to the second volume of the *Votos,* Vallarta makes direct reference to United States opinions and his attempts to reproduce this method in the sphere of Mexican constitutional law.

> If, as I well believe, I have never been able to imitate the conduct of the wise North American judges, who, with their "opinions," have formed the most complete constitutional jurisprudence of a free people, at least I have the satisfaction of having tried, and I am heartened by the hope that judges more capable than I will obtain this.[97]

Elsewhere in the *Votos,* Vallarta expands on this use of case decisions to develop rules of law:

> This is the way the North Americans have understood it, and with fewer constitutional laws than we have, and with more gaps in their Constitution than those contained in ours, they possess in the judgments of their tribunals the most complete constitutional jurisprudence a people could want. There, *one opinion* of Marshall is worth as much as a law, and laws are the *leading cases,* decided by its tribunals. Hundreds of judgments may be cited

[94] *Vallarta,* Votos, Tomo IV, pp. 129, 130.

[95] *Vallarta,* Votos, Tomo IV, pp. 130, 131.

[96] *Vallarta,* Votos, Tomo I, p. vi.

[97] *Vallarta,* Votos, Tomo II, pp. iv-v.

upon which to base their resolutions, not in laws that do not exist, but in prior judgments that settle the constitutional question they treat... Why among us does the opposite happen and it is said that the judgments of the Court are not authority nor doctrine to solve similar cases? We trust that once the ends of amparo are better known, it will not continue to be believed that it is limited to protecting an individual, but that it may be understood to extend to fix the public law by means of the interpretation it makes of the fundamental law.[98]

Vallarta saw the reports in the *Votos* as a step in building the constitutional jurisprudence of Mexico. He states that he undertook this work out of patriotic duty and to carry out his responsibilities as the President of the Supreme Court.[99] No doubt there were aspects of the project that advanced his professional and economic aspirations, but the business side of his reports has not been studied.[100] Furthermore, through these reports, Vallarta was certainly setting himself up as *the* central authority for constitutional interpretation in Mexico. His *Votos* are true to the method he proposed; their use of case law is not limited to United States opinions, but include many reference to prior decisions of the Mexican Supreme Court.

Although the scope and detail of Vallarta's project, and certainly his use and understanding of United States sources were novel, the general method of comparative constitutional analysis in Mexico was not. Indeed, in one passage, Vallarta states that he is going to "study the present question in the light of comparative legislation."[101] After comparing United States and Mexican constitutional texts and setting out several pages of John Marshall's opinion in *Brown v. Maryland*, Vallarta begins his analysis by stating "we can now make the observations suggested by the comparative study of the two texts."[102] The usefulness of "comparative legislation," and indeed of the study of English in understanding and interpreting the Mexican constitution, had already made some headway into Mexican legal curriculum by this point.[103]

Vallarta's assumptions about the usefulness of comparative study across countries and cultures provided the methodological underpinning for his second large written work during this period, his *El juicio de amparo y el writ of habeas corpus: ensayo crítico-comparativo sobre esos recursos constitucionales*. This comparative

---

98 *Vallarta*, Votos, Tomo IV, pp. 497–498. (Vallarta's emphasis. The term "leading cases" is in English in the original text.)

99 *Vallarta*, Votos, Tomo II, p. iv.

100 The development of case reports in the common law tradition seems always to have been linked to the sale of the reports and the potential for the reporter to earn some money. Vallarta may have been motivated by these concerns as well. I thank Professor Thomas E. Baker for reminding me of this aspect of law reporting. A quick reading of some of Vallarta's uncatalogued correspondence now at the Benson Collection at the University of Texas, Austin, indicates that Vallarta actively promoted the sale of his works.

101 *Vallarta*, Votos, Tomo II, p. 57.

102 *Vallarta*, Votos, Tomo II, p. 60.

103 *Mirow*, pp. 117–118.

treatise can be seen as the intellectual mid-point between the application of the Mexican constitutional law of amparo found in the *Votos* and the new law of general application found in the Amparo Act of 1882. It is Vallarta's opportunity to step back from praxis, to analyze, to expound, and to think about the broader application of constitutional protections within constitutional systems. It is a work that led directly to Vallarta's draft of the Amparo Act of 1882. Broadly speaking, the work covers the history, application, limits, and procedure of both habeas corpus and amparo.

One assumption of Vallarta's comparative method is that there are winners and losers, that when comparing one type of constitutional action to another, one will come out better. Not unexpectedly, Vallarta favors amparo over habeas corpus for numerous reasons set out in the work. In Vallarta's view, amparo covers more types of unconstitutional actions, is broader in its coverage of individuals, and requires fewer formalities. Vallarta also considered the nature of reviewing amparo actions superior to the procedure for reviewing habeas actions.[104] United States practices surrounding habeas offered Vallarta some useful suggestions for improving amparo actions. For example, Vallarta admired United States enforcement mechanisms that prevented the sidestepping of habeas remedies and suggested that Mexico follow such methods.[105] He also sought changes in Mexican law based on United States practice concerning the status of the claimant after the filing of the amparo action.[106]

The framework of comparing amparo to habeas corpus gave Vallarta an opportunity to explore various larger aspects of constitutional law and to revisit some of the principles he had set out in his *Votos*. For example, early in the book, he advances arguments for the power of judicial review for the Mexican Supreme Court.[107] He later makes it clear that the Supreme Court itself is not subject to amparo actions.[108] In another portion of the work he examines the nature and limits of the doctrine of judicial review within Mexican law.[109] Another chapter delves into the case and controversy requirement under United States law.[110] Federalism, in light of the Civil War and Reconstruction era cases from the United States, is addressed at length, particularly as the texts of the two constitutions led to different results.[111]

104 *Vallarta*, El juicio del amparo, pp. 286–290.

105 *Vallarta*, El juicio del amparo, pp. 165, 314–315.

106 *Vallarta*, El juicio del amparo, pp. 175–176.

107 *Vallarta*, El juicio del amparo, pp. 11–21.

108 *Vallarta*, El juicio del amparo, pp. 386–393.

109 *Vallarta*, El juicio del amparo, pp. 269–273. "Bien está que la Corte *juzgue de las leyes secundarias* para decidir si ellas son o no conformes con la fundamental: su deber es anularlas, cuando en algo la contradigan, y cumpliendo con ese deber, llena su elevada misión de interpretar final y decisivamente esa ley suprema . . . ." *Vallarta*, El juicio del amparo, pp. 269–270.

110 *Vallarta*, El juicio del amparo, pp. 120–126.

In other sections of the work, Vallarta attempts to build up support for the judgments of the court as sources for binding rules of constitutional interpretation.[112] In these passages, Vallarta carefully presses his desire for case-based constitutional jurisprudence in the style of the United States against the Mexican constitutional provisions that stated, "A judgment will always be such that it only addresses the particular individuals, limiting itself to protecting them and defending them in the particular case upon which the action is brought, *without making any general declaration regarding the law or act that motivated it.*"[113]

This is one of the great tasks of Vallarta's work. He wrote:

> To determine the effects of a judgment of amparo is the topic I wish to now address. The theories of our constitutional jurisprudence on this point are of the greatest importance, treating judgments that not only protect the individual against abuses of power, but also determine the public law of the nation, establishing the final interpretation of the supreme code.[114]

Vallarta pushed the bounds of the amparo judgments beyond judicial relief for the claimant. He wrote a bit later in the amparo treatise:

> And do not think that judgments of amparo by being trapped in the narrow limit of protecting a individual only in the particular are of little importance: they are, on the contrary, of the highest value, so high, that according to law, they ought to be published in the newspapers to determine the public law of the nation; they serve to nullify unconstitutional laws, to conserve the balance between the federal and local authority, avoiding their mutual collisions; they form the supreme, definitive and final interpretation of the Constitution, even above the interpretation that the legislator wanted to establish; through a peaceful process they resolve the most serious, the most difficult questions upon which the peace of the nation rests at times, the sovereignty of the states, the imperium of law over authority, the precepts of justice over the exigencies of political passion. Judgments of this transcendence cannot be but of the highest importance, much greater than the importance of judgments in ordinary trials.[115]

This second aspect of amparo judgments is carried out poorly if judges stick to "studied brevity" and "routine formulas" in deciding cases according to Vallarta.[116] Indeed, judges who do so are abandoning their duty and are refusing to recognize the important ends of such decisions.[117]

In an important move for establishing meaningful constitutional jurisprudence in Mexico, Vallarta took on the criticism that the method he proposed violated the

111 *Vallarta,* El juicio del amparo, pp. 364–374.

112 *Vallarta,* El juicio del amparo, pp. 272–273, 296–322.

113 Mexican Constitution, 1857, Art. 102 (Mirow's emphasis); *Vallarta,* El juicio del amparo, pp. 299–300, 310.

114 *Vallarta,* El juicio del amparo, p. 294.

115 *Vallarta,* El juicio del amparo, pp. 316–319.

116 *Vallarta,* El juicio del amparo, p. 320.

117 *Vallarta,* El juicio del amparo, p. 320.

constitutional prohibition of Article 102. Vallarta first cites one view that a judge who resorts to brevity and forms misunderstands the meaning of the constitutional provision, confusing the judgment and the reasons for the judgment. Vallarta, however, opted for an even narrower reading of the constitutional provision to justify his method. He quoted Lozano's *Derechos del hombre* for the proposition that "What the constitution prohibits. . .is that in the part of the judgment setting out the resolution, it is declared that the law or act that is judged is unconstitutional; the judgment must limit itself to declaring that the justice of the Union protects and defends the claimant against the law or act complained of."[118] Thus, when explaining the reasons for its judgment, the court ought to keep both ends of the case in mind. These ends are to protect the claimant and to determine definitively the meaning of a constitutional text.[119]

This work dovetails with the Amparo Act of 1882 itself. Numerous sections of the Act are cross-referenced to *El juicio de amparo* as well as to decisions in the *Votos*. The references provided to his work for the sections of the Amparo Act of 1882 unfortunately do not provide any further help in determining the sources of the specific provisions establishing jurisprudencia.

Vallarta's work after the Amparo Act of 1882 demonstrates that Vallarta never abandoned the United States as the primary source for his constitutional method. In 1885 in a speech outlining the jurisdiction of the Supreme Court and other federal courts, Vallarta noted that structural and jurisdictional provisions of the Mexican Constitution were based on the United States Constitution. Indeed, Vallarta turned to George Paschal's treatise on the Constitution and quoted Chief Justice John Marshall from Weaton's Reports to support his analysis. He comfortably and unabashedly turned to *"los jurisconsultos norteamericanos"* for authoritative interpretations of the Mexican Constitution on this occasion as he had for many years earlier.[120]

Vallarta's work leaves little doubt that the development of Mexican jurisprudencia is the result of direct borrowing from the constitutional methods of United States law. Certainly those legal scholars who found the roots of Mexican jurisprudencia in Roman law or autochthonous developments were mistaken.

Although the United States is the primary donor in this process, it may not have been the only donor. For example, Vallarta's use of the term "jurisprudencia" is not always as consistent as a reader of this article might assume. At one point Vallarta discusses "jurisprudence, whether doctrinal or flowing from judicial resolution." Some have seen this phrase indicating that Vallarta may have been following the Spanish notions of jurisprudencia as found in the Leyes de Enjuiciamiento Civil of

118 *Vallarta,* El juicio del amparo, p. 321.

119 *Vallarta,* El juicio del amparo, p. 321.

120 *Ignacio L. Vallarta,* Ocurso sobre una cuestión de competencia de tribunales, Archivo Inédito, Suprema Corte de Justicia de la Nación, p. 397.

1855 and 1881.[121] Indeed, the mid-nineteenth century witnessed the growth of notions of *jurisprudencia* or *jurisprudence* in European high courts.[122] Vallarta must have been aware of these developments and was certainly also aware of the Spanish Ley de Enjuiciamiento of 1855 that led to greater explanation and reasoning in judgments.[123] Spanish legal developments were generally important as Mexico sought to change its laws, and the Ley de Enjuiciamiento of 1855 was used by Mexico in drafting civil procedure rules in 1857.[124]

Another possible source for such developments is other Latin American countries. Jonathan Miller has fully explored the massive influence of the United States sources of constitutional law in Argentina during the same period that Mexico was rapidly adopting these "talismanic" sources for many of the same reasons.[125] To what extent the Mexican and Argentine embrace of the United States law was mutually influenced through translated sources in Spanish, news, and individual contacts presents an worthwhile avenue of investigation perhaps recognizing a transnational Latin American phenomenon during the period. Despite these possible secondary influences worthy of investigation, it is overwhelmingly clear from the works and statements of Vallarta that Mexican jurisprudencia in constitutional law is predominantly a product of direct borrowing of United States legal methods.

---

121 *Salinas Martínez,* La Suprema Corte y la jurisprudencia obligatoria, 19 Abril 1975, as cited in Zertoche, p. 74.

122 *J. Baró Pazos,* Notas acerca de la formación de la jurisprudencia del tribunal supremo hasta la codificación del derecho civil, in Anuario de historia del derecho español, vol. 66(2) (1997), p. 1511.

123 *J. Baró Pazos,* Notas acerca de la formación de la jurisprudencia del tribunal supremo hasta la codificación del derech civil, in Anuario de historia del derecho español, vol. 66(2) (1997), p. 1520.

124 *Mirow,* p. 114.

125 *J. M. Miller,* The Authority of a Foreign Talisman: A Study of U.S. Constitutional Practice as Authority in Nineteenth Century Argentina and the Argentine Elite's Leap of Faith, in: American University Law Review, vol. 46 (1997), pp. 1484 – 1572.

BERNARD DURAND

Motivations des décisions de justice et contrôle des motifs: la pratique judiciaire coloniale sous la troisième République

De valeur «modeste» en droit européen[1], la motivation des décisions de justice, en France, est récente. Elle ne date que de la loi des 16–24 août 1790. En droit positif, l'obligation de motiver est rappelée par l'article 455 du Nouveau Code de procédure civile dans son alinéa 1 («Le jugement doit exposer succinctement les prétentions respectives des parties et leurs moyens; il doit être motivé») et par l'article 593 alinéa 1 du Code de procédure pénale («Les arrêts de la chambre d'accusation ainsi que les arrêts et jugements en dernier ressort sont déclarés nuls s'ils ne contiennent pas de motifs ou si leurs motifs sont insuffisants et ne permettent pas à la Cour de cassation d'exercer son contrôle et de reconnaître si la loi a été respectée dans le dispositif»). Doctrine et Jurisprudence ont largement et précisément étudié ses applications, tandis que les historiens du droit ont partiellement déduit de l'Ancien régime les raisons qui militaient pour son absence et, par contre-coup, celles qui justifient son exigence en droit moderne.

On sait que l'Ancien Régime en France avait des motivations une conception étriquée: le juge ne devait pas motiver ses décisions au pénal, sauf à rappeler (comme obligation lui en était faite) le crime qu'il sanctionnait. Les raisons en étaient diverses[2]. Il fallait éviter le rebondissement des procès, empêcher que pour quelque mauvaise motivation au milieu d'un ensemble tout à fait justifié un procès ne soit annulé, affirmer l'autorité des juges, etc. Mais les inconvénients n'étaient pas négligeables, en particulier sur la science du droit: comment réguler une jurisprudence? Faire progresser le droit? En comprendre les évolutions?

A partir de la Révolution, l'obligation de motiver a fortement progressé, portée par une doctrine qui en recensait aisément les avantages. Enumérons-les rapidement. Soumises à l'appel et à la cassation, les décisions des juges, parce que motivées, peuvent être contrôlées (il suffit aux juges, observe-t-on avec un peu d'humour «de ne pas en dire plus qu'il n'est nécessaire du soutien du dispositif et d'en dire assez pour ne pas donner prise à l'annulation ou à la réformation pour

---

[1] *Serge Guinchard/Jacques Buisson*, Procédure pénale, Litec, 2000, page 266.

[2] Voir *Philippe Godding*, Jurisprudence et motivations des sentences du Moyen-âge à la fin du 18e siècle, in: La motivation des décisions de justice, Etudes publiées par Ch. Perelman et P. Foriers, Bruxelles, 1978, p. 37–67.

défaut ou insuffisance de motifs»). A cette première raison, qui pourrait dispenser les cours suprêmes de se contraindre à la motivation, on ajoute le besoin d'imposer à celui qui juge de maîtriser et de préciser son propre raisonnement, de lever toute obscurité et de contrôler, par lui-même, la validité de son argumentation, ce qui ne peut que renforcer la sécurité juridique. Pour les justiciables, en particulier, la motivation est une garantie contre la partialité du juge et son arbitraire; c'est, aussi, la preuve que le juge a examiné soigneusement les moyens soumis, qu'il a réfléchi à ses conclusions et qu'il peut ainsi les convaincre du fondement de sa décision. Par la même occasion, la motivation, en précisant aux plaideurs la solidité de leurs droits ou leur faiblesse permet aux parties de mesurer et d'apprécier leurs chances en appel ou en cassation. Enfin, sur le plan de la philosophie du droit, la motivation intéresse l'ensemble de la société, lui fait accepter l'adhésion au système de droit, la persuade, par une jurisprudence cohérente, de la saine interprétation de la loi qu'elle unifie[3].

Mais la question des motivations renvoie également à deux interrogations majeures.

L'une est relative aux juges. En France, la domination de la «loi», qui débouche logiquement sur des juges chargés de la «dire» et de l'appliquer (au point de leur interdire toute considération d'équité?), ne laisse habituellement aux magistrats qu'un rôle théoriquement modeste. Aux termes de l'article 5 du Code civil, il leur est interdit de se prononcer par voie de disposition générale et réglementaire sur les causes qui leur sont soumises, règle qui atteste du caractère «légaliste» de ce Code et de la réaction aux abus des Parlements d'ancien régime qu'il consacre. Dans notre système judiciaire, toutefois, le juge conserve dans sa fonction le pouvoir d'interpréter la loi faute de quoi disparaîtrait «l'art de juger à l'égard de chaque cas particulier». L'article 4 du Code civil lui fait obligation de pallier le silence, l'obscurité ou l'insuffisance de la loi. Le juge, en effet, par son jugement, dit le droit pour un cas particulier et il ne peut pas ne pas juger. Mais dans le même temps, les décisions rendues par les tribunaux finissent par constituer une jurisprudence, c'est-à-dire un ensemble de solutions de droit, dont on voit bien que, par leurs motivations et la continuité de celles-ci, elles finissent par constituer une interprétation du droit fort proche d'une règle générale et abstraite et donc fort proche d'une véritable source du droit.

La généralisation des motivations permet ainsi, en raison du rôle important qu'elles font jouer aux juges, de s'interroger sur leur rôle exact. De quelle marge d'interprétation disposent ces derniers dans une société dont la complexité est croissante? Un auteur parle du développement d'une «semi-législature» judiciaire, évoque la théorie de la «rechtsvinding» selon laquelle le droit n'est pas créé mais trouvé par le juge, celui-ci étant en quelque sorte le porte-parole d'un système ouvert dont la marge d'appréciation judiciaire fait partie intégrante[4]. Plutôt que

---

3 Les motivations des décisions de justice, études publiées par *Ch. Perelman/P. Foriers*, Bruxelles, 1978.

d'imaginer d'un côté la loi, de l'autre son interprétation, il invite à penser l'imbrication entre règle et décision, l'une n'étant rien sans l'autre. Ce droit vivant laisse au juge une latitude certaine, puisque le cas d'espèce le conduit à confronter les données concrètes au donné juridique (la loi ou les principes généraux du droit). Cet exercice l'amène à choisir, et c'est ici que s'inscrit son «intime conviction» mais en réalité la question est de savoir pourquoi le juge fait tel choix plutôt que tel autre. C'est là qu'interviennent les motivations, car le juge doit dire ce qui l'amène à considérer le cas sous telle perspective ou telle autre, à chercher tel résultat, que ce soit en inspectant le fait (ce qui est le plus facile) ou en inspectant le droit (et alors le juge devrait dire quelle valeur il met en œuvre, d'ordre social ou autre, équité, intérêt général), ce qui dans les motivations peut avoir des retombées bien plus riches.

La deuxième interrogation est relative au Droit. En effet, l'approche précédente, qui prend le juge pour cible, est aussi une invitation à scruter le système juridique dans lequel il évolue. Selon qu'il est limité dans ses pouvoirs et se trouve «esclave» de la loi (droit «autoritaire» ou d'inspiration rousseauiste qui limite au maximum les pouvoirs du juge), ou qu'il est au contraire investi du pouvoir de «déduire le droit» («droit démocratique»), le regard sur les motivations peut être différent. En dehors d'un tronc commun, n'y-a-t-il pas entre les pays anglo-saxons, où domine le droit de common law et les pays de tradition continentale romano-germanique, des différences tenant à la conception du Droit lui-même, d'où découlent une priorité à la motivation pour convaincre, dans les pays de common law (où la loi est moins présente, où le précédent joue un rôle essentiel, où le juge dispose du pouvoir important de déduire le droit des situations qui lui sont soumises) et, dans les pays du continent de droit écrit (où la loi joue un rôle majeur et le juge doit l'interpréter), une priorité donnée à la volonté de justifier la décision par référence à la règle de droit applicable aux faits[5].

Or, si ces deux approches sont exactes, il peut être intéressant de prendre pour objet d'étude un milieu original, les territoires coloniaux sous la troisième République, pour lesquels on trouve réunis tout à la fois, une tradition continentale érigeant en principe la primauté de la loi (mais contrariée en pratique par la diversité des législateurs), un milieu où la loi est souvent absente (parce que certains textes ne sont pas promulgués et les coutumes locales ne sont pas rédigées) et confuse (certains textes se contredisent), et enfin des juges dont les pouvoirs, en raison de l'éloignement de la Métropole et des difficultés de contrôle, sont importants (un véritable droit prétorien s'y développe) mais dont les décisions sont parfois contradictoires (jurisprudence erratique). Un témoignage, très bref, l'illustre: A la veille de la première guerre mondiale, le Président du tribunal de Majunga regrettait

---

4 *Visser't Hooft,* Vers un style de motivation plus concret?, in: Les motivations des décisions de justice, op. cit., p. 161 et s.

5 De fait, on peut expliquer l'absence de motivations sous l'ancien régime en France, en partie, par l'idée que la loi pénale y est rare, alors au contraire qu'elle devient la seule référence après la Révolution.

qu'on ne puisse disposer pour Madagascar – où depuis le décret du 28 décembre 1895 avaient été promulguées en bloc les lois civiles, commerciales et pénales françaises antérieures – d'un Code spécial «qui s'adapterait aux besoins du pays» et éviterait «ces discussions juridiques sur lesquelles les tribunaux de l'île, eux-mêmes, ne sont pas toujours d'accord»[6].

Les questions que nous essayerons de résoudre sont les suivantes: Le système colonial étant à mi-chemin entre un droit qui repose sur le principe de la loi et un système qui prend acte de leur rareté et de leur confusion, est-il possible, en scrutant la jurisprudence des tribunaux, des Cours d'appel et de la Cour de cassation, de déceler: d'une part, comment les magistrats, habitués aux usages métropolitains mais plutôt éloignés du contrôle de la Cour de cassation, vont se livrer à l'exercice des motivations (I)? Pour justifier plutôt, mais dans quels domaines? Pour convaincre, et dans quel domaine? D'autre part, comment la Cour de cassation, lorsqu'elle est saisie, réagit-elle devant les pourvois qui lui parviennent pour absence ou insuffisance de motifs (II)? En restreignant, ici, volontairement le champ des motivations, nous mettrons en valeur une dimension particulière: ce n'est ni l'incompétence, ni l'erreur de droit, ni l'excès de pouvoir, etc., qui sont au premier plan, mais le fait que les juges, dont les décisions ont fait l'objet d'un recours, n'ont pas permis, en raison de motifs absents ou insuffisants, à la Cour de cassation d'exercer son contrôle sur le respect du Droit, soit pour une raison de forme (il n'y a pas de motifs), soit pour une raison de fond (les motifs ne suffisent pas à expliquer le dispositif).

I. La nature des motivations en matière coloniale

Le principe de l'obligation de motiver, qui valait aussi bien pour les cours d'appel métropolitaines que pour les cours d'appel coloniales, fut affirmé très tôt. Dans les établissements de l'Inde, les jugements rendus par les tribunaux doivent être motivés à peine de nullité, aux termes de l'ordonnance du 7 février 1842[7]. Dans son arrêt en date du 25 août 1863, la Cour de cassation rappelait, à l'occasion d'un arrêt de la Cour de la Martinique qui n'avait pas examiné s'il y avait lieu d'ordonner ou de refuser la preuve d'une possession alléguée par les demandeurs, que cette Cour n'avait pas motivé sa décision, que «dans la colonie de la Martinique», les jugements qui ne renferment pas les motifs exigés par l'article 141 du code de procédure applicable à cette colonie en vertu de l'ordonnance royale de 1828, sont nuls, «quoique l'article 141 du code de procédure n'en prononce pas expressément la nullité et que l'article 7 de la loi du 20 avril 1810, qui l'a édictée, n'ait pas été déclaré exécutoire à la Martinique, les motifs étant une partie essentielle de tout

6 *F. Berge,* De l'application à Madagascar des lois françaises antérieures au 28 décembre 1895, Penant, 1911, p. 5 et s.

7 Penant 1909, Cass. Civ., 23 décembre 1908, page 93, art. 2774.

jugement»[8]. Position qui sera reprise en 1876 pour Saint-Pierre et Miquelon, où il est suppléé à l'article 7 de la même loi par l'ordonnance du 26 juillet 1833 concernant l'organisation judiciaire et l'administration de la justice dans ces îles. En l'occurrence, les juges du fond avaient omis de faire connaître les faits «dans lesquels ils ont vu les manœuvres frauduleuses», silence qui «met la Cour de cassation dans l'impossibilité d'exercer son contrôle»[9].

Avec la constitution de l'Empire colonial sous la troisième République, le rappel de cette obligation ira de soi. Dans un arrêt du 9 mai 1898, la Cour de cassation se réfère à «l'ordonnance du 22 novembre 1819 concernant l'administration de justice dans les colonies françaises, laquelle est applicable à la Guadeloupe et porte que tous les jugements doivent être motivés»[10]. Dans le même temps (comme le fait remarquer au Penant un annotateur), «la jurisprudence en matière de motifs, est tellement vaste et si aisée à trouver dans tous les recueils», que les commentateurs se contentent en général de ne citer que les derniers arrêts[11].

Devant cet ample matériel et sans donner à ces premières conclusions une valeur définitive, il est intéressant de noter, à la lecture des jugements et arrêts rendus par les tribunaux et les Cours d'appel, deux manières de motiver. Il apparaît que là où les textes sont très précis ou qu'est en jeu l'autorité de l'Etat, la mode est au laconisme, excessif même. La référence à la loi, impérative, s'impose et le juge se satisfait de s'y référer pour se justifier, allant jusqu'à oublier de rappeler les faits (I.1). En revanche dans les secteurs où la loi est absente ou mal comprise ou bien qui véhiculent les enjeux de colonisation ou bien lorsque les juges invitent à un revirement de jurisprudence, l'art de convaincre l'emporte. Les motivations, alors préparent d'abondance le dispositif (I.2).

1. Le souci de justifier par la seule référence à la loi: des juges parfois laconiques

Motifs évasifs ou quasi inexistants peuvent avoir pour cause des «raisons mystérieuses» qui laissent perplexe la doctrine elle-même, mais à laquelle elle finit par se ranger sans conviction! On en a un exemple en matière de douanes où, aucun texte n'ayant attribué aux tribunaux de première instance la compétence en premier et dernier ressort, leurs décisions devraient normalement être susceptibles d'appel. C'est pourtant à la solution contraire que s'est arrêtée «une jurisprudence aujourd'hui constante et qu'il serait superflu de contester». Pourtant, notait un auteur, ces arrêts «sont à peine motivés» et leur rédaction même laisse des doutes[12].

---

8 D. 1863, 1, 335.

9 D. 1876, 1, 139, arrêt de cassation du 22 mai 1874.

10 Penant, 1899, art. 1329, p. 148 et s.

11 Penant, 1925, p. 68 et s., art. 4542 note 5 sous arrêt du 2 juin 1924.

12 *Dareste*, Traité de droit colonial, § 179.

Plus intéressants sont les domaines où les textes sont abondants et précis, ce qui est en particulier le cas en matière pénale. Or, ici, témoignages de doctrine et jurisprudence attestent du caractère expéditif de certaines motivations. Le Traité de droit colonial de Dareste, en 1931, mettait en cause les chambres des mises en accusation d'Indochine, montrées du doigt pour des motifs on ne peut plus sommaires (§ 189): «Leurs arrêts, écrit l'auteur, sont soumis aux mêmes règles que dans la métropole» et doivent notamment contenir, à peine de nullité, l'exposé sommaire des faits qui font l'objet de l'accusation et non pas seulement leur qualification légale. Il ajoutait: «Ce principe mériterait à peine d'être énoncé s'il n'avait été nécessaire par des cassations réitérées de le rappeler aux juridictions de l'Indochine»[13]. Ainsi d'un arrêt de renvoi de la chambre des mises en accusation de la Cour d'appel séant à Hanoi qui ne contient «aucun exposé des faits» en violation de l'article 232 du Code d'instruction criminelle qui «exige, à peine de nullité», que l'ordonnance de prise de corps contienne l'exposé sommaire et la qualification légale du fait objet de la poursuite[14].

Un bref regard sur la jurisprudence rapportée au Recueil Penant comme au Recueil Dareste confirme cette attitude désinvolte, qui n'est pas (loin de là!) l'apanage des chambres des mises en accusation ou de l'Indochine. Ainsi de cet arrêt rendu par la Cour d'appel de la Réunion le 17 juin 1926 qui condamne un cuisinier de Saint-Denis, originaire de Chine, à quinze jours de prison et à 100 francs d'amende, en se contentant «de reproduire les termes de la loi» relatifs à la tenue d'une maison de jeux de hasard et d'une fumerie d'opium sans indiquer «ni la nature des jeux pratiqués, ni si le rôle du hasard y était prépondérant...(ni fait) connaître les circonstances desquelles (les juges) ont induit que le prévenu avait facilité à autrui l'usage de l'opium», ni d'ailleurs «expressément déclaré la culpabilité»[15]! Ainsi également d'un arrêt de la Cour d'appel de Saigon rendu le 27 mars 1928 qui relaxe trois prévenus en se contentant de dire que «des débats et de l'examen du dossier ne résultait pas la preuve... qu'ils se fussent rendus coupables de manœuvres susceptibles d'ébranler la fidélité et le loyalisme des populations, ne prenant pas la peine de faire connaître le contenu des articles de journal incriminés qui avaient motivé la poursuite[16].

En Guinée, la Cour criminelle, soumise aux formes de la procédure correctionnelle, doit motiver ses décisions et donc spécifier les faits: le 14 août 1903, la Chambre criminelle de la Cour de cassation casse un de ces arrêts qui condamne un accusé pour un attentat à la pudeur commis avec violence, sans spécifier les faits qui auraient constitué l'attentat, ce qui «s'agissant d'un crime qui se compose

---

[13] Voir les arrêts de cassation mentionnés à la Table 1898–1910, n° 64–68 et à a table 1911–1920, n°86 et 87.

[14] Recueil Dareste, 1910, p. 147 et s. Cour de cassation, Chambre criminelle, 13 mai 1909.

[15] Recueil Dareste, 1927, Cour de cassation, 10 décembre 1926, p. 39 et s.

[16] Recueil Dareste, 1930, p. 67 et s., arrêt du 8 décembre 1928.

d'éléments discutables, susceptibles d'influer sur la qualification», met la Cour de cassation dans l'impossibilité d'exercer son contrôle et de vérifier la régularité de l'application de la peine[17]. De nombreux autres arrêts viennent sanctionner par la cassation des décisions dans lesquelles les faits ne sont pas exposés ou les règles de droit sont purement et simplement oubliées[18].

2. Le désir de convaincre: des motivations surabondantes

Les questions de politique «coloniale», celles pour lesquelles une législation lacunaire place en désaccord administrateurs et magistrats ou même celles qui traitent d'un point de droit sensible, ou bien celles qui reflètent des différences de perception, liées à l'idée que le Droit doit protéger les indigènes, voilà des domaines qui incitent les juges à développer leurs arguments, répondant ainsi à un des buts de la motivation: établir et confirmer une jurisprudence ou bien, ce qui va dans le même sens, orienter une nouvelle jurisprudence.

a) Les revendications du domaine et le droit de propriété: interpréter les traités

Deux raisons ont fait de cette question une matière épineuse favorable à la «surabondance des motivations». D'une part, bien sûr, le fait que les textes en vigueur aient laissé longtemps planer un doute sur les véritables intentions du légis-

---

17 Recueil Dareste, 1904, p. 28 et s.

18 Même situation pour un arrêt de la Cour de cassation du 22 février 1902 qui casse un arrêt de condamnation de la Cour criminelle de Longxuyen pour vol qualifié, parce que la Chambre des mises en accusation dans son arrêt n'a exposé aucun fait et s'en réfère aux résultats de l'information (Recueil Dareste, 1902, p. 50 et s.). Idem contre un arrêt du 7 septembre 1906 par lequel la Chambre des mises en accusation séant à Hanoi a renvoyé le demandeur devant la Cour criminelle d'Hanoi, qui ne contient aucun exposé des faits (recueil Dareste, 1907, p. 123 et s., Cass. Chambre criminelle, 1 mars 1907). Idem pour la Guyane par la cassation d'un arrêt de la Cour d'assises de la Guyane du 25 août 1906: «Attendu que l'exposé sommaire des faits ne se trouve ni dans l'ordonnance de prise de corps, ni dans l'arrêt de renvoi devant la Cour d'assises et que l'arrêt se borne à énoncer des qualifications sur l'exactitudes desquelles la Cour de cassation ne peut, en l'absence de l'exposé, exercer son contrôle» (autre arrêt identique à la même date et pour la même Cour) (Recueil Dareste, 1907, p. 37 et s., Cass. Crim. 3 novembre 1906). De même peut on s'étonner de ce que la Cour d'appel de la Guadeloupe, en sa chambre correctionnelle se soit contentée, pour condamner un distillateur aux peines de la récidive, de déclarer «que Blandin avait été condamné 10 ans plus tôt par le tribunal correctionnel de la Basse-Terre à 2000 francs d'amende», sans faire connaître la cause de cette condamnation, ce qui est une violation flagrante du décret concerné qui prévoit que la récidive est spéciale, c'est-à-dire qu'il veut que les deux condamnations soient de même nature: Ne s'expliquant pas sur ce point, la Cour de Guadeloupe n'a pas permis à la Cour de cassation de vérifier si la peine de la récidive avait été légalement appliquée, casse avec renvoi à la Cour d'appel de la Martinique (Penant, 1896, Cass., article 849, Chambre criminelle, Audience du 27 décembre 1895).

lateur. Mais également le fait qu'est venue s'y greffer la question fort débattue du droit reconnu aux tribunaux de l'ordre judiciaire d'interpréter les traités, question sur laquelle la jurisprudence était contradictoire[19].

Le droit invoqué en vertu des divers traités passés avec les souverains, qui faisait de l'Etat français le subrogé à tous les droits des souverains régnants, fut longtemps invoqué en Afrique, tant occidentale qu'orientale. Il postulait qu'héritant de leur souveraineté comme de tous leurs biens parmi lesquels se trouvait le «domaine éminent» du sol, l'Etat pouvait prétendre à la propriété du sol et ne laisser aux individus qu'un droit d'occupation précaire. Or cette thèse a fortement opposé juges, doctrine et législateur. La jurisprudence, dans un premier temps, a accompagné les prétentions de l'Administration devant une doctrine, outrée des positions soutenues, et un législateur plus circonspect. La Cour de Bordeaux en 1903,[20] la Cour d'appel de Dakar en 1907,[21] le tribunal de Dakar en 1908,[22] ont posé le principe que l'Etat français avait succédé aux droits du Damel du Cayor, qui avait cédé son royaume à la France et que ces droits comprenaient la propriété de la terre. Ils s'appuyaient là, selon la doctrine, sur une conception erronée de la terre ainsi que sur une lecture formaliste des traités qui parlaient d'une cession «en toute souveraineté et propriété». Du reste, ces prétentions n'avaient pas seulement pour but le seul désir d'accroître le domaine privé ou de diriger la mise en valeur des terres mais elles s'inscrivaient dans un plan imaginé pour faire naître la propriété privée.

Cette question sensible, liée au domaine de l'Etat, fut donc l'occasion de motivations de «conviction», souvent appréciées par la doctrine comme autant «d'affirmations» justifiant mal la thèse soutenue. Par l'arrêt du 8 février 1907, la Cour d'appel de l'AOF, dans ces considérants invoquera successivement, pour débouter les requérants les traités passés avec les chefs indigènes, les historiens, les coutumes du Cayor, les ouvrages de doctrine, les arrêtés locaux, les arguments juridiques (Code civil et lois), tous arguments qui étayaient, selon elle, le bien fondé de la substitution de l'Etat français aux droits du Damel[23].

Mais de tout aussi abondantes motivations furent avancées lorsqu'il s'est agi de renverser cette jurisprudence. Dans l'arrêt «Etat français contre d'Almeida»[24], en

---

19 A propos de l'affaire Rawane Boye, on a laissé aux juges du fait le soin d'interpréter un traité et de dire si telle région faisait partie ou non du territoire cédé. Il y avait sur ce point jurisprudence en sens contraire et on se serait attendu à ce que la Cour de cassation ne s'en remette justement pas aux juges du fait. La doctrine critique cette vision (Voir Penant, 1910, p. 193 et s. il y est question de *motifs surabondants*).

20 Recueil Dareste, 1904, p. 159, arrêt du 24 juin 1903.

21 Cour d'appel de l'AOF, 8 février et premier mars 1907, Recueil Dareste, 1907, p. 78 et 97.

22 Tribunal de première instance de Dakar, 17 octobre 1908, Recueil Dareste, 1909, p. 260.

23 Arrêts du 8 février et premier mars 1907, Recueil Penant, 1907, p. 219 et 1908, p. 247, arrêt du 18 juin 1909, Recueil Penant, 1910, p. 62 et s.

24 Penant, 1933, 1, p. 252 et 2 novembre 1934, Recueil Penant, 1934, 1, 18.

des termes dénués de toute ambiguïté, sera niée la thèse de la subrogation. La Cour d'appel de l'AOF, sur la prétention de l'Etat à s'opposer à une demande d'immatriculation en invoquant «la substitution de l'Etat français à l'ancien souverain local, propriétaire du sol», y reconnaît bien qu'au Dahomey les anciens chefs indigènes se «considéraient et se comportaient comme étant propriétaires dans le sens le plus absolu du mot non seulement du territoire sur lequel s'étendait leur autorité mais encore de tous les biens de leurs sujets» et que si l'Etat français voulait prétendre la même chose «il ne rencontrerait aucune opposition de la part des populations indigènes qui, courbées si longtemps sous le joug de despotes et accoutumées à la plus sévère discipline, s'inclineraient encore comme par le passé devant la force». Mais c'est pour ajouter que «cet acquiescement passif à la substitution de l'Etat français... ne saurait justifier cette substitution», qu'il importait au contraire de «distinguer le droit de l'abus, la propriété régulièrement acquise de l'usurpation».

La Cour d'appel stigmatisait cette thèse «erronée au regard de la mission civilisatrice et colonisatrice» et rappelait que, par les textes de 1906, l'Etat avait reconnu le droit des indigènes d'exercer un droit d'usage capable d'être consolidé et d'accéder à la pleine propriété et que ce texte ne saurait être rendu inapplicable «par la seule permission arbitraire de l'Etat pour chaque cas particulier, solution contraire au bon sens et à tout esprit de justice» ce que ne peut avoir voulu le législateur. La Cour refusait alors à l'Etat de s'opposer à la demande d'immatriculation. Elle renouvela à quelque temps de là sa position, cette fois pour la presqu'île du cap vert, dans un arrêt du 2 novembre 1934: «considérant que l'Etat français soutient qu'il a comme successeur de l'ancien souverain indigène, le Damel du Cayor, sur l'ensemble des terres de cet ancien royaume, le domaine éminent qui ne laisse aux détenteurs qu'un droit précaire; que ce domaine éminent équivaut à un droit de propriété... mais considérant que cette prétention est en l'espèce basée sur une double erreur: d'abord de fait car le territoire où est situé le terrain litigieux était depuis des siècles soustrait à toute autorité du Damel..., puis erreur de droit parce que cet article 83 du décret du 26 juillet 1932 comme l'article 58 du décret du 24 juillet 1906 dont il est l'exacte reproduction, signifie que l'Etat n'a pas entendu revendiquer à son profit les attributions et prérogatives des anciens souverains indigènes et qu'il y a renoncé particulièrement à l'égard des terres qui sont détenues en conformité du droit coutumier local. Que l'article 10 du décret du 23 octobre 1904, qui a réglementé le domaine de l'Etat en Afrique, rapproché de cet article 58 du décret du 24 juillet 1906, fait ressortir que l'Etat ne saurait prétendre à aucune autre propriété privée que celle des terres vacantes et sans maître»[25].

---

25 Recueil Penant, 1937, art. 5704, p. 18–22.

b) Entre créanciers et débiteurs: protéger les indigènes

Il est clair qu'en ce domaine, le débat qui s'est focalisé sur la contrainte par corps a largement alimenté la jurisprudence et poussé les juges de première instance comme des Cours d'appel à développer de minutieuses motivations, parfois oublieuses des seuls arguments de textes[26]. Ce fut particulièrement vif en Indochine où une jurisprudence variable et une intervention tardive de la Cour de cassation (non saisie avant 1929) permit aux juges de participer à la controverse relative au droit d'un créancier français de bénéficier de la contrainte par corps (supprimée en France en 1867) et de la question de savoir s'il s'agissait, en cas d'affirmative, de la contrainte par corps française ou de celle annamite. Les décisions furent parfois l'occasion de longs développements sur le droit annamite et ses conceptions (ou sur les abus qu'il pouvait générer), motivations qui faisaient parfois office de petits traités de droit coutumier, utiles à fixer une jurisprudence.

A plusieurs reprises, les juges se sont employés à faire la clarté sur ces questions, maniant arguments de logique, d'opportunité, de morale, de principes, etc. Au milieu d'une abondante jurisprudence, on se contentera d'évoquer ici le très long jugement rendu par le tribunal de première instance de Cantho le 24 juin 1919 qui, après avoir rappelé les différentes modifications subies par la législation depuis 1832 et détaillé la jurisprudence antérieure, énumère les arguments utilisés par les juges, partisans et adversaires de la contrainte par corps.

Aux premiers, il reproche d'user de considérations de fait (instabilité de la propriété foncière, cadastre à faire ou à refaire, régime hypothécaire à organiser, insuffisance des garanties réelles, défaut d'état civil des indigènes, diminution de leur crédit, etc.) qui toutes «pourraient intéresser le législateur chargé de modifier nos codes mais qui ne sauraient, pour le moment, être retenues par nos tribunaux». Reprenant les arguments de ceux qui en désirent la suppression et ajoutant les siens propres, il met en cause «les capitalistes» qui n'ont jamais cru devoir porter le litige devant la Cour de cassation et se sont satisfaits de «décisions de justice intermittentes», critique l'arrêt rendu précédemment par la Cour d'appel, invite à la réalisation du programme de civilisation que s'est fixé la France, déplore le maintien d'une contrainte par corps «qui n'est que le dernier vestige des régimes d'esclavage où la liberté de l'homme était un bien dont on pouvait le dépouiller», arguments auxquels la Cour d'appel de Saigon répondra point par point, ne s'arrêtant pas à la lettre du texte mais dégageant les considérations juridiques justifiant l'intervention législative[27].

---

26 Voir sur cette question de la contrainte par corps, notre article «le juge colonial et la contrainte par corps en matière civile et commerciale», in: *B. Durand/M. Fabre,* Le juge et l'Outre-mer, Histoire de la Justice, 2004, p. 421–456.

27 Recueil Dareste, 1920, Arrêt du 19 septembre 1919, p. 173 et s. voir aussi Penant, 1925, p. 211, note d'André Dureteste sous jugement du tribunal de première instance de Hanoi du 20 septembre 1924.

II. Le contrôle des motivations en matière coloniale

L'originalité de la cassation en matière coloniale (II.1) produit ce résultat que l'éloignement, et les règles particulières qui président aux pourvois, en raison de leur imperfection, laissent aux juges locaux une grande liberté. Il est d'autant plus important que soit mis l'accent sur le contrôle des motifs (II.2) que ce contrôle, en raison de son caractère «formel» et des renvois qu'il génère, laisse aux juges coloniaux le dernier mot sur le fond.

1. L'originalité de la cassation en matière coloniale

La question des pourvois est, dans les colonies d'une complexité extrême. En effet, contrairement aux recours en Conseil d'Etat qui sont de droit, le pourvoi en cassation contre les décisions des cours et tribunaux n'est ouvert qu'en vertu de textes précis et il n'existe aucun texte général. De sorte que la règle fut à l'origine l'absence de pourvois, progressivement introduits dans les diverses colonies. Il en fut ainsi pour le pourvoi en cassation, celui en révision, celui en annulation pour incompétence ou excès de pouvoir, de telle sorte que si à peu près partout l'existence des pourvois est presque devenue la règle, cela ne fut qu'avec d'innombrables nuances. C'est ainsi que le pouvoir dans l'intérêt de la loi fut, sauf exception, réservé au Procureur général de la Cour de cassation.

a) Unité de contrôle par la Cour de cassation

Bien que tenté à plusieurs reprises (en 1789, en 1790, par exemple) de créer des Cours de cassation «locales», le législateur s'est toujours abstenu. Ce refus était justifié par un ensemble d'arguments, dont le principal était certainement le souci d'unité, commandé par la situation de diversité imposée par les territoires coloniaux[28].

De la même façon, refus fut également apporté à l'idée de créer une chambre spéciale. En 1902, un projet de réforme visait à créer une quatrième chambre chargée de régler les affaires coloniales en matière indigène tant au criminel qu'au civil. Mais la chose fut finalement écartée en raison du faible nombre de pourvois, les citoyens français continuant de relever des autres chambres. Projet repris en 1909, sous une forme un peu différente (sa compétence serait limitée à l'Indochine, à Madagascar, à l'AOFet au Congo), sans plus de succès.

Il est vrai que cette centralisation est atténuée par les recours en annulation qui frappent certains jugements devant les Cours d'appel locales.

---

28 Voir sur ces questions Martine Fabre, Le contrôle de la Cour de cassation: censurer le juge colonial, in Le juge et l'Outre- mer, op. cit., pages 221 et s.).

b) Compétence variable de la Cour de cassation

En métropole, c'est l'article 2 de la loi du 27 novembre / 1er décembre 1790 qui a posé la base du recours devant la Haute juridiction: la Cour connaît de tous les pourvois contre les jugements rendus en dernier ressort, à l'exception des décisions des juges de paix (article 4). La loi du 27 ventôse an 8 va ouvrir le pourvoi contre les décisions de juge de paix rendues en dernier ressort en cas d'incompétence ou d'excès de pouvoir. Cette compétence fut étendue aux colonies mais selon des modalités particulières qui en limitèrent les effets.

D'une part, le pourvoi en cassation n'est ouvert qu'en vertu d'un texte; à défaut le pourvoi est irrecevable. Le doute avait été un moment permis car un arrêt de 1911[29] avait semblé admettre que le pourvoi en cassation était ouvert contre toutes les décisions rendues par les tribunaux français pourvu qu'elles soient en dernier ressort, et que cette règle s'étendait aux tribunaux français établis dans les pays de protectorat, sauf dispositions exceptionnelles, mais cette jurisprudence est restée isolée.

D'autre part, le régime est différent selon qu'il s'agit de droit civil et commercial ou de droit pénal. Dans les deux première matières, il y a des colonies pour lesquelles on suit à peu près le régime de métropole (ainsi, par exemple, en Indochine à partir de 1868, à Madagascar à partir de 1897), d'autres au contraire pour lesquelles seules les décisions de Cour d'appel sont susceptibles de faire l'objet d'un recours (par exemple en AOF ou en Océanie). En droit pénal, il faut noter une situation encore plus complexe car, outre le fait que le recours ne sera admis que fort tard dans certaines colonies, il est, ici, le même qu'en métropole (AEF par exemple), limité, là, aux cours d'appel ou cours criminelles (AOF ou Océanie par exemple), limité, ailleurs, à certaines personnes ou à des motifs très précis (ainsi à la Réunion ou à Madagascar), toutes démarches commandées peut-être par le souci d'ordre public, mais plus sûrement par le souhait de maîtriser un procédé fort lourd dans sa mise en œuvre.

Enfin, la Cour de cassation, reconnaît aux juges du fond, en matière de droit coutumier, tout pouvoir de constatation des dispositions de la loi (par exemple, en terre de protectorats) ou des coutumes, comme s'il s'agissait d'une loi étrangère, solution inspirée de celle qui prévaut en métropole où, lorsque les juges se sont référés à une loi étrangère, il est satisfait aux exigences de la loi et il n'appartient pas à la Cour de cassation de rechercher si la loi étrangère a été bien ou mal appréciée et appliquée. Cette position, dénoncée par une partie de la doctrine comme étant «une abdication complète du droit de contrôle de la Cour de cassation» fut notamment appliquée en Indochine, en matière annamite, position en partie imposée par la difficulté à connaître cette loi en l'absence de codification. En pareille hypothèse, en effet, la Cour, dès lors que la décision est motivée, ne fait que l'enregistrer purement et simplement[30].

---

29 Cass. Crim., 15 novembre 1911, Recueil Dareste 1912, p. 43.

Enfin, le recours n'est pas ouvert ou au contraire ouvert, selon les pays, aux indigènes. Ainsi, les indigènes de Madagascar ne bénéficient pas, pour les peines afflictives, du contrôle de la Cour de cassation alors que ceux d'Indochine peuvent le revendiquer. En effet, le décret du 24 mai 1905 qui a organisé pour Madagascar le recours en cassation en matière criminelle et correctionnelle, ne l'avait prévu qu'à l'égard des européens et assimilés, termes si exprès que la Cour de cassation ne pouvait, lorsque la qualité d'indigène était acquise, qu'appliquer le décret[31].

2. Les motifs retenus par la Cour de cassation

Les lignes qui précèdent font mieux comprendre sans doute, l'importance que présente pour les colonies le contrôle des motifs. D'une part, en effet, ce contrôle supplée à la rareté des textes en matière coutumière, permettant ainsi à la Cour de cassation qui ne peut intervenir sur le fond de le faire sur la forme. D'autre part, certains indigènes ne bénéficiant pas des pourvois, la Cour de cassation a infléchi sa jurisprudence pour pouvoir contrôler les motifs. C'est ainsi que pour Madagascar, dès lors que l'arrêt attaqué ne constatait pas que le demandeur au pourvoi n'était ni européen ni assimilé[32] ou bien lorsqu'il ne résultait pas de l'arrêt attaqué que le requérant était indigène de Madagascar, la Cour de cassation, par cette subtilité juridique admettait la recevabilité du pourvoi[33], faisant ainsi bénéficier un indigène d'une cassation pour motifs insuffisants (renvoi devant la même Cour composée d'autres juges). C'est donc essentiel, dans un monde où les textes restent rares de pouvoir contrôler les juges sur absence de motifs, faute de pouvoir les contrôler sur les coutumes non rédigées ou sur la base d'un autre texte.

L'article 7 de la loi du 20 avril 1810 voulait l'annulation «pour défaut de motifs». En cas d'absence de motifs, la décision est dépourvue de toute motivation sur le point litigieux et le juge est directement passé de la présentation des faits et de l'exposé des parties à l'énonciation du dispositif. Ou encore les motifs existent mais ils sont contradictoires et la contradiction porte sur les faits relatés par les juges. Il s'agit d'un pur vice de forme.

---

30 Une solution identique valait pour les coutumes de l'Inde où, suivant une jurisprudence constante, l'interprétation et la prétendue violation de la loi indigène ou des coutumes indigènes dans les colonies échappait au contrôle de la Cour de cassation «à moins que la loi indigène résulte d'un texte formel, rédigé ou visé et promulgué par le législateur français» (confirmé par toute une série d'arrêts cités au Penant, 1922, art. 4253, arrêt Cass. Chambre Civile, 2 mai 1922, notes 1 et 2). Le contrôle de la Cour ne doit s'exercer que lorsque le législateur s'est «approprié les dispositions sur telle matière spécialement visée» (comme ce fut le cas pour le droit musulman en Inde et en Algérie). Mais si le pourvoi s'appuie uniquement sur des opinions de jurisconsultes, il n'y a pas lieu à cassation.

31 Arrêt du 6 mai 1911, Penant 1911, 3016, 6.

32 Arrêt du 22 juillet 1909, Penant 1910, 1, 2871, 349.

33 Penant, 1916, Article 3547, audience du 28 octobre 1915, cassation Chambre criminelle.

Mais motiver un arrêt, c'est le motiver complètement. A l'absence de motifs s'ajoute l'insuffisance des motifs: Le jugement manque de base légale. Il s'agit d'un vice de fond. Le juge ne s'est pas prononcé sur tous les chefs de la demande, les motifs existent mais, incomplets ou imprécis, ils ne permettent pas à la Cour de cassation d'exercer son contrôle sur le droit. Ce «défaut» révèle une carence des juges du fond dans la présentation des conditions d'application de la règle de droit qui avait vocation à régir la cause. Il apparaît lorsque le raisonnement du juge, à un de ses stades, est affecté par des insuffisances, soit au stade de la vérification des faits (le juge fait produire des effets juridiques à des faits non vérifiés), soit au stade de leur qualification juridique (le juge ne précise pas pourquoi telle qualification doit être retenue), soit, enfin, au stade du raisonnement *in fine* (le juge n'énonce pas la règle de droit sur la base de laquelle il tranche le litige, ou bien il omet de caractériser l'ensemble de ses conditions juridiques d'application)[34].

Ces deux approches, toutes deux relevant du pourvoi pour motivation inexistante et insuffisante, sont d'un intérêt majeur: elles confortent l'exercice d'un contrôle par la Cour de cassation, forcent le juge à prendre conscience de la valeur de son opinion, permettent au plaideur d'avoir une justification de la décision des juges et facilitent l'analyse scientifique de la jurisprudence[35]. Elles ont été manifestement l'un des moyens les plus fréquents de cassation, ce qui l'a fait qualifier par un auteur de «vulgaire»[36], signe sans doute de l'attention que prend la Cour de cassation à l'application stricte de la règle mais également indice peut-être, soit d'une négligence singulière des magistrats (ce qui peut toujours arriver), soit de leur embarras devant l'incertitude sur la teneur et les limites de la règle (il est vrai que la doctrine est souvent en désaccord sur ces questions, une partie d'entre elle proposant de renoncer à maintenir le manque de base légale parmi les cas d'ouverture à cassation, cas qui se ramèneraient essentiellement à la violation de la loi; quant à la jurisprudence, elle peine parfois à ranger clairement certains situations dans une catégorie ou dans l'autre).

Et pourtant, la distinction reste fort utile, car le défaut de motifs est considéré, majoritairement comme un vice de forme (et à ce titre, l'arrêt prendra en compte la règle du code de procédure civile), le manque de base légale est un vice de fond (et l'arrêt sera rendu au visa du texte de fond dont l'une des conditions d'application n'a pas été suffisamment caractérisée par le juge du fond). En tout cas, annotant un arrêt de la Cour de cassation du 14 décembre 1936, un professeur à la Faculté de droit de Bordeaux relevait qu'une «jurisprudence aussi abondante (autour de la règle sanctionnée par l'article 7 de la loi de 1810) et tant de recours en cassation... n'est évidemment pas un résultat dont il y ait lieu de se féliciter»[37].

---

34 Voir sur ces points *Jean Vincent/Serge Guinchard*, Procédure civile, Dalloz, 1994, n° 1521, p. 893 et s.

35 *J. Vincent/S. Guinchard*, Procédure civile, op. cit., n° 1232 et n° 1521 et s.

36 *L. Hugueney*, note au Sirey 1923, 1, 145.

37 Penant, 1938, art. 5847, Audience du 14 décembre 1936, p. 309 et s.

Il n'est pas certain qu'en matière coloniale, on ne puisse au contraire se féliciter de la fréquence des pourvois pour manque de base légale ou absence de motifs. Retenant la Cour de cassation comme seule compétente, ceci impliquait un contrôle attentif des arrêts rendus et une attention particulière portée aux motifs avancés et, compte tenu de la complexité du droit appliqué aux colonies et des incertitudes sur la législation elle-même, cela permettait de tenir la juges coloniaux sous la surveillance d'une Cour qui, bien qu'éloignée, pouvait veiller par ce canal au respect élémentaire de certains principes. La Cour de cassation leur rappellera continûment que, dans les décisions rendues, les motifs qui les étayent sont là pour «mettre la Cour de cassation à même d'exercer son contrôle»[38].

On ne saurait pour autant en conclure, *a priori*, que les juges coloniaux, souvent critiqués pour leurs connaissances modestes du droit (la rareté des magistrats impose des intérims exercés par des non professionnels), les difficultés qu'ils rencontrent dans leur carrière (déplacements fréquents) et dans l'exercice de leurs fonctions (manque de textes), aient été particulièrement sanctionnés. Sans donner à ces chiffres valeur certaine (mais le Recueil Penant dresse de la cassation en ce domaine un bilan systématique), on peut constater globalement que les pourvois en matière pénale sont très majoritairement sanctionnés par des rejets. En revanche, il est exact que les arrêts de cassation pour absence de motifs ou absence de base légale, parce qu'ils renvoient aux juges coloniaux (la plupart du temps d'ailleurs, la même Cour autrement composée), sont, à leur manière, une invitation à respecter le droit comme à le connaître, renvoyant au code de procédure civile ou au code pénal, ou pour les arrêts de rejet, «certificat de bon jugement». De sorte qu'en matière de motifs «coloniaux», plutôt que d'emboîter le pas aux distinctions habituelles entre le fond et la forme, nous préfèrerons mettre l'accent sur cette pédagogie mise en œuvre par la Cour de cassation. Sa jurisprudence varie entre rappel brutal des règles élémentaires, invitation à affiner l'analyse juridique et, bien sûr, confirmation des décisions des juges coloniaux, y compris pour motifs implicites ou par l'acceptation de suppléer aux motifs erronés.

a) Sanctionner les erreurs grossières

Nous signalions plus haut la motivation souvent négligente de quelques juges coloniaux. Ainsi de cet arrêt déjà mentionné par nous, dans lequel la Cour d'appel de la Réunion s'était contenté «de reproduire les termes de la loi» relatifs à la tenue d'une maison de jeux de hasard et d'une fumerie d'opium sans indiquer «ni la nature des jeux pratiqués, ni si le rôle du hasard y était prépondérant... (ni fait) connaître les circonstances desquelles (les juges) ont induit que le prévenu avait facilité à autrui l'usage de l'opium», ni d'ailleurs «expressément déclaré la culpabilité»! On voit mal comment la Chambre criminelle de la Cour de cassation aurait pu faire autrement que de conclure à la violation de l'article 7 de la loi du 20

[38] Penant 1896, art. 909, Audience du 29 avril 1896, p. 243 et s.

avril 1810 et de constater qu'elle était dans l'impossibilité de vérifier s'il a été légalement fait application des textes de loi visés par l'arrêt» et «qu'en cet état la décision attaquée manque de base»[39]. C'est en ce domaine une position constante car la Cour de cassation, qui se contente, en France, de l'énonciation du jeu (du moins quant il s'agit de jeux connus) mais refuse en matière indigène que l'on se contente de dénommer le jeu et de dire que c'est un jeu de hasard. Le caractère de jeu de hasard étant la condition de la pénalité, la Cour de cassation casse les arrêts qui ne lui permettent pas, par de suffisantes précisions, de vérifier que le jeu en question est bien un jeu de hasard. De nombreux arrêts décident, à défaut, qu'il n'est pas possible à la Cour de cassation de vérifier ce caractère[40].

Dans une autre affaire relative à la législation sur les débits de boisson, la Cour de cassation casse un jugement du tribunal correctionnel d'Oujda du 11 décembre 1924 qui avait condamné un marocain et son épouse (relaxés en première instance) pour «délit d'ouverture d'un débit de boissons à consommer sur place sans autorisation» en se contentant d'énoncer «qu'avaient été vues sur la terrasse des prévenus et assises à leur table des personnes devant qui se trouvaient des verres contenant un liquide ayant l'aspect de l'anisette». La Cour de cassation notera que l'arrêt, ne spécifiant aucuns faits permettant d'induire que cette boisson ait été servi moyennant paiement, manque de base légale[41].

Cette démarche, assez grossière, s'était produite devant la Cour de Nouméa en 1901. Deux accusés de vols avaient été renvoyés devant la Cour criminelle pour avoir «ensemble et de concert» soustraits frauduleusement argent, bijoux, papiers et valeurs, à l'aide de fausses clefs. Or, après avoir «successivement déclarés coupables les deux accusés sur le fait principal ci-dessus spécifié», la Cour avait décidé pour l'un qu'il l'avait commis seul et pour l'autre qu'il l'avait commis avec le premier! Irrégulière et contradictoire la déclaration de la Cour fut cassée avec renvoi devant la même Cour autrement composée, en raison d'une contradiction manifeste[42].

Ces cassations sont aussi l'occasion de rappeler aux Cours d'appel leur pouvoir de contrôle sur les premiers juges. Ainsi dans un arrêt de la Chambre correctionnelle de la Cour d'appel de Hanoi qui avait relaxé un dénommé Commans, accusé d'avoir abusé de son autorité pour inciter un délinquant à porter des coups à un tiers, sur la constatation qu'il n'avait en réalité «aucune autorité sur lui». Mais dans le même arrêt, la Chambre correctionnelle avait souligné «qu'il y avait doute sur le point de savoir si Commans avait donné l'ordre de frapper les indigènes... et que sur quatre plaignants un seul a été entendu... ce qui ne permet pas de contrôler les dépositions les unes par les autres», ce qui aurait été utile à la manifestation de la vérité! La Cour de cassation en conclura que «le doute dont la Cour a

---

39 Dareste, 1927 Cour de cassation, 10 décembre 1926, p. 39 et s.

40 Voir les références sous l'arrêt du 13 mars 1908, Penant, 1908, p. 270 et s. note 2.

41 Recueil Dareste, 1926, p. 24 et s., Chambre criminelle, 31 janvier 1925.

42 Recueil Dareste, 1902, arrêt du 10 janvier 1902, p. 47 et s.

fait bénéficier Commans a été motivé par l'insuffisance même de l'information suivie devant les premiers juges», qu'il appartenait à la Cour d'ordonner les mesures d'instruction qu'elle constatait avoir été omises et qu'elle déclarait être utiles à la manifestation de la vérité... «que faute par elle d'avoir ordonné les dites mesures, elle n'a pu légalement faire état pour infirmer le jugement de condamnation du doute qui lui paraissait exister en faveur de Commans; qu'il suit de là que la décision de relaxe est insuffisamment motivée et que l'arrêt doit être cassé»[43].

On peut rapprocher de cet exemple une autre affaire pour laquelle la Cour d'appel a fait preuve de nonchalance. Ainsi à l'occasion d'un arrêté du Gouverneur général de l'Indochine qui décide que la détention de substances en macération ou en fermentation constitue une infraction en matière de fabrication d'alcools et est imputable au propriétaire ou locataire du terrain sur lequel les substances sont trouvées. Il va de soi que cette présomption légale établie par la loi peut être écartée par le juge mais il devra alors apporter la preuve contraire et ne pas se contenter d'extraire des faits le moyen de «douter de la culpabilité». En l'espèce, la Cour d'appel avait prononcé la relaxe du propriétaire sur la seule constatation qu'un tiers avait fui au moment de la découverte, «ce qui pouvait laisser croire», selon la Cour d'appel, «qu'il avait dissimulé ces substances sur le terrain d'autrui». La Chambre criminelle trouvera que «le doute très sérieux» sur la culpabilité du propriétaire invoqué par la Cour d'appel ne constituait pas une preuve contraire et qu'en conséquence «l'arrêt attaqué n'a pas donné une base légale à sa décision»[44].

b) Invitation à affiner les motifs

Pour d'autres affaires, l'erreur sur les motifs semble moins étonnante et le juge de cassation, qui relève une erreur de raisonnement, indique la direction à suivre.

C'est souvent le cas lorsqu'un désaccord existe quant à l'application d'un texte à une situation donnée. On prendra pour exemple une affaire concernant l'Indochine. Le 4 septembre 1897, la chambre correctionnelle de la Cour d'appel de Saigon avait condamné à deux mois de prison deux annamites pour avoir négligé d'informer le procureur de la République d'un vol commis dans la commune. Elle s'appuyait sur le décret du 20 mars 1880 qui tout en rendant le code pénal applicable aux Annamites prévoyait que pour les délits et contraventions non prévus par le présent code les tribunaux continueraient d'appliquer les lois, règlements et coutumes annamites. Or l'article 63 du code annamite disait expressément que «lorsqu'il y aura lieu d'informer une autorité supérieure et que cette autorité ne sera pas informée, la peine sera...». Le procureur général quant à lui avait prétendu que

[43] Renvoi devant la Cour de Saigon, Penant, 1900, art. 1425, audience du 10 novembre 1899, p. 53 et s.

[44] Recueil Dareste, 1930, p. 147 et s., Cass. 11 avril 1929.

cette affaire relevait du pouvoir disciplinaire des administrateurs et plaidait l'incompétence. Quant aux deux demandeurs «cultivateurs lettrés» ils avaient invoqué l'article 7 de la loi du 20 avril 1810 (d'ailleurs à tort, ce texte n'étant pas applicable à l'Indochine mais bien l'article 2 du décret du 17 mai 1895 prescrivant de motiver les jugements dans la colonie). La Chambre criminelle de la Cour de cassation, négligeant le pourvoi du procureur avait, en revanche, estimé que la formulation du code annamite en termes très généraux ne permettait ni de spécifier «les cas dans lesquels cet avis à donner à l'autorité supérieure d'un fait qui vient de se produire est obligatoire sous une sanction pénale», ni de faire connaître à quelles personnes incombait, dans chaque commune, l'obligation de donner cet avis et que l'arrêt attaqué ne s'expliquait pas davantage sur ces deux points «d'une importance capitale». En conséquence, elle rappellera que la règle «*nulla poena sine lege*» était une règle d'ordre public et que «l'insuffisance des motifs de l'arrêt entrepris» ne permettait pas à la Cour d'exercer un droit de contrôle et de vérifier si le fait poursuivi était légalement punissable[45].

C'est aussi le cas pour la cassation pour contradiction de motifs, ou pour contradiction entre motifs et dispositif, parce que, plus subtiles, ces erreurs des juges du fond permettent à la Cour de cassation de leur rappeler la signification du droit.

Ainsi d'un arrêt de la Chambre des mises en accusation de la Cour d'appel de Madagascar, cassé avec renvoi à la même chambre autrement composée. Un colon avait tenté d'obtenir d'un chef de district et obtenu d'un chef de poste administratif par des présents un appui pour déterminer des indigènes à lui vendre des bœufs. La chambre des mises en accusation avait jugé que «les interventions d'un fonctionnaire auprès des particuliers pour favoriser des entreprises commerciales ne peuvent en aucun cas constituer un acte de la fonction», alors pourtant qu'elle avait également constaté l'existence de prescriptions émanant du Gouverneur et visant à inviter les «chefs de district et de poste administratif» à donner aide et secours «aux entreprises des colons». La Chambre criminelle de la Cour de cassation estimera quant à elle qu'il y avait contradictions de motifs et retiendra la corruption de fonctionnaires[46].

Ainsi également pour une contradiction entre motifs et dispositif, ce qui arrive lorsque la Cour d'appel infirme sur tel point la décision intervenue, mais ne dit pas pourquoi ou bien lorsqu'elle confirme le dispositif sans s'en approprier les motifs mais sans faire connaître ceux qu'elle entend y substituer. Lorsque cette règle n'est pas respectée, la Cour de cassation juge qu'il y a contradiction entre les motifs et le dispositif, ce qui équivaut à un défaut de motifs et donc à la nullité de l'arrêt. Cette jurisprudence constante fut évidemment transposée dans les colonies.

---

45 Recueil Dareste, 1898, p. 17 et s., Cass., 24 décembre 1897; voir au Penant, 1898, art. 1182, audience du 24 décembre 1897, renvoi à la cour autrement composée.

46 Arrêt du 12 décembre 1925, Penant, 1926, art. 4673, p. 127 et s.

Ainsi pour la Nouvelle-Calédonie en 1937, à la suite d'une convention intervenue entre deux colons. En échange du désintéressement de ses créanciers, le locataire d'un domaine (Blum) s'était engagé à livrer du bétail en remboursement de son dû, la moitié du prix des têtes lui étant seulement versée, l'autre moitié étant conservée par son créancier (Chabert). L'exécution de la convention posa vite problème, le créancier négligeant de verser la moitié du prix, le débiteur, par voie de conséquence ne livrant pas et s'opposant à la capture des bêtes par le premier... Le tribunal de Nouméa donna raison à Blum, estimant que Chabert avait commis toute une série de manquements. En appel, la Cour d'appel de Nouméa, estima que les deux parties étaient en faute... mais que Blum, le locataire, devait supporter complètement les conséquences de ces défaillances! La Cour de cassation n'eut aucune peine à constater que cette décision avait opéré «un renversement complet de la situation juridique, telle qu'elle avait été décrite et fixée par les premiers juges, sans réfuter ou même viser la plupart des griefs qui avaient été retenues par ceux-ci à la charge de Chabert»; qu'en outre, les juges en appel avaient fait allusion à la faute que Chabert aurait «commise en omettant de respecter l'une des clauses du contrat, sans préciser davantage à ce sujet et en passant sous silence les divers manquements au contrat dont ledit Chabert se serait rendu coupable... »; «que la Cour néglige de répondre effectivement au grief admis par le tribunal... d'où il suit que la Cour de Nouméa a rendu des arrêts qui sont dépourvus de motifs... introduisant dans sa décision une contradiction entre les motifs et le dispositif, laquelle équivaut à une absence de motifs» (casse et annule, renvoi devant la même Cour autrement composée[47].

c) Adhésion aux motifs satisfaisants

Les parties ne sauraient attendre de la Cour de cassation qu'elle suive systématiquement leurs demandes. Les arrêts de rejet, rapportés au recueil Penant entre les années 1895 et 1936 et ne retenant pas «la violation de l'article 7 de la loi du 20 avril 1810 pour défaut de motifs et absence de base légale», attestent de ce que les juges coloniaux «motivent suffisamment leurs décisions et échappent ainsi, sur ce point, à la censure de la Cour de cassation»[48]. Il faut reconnaître toutefois que ces arrêts confirment l'élaboration d'un droit conforme aux principes les mieux reconnus, car les pourvois présentés ne sont pas faits à la légère et la Cour de cassation en est réduite à rappeler les règles sur son droit à suppléer aux motifs erronés ou à valider les motifs implicites ou qui manquent de netteté.

Ainsi des motifs erronés. Le juge de paix de Saint-Louis avait, par décision du 26 février 1907, ordonné la radiation de la liste électorale d'un indigène, né dans la province du Gandiole, inscription qui avait été décidée par la commission municipale. En droit, la décision fut confirmée, cet indigène n'étant ni citoyen français ni

47 Penant, 1938, art. 5785, audience du 9 février 1937, p. 75 et s.

48 Environ 44 arrêts de rejet ainsi libellés.

originaire d'une des quatre communes organisées dans la colonie du Sénégal. Mais, le pourvoi en cassation reprochait aussi au juge de paix de ne pas avoir appliqué le décret organique de 1852 qui veut dans son article 2 que l'on renvoie les parties devant les juges compétents dans les cas où «la demande implique la solution préjudicielle d'une question d'état». Le juge de paix avait rejeté ce sursis en mettant en avant le fait qu'il était à la fois juge de paix et juge unique du tribunal civil et par conséquent qu'il ne pouvait renvoyer l'affaire à lui-même, confondant ainsi ses pouvoirs de président du tribunal civil et ses pouvoirs de juge d'appel en matière électorale, erreur manifeste. Le motif mis en avant était donc erroné. Mais, par ailleurs, d'autres raisons de droit militaient en faveur de la décision rendue. D'une part, les questions de capacité électorale (domicile, résidence, délais) ne sont pas des questions d'état (âge, ou nationalité) et la référence au décret de 1852 tombait d'elle-même. D'autre part, une jurisprudence constante de la Cour de cassation décidait que le juge de paix pouvait refuser le sursis lorsque la question soulevée pouvait être facilement résolue ou qu'il ne devait consentir au sursis que si la question préjudicielle était «sérieuse». En l'espèce le juge avait commis une erreur de doctrine. Or une jurisprudence constante décidait que «quelles que soient les erreurs de doctrine que contiennent les motifs, l'arrêt ne peut être cassé que s'il décide contrairement à la loi; donc maintenu si la loi n'a pas été violée». La Cour de cassation rejettera donc le pourvoi (tout en reconnaissant que c'est à tort que le juge s'est fondé sur un argument inexact) en affirmant que «ce motif erroné n'est pas de nature à vicier la décision qui est justifiée par un motif de droit qu'il appartient à la Cour suprême de suppléer»[49].

De même, la Cour se satisfait de motifs évidents même s'ils manquent de netteté. Le 4 juin 1896, la Chambre criminelle se satisfait de ce que la Cour d'assises de Constantine se soit appropriée les conclusions du Ministère public, se bornant à dire «que les faits allégués n'étaient pas nouveaux et que la fausseté en était démontrée»; il lui a donc paru qu'un supplément d'instruction n'apporterait aucune lumière nouvelle sur des faits déjà connus et examinés; d'où il suit que le refus de renvoyer l'affaire à une autre session «ne saurait être considéré comme insuffisamment motivé»[50]. De même, considère-t-elle qu'un arrêt peut être «régulièrement motivé sur des conclusions d'appel incident prises à la barre, alors surtout qu'il est constant, d'après l'ordonnance de règlement des qualités de l'arrêt, que ces conclusions ont été prises et que la Cour a statué sur le point spécial qu'elles visaient»[51]. De même, à l'occasion d'une action en recherche de paternité naturelle, la Cour de cassation considère que la décision rendue par le tribunal supérieur de Papeete, confirmée par adoption de motifs, n'a pas besoin d'indiquer quel est le cas sur les cinq retenus par la loi du 16 novembre 1912, modifiant l'article 340 du Code civil mais peut se contenter de dire «qu'il résulte de l'enquête que

49 Penant, 1908, Cass. Civ. 24 juillet 1907, art. 2582, p. 362 et s. Voir note 2.

50 Penant, 1896, p. 415 et s. art. 963.

51 Penant, 1908, art. 2535, Cass. Chambre des requêtes, audience du 30 mai 1907, p. 227 et s.

le défendeur» était fier de cet enfant, qu'il le considérait comme son fils, avait l'intention de le reconnaître, n'avait pas contesté avoir vécu en concubinage avec la mère pendant la période légale de la conception et n'avait pas apporté la preuve que celle-ci avait eu commerce avec un autre homme[52].

La Cour se satisfait enfin de motifs implicites. Ainsi un bailleur par la faute duquel un litige est survenu avec son locataire ne saurait prétendre que la Cour d'appel n'a pas motivé son refus d'accueillir sa demande de dommages et intérêts (pour dépenses et dérangements causés par le procès et difficulté de relouer l'immeuble) et, en conséquence, a violé l'article 7 de la loi du 20 avril 1810. En effet, en indiquant que le litige est «provenu surtout de la faute du bailleur» qui avait enfreint ses obligations contractuelles, la Cour a «d'une manière implicite» justifié le rejet de ses conclusions[53]. Il en va de même pour un litige né entre un propriétaire de navire et une compagnie mettant en cause sa responsabilité pour les avaries occasionnées aux marchandises transportées. Or, une clause du connaissement avait prévu que le propriétaire du navire ne répondrait pas, vis-à-vis des chargeurs, des fautes ou des négligences du capitaine ou des gens de l'équipage. Les chargeurs avaient dans un «deuxième moyen» invoqué la violation de l'article 7 de la loi du 20 avril 1810 en avançant «qu'en assistant à l'expertise et par leur correspondance, les propriétaires avaient renoncé à se prévaloir de l'article 2 du connaissement». La Cour d'appel de Bordeaux, quant à elle, avait jugé qu'était valable cette clause, et «en décidant qu'à aucun point de vue cet article ne saurait être écarté du débat» avait dès lors, implicitement motivé le rejet desdites conclusions et satisfait, par suite, à la prescription de l'article 7 de la loi du 20 avril 1810». La Cour de cassation estimera qu'en ce faisant, elle avait suffisamment motivé sa décision en «rejetant implicitement le moyen, présenté comme un chef distinct mais qui n'est en réalité qu'un motif de ces mêmes conclusions qui se rattache par un lien direct à la question de fond relative à la validité et à la portée de la cause». La Chambre civile rejettera le pourvoi[54]. A plus forte raison, la Cour de Saigon, en décidant que l'affaire était jugée selon les principes de droit annamite, avait, à juste raison, rejeté les règles du droit français relatives à l'arbitrage. En se fondant sur le droit indigène, le juge décide implicitement que les parties n'ont pas entendu se soumettre à l'application de la loi française et ne viole donc pas l'article 7 de la loi[55].

---

52 Penant, 1927, p. 187 et s., art. 4812, audience du 17 janvier 1927, Cass. Chambre des requêtes.

53 Penant, 1896, art. 885, Audience du 5 novembre 1895, Chambre des requêtes, p. 166 et s.

54 Penant, 1896, art. 852, Audience du 18 Novembre 1895, p. 58 et s.

55 Penant, 1900, Cass. Requêtes, 26 décembre 1899, p. 84–85.

Conclusion

Sans doute ne peut-il s'agir que d'une conclusion partielle, le sujet méritant l'exploitation d'un plus grand nombre de jugements et d'arrêts. En l'état, on peut toutefois rassembler quelques observations.

D'une part, la jurisprudence coloniale montre un grand respect de la légalité. Même le contrôle des motifs ne peut inciter les juges à trop s'éloigner du dispositif législatif dès lors qu'il est précis. On en a un exemple symbolique dans un arrêt de la Chambre criminelle du 26 juin 1897, d'une sobriété absolue, qui se prononce sur une affaire de spéculation ayant mis en émoi l'opinion publique à Saigon. Le secrétaire et interprète de l'administrateur était accusé d'avoir favorisé des adjudicataires en se faisant remettre des pots-de-vin et avait été envoyé devant le tribunal de Mytho sous prévention de corruption comme agent de l'administration (article 175 du Code pénal). Le tribunal s'était déclaré incompétent, estimant que l'administrateur avait seul qualité pour faire le contrat; sur appel du procureur général, la Cour de Saigon l'avait condamné à 6 mois de prison par arrêt du 13 mars 1897, arrêt qui fut cassé par la Chambre criminelle sur pourvoi de Tran-daï-Hoc, démontrant qu'il n'était pas fonctionnaire mais «que tous les décrets tendent à remettre tous les pouvoirs aux mains des administrateurs à l'exclusion des *phu* qui ne sont que de simples auxiliaires indigènes». L'annotateur, confirmera que «tout en déplorant sans doute sa décision... ne pouvait pas traiter Hoc comme fonctionnaire au point de vue de la responsabilité, alors que la Cour de Saigon elle-même n'avait point su caractériser la nature de ses fonctions». De fait la Cour de cassation (mais en renvoyant à la même Cour composée d'autres juges) prendra acte de ce qu'il n'était pas constaté que Hoc au moment de la perception d'un intérêt était dans ses fonctions de *phu,* ni même constaté d'ailleurs de quel type de fonctions il s'agissait. Elle en conclura que les éléments du délit n'étaient pas complètement établis et par conséquent que les faits de la prévention n'étaient pas suffisamment exposés par l'arrêt, et qu'à ce point de vue, «il ne fournissait pas les éléments nécessaires pour apprécier la légalité de la décision». Tout en reconnaissant que la Cour de cassation ne pouvait faire autrement, l'annotateur observait que «l'impression ressentie en Cochinchine à l'annonce de la décision n'en sera pas moins des plus fâcheuses»[56].

D'autre part, la jurisprudence relative au contrôle des motifs fait la démonstration qu'elle n'est ni plus abondante qu'en France ni plus spectaculaire. Cassations et rejets y sont assez semblables pour des raisons identiques, ce qui atteste sur ce point d'un transfert de droits tout à fait intéressant visant à une égalité de traitement des justiciables, compte tenu bien sûr de ce que nous avons dit de l'originalité de la cassation sur ces territoires.

Enfin, les motivations permettent de saisir l'originalité de la place des juges coloniaux dont l'indépendance reste grande tant en ce qui concerne certains indi-

---

[56] Penant, 1897, art. 1100, Audience du 26 juin 1897, p. 259 et s.

gènes, interdits de recours, qu'en ce qui concerne le fond du droit. Dans le même temps, parties prenantes à la politique judiciaire, ils font preuve d'une autonomie certaine, que leur procure l'obscurité des textes ou leur absence, pour justifier leurs positions, convaincre de la justesse de leurs motifs même si par ailleurs cette autonomie les fait pencher vers un certain arbitraire que dévoilent les erreurs grossières en matière de motifs. C'est tout le mérite du contrôle de la Cour de cassation sur l'absence ou l'insuffisance de motifs que d'avoir dégagé, pour les territoires coloniaux, une pratique du respect du Droit.

Summary

The study of motivations of judicial decisions in the colonies of the French Third Republic allows us to appreciate the role played by judges and the margin of interpretation available to them, in a society of increasing complexity; this is an example of «living law» which leaves judges a certain latitude, confronting specific facts with juridical concepts. The grounds of the judgment refer back to the juridical system itself. The grounds can be different in a country where the law depends on statutes (the priority is the will to justify the decision) and in a country where the law depends on the judge (the priority is the motivation to convince). What is the situation then in colonial territories subjet to legislative texts which do not cover all questions of law, and where the judges have more power than those in the home country?

A study of colonial jurisprudence under the Third Republic shows that in cases where the relevant texts were precise and where the authority of the State was at stake, the motivations were laconic. The reference to the statute was essential, and considered by the judge to be sufficient to justify his decision. But in cases where there was no pertinent statute, or where the statute was not well understood, in areas where colonisation was at stake, in questions of colonial policy, the judge resorted to the art of persuasion. The justifying motivation in this case was superfluously abundant. A study of judicial review of motivations in colonial matters, which was the prerogative of the Cour de cassation, shows that the court gave increasing importance to appeals on the basis of absence of legal justification. In this way, the jurisprudence of the Cour de cassation was the instrument of a perfect equality of treatment of subjects and a means of progress of law and of the respect of principles in colonial territories.

KNUT WOLFGANG NÖRR

Zur Bindungswirkung von Entscheidungsgründen: das Beispiel des deutschen Bundesverfassungsgerichts

I. Einführung

Im Vergleich zum Supreme Court der Vereinigten Staaten blickt das deutsche Bundesverfassungsgericht auf eine kurze Geschichte zurück: seine erste Entscheidung hat es im Jahr 1951 gefällt. Die deutsche Verfassungstheorie pflegt fünf Verfassungsorgane aufzuzählen, die sich die staatliche Macht und Verantwortung auf der Ebene des Bundes teilen: Bundestag, Bundesrat (hier sind die Länder vertreten, 16 an der Zahl), der Kanzler mit seinem Kabinett, der Bundespräsident (mit im wesentlichen integrativer und staatsrepräsentierender Funktion) und eben das Bundesverfassungsgericht. Zieht man den Vergleich genauer zwischen dem deutschen und dem amerikanischen Gerichtshof, dann fallen freilich bestimmte grundlegende Unterschiede auf; zu ihnen zählt die Tatsache, dass der deutsche Gerichtshof auf die Entscheidung über solche Fälle beschränkt ist, in denen die Verfassung als Prüfungsmaßstab in Frage kommt. Andere Fälle werden von anderen obersten Bundesgerichten entschieden, und hier hat die historische Entwicklung zu dem Ergebnis geführt, dass in Deutschland neben dem Bundesverfassungsgericht noch fünf weitere oberste Bundesgerichte bestehen, nämlich der Bundesgerichtshof für Zivil- und Strafsachen, sowie Bundesgerichte jeweils für Verwaltungs-, Steuer-, Arbeits- und Sozialversicherungsstreitigkeiten. Ein anderer grundlegender Unterschied zwischen dem deutschen und amerikanischen Gerichtssystem ergibt sich aus dem unterschiedlichen föderativen System der beiden Staatsgebilde. Denn eine genaue Trennung von Bundesgerichtsbarkeit einerseits und Gerichtsbarkeit der Einzelstaaten andererseits ist dem deutschen Modell fremd, hier sind die Gerichte auf Bundes- und Länderebene miteinander verwoben: alle Tatsacheninstanzen sind Gerichte der Länder, gegen deren Entscheidungen dann gegebenenfalls Rechtsmittel beim jeweiligen Bundesgericht eingelegt werden können.

II. Drei Kompetenzen des Bundesverfassungsgerichts

Die Kompetenzen des Bundesverfassungsgerichts sind an zwei Stellen geregelt: in der Verfassung selbst, das heißt dem Grundgesetz von 1949 (Art. 93 und 94 Abs. 2), und im Bundesverfassungsgerichtsgesetz von 1951. Mehr als ein Dutzend Arten von Streitigkeiten können vor den Gerichtshof gebracht werden, drei von ihnen sind für unsere Darstellung bedeutsam:

- Bestimmte politische Instanzen können das Bundesverfassungsgericht anrufen, wenn Streit oder Zweifel darüber bestehen, ob ein Bundes- oder Landesgesetz mit der Verfassung zu vereinbaren sind. Eine solche Prüfung können die Bundesregierung und die einzelnen Landesregierungen veranlassen, aber auch ein Drittel der Mitglieder des Bundestags. Letztere Möglichkeit wird natürlich von Oppositionsparteien genutzt, die verfassungsrechtlich zu erreichen suchen, was politisch ihnen nicht gelungen war. Diese Art der Streitigkeiten wird als abstrakte Normenkontrolle bezeichnet.
- Im deutschen Gerichtssystem ist die Prüfung der Verfassungsmäßigkeit von Gesetzen monopolisiert, das heißt der alleinigen Zuständigkeit des Bundesverfassungsgerichts übertragen. Daher haben Gerichte, die ein Gesetz für verfassungswidrig halten, das Verfahren auszusetzen und die Frage der Gültigkeit der anzuwendenden Norm dem Bundesverfassungsgericht vorzulegen. Dieses Verfahren nennt man konkrete Normenkontrolle.
- Die große Mehrzahl der Fälle gelangt an das Bundesverfassungsgericht auf dem Wege der Verfassungsbeschwerde. Dieses Rechtsbehelfs kann sich bedienen, wer behauptet, in einem seiner oder ihrer Grundrechte durch die öffentliche Gewalt verletzt worden zu sein. Da Verfassungsbeschwerden in aller Regel erst nach Erschöpfung des Rechtswegs erhoben werden können, handelt es sich ganz überwiegend um gesetzliche Normen oder um gerichtliche Entscheidungen, die angegriffen werden. So hat das Bundesverfassungsgericht auch schon Entscheidungen des Bundesgerichtshofs für verfassungswidrig erklärt.

III. Drei Gattungen seiner Entscheidung

Wenn das Bundesverfassungsgericht über Verfassungsmäßigkeit oder Verfassungswidrigkeit zu entscheiden hat, dann war es von Gesetzes wegen gewissermaßen binär programmiert, das heißt es konnte den in Frage stehenden Akt entweder wegen Verstoßes gegen die Verfassung für nichtig oder, weil kein Verstoß vorlag, für gültig erklären. Dieses Alles oder Nichts-Prinzip hat sich besonders dann, wenn die Gültigkeit von Gesetzen zur Prüfung anstand, als misslich und inadäquat erwiesen. Die Richter haben deshalb zwar nicht geradezu *contra,* wohl aber *praeter legem* eine Reihe von feiner gestimmten Instrumenten entwickelt, von denen drei im folgenden erwähnt seien:

- Wenn eine gesetzliche Bestimmung auf verschiedene Weise ausgelegt werden kann und die eine Auslegung mit der Verfassung übereinstimmt, die andere aber nicht, dann wählt das Gericht die der Verfassung entsprechende Auslegung und erklärt die Norm für gültig, soweit dieser Auslegung gefolgt wird. Das Verfahren wird als verfassungskonforme Auslegung von Gesetzen bezeichnet

Ein Beispiel (BVerfGE 64.229; 1983): Nach deutschem Recht sind alle Rechtsverhältnisse an Grundstücken im Grundbuch verzeichnet. In das Grundbuch kann aber Einblick nur nehmen, wer ein berechtigtes Interesse daran darlegt. In einer speziellen gesetzlichen Bestimmung war vorgesehen, dass öffentliche Behörden zur Einsicht befugt sind, ohne ein berechtigtes Interesse darlegen zu müssen. Die gängige Praxis hatte die Bestimmung dahin ausgelegt, dass unter öffentliche Behörden im Sinne der Bestimmung auch die Sparkassen fallen, da sie rechtlich als öffentlich-rechtliche Kreditinstitute organisiert sind. Hingegen müssen private Geschäftsbanken ein berechtigtes Interesse darlegen. Das wurde als Verstoß gegen den Gleichheitssatz (Art. 3 Grundgesetz) gerügt. Das Bundesverfassungsgericht hat die erwähnte Bestimmung als verfassungsgemäß aufrechterhalten und sie dahin ausgelegt, dass unter den Begriff der öffentlichen Behörde die Sparkassen nicht fallen, sie also wie die privaten Geschäftsbanken ein berechtigtes Interesse darlegen müssen, so dass beide Arten von Kreditinstituten gleich behandelt werden.

Es ist klar, dass in solchen Fällen auf die Urteilsbegründung zurückgegriffen werden muss, da sich aus ihr ergibt, welche Auslegung der Norm als verfassungskonform und welche als verfassungswidrig zu gelten hat.

- Nicht selten zögert das Bundesverfassungsgericht, eine Norm für nichtig zu erklären, und wählt stattdessen den Ausspruch der Unvereinbarkeit der Norm mit der Verfassung. Diesen Weg geht es vor allem aus zwei Gründen. Der eine Grund liegt in den Konsequenzen, die sich aus der Nichtigkeit einer Norm ergeben. Denn der Ausspruch der Nichtigkeit wirkt zurück, *ex tunc,* das heißt die Norm war von Anfang an nichtig, so dass unter Umständen alle Verwaltungsmaßnahmen, die auf der Norm beruhten, ebenfalls nichtig gewesen sind. Man stelle sich nur eine steuerrechtliche Regelung vor, die vielleicht erst nach jahrelanger Anwendung für nichtig erklärt wird. Der zweite Grund wirkt sich in solchen gesetzlichen Vorkehrungen aus, die eine bestimmte Gruppe von Personen begünstigen, eine andere aber nicht. Wird diese Differenzierung vom Gericht, weil gegen den Gleichheitssatz verstoßend, nicht akzeptiert, dann will es doch dem Gesetzgeber die Möglichkeit offenhalten, die Regelung entweder auch auf die bisher nicht einbezogene Personengruppe auszudehnen oder die Begünstigung überhaupt aus der Welt zu schaffen. Bisweilen wird dem Gesetzgeber eine Frist zum Tätigwerden vorgegeben. Die Erfindung des Bundesverfassungsgerichts, auf diese Weise Gesetze nicht als nichtig, sondern als verfassungswidrig zu erklären, kann man ihm als Exempel politischer Klugheit zugutehalten; jedenfalls hat der Gesetzgeber mittels Änderung des Bundesverfassungsgerichtsgesetzes 1970 den Ausspruch der Unvereinbarkeit mit dem Gesetzgeber rezipiert.

- Nicht weit hiervon entfernt ist der vom Bundesverfassungsgericht angewandte Kunstgriff, ein Gesetz für zur Zeit noch verfassungsmäßig zu halten, zugleich aber den Gesetzgeber davor zu warnen, das Gesetz würde in Zukunft als verfassungswidrig gelten, wenn er nicht tätig wird und das Gesetz entsprechend ändert oder ganz aufhebt.

  Ein Beispiel (BVerfGE 25.167; 1969): Nach dem Bürgerlichen Gesetzbuch (BGB) von 1896 waren uneheliche Kinder vom Erbrecht nach ihrem Vater ausgeschlossen; ihnen standen nur schuldrechtliche Ansprüche gegen den Erben zu. Das Grundgesetz von 1949 (Art. 6 Abs. 5) hat aber dem Gesetzgeber den bindenden Auftrag erteilt, den unehelichen Kindern die gleichen Bedingungen für ihre Entwicklung und ihre gesellschaftlicher Stellung zu schaffen wie den ehelichen Kindern. Der Gesetzgeber ist nun fast zwei Jahrzehnte lang untätig geblieben. Als in den späten 60er Jahren Verfassungsbeschwerde gegen das Urteil eines Zivilgerichts erhoben wurde, das auf der erwähnten Regelung des BGB beruhte, entschied das Bundesverfassungsgericht, dass zwar das Grundgesetz eine bestimmte Frist für das Tätigwerden des Gesetzgebers nicht gesetzt hat, ein angemessener Zeitraum aber nicht überschritten werden darf; den kritischen Zeitpunkt legte das Gericht auf das Ende der damals laufenden Legislaturperiode fest. Nach diesem Zeitpunkt tritt Nichtigkeit aller das uneheliche Kind diskriminierenden gesetzlichen Bestimmungen ein.

In diesem Beispiel stand fest, was der Gesetzgeber zu unternehmen hatte; in anderen Fällen boten die Richter dem Gesetzgeber Alternativen der Regelung an. Auch wurden ihm Fristen gesetzt. Für diese Variante der Entscheidungstätigkeit der Bundesverfassungsgerichts hat sich der Begriff der Appellentscheidung eingebürgert als einer Entscheidung, die an den Gesetzgeber appelliert, tätig zu werden.

IV. Drei Entscheidungswirkungen

Wenn wir uns nun den Wirkungen der Entscheidungen des Bundesverfassungsgerichts zuwenden, dann müssen wir drei Arten der Wirkung unterscheiden. Wir stellen sie im folgenden vor, doch wird uns von ihnen nur die zweite näher beschäftigen.

- Wie alle gerichtlichen Entscheidungen erwachsen auch die des Bundesverfassungsgerichts in Rechtskraft (*res judicata, estoppel by judgement*). Das ist nirgends gesetzlich festgehalten, weil als selbstverständlich vorausgesetzt. Es gelten dieselben Regeln wie im Prozessrecht aller anderen Gerichtszweige. So wird zwischen subjektiver und objektiver Rechtskraftwirkung unterschieden: subjektiv in dem Sinn, dass die Entscheidung nur für und gegen die Parteien wirkt, die den Rechtsstreit geführt haben; objektiv in Hinblick auf den Streitstoff, um den es gegangen ist und der dann jeweils genau zu definieren ist (sog. Verfahrensgegenstand). Der objektive Umfang der Rechtskraft ergibt sich aus dem Tenor der Entscheidung; handelt es sich um ein klage- oder beschwerdeabweisendes Urteil, dann ist regelmäßig die Urteilsbegründung heranzuziehen, um den Verfahrensgegenstand und so den Umfang der Rechtskraft festzustellen, ohne dass hierdurch die Entscheidungsgründe selbst in Rechtskraft erwüchsen.

- Von größerer Bedeutung für unsere Zwecke ist die sog. Bindungswirkung als eine Wirkung, die den Entscheidungen nur des Bundesverfassungsgerichts zu eigen ist. Gemäß einer Vorschrift des Bundesverfassungsgerichtsgesetzes – § 31 Abs. 1 BVerfGG – binden die Entscheidungen des Gerichtshofs „die Verfassungsorgane des Bundes und der Länder sowie alle Gerichte und Behörden" (nicht aber die Bürger und ihre Beziehungen untereinander). Das Bundesverfassungsgericht selbst ist an seine Entscheidungen nicht gebunden, ein Rechtsinstitut nach Art des *stare decisis* ist dem deutschen Recht unbekannt. Zu den Verfassungsorganen, die gebunden sind, gehört auch der Gesetzgeber, und die nähere Bestimmung dieser Bindung ist, wie man sich vorstellen kann, lebhaft umstritten.
- Schließlich wird durch § 31 Abs. 2 BVerfGG den Entscheidungen des Gerichtshofs Gesetzeskraft verliehen, soweit sie ein Gesetz für nichtig oder für mit dem Grundgesetz vereinbar oder unvereinbar erklären. Folgerichtig ist in diesen Fällen der Tenor der Entscheidung im Bundesgesetzblatt zu veröffentlichen.

V. Zur Bindungswirkung gegenüber dem Gesetzgeber

Wie schon angedeutet, ist die Bindungswirkung der Entscheidungen des Bundesverfassungsgerichts nach § 31 Abs. 1 BVerfGG besonders umstritten, soweit sich der Gesetzgeber daran zu orientieren hätte. Die Kontroverse erreichte hierbei die Richter selbst, als sie sich vor die Frage gestellt sahen. Noch nicht erwähnt haben wir, dass das Bundesverfassungsgericht in Wirklichkeit als eine Verknüpfung zweier Gerichte betrachtet werden kann, weil die Richter auf zwei Senate (von je acht Mitgliedern) verteilt sind und jeder Senat unabhängig vom anderen in ausschließlichen Zuständigkeit die Fälle entscheidet. Hierbei hat sich, aus welchen Gründen auch immer, umgangssprachlich für den 1. Senat das Attribut „roter", für den 2. aber „schwarzer" Senat eingebürgert, rot für eher den Sozialdemokraten (*liberals* im amerikanischen Sinn), schwarz den Unionsparteien nahestehend. Hat Bindung, so lautet die Frage, die Bedeutung, dass dem Gesetzgeber grundsätzlich nicht mehr gestattet ist, ein neues Gesetz desselben oder ähnlichen Inhalts zu erlassen, wenn das frühere Gesetz für verfassungswidrig erklärt worden war? Diese Ansicht, auch als Normwiederholungsverbot bezeichnet, hat der 2. Senat von Anfang an, freilich nur in knappen Sätzen, vertreten (BVerfGE 1.14,37; 1951), während der 1. Senat – inzwischen waren kritische Stimmen im Schrifttum laut geworden – in einer ausführlicheren Stellungnahme sich gegen das Verbot aussprach, BVerfGE 77.84, 103 (1987):

> § 31 BVerfGG und die Rechtskraft normverwerfender verfassungsgerichtlicher Entscheidungen hindern den Gesetzgeber nicht, eine inhaltsgleiche oder inhaltsähnliche Neurege-

lung zu beschließen. Das folgt bereits daraus, daß die gesetzgebende Gewalt im Unterschied zur vollziehenden und zur rechtsprechenden Gewalt in Art. 20 Abs. 3 GG nur an die verfassungsmäßige, nicht auch an die einfachgesetzliche Ordnung gebunden ist, als deren Urheberin sie gerade fungiert. Ebensowenig wie die von der Rechtskraft zu unterscheidende Bindungswirkung für das BVerfG selbst besteht (...), verwehrt diese einfachgesetzlich angeordnete Bindung es dem Gesetzgeber, seiner Gestaltungsfreiheit und Gestaltungsverantwortung durch Verabschiedung einer inhaltsgleichen Neuregelung nachzukommen, wenn er sie für erforderlich hält (...). Diese Beurteilung entspricht der besonderen Verantwortung des demokratisch legitimierten Gesetzgebers für die Anpassung der Rechtsordnung an wechselnde soziale Anforderungen und veränderte Ordnungsvorstellungen. Sie trägt zugleich den funktionellen und institutionellen Grenzen verfassungsgerichtlichen Rechtsschutzes, namentlich dem Umstand Rechnung, daß das BVerfG Akte der gesetzgebenden Gewalt an der Verfassung selbst und nicht an verfassungsgerichtlichen Präjudizien zu messen hat und seine Rechtsprechung nicht aus eigener Initiative korrigieren kann; sie beugt einer mit der rechts- und sozialstaatlichen Demokratie unvereinbaren Erstarrung der Rechtsentwicklung vor, ohne die Aufgaben und Befugnisse des BVerfG zur rechtsverbindlichen Auslegung der Verfassung und Gewährung wirksamen verfassungsgerichtlichen Rechtsschutzes zu gefährden.

In der Entscheidung wurde dem Gesetzgeber eine Neuregelung lapidar mit den Worten „wenn er sie für erforderlich hält", also seinem Ermessen anheimgestellt: eine Großzügigkeit, die dann doch einzuschränken der 1. Senat später für erforderlich hielt, BVerfGE 96.260, 263 (1997): Beim Erlass inhaltlich gleichlautender Bestimmungen kann der Gesetzgeber die vom Bundesverfassungsgericht festgestellten Gründe der Verfassungswidrigkeit des ursprünglichen Gesetzes nicht übergehen. Eine Normwiederholung verlangt vielmehr ihrerseits besondere Gründe, die sich vor allem aus einer wesentlichen Änderung der für die verfassungsrechtliche Beurteilung maßgeblichen tatsächlichen oder rechtlichen Verhältnisse oder der ihr zugrunde liegenden Anschauungen ergeben können.

Auf diese Weise wurde der Zwist zwischen den Senaten offenbar entschärft, der 2. Senat hat sich jedenfalls nicht gegen die Erwägungen des anderen Senats gewandt. Der Gesetzgeber selbst beherzigte dann die Forderungen des 1. Senats, wie einer Entscheidung aus dem Jahr 2000 zu entnehmen ist (BVerfGE 102.127, 141).

VI. Die Erstreckung der Bindungswirkung auf die tragenden Entscheidungsgründe I: zur Rechtsprechung des Bundesverfassungsgerichts

Als der 2. Senat in dem erwähnten Urteil von 1951 den Gesetzgeber streng an die Entscheidungen des Bundesverfassungsgerichts band, hat er zugleich, mit ebenso dürren Worten, die Bindungswirkung auf die den Tenor tragenden Entscheidungsgründe erstreckt. Weder die Verfassung noch der einfache Gesetzgeber im Bundesverfassungsgerichtsgesetz hatten diese Folgerung ausgesprochen; es handelte sich also um ein Postulat, eine Erfindung der Verfassungsrichter selbst (woran dann außer dem Gesetzgeber auch alle Gerichte und Behörden sich zu orientieren hätten). Die Sätze blieben nicht ohne Widerspruch; an der Diskussion beteiligten sich die Richter selbst in literarischen Äußerungen und begannen nun Argumente zu sammeln und vorzustellen, die die Gegner von ihrer Ansicht überzeugen sollten. Wenn hierbei die Notwendigkeit betont wurde, die Auslegung der Verfassung zu monopolisieren, damit Rechtssicherheit und Rechtsfrieden gewahrt würden und sich der Grundsatz der Gleichbehandlung durchsetzen könne, dann hatte sich im Grunde genommen der Bindungsmaßstab verschoben und war an die Stelle des Merkmals „tragende Entscheidungsgründe" die in der Begründung vorgenommene Verfassungsauslegung getreten. So oder so ist dann in der Einbeziehung der Entscheidungsgründe in die Bindungswirkung der 1. Senat bereitwillig den Spuren des 2. Senats gefolgt (BVerfGE 19.377, 392; 1966).

Gelegentlich haben sich die Richter konkret am Fall zum Thema geäußert. In einer Entscheidung zur Finanzierung politischer Parteien mit staatlichen Mitteln waren bestimmte gesetzliche Regelungen für verfassungswidrig erklärt worden, weil sie gegen den Grundsatz der Chancengleichheit der politischen Parteien verstießen. In der Begründung der Entscheidung hatte sich das Gericht mit der Argumentation auseinandergesetzt, Parteienfinanzierung mit staatlichen Mitteln seien per se durch die Verfassung verboten; dieser Ansicht waren die Richter nicht gefolgt. Ihre Ausführungen hierzu wären „tragend" gewesen, wenn die genannten Regelungen für gültig erklärt worden wären; sie waren aber nicht tragend, weil die Regelungen aus den erwähnten Gründen für verfassungswidrig erklärt worden waren (BVerfG 20.56, 87; 1966). Hatte eine Gesetzesnorm durch den Kunstgriff der verfassungskonformen Auslegung – siehe oben unter III – das rettende Ufer erreicht, dann umfasst die Bindungswirkung diejenigen Teile der Begründung, in denen eine an sich denkbare Auslegung als verfassungswidrig eingestuft worden war (BVerfGE 40.88, 93 f.; 1975).

Den Gegenbegriff zu den tragenden Gründen bilden die *obiter dicta,* die dem Bindungsgebot nicht unterliegen; aber sind die Grenzen immer eindeutig zu ziehen, bedenkt man nur die Freude am Argumentieren, zu der sich die Richter nicht selten in Dutzenden von Druckseiten bekannten? Fast skurril mutet es an, dass sich die beiden Senate über diese Frage in die Haare geraten sind. Hier ist zunächst nochmals ein Blick auf die innere Struktur des Bundesverfassungsgerichts zu werfen. Die zwei Senate hatten wir als selbständige und von einander unabhängige Spruchkörper kennengelernt, woraus natürlich unterschiedliche Ansichten über die Vereinbarkeit oder nicht eines bestimmten Aktes mit der Verfassung entspringen können. Für solche Fälle hat der Gesetzgeber die Einrichtung des Plenums vorgesehen, das unter Anwesenheit von mindestens zwei Drittel der Richter jedes Senats entscheidet (§ 16 BVerfGG). Weil den Entscheidungsgründen Bindungswirkung zugesprochen wird, ist es nur folgerichtig, dass das Plenum nicht nur dann anzurufen ist, wenn ein Senat von der Entscheidung, sondern auch wenn er von der tragenden Begründung des anderen Senats abweichen will. Und hier ist es nun eines Tages zum Konflikt zwischen den Senaten gekommen. Der 1. Senat hatte über Verfassungsbeschwerden zu entscheiden, die sich gegen Urteile der Zivilgerichte richteten, wonach die Unterhaltspflicht für ein Kind bei fehlgeschlagener Sterilisation oder fehlerhafter genetischer Beratung einen vom Arzt zu ersetzenden Schaden darstellen kann. Die Verfassungsbeschwerden wurden zurückgewiesen. An diesen Ausspruch sah sich der Senat nicht durch ein Urteil des 2. Senats gehindert, das zu verschiedenen gesetzlichen Vorschriften über den Schwangerschaftsabbruch ergangen war und in den Gründen (die mehr als 120 Seiten in der Entscheidungssammlung umfassen) die Auffassung verworfen hatte, die Unterhaltspflicht für ein Kind als Schaden einzustufen. Der 1. Senat hielt die Ausführungen nicht für tragend, der 2. Senat war gegenteiliger Ansicht und forderte die Anrufung des Plenums auch dann, wenn darum gestritten wird, ob das einschlägige Stück der Begründung diesseits oder jenseits der Grenze zwischen tragendem Grund und *obiter dictum* liegt. Verfahrensrechtlich konnte aber nur der „abweichende", das heißt der später mit dem Thema befasste Senat an das Plenum appellieren, aber gerade hierzu erklärte sich der 1. Senat nicht bereit, und gab so dem 2. Senat das Nachsehen. Beide Senate hatten übrigens nur mit knapper Mehrheit votiert (BVerfGE 96.375 und 409; 1997).

VII. Dito II: zur Kritik des Schrifttums

Der Zwist, den wir schilderten, bestätigt gewissermaßen die Stimmen im Schrifttum (es sich nicht wenige), die schon wegen der Schwierigkeit der Abgrenzung die Erstreckung der Bindungswirkung auf die Entscheidungsgründe verwerfen. Allerdings wird an der praktischen Bedeutung des Abgrenzungsproblems gezweifelt, da etwa von den Beamten in den Bundesministerien, die die neuen Gesetze vorbereiten, berichtet wird, sie würden die vom Bundesverfassungsgericht gelieferten Texte, ohne zwischen tragenden Gründen und *obiter dicta* zu unterscheiden, sorgfältigst studieren, um ihre Gesetzentwürfe gegenüber verfassungsrechtlichen Bedenken hieb- und stichfest zu schmieden. Wie dem immer sei, im Schrifttum wird das Abgrenzungsproblem angesprochen, freilich stellt es nur eines, und sicher kein hervorragendes, der Argumente dar, die gegen die Bindung an Entscheidungsgründe vorgebracht werden.

Von solchen Argumenten, die in erster Linie die Gebundenheit des Gesetzgebers im Auge haben, seien noch einige weitere erwähnt. Zunächst können Gesichtspunkte, die gegen das Normwiederholungsverbot sprechen, auch dem Bindungsgebot an Entscheidungsgründe entgegengehalten werden, also – um Erwägungen des Bundesverfassungsgerichts in der unter V erwähnten Entscheidung von 1987 wiederaufzunehmen – die besondere Verantwortung des demokratisch legitimierten Gesetzgebers; das Unvermögen des Bundesverfassungsgerichts, seine Rechtsprechung aus eigener Initiative zu korrigieren; die Gefahr der Erstarrung oder Zementierung der Rechtsentwicklung. Hinzu treten spezifische auf die Entscheidungsbegründung zugeschnittene Argumente. Auch wenn in den Gründen Sätze der Verfassungsauslegung in allgemeine Formulierungen gekleidet werden, hat doch immer hierzu die Betrachtung des Einzelfalls, die Betrachtung eines konkreten Vorgangs der Vergangenheit oder Gegenwart den Anstoß gegeben. Ein Gericht prophezeit hingegen nicht, sieht nicht die Lebensverhältnisse und Wertvorstellungen voraus, deren sich jedoch der Gesetzgeber, über kurz oder lang, zu vergewissern hat, wenn er durch neue Normen die Verhältnisse der Normunterworfenen gestalten will. Einem Gericht fehlt das ganze Arsenal von Methoden, mit deren Hilfe der Gesetzgeber die Risiken seines generell-hypothetischen Vorgehens zu verringern sucht: Methoden eines auf langen Erfahrungen beruhenden und institutionell nach vielen Seiten gesicherten Gesetzgebungsverfahrens.

Wenn demgegenüber dann die Befürworter der Bindungswirkung replizieren, es werde alles nicht so heiß gegessen wie gekocht, da die Änderung der Verhältnisse ein Abweichen von den Entscheidungsgründen gestatte, so duplizieren die Gegner zum einen, dass „wesentliche", „erhebliche" Änderungen vorausgesetzt würden und vage Maßstäbe wie diese niemanden zur Annahme verleiten könnten, das Bundesverfassungsgericht würde, wenn angerufen, aller Voraussicht nach am gleichen Strange ziehen; zweitens gingen die Richter selbst nicht mit gutem Beispiel voran, da sie selten genug einen Wandel der tragenden Begründung in Angriff nähmen und überdies sich zierten, einen solchen Wandel dem lesenden Publikum kenntlich zu machen. Nur brüskieren oder ignorieren sollte niemand die Begründungen des Bundesverfassungsgerichts, sagen auch die Gegner des Bindungsgebots; das heißt wer abweicht, hat sich mit den Texten der Entscheidungen eingehend auseinanderzusetzen und nun seinerseits die Gründe zu entwickeln, die ihm den Texten zu folgen verwehrt haben.

VIII. Schluss

Wird es in diesem Für und Wider jemals zu einer Einigung kommen? Hinter der Kontroverse verbergen sich zwei grundlegende – und allen wohlbekannte – Positionen institutioneller und politischer Art. Institutionell: die Doppelnatur des Bundesverfassungsgerichts als Verfassungsorgan und als Gericht lässt es zu, entweder die Organ- oder die Gerichtsqualität zu betonen; im ersten Fall steht dann das Bindungsgebot auf festerem Boden als im zweiten. Und politisch: weil den optimalen Staatstypus die „verfasste Demokratie" darstellt, können auch hier die Akzente verschieden gesetzt werden; je nachdem wird das Bindungsgebot hervor- oder in den Hintergrund treten. Dass soeben eher grobmaschige Einordnungen übernommen worden sind, liegt freilich auf der Hand; und so würde zu nicht unerheblichen Differenzierungen die Untersuchung der einzelnen Stellungnahmen führen (wenn solches überhaupt angezeigt wäre).

Aus dem Schrifttum

Geiger, Willi: Die Grenzen der Bindung verfassungsgerichtlicher Entscheidungen (§ 31 Abs. 1 BVerfGG), in: Neue Juristische Wochenschrift 7, 1954, S. 1057 ff.

Hoffmann-Riem, Wolfgang: Beharrung oder Innovation: zur Bindungswirkung verfassungsgerichtlicher Entscheidungen, in: Der Staat 13, 1974, S. 335 ff.

Sachs, Michael: Die Bindung des Bundesverfassungsgerichts an seine Entscheidungen, München 1977

Wischermann, Norbert: Rechtskraft und Bindungswirkung verfassungsgerichtlicher Entscheidungen: zu den funktionsrechtlichen Auswirkungen der extensiven Auslegung des § 31 Abs. 1 BVerfGG, Berlin 1979

Gusy, Christoph: Parlamentarischer Gesetzgeber und Bundesverfassungsgericht, Berlin 1985

Ebsen, Ingwer: Entscheidungsspezifische und adressatenspezifische Durchsetzungsbedingungen der Judikate des Bundesverfassungsgerichts, in: Durchsetzung und Wirkung von Rechtsentscheidungen, hg. von Thomas Raiser / Rüdiger Voigt, Baden-Baden 1990, S. 167 ff.

Luetjohann, Eberhard: Nicht-normative Wirkungen des Bundesverfassungsgerichts: ein Beitrag zur Rechtsprechungslehre, 1991

Detterbeck, Steffen: Streitgegenstand und Entscheidungwirkungen im Öffentlichen Recht, Tübingen 1995

Schulze-Fielitz, Helmuth: Wirkung und Befolgung verfassungsgerichtlicher Entscheidungen, in: Festschrift 50 Jahre Bundesverfassungsgericht, hg. von Peter Badura / Horst Dreier, Tübingen 2001, Bd. 1, S. 385 ff.

Bauer, Thorsten: Die produktübergreifende Bindung des Bundesgesetzgebers an Entscheidungen des Bundesverfassungsgerichts: zugleich ein Beitrag zur Prozeduralisierung des Rechts, Berlin 2003

Schlaich, Klaus / *Korioth*, Stefan: Das Bundesverfassungsgericht: Stellung, Verfahren, Entscheidungen, 6. Aufl. München 2004

Further Reading

McWhinney, Edward: Constitutionalism in Germany and the Federal Constitutional Court; with an Introduction by Gerhard Leibholz, Leyden 1962

Rupp-v. *Brünneck*, Wiltraut: Germany: the Federal Constitutional Court, in: Admonitory Functions of Constitutional Courts, American Journal of Comparative Law 20, 1972, pp. 387seqq.

Kommers, Donald P.: Judicial Politics in West Germany: a Study of the Federal Constitutional Court, London 1976

– The Constitutional Jurisprudence of the Federal Republic of Germany, Durham 1989

Currie, David P.: The Constitution of the Federal Republic of Germany, Chicago 1994

Starck, Christian: The Legitimacy of Constitutional Adjudication and Democracy, in: Constitutionalism, Universalism and Democracy: a Comparative Analysis, Baden-Baden 1999, pp. 13seqq.

W. HAMILTON BRYSON

Summary Conclusion

Ratio decidendi is the reason of the decision, the ruling, of the judge of a court of law in a particular adjudication. It is to be distinguished from *obiter dictum,* a judicial comment that is not the foundation for the judge's order to the parties to the litigation.

A judge may rule without having a reason. A judge might leave the decision to chance by flipping a coin or by consulting the omens. A decision based upon whim rather than upon the rule of law is not acceptable because it is both unjust and unpredictable. People have an innate sense of justice, a conscience, and people have a need to order their future affairs, whether social or economic, upon a knowledge of what will occur in the future. When judicial decision-making is random, this cannot be done, and, where plans for the future have been made in reliance on the rule of law, unfulfilled expectations create discontent. Such an irrational approach to law leads to anarchy, the opposite of law, which is clearly a bad thing. This is useless in a rational world.

A judge may rule according to rational, but unlawful, principles, such as personal self-interest, bribery, fear, personal prejudice, or a pre-disposition that is based upon social, economic, or political factors. Such judges are the bad judges. The good judges rule according to the general principles of law as applied to the particular facts of the individual parties in court. Of course, judges – all of them – are human and thus not perfect. Some few judges are evil; some are lazy; certainly, these should be removed rather than tolerated. The judges should be encouraged to put aside their natural inclinations of self-preservation and not to act according to any personal inclination, but to rule according to the law and the evidence.

There are legal philosophers who have observed the imperfections of the judiciary and have concluded that all judges are guided by these improper external forces rather than by the rule of law. They conclude that this is the way it was and is and always will be. By their acceptance of imperfection in judges, they encourage judges to serve themselves rather than to serve the rule of law and the general public. This cynicism overlooks the clear fact that many judges can, have, and do recognize their own personal interests and consciously set them aside while they are acting as a judge. If we have high expectations of judges and clearly state them, then most judges will make an effort and will succeed in the administration of justice according to the rule of law. Those few who fail to do so should be removed from their positions on the bench. The opinion that judges cannot rise above their own personal interests is truly cynical, negative, and useless, and it undermines the faith of the general public in the rule of law and thus it undermines the rule of law itself. Such a nihilistic approach to law allows for tyranny and leads to oppression, the opposite of law, which is clearly a bad thing. This is useless in a just world.

The reason of the judge must be based upon the law. What, then, is the law?

Some say that the law is the will of the sovereign, whoever that might be, a prince or a group of people or all of the people. *Quod principi placuit legis habet vigorem.*[1] Whatever pleases the prince, or the sovereign, has the force of law. This is because the sovereign has the physical power to force its will upon those who disagree or disobey. Where there is no other concept of law, then, might makes right, and the big fish eat up the little fish; *vae victis.*

If might makes right, then the prince or a majority of the sovereignty can force its will on a minority or an individual without regards to any concept of innate or absolute right or justice. In times of danger and war, justice and right may have to be given up temporarily rather than be lost forever; *inter arma silent leges.*[2] But in times of peace and civilization – and war is not civilized; "war is hell"[3] – the rule of law should prevail over the rule of force, even majoritarian force that is against right.

If the law is the will of the sovereign or of the sovereignty, then it is the will of imperfect humans and thus is itself imperfect. And clearly human beings are not perfect. The concept of imperfection implies that of perfection. While it is beyond the scope of this essay to speculate on the nature of perfection, i.e., God – indeed, it is beyond the comprehension of this imperfect writer – we might recall the words of Sir Edward Coke quoting Bracton to King James I, *non sumus sub hominem sed sub Deo et lege.*[4] We are not under man but under God and the law. To say otherwise and to say that might makes right is to deny both the rule of law and God. (To deny God is to deny rationality, order, and purpose, which is too difficult a leap of faith for this writer.) Such an approach to the law will certainly result in brutality and the destruction of civilization. Human civilization is based on the rule of law, and the *ratio decidendi* of the judges should reflect the ultimate rule of law.

---

1 Digesta, 1.4.1. (This is denied in Bracton on the Laws and Customs of England (*S. E. Thorne*, ed., 1968), vol. 2, p. 305.)

2 Barwis v. Keppel (1766), 2 Wilson K.B. 314, 318, 95 English Reports 831, 833, quoting *Marcus Tullius Cicero*, Pro Milone.

3 So said Gen. William T. Sherman, U.S. Army, who knew well whereof he spoke.

4 Bracton on the Laws and Customs of England (*S. E. Thorne*, ed., 1968), vol. 2, p. 33; *C. D. Bowen*, The Lion and the Throne, The Life and Times of Sir Edward Coke (1957), p. 305.

Thus, the law must be something superior to the force of the state and the will of powerful people. It is a system of good order that is superior to mankind.

Where, then is the law to be found?

Legislative Sources of the Law

The supreme source of legislation is a formal constitution that is intended to be the statement of the fundamental law in force. Constitutions are usually the work of broad based conventions and are usually formally ratified by all of the people to be governed by it in a referendum open to everyone. Although such ratification is not necessary, it is considered helpful in obtaining broad and voluntary support for it as law.

While most constitutions have been written down, the constitution of Great Britain is only partially written, but the customary parts of it are well known and well respected. On the other hand, the constitution of the former Soviet Union was written down, but it was ignored in practice.

Constitutions can be ignored, amended, or replaced with new (and, one hopes, better) ones. Constitutional ideas and principles are not always good nor above criticism; on the other hand, successful clauses have been copied from old by new constitutions and from one nation by others. Not only are constitutions printed, but frequently the debates and subsidiary documents of the constitutional conventions are published as well, and these can be informative of the meaning of the words of the constitution.

National and provincial legislatures enact statutes, and local governing boards and councils enact ordinances, within their political boundaries. Administrative agencies create law in the form of regulations. This legislative activity has generated a substantial literature.

At the end of each session of the legislature, there appears the chronological publication of the legislative enactments. Statute law in force is frequently compiled into codes organized by subject matter. Codes can be abridged in various ways for the convenience of particular classes of user; a good example of this are tax codes, commercial codes, and criminal codes. In Anglo-American jurisdictions, the codes are only a collection of all of the statutes in force. In the Continental jurisdictions, the codes are a statement of all of the law in force.

The various administrative agencies issue printed editions of their rules and regulations.

These legislative forms of law – constitutions, statutes, ordinances, and regulations – are statements of the law. They are subject to change by repeal by the legislative body that created them or by a superior one. A national or state legislature, for example, can declare a local ordinance to be invalid because the local governments are created by the national or state governments.

On the other hand, where the Corpus Juris Civilis was in force but the medieval emperors did not have the political power and ability to legislate and change it when needed, the principle arose that local laws prevailed over it in cases of conflict.

Furthermore, a court can declare a statute to be void as violative of a superior constitutional law. It would not be reasonable or logical for a legislature to make the ultimate determination of the constitutionality of its own statute. It must be presumed that its own statute was considered to be constitutional when it was enacted, or else it would not have been made. Furthermore, a constitution is a legal document and thus it is appropriate that the courts of law should rule as a matter of law what the constitution does and intends and whether an inferior legislative enactment is in violation of it. It is the function of the courts to say what the law, including constitutional law, is.

However, it is the purpose of a legislature to change or to create the law applicable to the community. The instrumental approach to law making is the constitutional province of the legislature. Thus, the courts should acknowledge the superiority of a statute to case law declared by judges. It is not the function of the courts to say what the law ought to be. The popularly elected legislature is to declare public policy. However, as Professor Charles Hobson has pointed out,[5] when the judges are called upon to interpret a constitution, as opposed to the common law, whether declared by the courts or the legislatures, there is not the same amount of precedent available for guidance, and they are necessarily required to be more creative in dealing with a new argument.

Applying the general statutory law in specific factual disputes in the law courts is not always as straightforward as one might think. Perhaps, the legislation was badly drafted; perhaps, the statute results in a gross injustice through over-inclusion. Over the centuries, the courts in the civil law countries, as well as the common law countries, have developed rules of statutory interpretation that are subtle and learned.[6] Simply to state that the statute is the *ratio decidendi* of a court's judgment may overlook many subtle and difficult issues as to how the general statute was applied to the specific case at hand.

Judicial Sources of the Law

The primary function of legislative bodies is to declare the general law. The primary function of the law courts is to apply the general law to specific, individual situations.[7] The courts, in the process of adjudication, state general principles

5 See above, the chapter by *C. Hobson*.

6 E.g. *R. Cross*, Statutory Interpretation (1987).

7 Of course, the legislature can enact a private bill, and the court can declare a general law to be invalid.

of law and state the specific application of the law. Therefore, whether a judge is creative or not, adjudication states the law and is thus a source, whether original or not, of the law.

As with legislative bodies, there is a hierarchy of courts. Naturally, the statements of the higher courts will be accorded greater deference as to the validity of their statements of the law. However, all courts, appellate, trial, and administrative, are actively involved in the process of stating and restating the law, declaring what the unwritten common law is and what an act of legislation means.

The opinions of the judges are printed in books called reports of cases. The courts also publish their general rules of court, which dictate the procedure to be followed in the litigation of a particular matter. The publication of judicial decisions is vitally important to the statement and understanding of the case law. Otherwise, the advocates and judges have to rely on memory, which can be selective and self-serving. The common law is an accumulation of case law. How later judges deal with the decisions of the earlier judges is a matter of jurisprudence. This is an inductive, *a posteriori,* approach to the law.

In the common law countries, the case law is the statement of the law; the case law is the law. The later judges should follow the law already stated by former judges; this is the principle of *stare decisis.* However, there are many difficulties with applying the rule of *stare decisis* as Lord Mansfield and John Marshall were well aware.[8] As noted by J. Oldham, T. Wren, and C. Hobson,[9] the judges thought that the cases were not themselves the common law of England, but are only evidence of the common law. The quality of the reporting of cases was an important factor to be considered by the judges. Whereas, today, there is a tendency to think that any opinion of the highest court of the nation is the law.

In the civil law countries, the statutes, the codes, are the law. However, statutes cannot be perfect or complete; the legislators cannot foresee the problems of the future. Therefore, the judges who are called upon to put the statutes into force in an individual case must frequently resort to legislative interpretation. There is a large body of legal learning in the common law countries as to statutory interpretation; this body of law is case law also.

In addition, the chapters by R. H. Helmholz, J.-L. Halpérin, and M. C. Mirow demonstrate the use of case law in the canon law courts[10] and in the civil law countries.[11]

---

8 *R. Cross,* Precedent in English Law (1991) gives a good exposition of these issues.

9 See above, the chapters by *J. Oldham, T. Wren,* and *C. Hobson.*

10 Note also *G. Dolezalek* and *K. W. Nörr,* "Die Rechtsprechungssammlungen der Mittelalterlichen Rota" in H. Coing, Handbuch der Quellen und Literatur des Neueren Europäischen Privatsrechtsgeschichte (1973), vol. 1, pp. 851–856; *G. Dolezalek,* "Reports of the 'Rota' (14th – 19th Centuries)" in *J. H. Baker,* Judicial Records, Law Reports, and the Growth of Case Law, Comparative Studies in Continental and Anglo-American Legal History (1989), vol. 5, pp. 69–99, esp. 81–82; *G. Dolezalek,* "Litigation at the Rota Romana Particularly

Legal Scholarship

Even though the work product of the legal academic community has no official, binding, or legal authority, the opinions of legal scholars (and of the general public) are statements of the law. The difference between a professor of law and a plowman is only one of education and experience.

The statement of the law by an academic lawyer will be given the consideration that it deserves. Some academic statements of the law are, in fact, accorded great weight, and some are considered to be authoritative. This was especially true of the academic exposition of the *ius commune* and the *usus modernus pandectarum* of continental Europe before the codification movement of the late eighteenth century which culminated in the napoleonic codes and the *Bürgerlichesgesetzbuch.*

Academic or secondary legal authority has its own hierarchy. Jurisprudence, the philosophy of law, is the statement of the ultimate and fundamental law. Legal writers also set forth the principles of the substantive law, for example, the rules governing the enforceability of contracts, the definitions of crimes and torts, and so on. They expound upon the procedural law of the courts, without which the substantive law could not be put into effect. Finally, there are legal scholars who edit and publish the primary statements of the law, the statutes of the legislatures and the judgments of the courts. These humble editors make feasible the statement and restatement of the law by all of the others. In fact, the practitioners of the law value the various classes of legal scholarship in inverse order from the academic scholars of the law.

The legal academics are an important part of both the statement and of the restatement of the law. Their treatises on the law help bring it into focus. The explanations of the statutory law and the unwritten law as declared by the courts are statements of the law. If the law is not stated and agreed upon, then the administration of the law deteriorates into the personal whim of the individual judge. The statement of the law in the secondary legal literature makes it possible to know the law. If the law is known, it can be discussed and criticized. Academic and public criticism can lead to the change or restatement of the law.

---

around 1700" in A. Wijffels, Case Law in the Making, *ibidem* (1997), vol. 17/I, pp. 339–373, esp. 373.

11 See also generally *J. H. Baker,* Judicial Records, Law Reports, and the Growth of Case Law, Comparative Studies in Continental and Anglo-American Legal History (1989), vol. 5; *A. Wijffels,* Case Law in the Making, *ibidem* (1997), vol. 17; *P. Stein,* Civil Law Reports and the Case of San Marino, in The Character and Influence of the Roman Civil Law (1988), pp. 115–130 *S. Dauchy* and *V. Demars-Sion,* Les recueils d'arrêts et dictionnaires de jurisprudence, XVIe – XVIIIe siecles (2005).

Legal Argument

The primary function of the practitioners of the law, the lawyers, is the statement of the law in arguments made on behalf of their clients. This class of legal statement is at the lower end of the scale because the lawyer's duty is to represent his client's position so long as it is a plausible one. The lawyer in the courtroom is a partisan stating his client's legal positions, which are not necessarily his own. However, the written briefs of counsel and the legal dialogue in the courtroom between opposing counsel is very useful in guiding the impartial judge in his or her statement of the law as it applies to the parties in court. The practicalities of the current situation of the courts in America are that the lawyers usually have much more time to study the applicable law than does the judge. Thus, the research and scholarship of the lawyers, though partisan, is vital to the process of stating the law in the individual case. The written arguments presented to appellate courts in the lawyers' briefs are usually required to be printed. They are not widely available, but they are preserved in the archives of the courts and in some academic law libraries. They are frequently interesting and useful as precedents where the court agreed with the position taken.

In Virginia and in many other American states, the formal opinions of the attorneys general are published. Although they do not have the weight of a judicial opinion, because of the importance of the Attorney General of Virginia as an elected constitutional officer, they are considered as worthy of credit. In France, collections of *plaidoyers* have been published, and Professor J.-L. Halpérin has shown how the opinions of the *procureur général* Dupin, in particular, have been the foundation of later judicial opinions.[12] There are many collections of *consilia* and *responsa prudentium.*

Natural Law

The law of nature and the fundamental rules of law may be discovered by intelligent and rational people of good will. Conscientious philosophers may upon reflection be able to discover the law. This is a matter of deductive, *a priori,* legal reasoning. This is the law that was expounded by Aristotle, Thomas Aquinas, Samuel Pufendorf, Hugo Grotius, and their followers.

Natural law can be declared by divine revelation. The giving of the Ten Commandments to Moses[13] is an example. The authority of such law is unassailable. The problem with divine revelation is the credibility of the person claiming to be God's messenger; it, then, is a question of belief in God and in the prophet. Jesus himself warned of false prophets.[14]

12 See above, the chapter by *J.-L. Halpérin.*

13 Exodus 20.

In conclusion, it is interesting to note that, in the historical statement and development of the law, it has been done over time in the reverse order from that just given. First came the law said by the priests to have been given by God, then the law was presented by the elders of the community, then it was stated by the judges as officials of the king or of the state, then enacted by the legislators as official representatives of the people, and finally promulgated by constitutional conventions acting as superlegislatures.

These are the sources of the law that the judges should use in coming to their judgments.

If the judges give their reason for their decisions, then it can be seen whether or not they have followed the rule of law and decided according to the law or not. If the judges do not give their reasons, then it will be presumed that they came to the correct judgment for the correct reasons.

The judges of the parlements of France in the *ancien regime* were forbidden to give their reasons.[15] Juries in the United States at this present time are encouraged not to give special verdicts that explain their reasons, but are strongly urged to give general verdicts that merely find in favor of one party or another. This is favored by the public policy in favor of finality of judgments. If the reasons are not known, the results cannot be attacked and set aside upon a rehearing or an appeal to another court. Nor can they be brought into public disrepute. If there is no finality of judgments, the purpose of the courts will be totally frustrated, there will be no judgments, the rule of law would be destroyed because there would be no institution to administer it. *Expedit rei publicae ut sit finis litium.*[16]

On the other hand, not only should justice be done, but also justice should be seen to be done. Thus, the judges should give their reasons; they should express the *ratio decidendi.* Today, it is believed that a person is entitled to one fair trial and one fair appeal. To have a fair appeal, the appellate judges need to know the *ratio decidendi* of the trial judge, the judge of first instance. For justice to be seen to be done, all judges must give their opinions. Such a judicial process will not delay the final judgment to an unacceptable degree.

Furthermore, the expressing of an opinion will show to the judge himself or herself an initial error of thinking. A later reading of one's own opinion often exposes irrationality and mistakes initially made in a first draft. Thus, the setting down in words of the reasons for an opinion will certainly aid the judge in coming to the correct result.

Secondly, the publication of the judges' reasoned opinions is a major contribution to the furtherance of the study of jurisprudence. The open and free discussion of the law by many different persons, especially those educated and experienced in

---

14 Matthew 7:15.

15 See above, the chapter by *V. Demars-Sion* and *S. Dauchy.*

16 Berry v. Perry (1615), 3 Bulstrode 62, 68, 81 English Reports 54, 59.

the law, leads to a better understanding of the law and, perhaps, law reform. If a judge gives the reason for his or her judgment and the reason is a correct application of the law but the result is undesirable, then this could be an impetus for a legislative change in the settled law to make the law more just.

The chapters of this book demonstrate how these issues have been solved by various western legal systems at different periods in history.

It is an easy thing for the academic lawyers and philosophers to state legal theories in a classroom, but it is a difficult thing for the judges to put the legal theories into practice and come to a just decision in a courtroom. For the judiciary to lead us from chaos to order, from anarchy to justice, *hoc opus, hic labor est.*

Contributors

Brand, Paul, Dr., All Souls College, Oxford OX1 4AL, Great Britain (paul.brand@all-souls.oxford.ac.uk).

Bryson, W. Hamilton, Professor at the University of Richmond, School of Law, Richmond, Virginia 23173, USA (hbryson@richmond.edu).

Dauchy, Serge, Prof. Dr., Directeur du Centre d'Histoire Judiciaire (UMR 8025), Faculté de droit, 1 Place Déliot, BP 629, 59024 Lille Cedex, France (serge.dauchy@univ-lille2.fr).

Demars-Sion, Véronique, Professeur à l'Université de Lille 2, Centre d'Histoire Judiciaire (UMR 8025), Faculté de droit, 1 Place Déliot, BP 629, 59024 Lille Cedex, France (veronique.demars@univ-lille2.fr).

Durand, Bernard, Professeur à l'Université de Montpellier 1, Dynamiques du droit (UMR 5815), Faculté de droit, 39 rue de l'Université, 34060 Montpellier Cedex 1, France (UMR5815@univ-montp1.fr).

Finlay, John, Dr., School of Law, University of Glasgow, Glasgow G12 8QQ, Great Britain (jf58c@udcf.gla.ac.uk).

Halpérin, Jean-Louis, Professeur à l'Ecole Normale Supérieure, 45 rue d'Ulm, 75230 Paris Cedex 05, France (jean-louis.halperin@wanadoo.fr).

Helmholz, Richard H., Professor at the University of Chicago, Law School, 1111 East 60th Street, Chicago, Illinois 60637, USA (dick_helmholz@law.uchicago.edu).

Hilaire, Jean, Professeur émérite de l'Université de Paris 2 (jeanyveshilaire@numericable.fr).

Hobson, Charles F., Dr., Institute of Early American History, P.O. Box 8781, Williamsburg, Virginia 23187, USA (chhobs@wm.edu).

Martyn, Georges, Professor at the Ghent University, Faculty of Law, Universiteitsstraat 4, 9000 Ghent, Belgium (Georges.Martyn@UGent.be).

Mirow, Matthew C., Professor at the Florida International University, University Park Campus, Miami, Florida 33199, USA (mirowm@fiu.edu).

Nörr, Knut Wolfgang, Professor at the Eberhard Karls Universität Tübingen, Forschungsstelle für internationale Privatrechtsgeschichte, Wilhelmstraße 7, 72074 Tübingen, Germany (fip@jura.uni-tuebingen.de).

Oldham, James, Professor at the Georgetown University, Law Center, 600 New Jersey Avenue, Washington, DC 20001, USA (oldham@law.georgetown.edu).

Winkel, Laurens, Professor at the Erasmus University Rotterdam, Faculty of Law, P.O. Box 1738, 3000 DR Rotterdam, The Netherlands (winkel@frg.eur.nl).

Wren, J. Thomas, Dr., Jepson School of Leadership, University of Richmond, Richmond, Virginia 23173, USA (twren@richmond.edu)

MIX
Papier aus verantwortungsvollen Quellen
Paper from responsible sources
FSC® C105338

Printed by Libri Plureos GmbH
in Hamburg, Germany